The Most Intentional City

The Most Intentional City

St. Petersburg in the Reign of Catherine the Great

George E. Munro

Madison • Teaneck
Fairleigh Dickinson University Press

Associated University Presses
2010 Easpark Boulevard
Cranbury, NJ 08512

The paper used in this publication meets the requirements of the American National Standard for Permanence of Paper for Printed Library Materials Z39.48-1984.

Library of Congress Cataloging-in-Publication Data

Munro, George E.
The most intentional city : St. Petersburg in the reign of Catherine The Great / George E. Munro.
p. cm.
Includes bibliographical references and index.
ISBN 978-0-8386-4146-0 (alk. paper)
1. Saint Petersburg (Russia)—History—18th century. 2. City planning—Russia (Federation)—Saint Petersburg—History—18th century. 3. Catherine II, Empress of Russia, 1729–1796. 4. Saint Petersburg (Russia)—Social conditions—18th century. I. Title.
DK565.M86 2008
947′.21—dc22 2008010063

PRINTED IN THE UNITED STATES OF AMERICA

Contents

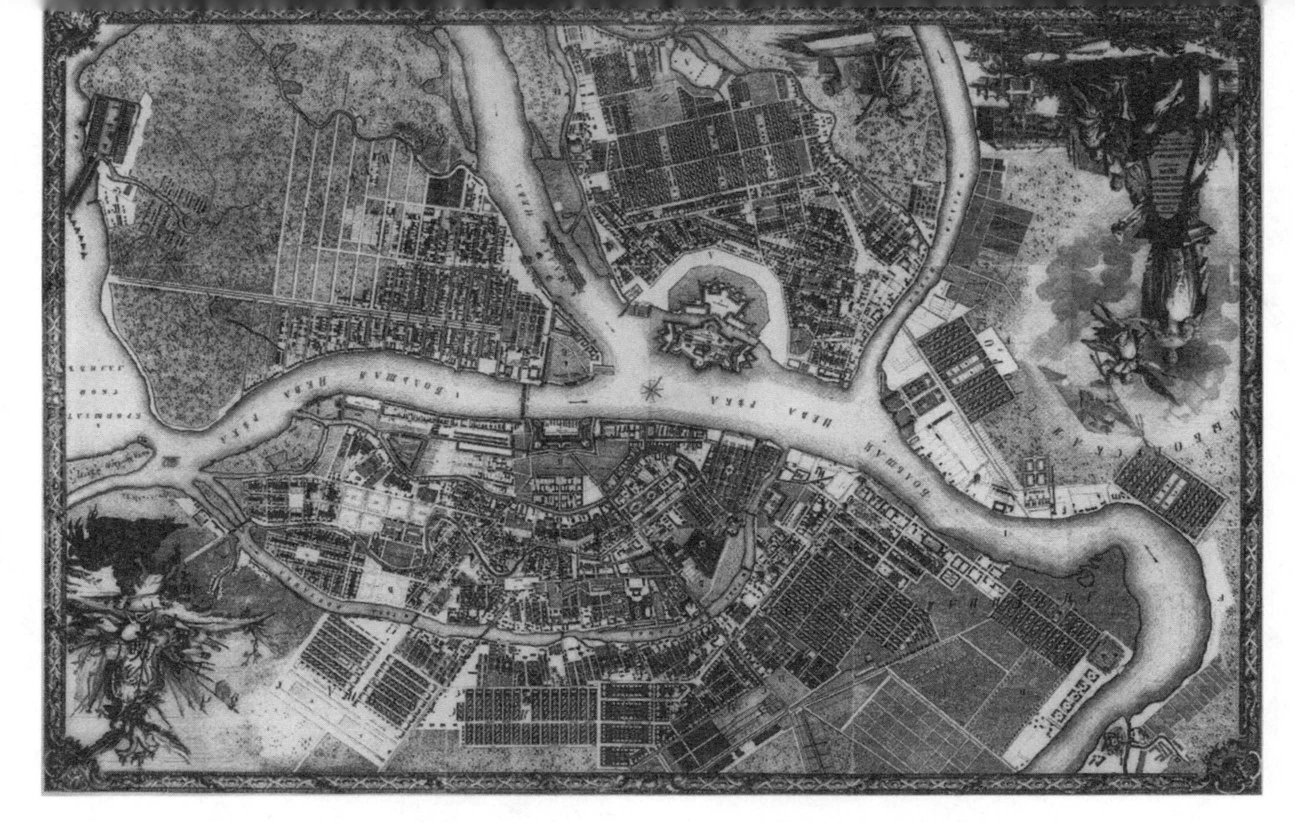

The map was produced by the Geographical Department of Academy of Sciences under the direction of John Truscott for the fiftieth anniversary of the city's foundation. Its original orientation was south up, north down. It has been turned upside down here to conform to the way we usually view maps, with north up. Reproduced with permission of the David Rumsey Map Collection, www.davidrumsey.com.

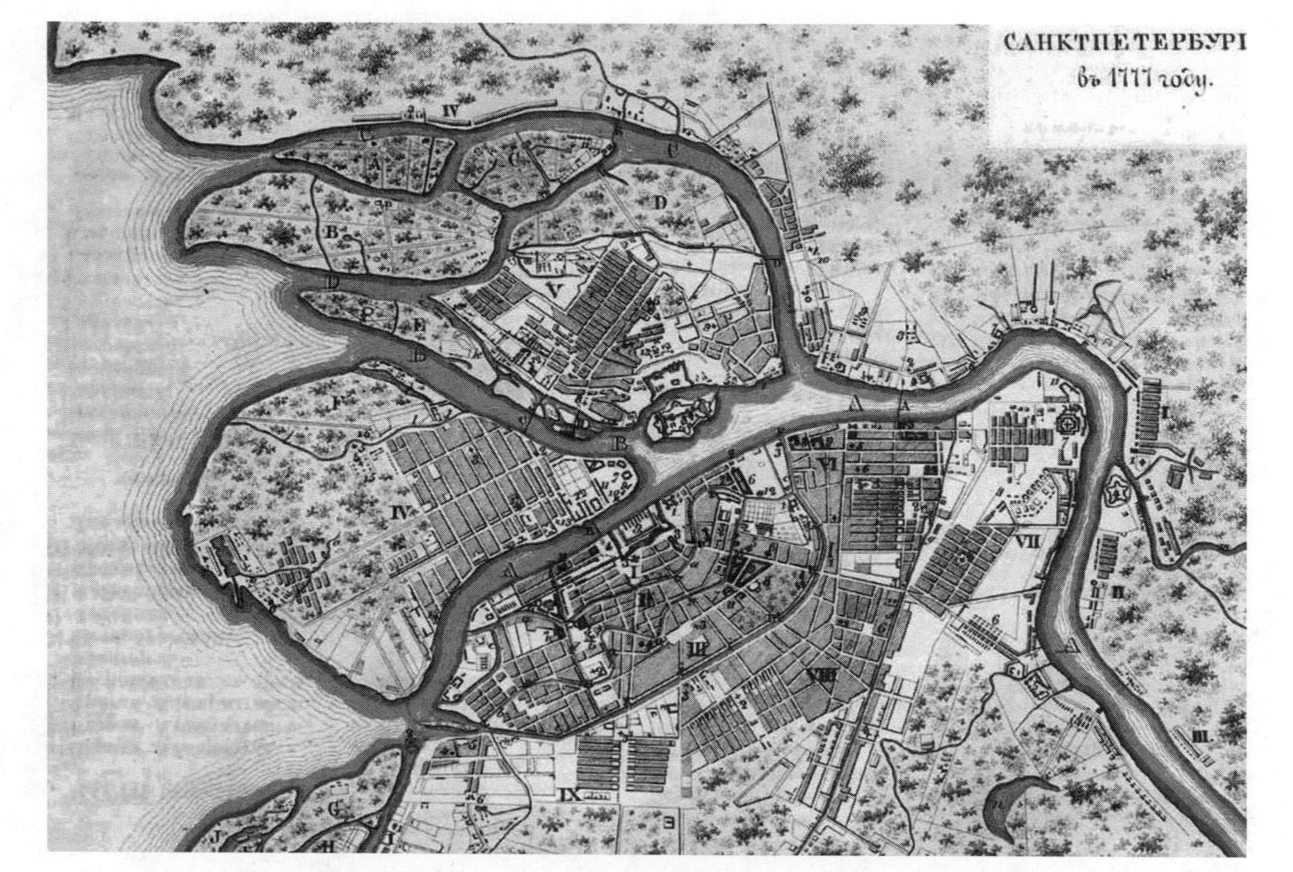

Plan of St. Petersburg in 1777. The source is Niklai Ivanovich Tsylov, ***Plany S.-Petersburga v 1700, 1705, 1725, 1738, 1756, 1777, 1799, 1840 i 1849godakh, s prilozheniem planov 13 chastei stolitsy 1853 goda*****. St. Petersburg, 1853.**

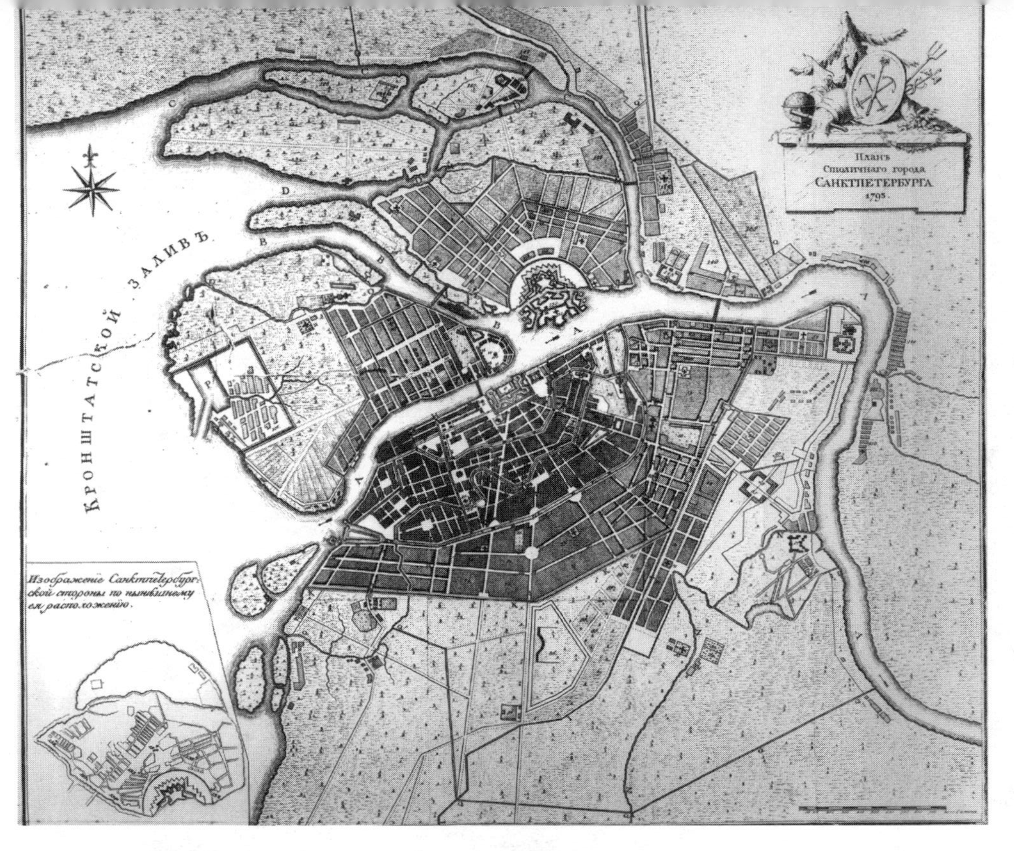

Plan of St. Petersburg in 1793. The plan was originally published in Johann Gottlieb Georgi, *Opisanie rossisko-imperatorskago stolichnago goroda Sankt-Peterburga i dostopamiatnostei v okrest-nostiakh onogo*. 3 vols. in 1. St. Petersburg, 1794.

Acknowledgments

THIS BOOK WAS LONG IN THE MAKING. TAKING ITS ORIGINS FROM A graduate seminar paper on foreigners' accounts of St. Petersburg in Catherine's reign, the book was in preparation for more years than Catherine was on the throne. Growing out of a doctoral dissertation, it underwent several significant makeovers as archival research in subsequent decades added depth and perspective. My Russian colleague Grigorii Kaganov noted that one of his books received its particular form because he wrote it at the time when he did. Written ten years earlier it would have been a different book. Likewise had it been written ten years later. This book has been reshaped more than once. It surely benefited from the changes in approaches to the city's history and the interpretations of its past as Leningrad suddenly emerged as St. Petersburg again as one of the results of nationwide political changes. The historical city and the contemporary city once more share a single name.

Over the decades many people contributed support in various ways, for all of whom I am grateful. For guidance in the early stages of preparation, I am deeply obliged to Josef Anderle, Willis Brooks, Clifford Foust, and David Griffiths. For many years John T. Alexander lent encouragement to continue and complete the project. Among others who read the manuscript in whole or in part at various stages are Judith Bruce and the late Raymond Fisher, along with Foust, Griffiths and Alexander. I profited enormously from conversation with and reading the works of Evgenii Anisimov, Robert E. Jones, Grigorii Kaganov, Isabel de Madariaga, and Gary Marker, as well as many other colleagues in the Study Group on Eighteenth-Century Russia. Any remaining errors of fact or interpretation are of course my own.

I want to thank Robert D. Andrews and Sergei Shevchenko for help with the graphs and Anastasia Budanok and Thomas Scott for help with photographs. Thanks to the David Rumsey Map Collection (www.davidrumsey.com) for permission to use maps from 1753. For emotional support over the years I want to thank Sue Munro, especially for the year in Leningrad, and Emily Scott.

I also am extremely grateful for financial support at various times from a variety of sources, including the International Research and Exchanges Board, the Council for the International Exchange of Scholars, the National Endowment for the Humanities, and Virginia Commonwealth University's grants for faculty research. I owe special thanks to librarians at the University of North Carolina at Chapel Hill and the Slavic collections of the University of Illinois at Urbana and the University of Helsinki. Angelika Powell of the University of Virginia and the interlibrary loan staff at Virginia Commonwealth University were unstinting in providing me quickly with needed books and articles. The administration and workers at various archives and libraries in Russia were extremely professional in finding sources, often with minimal direction. They include in St. Petersburg the National Library of Russia, the Russian State Historical Archive, the archive of the St. Petersburg branch of the Russian Academy of Sciences, and St. Petersburg State University; in Moscow, the Russian State Archive of Old Charters and the former Lenin Library; and in Iaroslavl' the regional archive. My editors at Associated University Presses, Cathy Slovensky and Christine Retz, were efficient and gracious.

My colleagues in the Department of History at Virginia Commonwealth University have been supportive over many years, especially James Tice Moore, Philip Schwarz, and my current chair, Bernard Moitt.

Finally, my deepest appreciation to Natasha Illenzeer Munro for believing in me.

The Most
Intentional City

Introduction

IT WAS THE RUSSIAN WRITER FEDOR DOSTOEVSKY WHO FIRST TERMED St. Petersburg "the most intentional city," nearly a century and a half after the city was founded and fifty years after the death of Catherine the Great.[1] St. Petersburg was by that time very much a city of officialdom. To many people it seemed un-Russian. It was somehow false, unnatural, an artifice. Dostoevsky's comment was not intended to be complimentary.

One of the things most widely known about St. Petersburg is that it was a planned city. An intentional act created a new capital for a new empire. It was an act of supreme confidence in a ruler's ability to shape the dominion under his authority. The intentionality extended beyond simply creating a new residence for the court and its appurtenances. Other rulers of the time were doing that. This was to be a most intentional *city*, bringing urbanism into an overwhelmingly rural society. The *city* had never really developed in Russia, although elsewhere it was a favored form of human habitation that had for ages been coveted by conquerors, condemned by moralists, depicted by artists, lauded or lamented by poets, resented by rustics, and sought out by fortune-seekers. In characterizing St. Petersburg as "intentional," Dostoevsky implicitly recognized it as an object to be examined, studied, and analyzed.

Dostoevsky concerned himself with one particular city that he found not entirely to his liking. It was only in the twentieth century that scholars in general discovered the city as an object of study. To a great extent it was the seemingly intractable problems of city life that turned consideration to efforts to define precisely what the city is, how it develops, its relationship to rural life, and the role it plays as a part of a larger human society. Answers to these issues extend inexorably into the historical dimension, and a rich literature studying the city in various contexts and from different perspectives has made its appearance in recent decades.[2]

Closely related to the history of particular cities is the history of urbanization, the process of becoming urban. The distinction between the two rests on the assumption that cities can exist in nonurbanized societies, and that a center of population need not necessarily be urban. Urbanization involves not only an increase in population and population density but also qualitative changes in economy and society.[3] It is characterized by extensive specialization of labor, increased cultural, educational, and public welfare activities, and often a change in values. Prior to the Industrial Revolution the term could be applied to a limited area within an otherwise nonurbanized population, but an entire society could not be urbanized simply because it would be unable to feed itself.[4] In the latter case, the urbanized area is generally the most complex economically if not socially, tending to influence and guide the development of society as a whole to an extent far out of proportion to its size alone.[5]

Closely linked to urban history is urban planning. Dostoevsky in his novels examined social problems identified with what seemed to him perhaps a hyperplanned—intentional—city. Modern urban planning rests on the assumption that if specialists can understand the phenomena of the growth and development of the city and the process of urbanization, it should then be possible to induce them into existence and nurture them into success. To be sure, sovereigns of the ancient as well as the early modern world attempted to will cities into being long before scholars undertook their systematic and analytical studies. How many cities did Alexander the Great establish and name in some way for himself? Such attempts by Alexander and other rulers failed far more often than they succeeded. This did not prevent them from trying. Their efforts provide rich and diverse raw material for studying what did and what did not work.

To establish a city intentionally was one thing. To oversee its successful growth—or, to put it differently, not to blow out the spark of life unintentionally through misguided and misdirected policies—was another. Rarest of all was to see the resulting municipality begin to transform the environment of which it was a part, for the town to become urbanized itself and extend that quality to the realm beyond. What conjunctures permitted this to happen? Was the planning especially prescient, or did the city develop for other reasons? Were policies developed and applied more wisely in these cases than in others, or was it possible that there was little relationship between governmental policy and urban dynamics?

The planned city was far outnumbered by those that grew indigenously, of their own accord. Because human societies differ so greatly, the city and urbanization have taken various forms and followed different paths of development. Obviously a wide range of studies of urban life in disparate settings is essential for general outlines of urban development to be posited or a comprehensive model of the city in history to be drawn. Of particular value are studies of cities unique in their characteristics, for they help define the interpretive parameters. If some cities arc of interest for their typicality, others are important for their singularity.

In this regard, eighteenth-century St. Petersburg is one of the first cities to merit our attention. It was one of Europe's great cities, not only in population but in architecture, commerce, culture, and politics. It attained this prominence during the reign of Catherine II (1762–96). During her thirty-four-year reign administrative bodies began to govern more effectively and efficiently, planners attempted—with some success—to direct the city's growth, the street pattern was essentially completed, urban services eased many inconveniences of city life, and the city became culturally more sophisticated. As the new imperial capital, St. Petersburg served as the locus of town planning and experimentation. More than once the government tested new ideas and policies there before attempting implementation in other cities.

Founded in 1703, St. Petersburg was the first modern capital planted in a wilderness, an auspicious experiment in city building that anticipated such subsequent planned capital cities as Washington, D.C., Canberra, New Delhi, and Brasília. Not only was St. Petersburg the first national capital created ex nihilo, but the Russian government, having successfully willed one city into being, founded others by decree, including Orenburg, Odessa, Nikolaev, and Ashkhabad.[6] Soviet planners later added to the tradition many such cities, including Magnitogorsk, Noril'sk, Novosibirsk, and Tol'iatti.[7] As the prototype of the modern planned city, St. Petersburg would have to figure large in a study of the suitability and adaptability of the planned city as a human habitat.

But the planned city is not always the city that results. In eighteenth-century St. Petersburg there was a constant tension between the statist conception of the nature and role of urban life and the living, vital city. This tension was mirrored in the frequent breach of laws and ordinances pertaining to economic life in the city. The people who congregated there were determined to make a life for themselves regardless of the orderly scheme for organizing and controlling urban life that the state was projecting. A study of St. Petersburg's history must contain the story of its people as well as the development of administration and architecture.

The history of the city can be written from many different perspectives. Prerevolutionary Russian and, more recently, Soviet historians frequently addressed the city, but rarely from the approach of an urban history that included an examination of the growth and impact of urbanization on their country. A number of the earlier histories only chronicled the important events that took place in cities. In the case of St. Petersburg, emphasis centered on what happened at court.

The first history of the city, written by A. P. Bogdanov a mere half century after its founding, followed this pattern.[8] A second edition, edited by V. G. Ruban, brought events up to the start of Catherine's reign in 1762.[9] Other works toward the end of the eighteenth century included considerable historical information, although they were cast as descriptions of the city or as reference works on other topics. Most of these works came from the pens of non-Russians who had spent a number of years in St. Petersburg. Written in western European languages, primarily German, they were intended for a foreign audience requiring or desiring knowledge about economic, social, political, and cultural conditions in St. Petersburg. Among such works are the detailed, accurate, and information-laden descriptions by A. F. Büsching, J. G. Georgi, G. F. Müller, H. von Reimers, B. F. Hermann, and H. F. von Storch.[10] They were supplemented by a few works by Russian authors, especially M. D. Chulkov and A. Shchekatov.[11] Some of these authors, especially Hermann and Storch, faithfully collected statistical information on a variety of subjects, although their figures must be used with caution, as is noted below.

The descriptive-historical-statistical approach continued in the nineteenth century with other writers on St. Petersburg. A. P. Bashutskii followed this path in his *Panorama of St. Petersburg,* in combination with the anecdotal approach.[12] More purely anecdotal, drawn principally from literary sources and the abundant fund of popular culture, was the history by M. I. Pyliaev.[13] Most of the books celebrating the city's two-hundredth anniversary can be placed in the same anecdotal category.[14] A few of them did begin to break new ground, such as P. N. Stolpianskii's history of industrial activity in St. Petersburg.[15] In preparing this work, Stolpianskii was the first to make extensive use of the advertisements section of the newspaper *Sanktpeterburgskie vedomosti* (St. Petersburg Gazette) as a rich source for social and economic history. Unfortunately he did not live to publish a fuller account of the city's history based on such sources. But his bibliographical essay on the writing of St. Petersburg's history survives in typescript in the library of the Museum of the History of St. Petersburg.

As Stolpianskii's example suggests, historical works written from a more analytical perspective began to appear in the last third of the nineteenth century. The centenary of Catherine the Great's principal legislation for towns in 1885 attracted the attention of P. N. Petrov, who wrote the most comprehensive prerevolutionary history of the city from its establishment to the midpoint of Catherine's reign.[16] His history ended with the formal opening of the *guberniia* (province) of St. Petersburg in 1782. Also in 1885 the historian of Russia's cities, I. I. Ditiatin, brought out a history that carried Petrov's work forward another century.[17] Ditiatin's history, commissioned by the St. Petersburg city council to mark the centenary of its founding under the terms of Catherine's municipal charter of 1785, necessarily devoted itself to administrative history. The paucity of archival materials on the city's administrative life for the period from 1785 to 1801 drove Ditiatin to the conclusion that the newly created administrative system did not function well at first, and he therefore concentrated on the nineteenth century.

Similar in design and highly complementary to Ditiatin was the early work of A. A. Kizevetter. His studies of Catherine's Charter to the Towns and of the society of *posad* people (defined and discussed in chapter 2) in the eighteenth century were classics of administrative-institutional history.[18] Although not focusing directly on St. Petersburg, they provide a framework for evaluating the relationship between what planners intended to bring about and what actually occurred in the organic development of Russian urban life. Both Ditiatin and Kizevetter looked for, and were disappointed in, the failure of Catherine to grant substantive autonomy to Russia's towns and cities. They viewed cities principally as administrative organisms. The peculiarity in Russian urban administration by which no city had its own municipal government before 1785 forced these historians either to limit their research to the nineteenth century (Ditiatin) or concentrate in earlier periods on those institutions that did exist in towns (Kizevetter). They believed that the failure—in their view—of Russian town life to develop sufficiently was attributable to Catherine's failure to permit such autonomy. This rather narrow administrative view of the vitality of urban life has colored subsequent interpretations by Western historians in particular.

A final category of histories of St. Petersburg that originated before the revolutions of 1917 consists of those works concentrating primarily on architecture. Frequently emphasizing the importance of spatial planning in the city's development, these works tended to treat the city primarily in terms of its buildings.[19] St. Petersburg, for their authors, was worthy of study because of its monumental buildings and its "architectural ensembles," a term particularly applicable to St. Petersburg. By focusing on the physical appearance of the city frozen in wood, brick, and stone, these works tended to miss the living, breathing city that was unplanned and unexpected, but in a sense more authentic than squares, palaces, and embankments.

In contradistinction to prerevolutionary historians, Soviet scholars showed considerable interest in social and economic factors in history. Only a few, however, most notably Iu. R. Klokman, P. G. Ryndziunskii, and S. P. Luppov, wrote extensively on cities as such.[20] Other Soviet historians concerned themselves with industrial and commercial history.[21] The laboring poor received their share of attention in several notable studies, but in the context of class relationships and class conflicts rather than urban history.[22] In recent years a younger generation of scholars has undertaken work more similar in methodology and approach to the work of urban historians in the West.[23] Multivolume cooperative histories of Petersburg-Petrograd-Leningrad, Moscow, and other cities appeared in the 1950s and thereafter.[24] They contain much of value to both general reader and specialist, but suffer from a lack of continuity. In the case of St. Petersburg, the work also pays insufficient attention to a number of critical issues, such as the relation between the capital and the rest of Russia and the peculiar logistical problems of the capital.

Three works published in the 1990s that treat the cultural history of St. Petersburg bear mention. Two of them purport to encompass the entirety of the city's history under all three names that have been bestowed on it.[25] Solomon Volkov, however, treats the eighteenth century as little more than a prelude to the nineteenth, when the real cultural significance of St. Petersburg began. Moisei Kagan gives considerably more play to the eighteenth century and devotes an entire chapter to the importance of St. Petersburg as a work of city planning, including not only architecture but also conceptualizations of plasticity and the "expanding universe" of the city. Kagan also deals much more with the importance of cultural institutions than does Volkov. The third work, by G. Z. Kaganov, examines the treatment not of buildings, streets, and geography, but rather of open space and perspective in the work of selected artists and writers who took St. Petersburg as their theme.

Several books from the perspective of urban historical studies published since the mid-1970s by North American scholars deal in whole or in part with St. Petersburg. For example, the role of factory workers in the city's life in the mid-nineteenth century is the focus of studies by Reginald Zelnik and Victoria Bonnell, and James H. Bater examines the changing patterns of land use during the rapid industrialization at the end of the nineteenth century. More to the point of the eighteenth century, Gilbert Rozman places St. Petersburg—as he does all other Russian cities—into his schematized model of the stages of urban development that he likewise applies comparatively to China and Japan. Josef Konvitz deals with St. Petersburg as a type of port city, noting its similarities and differences with other European cities created for the same purpose. And J. Michael Hittle uses St. Petersburg frequently for illustrative material in developing his thesis of the Russian "service city" in the seventeenth and eighteenth centuries.[26] Each of these works, in analyzing a segment of St. Petersburg's development, points to the need for more comprehensive and detailed studies of the critical periods in the city's growth.

The three-hundredth anniversary of the city's founding was greeted by a spate of books in Russia addressing the history of the city as a whole or various aspects of it.[27] Each district had its own book dedicated to it, as did features and institutions ranging from bridges to banyas (baths), from banks to breweries. The legends and myths of Petersburg summoned forth their own literature.[28] Guidebooks of all sorts abounded. Books were produced on the Finns of Petersburg, the Swedes, the Germans, the British, and the Dutch, among others. The history of homosexual life in the city found an author.[29] The very history of commemorative books about St. Petersburg, local history for locals, found its study.[30] Most of the commemorative works were intended for a popular rather than a scholarly audience. The anniversary attracted less attention outside Russia, but among the books marking it, mention should be made of Bruce Lincoln's *Sunlight at Midnight*.[31] Lincoln deals far more substantively with the nineteenth and twentieth centuries than the eighteenth, devoting only a few impressionistic pages to the reign of Catherine II. The mental image of the city is explored provocatively in Julie Buckler's *Mapping St. Petersburg*.[32] Like Lincoln, Buckler has far more material to deal with in the nineteenth and twentieth centuries than the eighteenth.

The present study draws not only from published works, but also is based significantly on unpublished manuscripts and documents preserved in the Russian State Archive of Old Documents in Moscow and the Russian State Historical Archive in St. Petersburg, as well as other archives. These sources are supplemented by contemporary laws, newspapers, journals, memoirs, travel accounts, and other published sources that provide insights into the city's life. The accounts of foreigners proved invaluable, for they frequently noted features and characteristics of the city that were invisible to Russians because of their very familiarity. The most significant foreign authors, Storch and Georgi, themselves belonging to the eighteenth century, benefited from years of residence in St. Petersburg and their trained powers of observation as scholars but were also informed by their familiarity with cities elsewhere in Europe. Much of this material, archival and published, is now used for the first time in a study of St. Petersburg.

Among the perils that can confront the historian, three in particular made their appearance early in this study and hung around until the end. The first is the matter of terminology. Eighteenth-century Russia was far removed in most ways from the world of the twenty-first century. It also bore little resemblance in its social structure, local governmental system, and economic life to the western European societies of that day for which our knowledge is greatest. Terms and concepts that historians are used to employing with regard to France or Germany or England can be fitted only with difficulty into the Russian context, and then only with grave potential for misconception and misconstruance. As examples, one can mention the very word "town" or "city." Its equivalent term in Russian, *gorod,* had a limited legal usage that neither extended to every center of population above a certain size nor necessarily meant a population center at all. Similarly, the Russian equivalents of "merchant," "factory," and "peasant," to name just a few, convey certain nuances in English that the Russian words do not really imply and fail to sustain in English part of the connotation in Russian. The impossibility of establishing exact meaning in translation is fully confronted in such terms as *posadskie;* the English equivalent "suburbanites" is so inappropriate that the term is better left in Russian as "*posad* people."

Imprecision or uncertainty in matters of terminology is not eased by the knowledge that the Russian government defined in law certain social and economic categories that did not correspond identifiably with living reality. Thus, to cite only a few examples, there were people identified as *kuptsy* (merchants) who never bought or sold; there were *krest'iane* (peasants) who had not been in a village in years; and there were numerous prohibitions against peasants operating in the money market while they continued to do so. All of these are problems that must be dealt with, and I have sought to respond to each in the manner that seemed most appropriate to its own context.

The second persistent problem is the uneven distribution of material on the city's history. The pretension to write a comprehensive survey of St. Petersburg's history for the last third of the eighteenth century is soon forced to yield to the realization that there are major aspects of the city's life about which little is known or in some cases can be known. It would undoubtedly be easier to produce a more limited monograph on well-documented phases of the city's development, yet to do so would also be to avoid the need to present as full a picture of the city's history as is possible at present. Much more could have been said in certain areas than is presented here. For other segments of the city's life one could only speculate if one wanted to go further. My attempt has been at least to touch on what seem to me to be the significant aspects and issues of the city's life and the changes in them during Catherine's reign.

The third difficulty has to do with the use to be made of statistical evidence for the eighteenth century. Whether one is dealing with the population of the city, the quantity of goods supplied to it, the values of imports and exports, the number and size of economic enterprises, or the levels of wages and prices, one is confronted with differing and contradictory sets of figures. Even in the eighteenth century enough questions were raised about some of these statistics to cast considerable doubt on their validity. For example, import and export figures show only those goods that passed through the custom house, yet smuggling was reported to be of great proportions and so heavily weighted to imports as to reverse a favorable balance of legally conducted trade. If the numbers are so wildly inaccurate in some cases, can they be trusted in any? And if they cannot be relied upon for accuracy, what is the point or the justification in using them?

Obviously, statistical information from the eighteenth century must be used with care. To ignore it entirely, however, would be foolish. When it appears in such works as Georgi's and Storch's, both of them scientists, and Storch, in fact, trained as a statistician, it can be given a strong measure of trust. Most official figures should be used—judiciously—in one of two ways. They give a strong indication that activity of a certain type did exist at a certain numerical level; the count may not have been complete, but it does establish a minimal figure. For example, there may have been commercial exchanges that remain hidden from us, but we do know that trade existed at least at a certain level. Then it is a matter of judgment as to how much else there was, how much remained uncounted. The other approach is to assume that statistics show, at least to a certain degree, relationships or ratios between kinds of activities. The recorded numbers of births and deaths may not be accurate, but the change they show over time can be assumed to reflect the real shift in rates. No single set of figures may be absolutely verifiable, but the assumption has been that they may be used, with implicitly understood caveats, unless there is evidence to cast doubt even on their degree of accuracy. They are the only figures we have, and they may be used with no less validity than the subjective and impressionistic observations that have come down to us in narrative form.

In order to comprehend the economic and social development of St. Petersburg, one must first be familiar with the city. For this reason, the first chapter describes the physical appearance of St. Petersburg in 1762. The people of St. Petersburg are the subject of the second chapter, which deals both with numerical growth and social composition.

The third part of the study, chapters 3 and 4, examines the structure and functions of city administration, with particular attention to the changes brought about in each under Catherine's leadership. The next three chapters deal with the economic life of St. Petersburg. One peculiarity of the city was its distance from the sources of its everyday necessities. Chapter 5 relates the solutions to problems of sustenance, of ensuring economic viability. Chapters 6 and 7 detail developments in the commercial and industrial sectors. The fourth section of the study, chapter 8, returns to the physical appearance of the city at the end of Catherine's reign, showing the imprint of the changes occurring in the intervening years after 1762. Finally, chapter 9 places St. Petersburg in perspective with the rest of Russia.

The system of transliteration followed throughout the text is that of type 3 as formulated by J. Thomas Shaw.[33] Russian words, whether or not familiar to those not reading Russian, are italicized. Such frequently cited names as Peter and Catherine are rendered in their English variant. All transliterations have been standardized according to modern Russian. All dates are by the Julian calendar, in use in Russia throughout the eighteenth century. The Julian calendar lagged eleven days behind the more familiar Gregorian calendar in the eighteenth century.

1

"I Found Petersburg Virtually Wooden . . .": St. Petersburg in 1762

Founded in 1703 on the banks of the Neva River, St. Petersburg was characterized from its inception by overwhelming spaciousness. Within the city's first year, it began to sprawl outward from three separate areas. The city's military garrison bristled on the Neva's north bank in the Fortress of St. Peter and St. Paul. Across the river's main channel on the south bank lay the navy's industrial shipyard called the Admiralty. And the intended residential district sprouted to the west on large, roughly diamond-shaped Vasil'evskii Island. Three distinct sites rather than one ensured from the beginning that the city would not be a compact center of population.

The initial tendency to spread over a wide area became even more pronounced as the city grew, both according to plan and beyond the foresight of planners, during its first sixty years. Majestic baroque two- and three-story palaces were diminished by the vast open spaces between them. Whereas almost every other European city from Moscow to London was characterized at the time by narrow streets, often with overhanging upper stories, St. Petersburg presented a singularly un-urban view. Vacant lots interspersed houses even in the center of the city. Cows grazed immediately to the south of the Admiralty and the Winter Palace in an open, grassy area called Admiralty Meadow. Sweeping avenues rather than constricted and congested streets typified St. Petersburg. In summer they often became dusty plains, in spring and autumn expansive mud flats, and in winter sheets of ice and snow. Even where streets were narrow, as along the embankments of canals and rivers, the presence of water lent an impressive feeling of breadth.

At least one provincial Russian landowner who served in the capital in the early 1760s found reason to complain about the distances that had to be traveled within the city to conduct business. A. T. Bolotov, an aide to police chief N. A. Korff, was astounded on his first day of work by the amount of time it took him to ride back and forth across town. The second day was even harder on him. When asked in the evening by the adjutant general how he liked service in St. Petersburg, Bolotov, painfully attempting to bow low, replied, "Well, Sir, I am glad you asked. If everything here is going to be like this you and your way of living can go to hell! And may the devil take it! I hurt so bad that my arms and legs are growing numb, and I can't straighten my back. Never in my life have I had to ride so much. I'm not so sure I'll even be able to get up tomorrow."[1] On his first ride across the length of Admiralty district, galloping close on the wheels of Korff's carriage, Bolotov wondered, "Good Lord! How spread out is this place? Does it even have an end?"[2]

Geographical Setting

The sense of spaciousness that both impressed and irritated Bolotov resulted not only from the sprawling nature of the city's construction by 1762, although that alone might have sufficed. The feeling was intensified by the surrounding landscape, which was almost totally flat, broken not far to the north and at a greater distance to the south by moraine-deposited hill lines. Poor drainage and numerous marshy areas impeded the intensive agricultural use of land. The city's locale had numerous rivers and streams. While the Neva and its branches flowed swiftly enough, many bogs, swamps, and creeks moved sluggishly if at all. The clayey substrata, in most places over a hundred feet in depth and interspersed with glacial boulders, prevented efficient drainage of rainwater. The swampy characteristics of the city's situation did not especially draw the attention of eighteenth-century observers; only later, in the nineteenth century, was criticism leveled at Peter's selection of a swamp for his new capital city. It is almost as though the marshiness of the city's location represented a larger and larger problem in the minds of observers at the very time that the problem was diminishing as more and more areas were drained.[3] The immediate region was partially forested with the remainder given over to scrub wood, bushes, and grass. The wooded areas included both coniferous and deciduous trees, especially the alders that prefer lots of moisture, but in the severe climate no trees grew very tall. These limiting climatic and geographical characteristics forced a unique mold of development upon St. Petersburg.

The natural feature with greatest importance in defining St. Petersburg was its river, the Neva. The delta and tributaries of the Neva divided the city's site into numerous islands, some quite small. The number of islands has fluctuated as nature has gradually raised the level of the earth in the Ingrian isthmus, a process that continues to this day, bringing sandbars to the surface of the river and creating new islands. According to Russian geologists, in fact, the Neva's delta was formed in most recent times by this process of uplifting rather than by sedimentary deposits. So much of St. Petersburg's total area was taken up by its water courses that toward the end of the eighteenth century, this was already cited as one reason that St. Petersburg showed lower population density overall than other European cities.[4]

The river itself, so vital to the city's life, flows less than forty-five miles from Lake Ladoga to the Gulf of Finland, in which distance it falls only fifteen and a half feet. Yet the river carries a remarkable volume of water, flowing three to four feet per second at the surface and emptying almost ninety thousand cubic feet of water per second into the Gulf of Finland, an amount equal to the combined volumes of the Dnepr and Don rivers and their tributaries. The force of flow results more from the river's shallow bed than its fall. The river's greatest depth in the city's limits reaches about eighty feet, in most places varying in depth from twenty-five to forty. The river's widest point, at the branching of the Large and Small Neva, exceeds four thousand feet, more than three-quarters of a mile. At its narrowest it constricts to just under 700 feet, but the Neva averages 1,300 to 1,900 feet in width. These figures, which pertain to the twentieth century, are confirmed by the less-exact observations of the eighteenth.

The Neva drains an enormous territory in northwest Russia and southeastern Finland. It is also the outlet to the sea for Europe's two largest lakes, Onega and Ladoga. The river's water today contains, as it undoubtedly did in the eighteenth century as well, the protozoan parasite *Giardia lamblia,* the zoolite spread by animal fecal matter that is responsible for most of the world's diarrhea. The many references in written sources throughout the eighteenth century to stomach troubles on the part of residents of St. Petersburg are the surest indication that giardiasis has been a persistent problem from the beginning. Catherine herself often complained of "the colic" and stomach troubles.

Whatever else the Neva has provided the city, it has never been rich enough in fish to sustain significant commercial fisheries, even for local consumption. Prior to the founding of the city, the local Finnish inhabitants supplemented their diets with fish from the river. Several attempts were made in the eighteenth century to capitalize fisheries. Stretches of the river known to be especially rich in fish were leased to various entrepreneurs. In season, when fish were running to spawn, catches were sufficient enough that holding tanks were built in the principal fish markets to keep fish alive until marketed. The fish used the river primarily as a conduit to pass from the gulf to Lake Ladoga. Smelt ran in the late spring and were particular favorites in St. Petersburg, with their unique smell when freshly caught similar to that of cucumber. Sig, a type of salmon, was relatively abundant in the eighteenth century, although it has since virtually disappeared. Among the other twenty-five or so varieties of fish that could be found in the river were sprats, pike, whitefish, perch, ruff, lamprey, and bream. The seals living in Lake Ladoga occasionally chased schools of fish all the way to the Neva's mouth during the spring passage of the lake's ice down the river.[5]

By eighteenth-century standards the river was well suited for transportation of wares. It easily accommodated a large number of ships. An extensive harbor for merchant vessels lay just off the eastern end of Vasil'evskii Island, where the Neva was widest.[6] Engravings from the middle of the eighteenth century, while undoubtedly stylized, depict the Neva as quite full of traffic, including massive ships of the line, merchantmen, heavily laden rafts and barges, and small oared- and sailboats used for intracity transportation.[7] Despite the depth and width of the river, however, care had to be taken not to block the channel. As early as 1727 laws regulated the freight that might be ferried on various types of river craft. In later years these regulations were amplified. In 1736, for example, Empress Anna Ioannovna (ruled 1730–40) ordered that all older vessels laden with rock or brick ballast be taken immediately to the privately operated shipyard, unloaded, and the owners assessed stiff fines.[8] Sandbars at the river's mouth downstream from the city prevented heavily laden ships from entering or leaving the city, despite efforts to dredge a channel. Lighters, particularly the galleys that had their own harbor at the southwestern tip of Vasil'evskii Island, were used to carry wares to and from the large ships moored in Kronshtadt, the port and naval base some ten miles west of St. Petersburg in the gulf. The largest naval vessels built in the city's naval shipyard made it over the shoals with the help of "camels," large floating devices similar to dry docks that could be lashed to the beams of ships for that purpose.

By the late 1770s river traffic was extensive and varied. Rafts, barges, and other craft loaded with wares from Russia's interior arrived in caravans of as many as several hundred vessels, needing access to warehouses and other storage areas. Their off-loading competed for space with the comings and goings of lighters and seagoing merchant ships. Waterways were becoming so crowded that Empress Catherine proposed at the end of the summer of 1778 the creation of a captain of St. Petersburg port, whose responsibility it would be to regulate all water traffic in the city from the brickyards on the Neva well above the city itself to a point beyond the last projection of land downstream.[9] After considerable discussion and revision, the proposal was not put into effect.

In addition to its commercial and transportation uses, the river provided a vista useful in various other ways. Its possibilities as a tableau for imperial architectural ensembles was only beginning to be developed, but the expanse of water fronting the Admiralty often provided the setting for the festive launching of warships. During Empress Elizabeth's reign (1741–61) in particular, illuminations and fireworks enjoyed great popularity. The mirroring of the brilliantly colored flashes of light on the river's surface provided much of the entertainment. Preparations for such spectacles could employ up to a thousand workers for a few days' time.[10]

Eighteenth-century technology was not capable of building a permanent bridge across the Large Neva. The only access from one side of the river to the other from spring to fall was by boat or, in summer, via pontoon bridge—more precisely, over planking laid across some twenty semifinished boat hulls. There were two such bridges over the Neva in fixed locations, both of which could be opened to allow river traffic to pass. When floating ice made the river hazardous and the bridges were dismantled (usually in October), hardly anyone dared attempt a crossing. In winter, however, the river froze solidly with ice fifteen to twenty inches thick and presented no obstacle to surface transportation. On the contrary, such public entertainments as ice hills for sliding were built on the river, which, along with the greenery stuck in the ice, gave the aspect of a winter park. Smaller branches of the river were bridged permanently by 1762, as were other rivers and streams.

Aside from the natural watercourses, by 1762 the city boasted several canals. One of the oldest, destined for frequent reference in song and poem, was the Moika, a deepened and partially rechanneled stream formerly called the M'ia. Another was the Fontanka, so named because it was the source of water for the fountains in the Summer Garden before their ruin in the flood of 1777. Although the Fontanka was somewhat widened and straightened during the reign of Elizabeth, both the Moika and the Fontanka remained pestilential and swampy, repeatedly becoming choked with refuse and alluvial sand.[11] The existence of these and other canals dated in part from the attempt by Peter I (reigned 1682–1725) to model his new capital after Amsterdam, for the sites of the two cities are topographically quite similar.[12]

Canals in St. Petersburg served at least three purposes. They represented a means for draining bog-filled land, particularly on Vasil'evskii

Island, where canals delineating the various "lines" were dug early in the century. Canals also acted as a reservoir against inundations, annual occurrences in St. Petersburg. And canals served as extensions of the water communications system linking the city both to the interior of Russia and, via Kronshtadt, to seaports throughout the world.[13] Peter had intended for canals to constitute the major system of transport and communication in the northern capital, as is apparent from the well-known plan for the city published in 1717 by J. B. A. Leblond. His plan called for wholesale reshaping of Vasil'evskii Island into an oval form, fortified according to the latest doctrine of military science. Within the island he wished to create a grid-pattern of city blocks delineated by canals.[14] Several of the latter were actually dug during ensuing years but had been filled in by 1762.

Human Geography

In order to administer the growing city more effectively, it was divided during the 1750s into six sections along its most obvious physical boundaries. Vasil'evskii Island and St. Petersburg Side were set off from other districts by branches of the Neva River. Admiralty Side encompassed the territory south of the Neva extending to the Fontanka. Liteinaia, or "Foundry" district, so called because of the large armaments plant located within it, covered the area lying north of Nevskii Prospect and east of the Fontanka, tucked beneath the sweeping ninety-degree bend of the Neva. Moscow Side was the part of town along the road to Moscow, that is, south of Nevskii Prospect and east of the Fontanka. Vyborg Side lay north and east of the Neva's branches at the beginning of the overland route to the town of Vyborg. In later years Admiralty Side was to be subdivided into first three and then four administrative sections as the city's population grew. Foundry district was later split into two sections, as was Moscow Side. In each case the original name was retained for one of the districts. Those designations will serve as a guide and frame of reference throughout this work, but for purposes of describing the human geography of the city, an analysis of land use is perhaps more meaningful.

In Russia's new capital, the land use pattern was far from static. In a city growing as rapidly as St. Petersburg, the ways in which land was used, the purposes to which it was put, changed constantly. A detailed look at usage not only identifies the places where various urban activities were situated but also sheds light on the everyday mental orientation of the people who lived in St. Petersburg. An examination of land use can also tell us much about the relative importance placed upon the various aspects of the city's life in competition for space, such as the imperial court and its appurtenances, housing for the city's population, the organs of city administration, commercial activities, productive enterprises, institutions of public welfare, areas set aside for leisure-time activities, and consecrated buildings for the exercise of religion. The pattern of land use thus reveals not only the locus of each type of endeavor but also the relative importance assigned to each and the degree of differentiation among them.

The city's administrators were very early interested in the pattern of land use. In conjunction with the major celebration in the early 1750's honoring the first fifty years of St. Petersburg, a detailed map was drawn of the city and commemorative paintings were made both to glorify the city's physical appearance and to enable future generations to remember it. All sorts of information were gathered and analyzed, including the ways in which land was used. The city police provided a report on the pattern of land distribution indicating the number of square *sazhens* (a *sazhen'* was seven feet long) given over to particular uses for all six districts of town (Admiralty, Vasil'evskii Island, Petersburg Side, Vyborg Side, Foundry, Moscow). The report identified broad categories of usage, indicating the amount of land still owned by the state, the amount in private hands, and the amount controlled by religious and cultural organizations (churches, schools, monasteries, almshouses, cemeteries, and the like), the amount used by the city's major markets, and the areas assigned earlier for the workers of specific organizations (in Russian called *slobody:* the artillery foundry, the military garrison, Galley Haven, and the military and naval hospital).[15] According to this information, the land surface of the city encompassed 20.24 square kilometers (7.7 square miles). More than half of that land was owned by the city's residents (53.8 percent). Another 39 percent remained under the state's control. Religious and cultural institutions controlled 2.7 percent of land, the four former *slobody* accounted for 1.7 percent, and the three large markets 0.5 percent.

The police report divided the state-owned and privately controlled land by further distinguishing land that had been given over to buildings (on private land, houses, and all sorts of shops, warehouses, smithies, and so forth, and on state land, offices, warehouses, grain storage houses, and other buildings), land used for cultivation and gardens (including the botanical garden belonging to the College of Medicine), land in meadow or pasturage, and vacant land (table 1.1). The fact that nearly half of the available land was used for housing seems an improbably high figure in light of what was noted above about St. Petersburg's sprawl. The figure does not distinguish the land

Table 1.1. Usage of State- and Privately Owned Land, 1752

	State-owned land		Privately-owned land	
	of state-owned	Of total 39%	Of total 53.8%	of privately owned
Buildings	86.5%	33.7%	47.9%	89.0%
Gardens	6.1%	2.4%	2.3%	4.2%
Shops	neglig.	neglig.	0.5%	0.9%
Meadow/Grazing	1.7%	0.7%	——	
Vacant	5.7%	2.2%	3.2%	5.9%

actually under houses from the plots of land upon which they sat. Nonetheless it stands in stark contrast to the popular notion that St. Petersburg was a creation exclusively of the imperial government, which alone provided the city's viability. This evidence that the preponderance of land in the city was given over to buildings and purposes presumably financed from nongovernmental sources and erected by workmen procured outside the state's power to requisition labor demonstrates that the state was not the sole sponsor of physical growth.

After privately owned housing, the second most widespread use of land identified in the capital city was for the offices, chambers, bureaus, and halls of the state and the crown. In 1752 government buildings reportedly accounted for more than a third of the city's area. They included not only the palaces for the imperial family but also office buildings, military and naval facilities, including barracks for servitors, and even state-owned warehouses. The governmental apparatus thus appropriated a large proportion of available land, although the point is well taken that the treasury's hunger for land had not yet approached anywhere near its appetite in total land area during the following century.

The 1752 accounting for land distribution indicated that gardens and orchards producing vegetables, fruit, and herbs took up less than 5 percent (4.7 percent) of the city's available land. Publicly owned pastureland, 0.7 percent of the city's total area, was far less than residents wanted, as was soon to become clear in city planning proposals of the 1760s. The category of vacant, or waste, land (5.4 percent in all) would seem to be underestimated. Much of it was undoubtedly the marshy and boggy ground that typified the city's location. Taken together with what the police labeled as garden plots, open areas accounted for nearly 11 percent of the city's area. Only 1 percent was represented as being used for commercial purposes.

What is most striking about this police accounting for land distribution is that it omitted as a category land use related to most of the city's vital economic functions. The three major market areas of town where residents purchased the necessities of life were identified. The city's importance for maritime trade, however, was hidden by the fact that the port facilities and warehouses were all state-owned and thus subsumed within a larger category. Besides wholesale commercial enterprises, the other "unseen" usage of land in the 1752 accounting was for industrial purposes. It is impossible to intrude into the 1752 accounting an exact percentage of land used in commerce and industry because those functions often shared buildings with other uses. Small-scale trading and productive enterprises were often located in the modest houses where their owners lived. Manufactories often occupied one or more rooms in larger buildings serving primarily other purposes. It is, however, not unreasonable to suggest that at least another 3 to 5 percent of the city's territory could be considered as dedicated to the economic enterprises of commerce and production.

Land distribution is just one way to gain an orientation for characterizing the appearance of St. Petersburg at the beginning of Catherine's reign. As defined by the summary made in 1752, the various uses of land would have been easily observable to someone strolling through the city. The stroll (*progulka*) has in fact been a device often used for looking at St. Petersburg through books.[16] One who strolls makes evaluations as he walks, but the evaluations are usually impressionistic, not scientifically analytical. The stroller through mid-eighteenth-century St. Petersburg would clearly have seen differences between the central part of the city and those parts lying farther from the center. A Russian stroller familiar with Moscow and small Russian towns would have seen other differences immediately.

Before St. Petersburg came on the scene, the traditional Russian town, familiar to our Russian stroller, could be viewed paradigmatically as having not two concentric divisions—center and outskirts—but three. At the center lay the fortified kremlin (in the northwest called the *detinets*), in which lived the hereditary or appointed governmental administrators, the local ecclesiastical hierarchy, and special military units. In earlier times the kremlin also provided a place of refuge for the surrounding local population in time of danger. Outside the kremlin was the *posad,* where the *posad* people, primarily merchants and craftsmen, lived.[17] These were the tax-liable urban population, and their places of business—arcaded bazaars (*gostinye dvory*), markets, and artisan shops—were also situated in the *posad,* as were *posad* administrative organs. Beyond the *posad* were individual *slobody* that were generally under the administration of bureaus and chancelleries of the state, and where also laborers, peasants, part-time soldiers, and newcomers to the town might live, and where life—semirural even at the center of most towns—resembled that of the village to a still greater degree.[18]

By the beginning of the eighteenth century this traditional pattern had begun to break down, from the kremlin outward. The extension of the state's secure boundaries had rendered the kremlin less essential as a defensive bastion against attack. Furthermore, a quickening economy, an expansion of the use of money, an increase in trade, and a growing complexity within the state that included changing revenue needs, combined by midcentury to undermine the usefulness and distinctiveness of both *posad* and *sloboda.* Their identity already blurred by economic and social developments, both designations were rendered obsolete by the tax reforms of 1775 and the municipal charter of 1785.[19] In St. Petersburg, where the *posad* never had an indigenous existence, and where the fate of outlying *slobody* was to be swallowed up by urban sprawl, a new type of city was introduced to Russia, a city without walls and defying the traditional pattern of land use.[20] In place of the three schematic concentric circles of the older Russian city, the St. Petersburg pattern consisted of a center, sometimes called the city proper (*sobstvennyi gorod*), and outskirts (*predmest'ia, forshtaty*).[21] Although the rigid concentricity of the older pattern was no longer appropriately descriptive for Moscow and other towns in the eighteenth century, basic differences in land use and appearance did exist between central city and outskirts.

Central City

In reality, several distinct parts of town within St. Petersburg comprised the city proper. These districts maintained a relative degree of autonomous existence from each other because each was situated on its own island, which could be cut off from almost all intercourse with other quarters at certain times of the year by floating ice or broken bridges. Each of the central quarters possessed its own market, provisions warehouses, church parishes, and shops.[22] A contemporary stroller would feel that the flavor of one section was often entirely different from that of another. It was already possible to label a person by the neighborhood where he lived, or to evoke emotional associations simply by dropping a geographical name. Administratively, the

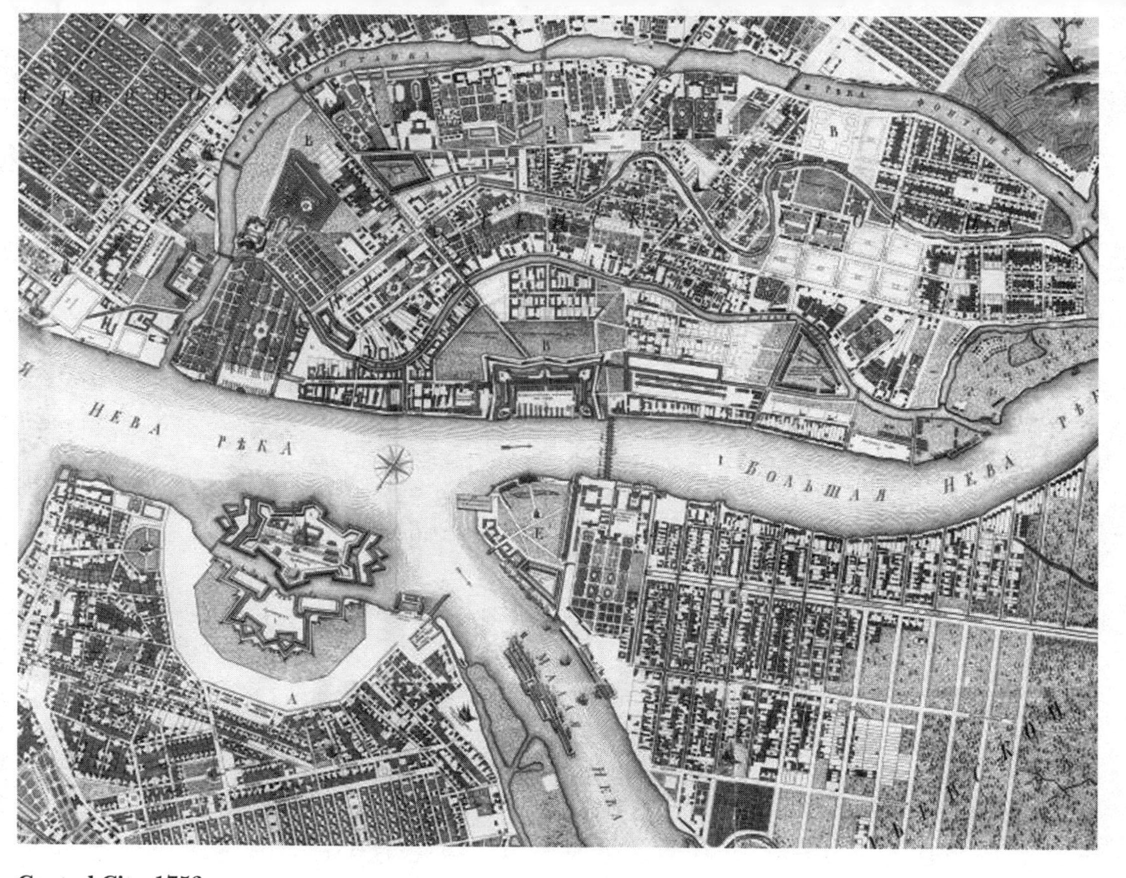

Central City, 1753.

districts making up the central city were Admiralty, Foundry, the southern half of St. Petersburg Side, and the eastern third of Vasil'evskii Island. These were the oldest sections of the city, each having become quite built-up before the end of the reign of Peter I in the mid-1720s.[23] Along a few of their streets a second or even third generation of buildings had replaced earlier structures.

Regardless of these changes, the point remains valid that land use in St. Petersburg was not intensive. Streets in the center of the city were broad and buildings widely spaced. The absence of dense construction was sometimes intentional, as three examples will illustrate. The structures immediately surrounding the Admiralty were razed in 1741 during the war with Sweden because of the potentially serious hazard to defenders of the Admiralty should those buildings be set afire by the enemy. Furthermore, those houses blocked lines of fire for the cannon within the walls of the Admiralty fortress. As a result of that measure, in 1762 a wide glacis covered only by grass gave perspective on the Admiralty's earthen walls (map 4). On the opposite side of the river a second large area behind the Fortress of St. Peter and St. Paul and the Kronverk (a munitions warehouse and powder factory) remained empty for the same reason. An additional consideration in this instance stemmed from the danger to nearby inhabitants of explosion from the artillery and gunpowder factory and magazine in the Kronverk. The third area, previously noted, was the wide marshy meadow extending from the Winter Palace to Nevskii Prospect, used for grazing cows belonging to the imperial kitchens.[24]

Despite the unevenness and occasional absence of construction, by 1762 the center of the city boasted a full complement of streets.[25] To the north, on St. Petersburg Side, our Russian stroller might feel the most comfortable, for there the street pattern came closest to resembling that of Moscow and other older Russian towns. Not only were streets narrower than elsewhere in St. Petersburg, they also met at odd angles and frequently were very short. St. Petersburg Side had few symmetrical four-way intersections. Vasil'evskii Island, on the other hand, was laid out most geometrically, conforming almost everywhere to the rectangular grid pattern introduced there by Peter I. Admiralty and Foundry displayed elements of both planned and natural growth. The three "ray" streets extending outward from the central focus of the Admiralty—Nevskii Prospect (already the grandest boulevard in the city), Gorokhovaia Street, and Voznesenskii Prospect from east to west—stretched at least as far as the Moika. They were the results of city planning laid out during the reign of Anna Ioannovna following the destructive fires of 1736 and 1737. Most other streets, if neither geometrically straight nor abutting each other precisely at right angles, were broad and lent a definite feeling of openness. To judge from appearances alone, St. Petersburg Side seemed to be the only central section not to have benefited from having its street pattern laid out prior to considerable building activity, a condition to be deduced from its not having suffered from fires that consumed almost everything. Moreover, there was little incentive to give that part of the city a parade appearance. Few governmental agencies were located there and no palaces. The population consisted primarily of middling to poor merchants and craftsmen.

With few exceptions the largest buildings a stroller would walk by housed government agencies and offices, each edifice erected freestanding in the center of its own plot of land, not abutted or hemmed in on any side. The largest number of government buildings was situated in Admiralty district, where the two most important structures—the Winter Palace and the large residence of the former chancellor A. P. Bestuzhev-Riumin, destined from 1764 to house the Ruling Senate—flanked the Admiralty itself. The Winter Palace, the fourth to stand on that site, was finally completed in 1762 after eight years of construction. Leftover building materials from that work were still strewn around it until shortly before Catherine came to power. Far more than simply a residence for the imperial family, it also housed the apartments of high government officials, numerous governmental offices, storerooms for clothing, furniture, ambassadorial gifts, and assorted collections of table service, porcelain, machines, and whatever else the imperial household had amassed in previous decades as well as living space for a large number of servants. Livestock—chickens, ducks, rabbits, sheep, goats, and pigs—were crowded into the building's attic. Other office buildings were located nearby.

The most significant exception to the location of government offices in Admiralty district was the elongated, narrow, three-story edifice on Vasil'evskii Island, the so-called Twelve Colleges Building housing many of the colleges, or ministries, of the central government. The colleges remained in that location, across the river from other central governmental offices, because housing for the hundreds of petty officials, clerks, and copyists employed there was cheaper and more readily obtainable on the island than would have been the case across the river.[26] Military installations in the center of the city included the Admiralty, the Kronverk, the Fortress of St. Peter and St. Paul, and military and naval academies along the Neva embankment on Vasil'evskii Island. A large stable near the Moika provided both the imperial court and the military with horses, equipage, and carriages. Still another area used by the army was Tsaritsa's Meadow, located on Admiralty Side immediately to the west of the Summer Garden (map 4 shows the Kronverk, imperial stables, and Tsaritsa's Meadow). Guards regiments utilized the meadow in summer as a drill field, giving rise to its later name of Mars Field.

Much of the land in each quarter of the central city found use as residential areas. Because the official imperial residences—the Summer and Winter palaces—were on Admiralty Side, most of the favored nobility, who themselves commonly owned large palaces with extensive grounds, followed suit. Here were found, in 1762 or later, the urban villas associated with the well-known surnames of Bestuzhev, Naryshkin, Osterman, Razumovskii, Sheremet'ev, Shuvalov, Stroganov, and Vorontsov from earlier in the century, with those of Bezborodko, Orlov, Panin, Potemkin, and Viazemskii added later. Other eminent people living on Admiralty Side included prominent Russian merchants (Shemiakin, Demidov, Miliutin), members of foreign embassies and consulates, and British merchants, whose preponderance was so great along the bank of the lower Neva that it came to be called *Angliiskaia naberezhnaia,* the English Embankment.[27]

Home for most foreigners living in St. Petersburg, however, was on Vasil'evskii Island. The merchants among them were attracted by commercial activity in that quarter of the city. In addition to the harbor for merchant ships, situated at the eastern tip of the island were the customhouse, commodity exchange (bourse), and a number of large warehouses. Scientists and scholars preferred the island because the Academy of Sciences was located there along with military academies and schools. Houses on the island, although not as large as those on Admiralty Side, were spacious enough.[28]

Early in the century, Peter I had caused plans and facades of model homes to be drawn up in order to ensure that privately built houses measured up to the size, type of design, and quality of construction that he envisioned for his new capital. Three basic designs were approved, for common (*podlye*), prosperous (*zazhitochnye*), and eminent (*imenitye*) people.[29] Such concern for minimal standards was no longer necessary by 1762 for the better parts of the central city, where the congregation of people of means had raised land values, and where new construction far exceeded the minimal standards of Petrine model houses. Homes in Foundry district and on St. Petersburg Side were somewhat smaller. In those areas the houses belonged to artisans, less-affluent merchants, a small number of government clerks, and even some laborers.

A few large industrial enterprises were located in the central parts of St. Petersburg; most visible were the armaments foundry in the eponymous district, the munitions plant on St. Petersburg Side, and the Admiralty shipyard. The attentive passerby could hardly miss noting the small privately owned shipyards, or the ropewalk and cable factory, or the imperial glassworks, among others. Numerous small workshops and factories found space in buildings utilized for the most part in other ways. It was not uncommon for wealthy people to rent a room or two to craftsmen, who both lived and worked in their apartments. Empress Elizabeth became concerned about the number of "factories" in the central areas of St. Petersburg in the mid-1750s and issued an order banishing them to outer areas. But as in the case of many ordinances and regulations in the eighteenth century, nothing substantive had been done by 1762 to carry out her will.

Commercial activity centered in two areas, the eastern tip of Vasil'evskii Island and along Nevskii Prospect on Admiralty Side. The former primarily handled goods involved in international trade and the latter those consumed domestically. The concentration of such activity in the area along the Nevskii by no means implies an absence of trading elsewhere. As has been noted, each administrative quarter possessed its own retail markets. But the area on Admiralty Side turned over a significantly greater volume than similar markets in other quarters of the city. As a sort of central marketplace, it dealt in specialized goods and in those products for which demand was irregular and soft. If an item was to be had anywhere in St. Petersburg, it was most likely to be found in the shops in and around the Admiralty Side bazaar, the *gostinyi dvor.*

Both waterways and roadways served as means of transportation and communication. Canals provided a convenient and inexpensive medium for moving large quantities of goods or bulky wares, which generally arrived in St. Petersburg by water. But facilities for transferring goods from one system to the other remained primitive. In 1762 even the best-developed banks of waterways were reinforced only with timber pilings, which seemed always to be rotting or otherwise falling into disrepair. People had to be careful not to approach too closely to the water's edge or risk the consequences of a crumbling bank. Furthermore, canals and streams were usually shallow, clogged with garbage and refuse, or otherwise noisome. Since they served partially as a sewer system, strollers found it unpleasant to walk too extensively along the canals.

The condition of streets was often worse. Most streets were unpaved and littered with horse droppings and whatever wastes people threw into them. Well traveled, they became rock-hard and rutted in the sun, a morass of mud in rain. Unused, they were soon overgrown with grass. Improved streets were usually cobbled. In that state they became so slippery from snow, ice, or rain that often it was impossible to ride horses on them; like Bolotov, riders might prefer to negotiate the wooden sidewalks where it was safer.[30] Some attempt had been made to embellish streets. Nevskii Prospect, already distinguished by its appearance, exemplified the best in street beautification. A spacious boulevard, it was bordered on either side by two rows of young trees, beyond which lay a drainage ditch and a sidewalk.[31] Most streets, unfortunately, were not as grand. They are best described as resembling raised driveways wide enough for two vehicles to pass and with ditches along either side. Grass grew between the ditches and the sidewalks, which were usually built of rough lumber, bordering the fronts of houses and fences.[32]

Streets provided access to another form of communication in the city, the signboard. Erected in places where crowds were likely to pass, these sidewalk newspapers contained news articles and important announcements. News of particular significance or timeliness was read aloud by government officials accompanied by drummers.[33]

Despite St. Petersburg's reputation as a wholly planned and artificial city, there were far more instances of planning not carried through to completion than there were of plans meticulously followed. The great fire of 1737 had given opportunity to replace inferior housing in the Admiralty district with buildings more in line with Peter's original intentions, but for the most part St. Petersburg was still far from being the well-planned residence city Peter's architects had envisioned, especially in backstreets off the grand "perspectives" (*pershpektivy*) such as the Nevskii.

By the early 1760s residential buildings followed three basic forms of construction. The largest and most expensive were those made of masonry (*kamennyi:* brick or stone). They were most visible in the area bounded by the Moika and the Neva and to a lesser extent Murky Run (*Glukhoi protok*), later the Catherine Canal.[34] In addition, a few blocks (lines) near the eastern end of Vasil'evskii Island also corresponded to this pattern. The houses there tended to exemplify baroque architectural forms, with lavishly decorated window frames, corners, cornices, and eaves. An English commentator noted that the structures mixed Italian and Dutch styles, albeit, he thought, unsuccessfully.[35] Masonry houses rarely exceeded two stories. They were closely spaced, commonly built flush with the sidewalk, but did not yet present a single unbroken facade. In a typical house for this area, the basement, raised one or two feet above street level and finished in stone, was used as apartments for servants or rented out as shops to merchants and artisans. Rooms on the first floor were commonly used for storage or pantry space. Usually the owner and his family actually occupied only the second floor. Rooms were large, walls thick. Roofs on more expensive houses consisted of sheet iron or sheet copper. On less-expensive ones, roofing tiles were used.[36] A carriageway at one side led behind the house to the yard, carriage-house, kitchen, woodshed, and other outbuildings. Although the view from the street gave the impression that houses were relatively close together and that all available land was economically used, a bird's-eye view would have dispelled this misconception. In fact, the houses extended only about two rooms deep away from the street. The yard and scattered outbuildings took up the remaining space. Contrary to the view from the street, and despite its larger houses, the Admiralty district had less square footage of land under buildings—because of its more spacious lots—than did the other quarters in the center of the city.[37]

The most prosperous citizens in Admiralty district lived in virtual palaces on lots that sometimes encompassed entire blocks. Their presence was most visible along the Fontanka Canal south of the Nevskii Prospect, where individual holdings stretched from the canal to Great Garden Street. A detailed survey of one of these properties, Anichkov Palace, gives proper appreciation of their size. Situated on the corner of Nevskii and the Fontanka, Anichkov Palace was one of several built for the imperial family, although it belonged briefly at this time to a wealthy St. Petersburg merchant named Shemiakin and later to Prince Grigorii Potemkin.[38] Its property was more than one thousand feet deep and five hundred feet wide at its greatest extent (map 4). Most of the land remained open, given over to trees and grass if not a formal park. But this does not mean that there were few buildings on the territory or that they were small. Just off Nevskii and facing the canal, although set back a considerable distance from it, reposed the palace itself, flanked on one side by a winter garden and on the other by a terrace. Between the winter garden and the Fontanka was situated the kitchen, the third-largest structure on the grounds. A canal thirty feet wide led to a large, oblong pond behind the palace. To the rear of the pond rose a multipurpose structure containing, among other things, an art gallery and an "Italian house." Still other outbuildings included a theater, a colonnade, living quarters in three separate structures (undoubtedly for servants), a storage cellar for food, a carriage garage, two houses with stores on the first floor and living quarters in the upper stories (these latter two opposite the bazaar on Great Garden Street), and a general warehouse. Near Nevskii stood a small gazebo, dwarfed by all the open space around it.[39] From this precise enumeration of buildings, it is clear that the property was more representative of a nearly self-sufficient rural estate than of an urban residence. The latter, to be sure, might be grandiose, yet the use of land and the buildings present on the estate betrayed the essentially rural character of the residence. Its presence serves to underline the fact that while by 1762 land in the city center had been distributed, the problem remained to persuade or force landowners to use their property more intensively.[40]

The second architectural model, a house with stone or brick foundations and wooden frame and superstructure, was used quite extensively because of its practicality. It typified the fringes of Admiralty district and parts of Vasil'evskii Island and Foundry district. Since the city lay on such low land and was subject to annual flooding, stone provided foundations durable enough to withstand these annual inconveniences as well as the year-round dampness. Most of the stone for foundations came from the Putilovo limestone quarry located some forty miles to the east of the city, which continues to this day to provide building blocks. Wood provided a less-expensive and more readily available material, allowing faster completion of superstructures on such houses. With a rock or stone foundation, a wooden house could be fronted in brick at a later date without too much difficulty. Wooden houses on stone foundations and masonry houses were of approximately equal size.[41]

The third type of dwelling was constructed completely of wood. Wooden houses were smaller than the others and made up a greater proportion of buildings the farther one traveled from the heart of the city. In outer parts almost all construction was with the ubiquitous wood. Such houses were not always small or built by less-wealthy citizens. Timbered houses were similar in style to American log cabins, with rounded logs laid one on another, mortised at the corners, the cracks filled with hemp, flax, and moss. Frequently the logs were covered over with boards on the exterior, both to conserve heat and to enhance appearance. Wooden houses ordinarily were set toward one side or corner of their small lots, in order to put the open yard to use as kitchen garden. The historian P. N. Stolpianskii provides a vivid description of such a building: "The little house (*domik*) was of wood, small, a typical cottage of old Kolomna; up top on the roof trotted a tiny carved steed; there was also carving under the windows. Toward the street ran a little wing with wee steps made rickety by time. A stairway led in two flights to the second floor; the steps quaked and creaked and gave rise to unwilling fear—will the steps bear the weight of the person ascending them? Only for special events in the evening was the stairway lit up by a putrid night lamp in which hemp oil smoked and sputtered."[42] Most wooden houses had four to seven feet of cellar (usually only a root cellar) and one story. Wooden houses were warm, relatively inexpensive, and relatively long-lasting. For those with brick foundations, sixty years was not an unusual life span for wooden houses. Furthermore, they could be transported from one place to another; apparently this was done fairly frequently.[43] Whole houses were sometimes sold in prefabricated sections in the city's larger markets, a practice common in other Russian towns as well.

At the start of Catherine's reign, the central sections of town had the aspect of a city, if somewhat unevenly. Unlike Moscow, St. Petersburg was more than a village writ large. It had enough of the hallmarks of princely splendor, commercial activity, and architectural creativity to impress even the most jaded eighteenth-century traveler. But not everything looked like the center.

Outskirts

Whereas most older Russian towns boasted walls that more or less delineated the boundary between city and suburb, St. Petersburg had no such definite limits. Thus to a greater extent than usual, the center and outskirts blended together with no sudden break. There were, though, distinct differences in land use between center and outskirts, and in its outer extremities especially, St. Petersburg was indistinguishable from many other preindustrial cities.

The outlying sections of eighteenth-century cities provided space for activities not welcome in the central cities for various reasons. For example, the higher valuation of land in central areas tended to force to the outside those undertakings requiring an extensive amount of land. Thus pasturage for animals was more apt to be located near the edges of cities than in centers. In addition, certain industrial processes were by that time deemed too noisome or otherwise inappropriate for the central city. For this reason plants and factories that polluted air or water were more often located away from the centers of cities. Furthermore, the preference by wealthier and more prominent residents to live in the cores of cities forced the residences of poor people from the centers and into the outskirts. This occurred in many cities and of course ran counter to the demographic movement pattern of contemporary urban life in the United States. The trend to push poorer elements from the center toward the city's edges can be dated from at least the 1730s in St. Petersburg.[44]

The dynamics of suburbs were such that they seemingly sprang up overnight, peopled by peasants fresh from rural areas. Buildings were haphazard structures made of whatever materials people could lay hands on. The crime rate was high, filth omnipresent. However, these slum areas did not necessarily retain these characteristics for long. As they became established, they often began by degrees to achieve respectability. Hovels and shacks seemingly metamorphosed into cottages; streets displaced some of the dwellings and attained regularity and permanence; the standard of living rose as men found work. This process has been noted many times in preindustrial cities. In the case of St. Petersburg, the ring of slums steadily drifted outward as more and more people migrated to the capital.[45]

As for their geographical limits, the outskirts of St. Petersburg enclosed the administrative areas of the city not previously described as belonging to the center: Moscow, Vyborg and the upper half of St. Petersburg sides, and the western parts of Vasil'evskii Island (map 4 shows lines laid out on Vasil'evskii Island along Bol'shoi Prospect but no buildings). Other areas also may be considered functionally a part of the city outskirts even though they were excluded administratively. For example, Okhta, founded by Peter I upstream from St. Petersburg on the site of the old Swedish fort Nienshants (Swedish Nyenskans), served as a residential area for shipbuilders and carpenters. Heads of most of the more than eight hundred households who lived in Okhta worked in St. Petersburg. Certainly with an economy so closely tied to that of the city, the *sloboda* of Okhta must be considered as having been part of the city. Kronshtadt is another example. Serving as the outlying port for the capital and a major naval base, its relationship to St. Petersburg was comparable to that of Piraeus to ancient Athens or Ostia Antica to Rome. Also immediately outside the built-up areas of the capital were the dachas and summer homes of the wealthy. They encompassed most land on the islands of the Small Neva and both riverbanks above Smolnyi, the point of land inside the elbow of the Neva's final bend before its delta fans out westward. Dachas extended as well along the roads to Peterhof and Tsarskoe Selo west and south of the city. Industrial enterprises were located along rivers and roads along with the summer homes.[46]

Maps dating from the 1750s and early 1760s corroborate the observation that land was used less intensively in the outskirts of St. Petersburg than in the center of the city. The most intensive utilization was by markets, shops, and factories. Residential areas, interchanging tiny peasant cottages and the barracks of various military units, took up most of the land that was in use. There were also peasant gardens and pasture areas.[47]

It may seem contradictory, first to assert that land in outlying areas of St. Petersburg was not used intensively, and then to contend that there was to an extent a shortage of land in these areas, yet both statements are true. More land was needed, both for extensive exploitation and for less-intensive utilization. There were several reasons for this. As the city grew, new areas were being taken up for houses and other buildings. However, the city required at the same time more land for vegetable gardens, pasturage for animals owned by citizens, cemeteries, and other nonintensive usages. There were clear limitations on the total amount of land that the city could utilize. Rivers and swamps could be channeled but never completely eliminated, even if that were desirable. There was no legal mechanism that the city could employ to claim vacant lands held by the two monasteries in the area. Nor could land on which there were dachas and summer homes be taken over by the city and redeveloped. And, of course, limited technology in transportation restricted the city to an area that could be traversed by boat and horse easily and relatively quickly. These problems of size and land use intensity were already in evidence in 1762. During Catherine's reign the government attempted in various ways to deal with them.[48]

Examination of existing maps and descriptions of the outskirts of St. Petersburg at the time when Catherine II became empress reveal that few outlying areas were well developed or even planned. The 1753 map of the city indicates that buildings on Vyborg Side were for the most part small. Traces of planning were evident in the street pattern, but in the main growth had been haphazard. Okhta, on the other hand, appeared as a well-planned block-wide strip along the right bank of the Neva.[49] Also neatly laid out were the *sloboda* of the Chancellery on Construction and such military barracks as those of the Preobrazhenskii and Izmailovskii regiments.[50] The outskirt portions of Vasil'evskii Island, St. Petersburg Side, most of Moscow Side (including the postmen's *sloboda*)—in short, all but the few exceptions mentioned—had developed with no plan. In fact, much of the outskirts were as yet undeveloped. Most of Moscow district remained in pasture or under hoe and plow; the western half of Vasil'evskii Island (except for Galley Haven next to the gulf) and the upper portions of St. Petersburg Side were covered by nothing more than scrub bushes and trees.[51]

A few areas in the outskirts had been used for one or another purpose in the past, but were now lying idle. The strangely named Elephant Yard between Foundry district and Smolnyi was where Empress Elizabeth had quartered her elephants until the northern climate killed them. Southwest of the city lay Ekaterinhof, built for Catherine I (reigned 1725–27) by Peter the Great, but in a low-lying area that flooded frequently, for which reason the palace had been allowed slowly to fall into ruin.

In addition to those functions already mentioned, at least three others must be added. Industrial concerns were located in the outskirts to a greater extent than in the central parts of the city. Vyborg was then (and still is) a quarter largely given over to heavy industry.

It housed mills, brickyards, a small shipyard, tanneries, a gunpowder enterprise, a wax factory, breweries, and distilleries. Similar enterprises operated on St. Petersburg Side and on Vasil'evskii Island. Far fewer industrial concerns could be found in 1762 in Moscow administrative district. Second, religious and semireligious institutions controlled larger tracts of land in the outskirts than in the center. The two most notable monasteries in St. Petersburg, the Smolnyi for women and the Alexander Nevskii for men, lay in the outskirts.[52] With one or two exceptions all cemeteries were there also. The few cemeteries within the central city continued in use only until the early 1770s. Finally, at certain times of year designated areas of land came into extensive use as special markets. Their territory lay adjacent to routes of transportation, that is, the highways leading to the interior and the Neva. These seasonal markets specialized in supplying certain of the city's essential needs. Thus firewood when brought to market in the city was unloaded along the Neva upstream from Smolnyi and sold there during the summer months. In the early winter, before Christmas, and again before *maslianitsa* or Shrovetide, prior to Lent, merchants from the interior of the country transported the frozen carcasses of cattle, sheep, swine, poultry, game birds, deer, rabbit, and other animals across the snow and ice to St. Petersburg and displayed them picturesquely for sale along the Moscow highway.[53]

In outlying districts the network of communication was not as well developed as in the center. Besides the Fontanka—which bordered the area—the outskirts contained only one canal, the Ligovo, located east and south of the Fontanka. The Neva was nowhere spanned, not even by the pontoon-type bridge. Defects noted in the central city's street system were worse in the outskirts. The lack of linking-roads forced circuitous routes of travel from one point to another. To go from one place in the outskirts to another, it was almost always necessary to travel into the center along one street and then back out by another to reach one's destination. Pavement, usually corduroy rather than cobblestone, was to be found exclusively on main streets and across a few swampy areas. Only on the main roads leading out of the city did the government attempt to render streets more beautiful, provide ditches, or clean up filth. Those roads, five in number, led to Moscow, to Riga, along the south bank of the Neva to Shlisselburg, due south toward Pskov, and north to Vyborg. Nearly impassable in spring and fall because of mud, they attained their best condition in winter. Indeed, only when hardpacked with snow did the roads carry significant quantities of goods from the interior to St. Petersburg. They were nevertheless in use year-round to carry wares inland from the city because it was easier to use roads, no matter how bad, than to fight river currents upstream.[54]

In 1762 people in the outskirts frequently still lived in *slobody,* small neighborhoods with high population density. A *sloboda* commonly contained people employed by and under the jurisdiction of a single state agency, such as the Admiralty or the postal service (*iam*). This fact makes it rather uncomplicated to reconstruct a typical residential neighborhood in the outer sections of St. Petersburg during its early decades.

A map of St. Petersburg Side provides the best example from contemporary sources. Lots were laid out either adjacent to the riverbank or within two blocks of it. Inland, main roads played the same role as the river. Blocks were divided into long and narrow strips of land. Sometimes one lot extended from street to street; at other times a block was two houses deep. The structures themselves covered only a small fraction of the land in each plot. Average house size ranged from 15 by 30 feet to 20 by 50 feet.[55] In other *slobody,* however, houses crowded together dangerously, creating potential fire hazards. This was notably true in the Moscow postmen's *sloboda.*[56]

Houses themselves can readily be described. They were normally of the third type mentioned above, all wooden. Obtaining building materials was an overriding, ever-present problem. Bolotov vividly described one solution to the dilemma. In the spring of 1762 the work on the Winter Palace was finally completed. In the large meadow on the land side of the palace remained piles of unused building materials, bricks, stone, and just plain rubbish. The authorities wanted to clear the area in time for Easter, but both the cost and the shortness of time prohibited the use of hired laborers to remove the materials. So the police chief devised a plan to allow residents of the city to take away anything they were physically able to remove. On the appointed day, according to A. T. Bolotov, "thousands of people hurried to the spot from every direction. Each one, hoping to get something of value, seized the first things he came upon; having taken them home, he returned for more. The noise, the cries, the clamor, the general happiness and exclamation filled the air . . . By evening the whole place was cleaned out—even the shacks and huts were totally removed."[57] Under normal circumstances it was much more expensive to acquire materials, and many newcomers lived in the crudest of hovels. A picture of the outskirt areas of the city, therefore, would show simple homes of one and two stories, wooden fences, unpaved streets, no streetlights, and dirty gutters filled with garbage.

In 1762, at the beginning of the period here under study, the city was divisible into two distinct parts, the center and the outskirts, differentiated both by function and by intensity of land use within them. The center of the city was distinctly more advanced than the outskirts in terms of urban development, yet its available space was still used much less intensively than land in other large cities of Europe. City planning had affected no more than street patterns, and then only in parts of the capital. The city was rough-edged, still a frontier town, despite its role as one of Russia's two imperial residences. In this regard, it was not dissimilar from its contemporary Berlin. Over the next three decades, however, St. Petersburg changed dramatically. Those changes were driven by a rapid increase in population unprecedented in the history of Russian towns.

2
“’Tis Pleasant There to Dwell for Each and All. . . .”: Population and Society

St. Petersburg’s population increased dramatically during Catherine’s reign. This constant growth in numbers was accompanied by far-reaching changes in societal relationships. The Russian state had long tried to fit people into a few legal categories (estates) in order to meet the fiscal and service needs of state and to maintain social control, a process culminating in Peter the Great’s “all-Russian subject people.”[1] The legal estates recognized in law, while they may have been descriptive of an overwhelmingly rural society, proved neither appropriate nor adaptable to the urban environment of St. Petersburg. In the countryside change in the relative distribution of wealth occurred slowly and evolution in the hierarchy of social relationships more slowly still, but in the city the financial rewards of commerce and production continually redistributed wealth and thereby placed pressure on the accepted social order, if not actually necessitating readjustments in it. These fluctuations did not affect all citizens equally, of course. Merchants and artisans coming to the city were absorbed into its life more quickly than peasants, who frequently spent only half of each year in the capital and thus retained much firmer ties with their native villages. The substantial foreign-born population also maintained ties with their homelands, often returning there following years of residence in St. Petersburg. Regardless of place of origin and reasons for staying, the people who came to live in Russia’s new capital raised it to the status of Europe’s sixth- or seventh-largest city by the end of Catherine’s reign. Life in St. Petersburg may not have been as pleasant “for each and all” as Vasilii Trediakovskii claimed in his poem of 1752 cited in the chapter title, yet to the city they came.[2]

The Numbers Game

The size of St. Petersburg at any given time has proven extremely difficult to estimate, with wildly varying results. Many historians have accepted population statistics showing some 120,000 people living in Russia's capital at the beginning of Catherine's reign and nearly 220,000 at its end.[3] These figures were published most notably by the Ministry of Internal Affairs in the 1830s and generally accepted thereafter. Their accuracy may be questioned on several counts. They are presumably based on pro forma police reports. The police were required to report periodically on the city's population as part of the mechanism for providing for emergencies, as for example in case of food shortages. The authorities needed to know how much to lay by in warehouses for such situations. One does not have to read very long through these reports to receive the distinct impression that each weekly report was based on the one preceding it. Recounts were too cumbersome and time-consuming to make. With time, the figures reported by the police and the actual size of the population diverged sharply. Police statistics failed to keep up with real growth. They are at considerable variance with other special reports filed by police officials with regard to the population. Weekly police reports, furthermore, were based only on the area within the administrative city limits, even though the built-up populated area included settled areas beyond those limits. Already at the time when the lines were drawn, they excluded several neighborhoods, among them the Okhta settlements and Galley Haven, whose residents were at least in an economic sense a part of the city. The metropolitan area, "greater St. Petersburg," thus included people living outside the administrative limits of the city.[4]

It is more than likely that the figure of 120,000 for 1762 is too high and that of 220,000 for 1796 is too low. Research undertaken by N. A. Varlamova found that parish records counting the number of Orthodox Christians who made confession and took communion did not exceed 70,000 into the early 1770s.[5] Starting in the 1730s the Holy Synod used a uniform reporting mechanism that was supposed to include everyone of both genders and all ages, from infants to oldest people. They were listed in categories starting with ecclesiastics, then military people, then civilians in the city under governmental orders, and so on through the entire population. The accounting included everyone living in a dwelling, whether a private house, a government building, a military barracks, a barracks for other state workers, a hospital, an almshouse, a monastery, an educational institution, even the house of someone of another faith. The names of people who said confession in a parish other than their home parish were supposed to be sent to their home church for inclusion on the list. Although the materials for thirty-eight parishes in St. Petersburg in 1762 admittedly are incomplete, counting only 52,298 Orthodox, it is unlikely that the actual number would have been as much as one and a half

Table 2.1. Orthodox Communicants in St. Petersburg[6]

Year	1737	1740	1750	1762	1772
Parishes	35	29	33	38	44
Houses (*Dvory*)	6,151	4,816	4,319	2,281	3,216
Souls (both sexes)	68,141	52,319	60,901	52,298	62,722

times larger (table 2.1). The number of military troops in the city was undoubtedly slightly lower in 1762 than in 1750 because of the demands of the Seven Years' War, and similarly deflated in 1772, when military garrisons were depleted to man the armies in the south against Turkey and in Poland to implement the first partition of that state.

Regardless of how the church counted its communicants, for our purposes temporary residents of St. Petersburg should also be included in an estimate of the city's population, even though they lived almost half of each year away from the city. These people contributed greatly to the workforce of the capital during their six to eight months' residence there each year. Temporary residents divided their lives between the city and a smaller town or village primarily because little work was available for them in winter in St. Petersburg, just at the time of year when living expenses rose. Their presence was also required periodically in their villages, and it was more economical to journey to and from the city each year than to maintain permanent households in the capital.[7]

Soldiers garrisoned in the city were sometimes included in population estimates, sometimes not. During Catherine's reign the city served as a permanent station for the guards regiments—the Preobrazhenskii, Semenovskii, Izmailovskii, and Horse—almost all of whom lived in regimental barracks. In addition, regular army troops were rotated from garrison to garrison, and at any time there would have been posted in St. Petersburg units of cavalry, several infantry regiments, artillery, engineer, and Cossack units, and naval and marine forces. Regular soldiers for most of Catherine's reign lived in private housing, not barracks, and their families, whether or not a *venchanie,* or church wedding, had taken place, often lived with them. The troops alone usually totaled about 25,000 early in Catherine's reign and upward of 40,000 by its end.[8] Because their number remained relatively stable and their dependents often became involved in the city's economic life, they too must be included in population figures that would lay claim to inclusiveness.

The addition of these groups to the figures supplied by police yields a metropolitan area including at least 100,000 people at the beginning of Catherine's reign. By its end, in a slightly larger area, the population had increased by about 150,000, now totaling approximately 250,000. In fact, the increase might have been even greater. In reports dating from 1786, Police Chief Ryleev by count and estimation arrived at a figure of 247,572 in January, when population was at its lowest, and 300,000 in late June and extending through the summer, then declining to 255,696 by the end of the year.[9] Alternatively, J. G. Georgi, in his lengthy published description of the city, played with figures for 1784–92 provided him by the police, the fourth "revision" or census of the soul tax–paying population, and statisticians in the Academy of Sciences, consistently coming up with totals of more than 200,000 up to nearly 228,000, a figure that he said "did not include the majority of the staff at court, the infantry and cavalry regular line regiments, and others."[10] When measured against the figures of Ryleev and Georgi, the estimate of a quarter million people living in the city by the end of Catherine's reign is conservative.

It goes without saying that any of these population figures for eighteenth-century St. Petersburg, as for Russia generally during that period, must be used with caution. Their accuracy is highly questionable, and they can only be considered to be approximate. Their greatest utility lies in the fact that they demonstrate the fluidity of the city's population. It was almost impossible to freeze a precise number in time even within a given year because of the vitality of the ebb and flow of people to and from the city. All of the figures given above were recognized by someone as having validity for late eighteenth-century St. Petersburg. Even if they cannot be regarded as accurate by today's statisticians, they do indicate what was generally the case, or show proportional relationships. They are the only figures we have, and however partial the picture may be that they give us, they are better than nothing.

All of the sets of figures compiled in the eighteenth century agree that St. Petersburg's rate of growth was uneven. The years 1770–75, for example, show a decline of about two hundred people, attributable primarily to stringent measures enacted in 1771–72 to protect the capital from plague and to increased military recruitment and troop transfers for fighting the war against Turkey. During the first five years of the 1780s, on the other hand, the population grew by eighteen thousand (a 10 percent rise) in the most rapid increase of Catherine's reign to that time (see table 2.2).[11]

Graph 2.1[12] contains the birth figures for St. Petersburg from 1764–90 as kept by the governors.[13] While it is impossible to ascertain their accuracy, at least some measure of reliability is suggested by the aggregate ratio of male to female births over the entire period

Table 2.2. Birth, Death, and Natural Change (per 1,000)

Years	Births	Deaths	Change
1764–70	31.9	29.2	+2.7
1781–90	30.5	31.4	-0.9
1791–1800	32.3	31.5	+0.8
AVERAGE	31.7	29.75	+1.95

(105.1:100), a figure that coincides with the natural ratio. Since the births of both sexes were apparently being reported, presumably the annual figures can be compared with some confidence. What is most noteworthy from the figures is that the number of births per thousand population, while remaining relatively steady, was about one-fourth lower than the traditional birthrate for rural societies (40 per 1,000). This phenomenon is most easily explained by the persistent disproportion of men to women in St. Petersburg, for fewer women than men migrated to the city. With most of the population growth limited to men, the birth rate per thousand of population could hardly be expected to increase. To know whether the fertility rate declined, one would have to be able to break down the population by gender, a process that the surviving population figures unfortunately will not support.

The increasingly male cast to the city's population is brought out by the city's statistics on deaths (graph 2.2), which reveal a much higher ratio of males to females than the figures for births. When birth figures are compared with those for deaths, it becomes clear that overall there was only a slight natural increase in population, far from enough to account for the total increase in population from 100,000 to 250,000 or more. In nineteen of the twenty-seven years, births exceeded deaths. The eight years of high mortality include two when there are known to have been grain shortages or at least excessively high prices (1766 and 1786), and six were war years (1770–72, 1788–90). The extremely sharp increase in male deaths at the end of the 1780s undoubtedly resulted from the number of soldiers wounded or taken ill in the nearby military campaigns against Sweden who were returned to the city to die. Excluding the war years, the excess of births over deaths averaged 977 per year. When the war years are included, some 367 more people were born each year in St. Petersburg than died. Because of the preponderance of males, St. Petersburg had significantly fewer births per capita than did other large European cities. It also seems to have had a lower incidence of child and infant

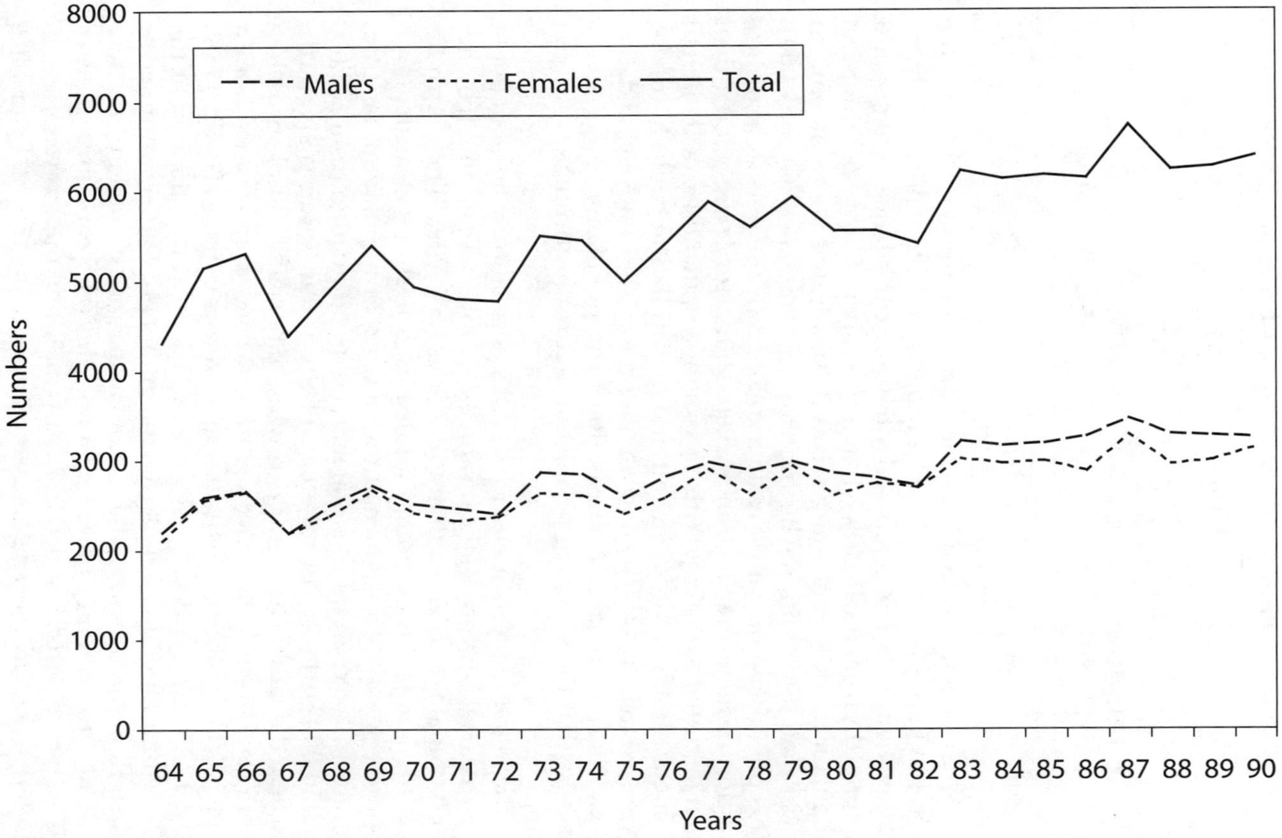

Graph 2.1. St. Petersburg Births, 1764–90

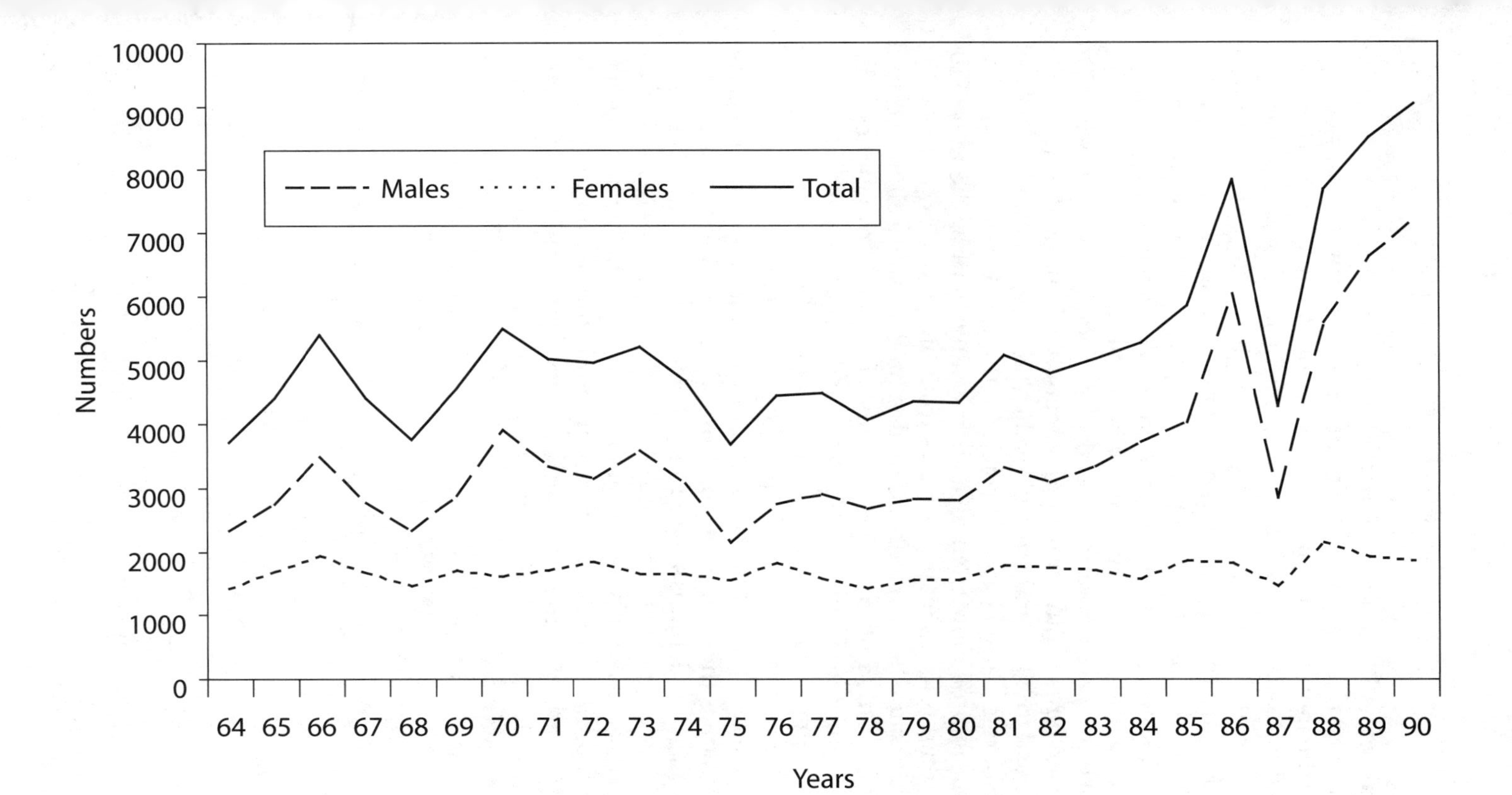

Graph 2.2. St. Petersburg Deaths, 1764–90

mortality.[14] All this considered, the impressive growth rate of St. Petersburg cannot be attributed in the main to natural expansion.

For the most part, the increase resulted from migration to the city from the Russian countryside, primarily by familyless males seeking employment. Many came (or were sent) at an early age as apprentices. For this reason the preponderance of males was clearly established by the mid-teenage years (60 percent against 40 percent female). Among adults the disproportion was even more pronounced, reflecting also the presence of the large military garrison.[15] The imbalance increased toward the end of the century. Whereas in 1750 the male-female ratio was approximately 14:10, by the mid-1780s it climbed to 20:10 and was still rising.[16] The male domination of St. Petersburg's statistics is confirmed by the death rates. Annually at least two-thirds more men died than women, and by the mid-1780s more than twice as many. Statistics from other Russian towns fail to show the same heavy majority of males. St. Petersburg alone received this large influx of male laborers unaccompanied by families.[17] Established in Catherine's reign, this pattern characterized St. Petersburg throughout the next century, providing the capital's manpower needs for construction and industrial production.

The excess of births over deaths, however slight, is striking because it contradicts the experience of most other early modern European cities. In general, towns showed a marked excess of deaths over births, which has led most observers to conclude that cities were less healthy places to live than the countryside. This view has been challenged by Allan Sharlin, who argued that migration to the cities caused the higher death rates there, because most migrants did not bring families with them and thus did not contribute to a higher urban birth rate.[18] But in St. Petersburg, apparently, despite an influx of people as great as any European city experienced at the time, births still outnumbered deaths. The ratio held despite evidence from the 1790s and the early 1800s that St. Petersburg had a lower percentage of population over age sixty than anyplace else in European Russia. Contemporaries attributed this to the insalubrious climate in St. Petersburg.[19] But the fact that the capital city's low birth rate still exceeded its death rate suggests other possible explanations as well. Was it because those who came to the city during the course of their productive lives left it in old age to return to their Russian villages or native homes in western Europe to die? Impressionistic evidence suggests that as a possibility. It is also possible that the city was so young and the migratory process so recent that no old-age cohort of migrants yet existed. Since it was young men who sought job opportunities in the city, one could not expect a sharp increase in the death rate attributable to natural

Table 2.3. St. Petersburg's Population in 1801, by Categories

Category	Number	Percentage
Nobles (*Dvoriane*)	13,200	6.5
Ecclesiastics	500	0.2
Merchants	14,300	7.1
Artisans and petty townsmen	23,400	11.6
Raznochintsy	35,000	17.3
Peasants	50,500	25.0
Domestic servants	26,100	12.9
Military personnel	39,100	19.4
TOTALS	202,100	100.0

mortality of migrants until several decades after the process of massive migration began.

Peasants—simple laborers—composed the largest group of migrating men, but there were also people in other categories, as is clearly demonstrated by the Soviet historian A. G. Rashin's estimate of the comparative sizes of various legal categories in 1801 (table 2.3). According to this estimate, upward of three-eighths of the city's inhabitants were peasants, since most domestic servants also belonged to that category.[20] Almost one-fifth of the population served in the army and navy. Twice as many servants as *dvoriane* lived in St. Petersburg. In most of these relationships the capital differed from other Russian towns.

Social Composition

In the course of the eighteenth century in Russia, the state attempted to differentiate its subjects into mutually exclusive categories based on their form of service to the state. To be sure, prior to the Petrine reforms early in the century, most of the population had already been placed into one or another of several broad categories. At the top were the nobles or gentry (*dvoriane*), required to give personal service to the state, generally in the form of military duty. At the bottom were the peasants, assorted into various subgroups according to whom their labor belonged—primarily the state (state peasants), noble landlords (serfs), or the Church (ecclesiastical peasants). The small number of townsmen (*gosti, gostinnaia sotnia, posadskie liudi*), around 3 percent of the population, were from time to time obligated to provide both monetary and service duties. People employed in the Church served the state by offering spiritual sustenance to the general population and also paid taxes. Peter's reforms simplified this system, introducing more standardized obligations from each category in the population (including the soul tax from most of them), while at the same time attempting to place into a fixed niche any group that had theretofore escaped categorization and the imposition of obligations. The whole system was imposed in order to marshal resources for the state.

In defining an official station for every social group, the state left open small windows of opportunity to move from one designation to another. But the goal overall was to set up a system not conducive to change, to maximize resources for the state from a fixed ordering of society. "Status" or "station" (*sostioanie*) slowly evolved into estate (*soslovie*), the concept that historians of the nineteenth century generally use for social analysis.[21] In the eighteenth century, however, the groups were more amorphous as the process of their definition and qualities of mutual distinctiveness were being defined. The legal definitions were clearer than the distinctions among them in reality. Each category was assigned its own rights and privileges, its own obligations to the state, and its own niche in the social hierarchy. People not fitting into any other major classification were grouped into a common category, the *raznochintsy*.[22] This legalized system of social differentiation was designed for a static society, one in which each category generally kept to its own established role, although such a situation never existed in Russia, rural or urban.

The system, as indicated, was even less suited to growing St. Petersburg than to the relatively stable countryside. The legal category a person belonged to did not always coincide with how he earned his living. For example, the merchant and artisan designations legally included only those people who had registered in merchant guilds or craft corporations (*tsekhi*). People practicing those occupations but unregistered for whatever reason were not considered to be merchants or artisans. Although exact figures cannot be ascertained, apparently significant numbers of people who were engaged in commerce and the trades in St. Petersburg never registered.[23]

Furthermore, the rural classification of "peasant" had no place in the city. Peasants living in St. Petersburg, therefore, to be considered city residents, had to register in some other, officially recognized category of the urban population. If they did not so register, they were not considered to be "citizens" (*gorozhane*). In gaining classification as urban residents, peasants were divided among other groups. Those not registering in guilds or *tsekhi* were included among the *posad* people. After 1785, owning their own homes placed them in the category of "genuine town residents." Domestic servants fit into no classification whatever, not even the lowest *posadskii* designation.

The classification system also failed to recognize new occupations. At least one group of growing significance, the government bureaucracy, comprised people from several legal categories—the nobility, the merchants, the clergy, and so forth. Not recognized legally as an estate, the bureaucracy was nevertheless beginning to develop into a distinct group in the city with its own values, interests, and motivations.[24]

To repeat, the eighteenth-century system of social differentiation was by legal estate, not economic function. Because those estates could not really circumscribe the roles filled by St. Petersburgers, however, this study lays more stress on economic and social function than estate classification. The discussion of population will pay less attention to the eighteenth-century system of division according to legal estate than to one that groups the population by the social and economic roles they played in the city's life. It was their occupation, not their estate, that brought people to St. Petersburg. Their roles in the city's life are better understood through a division by economic function than social station as determined by birth. The necessity of redefining social categories in order to understand the city on its own terms serves as a clear indicator that the city's vitality was constantly straining the state's ability even to understand the process of urbanization, much less control and direct it through planning. In the new system of classification, some groups remain essentially the same, but others overlap several eighteenth-century categories. The six defined and considered here are the urban aristocracy, government civil employees, people participating in commerce, artisans (including those not registered), the military, and laborers (including day workers and servants). The number of ecclesiastics was so small that they are discussed only as a sidelight. These divisions by no means represent social classes, yet the categories were distinct in their manner of living. The place in the social order and role in economic life of each group can be defined generally.

The group here called the urban aristocracy could also be understood as the wealthiest nobility or gentry, to whom might also be added the most prominent merchants. It stood at the top of the economic hierarchy as well as the legally recognized social order. It enjoyed more extensive legal rights and privileges than any other group. Indeed, the nobility derived its privileged social position from its more basic legal superiority endowed by the state. The urban aristocracy owned half the masonry houses in the city, generally those nearest the center and on choice properties overlooking the river and canals. Many of them also owned country houses beyond the outskirts of the city or along the shores of the gulf.

The urban aristocracy affected a more luxurious manner of living than any other group. The wealthiest of this group, the noble magnates, attempted to surpass each other in opulence, surrounding themselves with large numbers of servants. The best known and wealthiest aristocrats displayed, besides normal household staffs, large numbers of uniformed servants to fulfill such specialized roles as horsemen, coachmen, huntsmen, and tapsters. K. G. Razumovskii maintained more than two hundred servants in town and the Sheremetevs were rumored to have no fewer than three hundred.[25] Such ostentation could be duplicated by no other category of the population. It was these people who were invited most often to receptions, masquerades, and balls at court, and to their houses that Catherine frequently repaired for dinner, or an evening at cards, or some other social gathering.[26]

What family names can be associated with this group? They were, first of all, the houses that were deeply involved in life at court. They were the owners of palaces. They included not only the names of figures holding the highest governmental offices, but also those with appointments at court, as well as members of their extended family networks. David Ransel's study of "party" politics in Catherinian Russia names many of them, most prominently the Bestuzhevs, Dolgorukiis and Dolgorukovs, Kurakins, Orlovs, Panins, Potemkins, Sheremetevs, Shuvalovs, Trubetskois, and Vorontsovs, but there were others who did not figure large in his study, such as the Belosel'skiis, Betskois, Demidovs, Naryshkins, and Iusupovs. High-ranking military officers often maintained houses in St. Petersburg, where members of their extended family might live during the long periods of time when they themselves could not. For example, M. I. Kutuzov, the future vanquisher of Napoleon, inherited a riverbank house from his father in the late 1760s and continued to maintain it despite his long absences from the city.[27] Among the merchant-aristocrats were the Russian names Bolin, Chulkov, Severin, and Shemiakin, the Dutch surnames Bacheracht and Boehthlingk, the British houses of Cayley, Gardner, Gomm, Shairp, Sutherland, Swallow, and Thomson, and the Armenians Manichar and Lazarev.

These urban aristocrats were more aware than anyone else of the latest styles from western Europe and therefore those most devoted to them. From time to time well-dressed ladies might appear at the merchant harbor in order to ascertain all the sooner the latest Parisian fashion. Tailors and wigmakers—usually foreign by birth—thrived in the city. Barbers were retained by the wealthy at substantial salaries. Quite naturally, people less habituated to following the whims of Lady Fashion found much to satirize in the behavior of their fellow subjects. To cite only one example, the editors of the journal *I to i se* (*Both This and That*) pointed out in one issue that people in high society did everything *po modu* (à la mode, fashionably). They dressed *po modu,* walked *po modu,* spoke and thought *po modu*—even cursed *po modu.* Revealing the path of cultural influence, the article concluded by asserting that Petersburg attentively followed changes in Paris, Moscow imitated Petersburg, and the provinces strove to mirror Moscow.[28] This group alone had both the desire and the means to follow Western fashions so slavishly.

The urban aristocracy included many but certainly not all of the nobles living in St. Petersburg. By no means were all of them able—assuming they even wanted—to follow this style of living. Many nobles did not possess sufficient wealth to pass their time at ease. For that matter the poorest *dvoriane* frequently engaged employment as petty government officials and had difficulty making ends meet. The evidence of those involved in borrowing money through promissory notes indicates a high participation by lower-ranking military and civil servants with noble titles.[29] Despite this fact, the percentage of nobles who might be deemed poor was undoubtedly much lower in the capital than in rural areas, for St. Petersburg attracted primarily those interested in acquiring wealth, status, and power.

Urban aristocrats were primarily consumers, not producers. They sustained numerous artisans and merchants through their demand for luxurious furniture, clothing, and exotic food. The money paid for these goods came, for the most part, from rural landholdings outside the St. Petersburg area. Of course, many nobles also earned substantial incomes within the city. Some ventured into commerce, selling products from their estates to wholesale buyers, or underwrote industrial enterprises, like Count Iaguzhinskii, the silk stocking factory owner (until debts arising from his dashing lifestyle forced creditors to foreclose on the factory), or Prince Potemkin, who owned a glass factory and several brickyards, or Prince Nesvitskii, who headed a company that built merchant ships. In the end, whether wealthy or poor, the *dvoriane* among the urban aristocrats could always lay claim to the superior legal and social status commensurate with their birth or achievement.

Government employees made up a second identifiable group in St. Petersburg's population. This classification included high-level administrators, managers, and decision makers, to be sure, but in far greater number, it comprised the clerks, copyists, secretaries, and other bureaucrats who make up any governmental apparatus. Contemporary thinking did not distinguish this group as a category of town dweller. By the 1830s a writer like Nikolai Gogol' could lampoon them in his stories, but in the eighteenth century their existence was only intimated in statistics by words such as *chinovnik* or, more rarely, *raznochinets,* terms referring to government employees from non-gentry families.[30] The gentry also provided many bureaucratic employees; even functionaries at the lower end of the service ranks were often of noble extraction. As the number of government employees rose during this period, employment in the civil service increasingly assumed the trappings of a professional career.[31] Early in Catherine's reign civil service employees in St. Petersburg totaled fewer than ten thousand. By the end of the century some thirty-five thousand government employees labored in the capital. The increase raised the percentage of the population in government employ from about 7 percent to nearly 14 percent, a significant bureaucratization of the city's population. *Chinovniki* by 1796 made up the third-largest group in the city, after peasants and the military, and were rapidly approaching the size of the latter.[32]

Most civil servants lived near the buildings in which they worked. Since Vasil'evskii Island was home to the administrative nucleus, the building housing the "twelve colleges," many petty officials chose to live in that section of the city. Many also resided on St. Petersburg Side. Because lower-ranking officials could not afford to buy land and houses on their notoriously meager salaries, large numbers of them rented their quarters, ranging from comfortable apartments to single rooms. On occasion *chinovniki* worked and resided at the same address, sleeping in attics or basements of state office buildings.[33]

The bureaucracy held a peculiar position in the city after the Charter to the Towns was issued in 1785 (see chapter 3, 101ff). The charter completely ignored them in defining the groups that were to comprise the urban corporation and participate in town government. The oversight was significant, for preliminary studies have suggested that the civil bureaucracy was basically a self-perpetuating group by the end of Catherine's reign.[34] Their social origins were diverse. One-third came from noble families and another third from non-noble service people, both military and civil. The remaining third were from merchant, artisan, foreign, *meshchane* (petty townsmen), or peasant backgrounds. The vast majority had no income other than their state salary, indicating that few could have registered as merchants, artisans, or *posad* people. Few owned real estate, which excluded them from registering as genuine city residents, the first category of citizens as defined in the Charter. The fact was that the Charter made no provision for including civil servants among legally registered city dwellers. Although they made up a sixth of St. Petersburg's population, they were unable to participate in city affairs unless registered in a recognized category, a possibility open to only a few of them. Undoubtedly most remained unregistered, city residents in fact but excluded from the urban corporation.

Like civil servants, buyers and sellers of goods had a significant presence in the city's life. More people engaged in commerce than eighteenth-century statistics indicate, principally because the term "merchant" (*kupets*) was applied solely to people registered in one of the three guilds. Only guild members enjoyed the legal rights and privileges of merchants, but several thousand unregistered petty townsmen or *meshchane* (traders lacking the capital—500 rubles before 1775, 1,000 thereafter—to register in a guild) and their families greatly swelled the mercantile classification. Six to eight thousand seems a reasonable estimate of the total number of people whose livelihood depended on commerce at the beginning of the period under study. That figure more than doubled during the next thirty years to seventeen thousand by the end of Catherine's reign.[35] Merchants from interior Russian towns resettled in St. Petersburg in ever-increasing numbers. In 1781, a year of peak migration, three hundred merchants moved their official registration to the capital.[36] Many other merchants resided temporarily in the capital each year until their goods were sold.

The incomes of people in commerce varied widely. At one end of the spectrum were those eminent citizens active in commerce, legally the most privileged after nobles, worth perhaps a hundred thousand rubles. At the other end, street peddlers (*raznoshchiki*), usually fresh from the countryside, could not afford to rent shops, much less enter guilds. They walked the city's streets, hawking the wares that they carried with them, perhaps displayed on a board supported by a cord or rope tied to either end and strung around the backs of their necks, or carried on baskets, barrels, or boxes. The vast majority of traders fell between these two extremes, above subsistence level, yet not free from the threat of insufficiency. Wealthy merchants attained a level of living comparable to that of the nobility (whom they emulated), particularly after the clarifications of mercantile legal status in 1775 and 1785. They were invited from time to time to social affairs at court, for which they often had to purchase tickets—an effective method of excluding those lacking the means really to belong. Wealthier merchants owned houses in respectable central sections of the city and participated in city government. Among the most prosperous were merchants from England, who inhabited one of the most admired streets in the capital on the left embankment of the Neva below the last bridge. Already known colloquially as the English Embankment, it was deemed by those who wrote descriptions of St. Petersburg as the equal of any street in the world in its splendor.

Merchants of middling means made their homes in all parts of the city, with larger concentrations in the area known from the 1770s as Third Admiralty, in Moscow district, and on Vasil'evskii Island. Residents from western Europe thought such merchants able to live in higher style in St. Petersburg than in many other cities. The plentiful supply of servants for hire willingly worked for extremely low wages, enabling many merchant families to maintain staffs of ten to fifteen domestics.[37] The good life could be transitory, however, and merchants more than others all too often overextended their means and fell into bankruptcy.[38]

Since the relatively large sum of five hundred rubles in capital was necessary even to register as a merchant, many commercially active people traded illegally, without registering. Their number included not only those who simply lacked the minimal capital, but also people who had fled the obligations of another category. If registered at all, these people were petty townsmen or *posad* people, categories whose rights in mercantile relationships were less clearly defined and protected than those of registered merchants. Peasants living outside the city but who regularly sold their produce in town failed to qualify for registration in any classification. As a rule, neither petty townsmen, *posad* people, nor peasants rented shops. Open areas in markets and bazaars were reserved for their wares, however, with the stipulation that no permanent or semipermanent structures be built in such areas.[39] Other traders rented corners of basements in large houses, which served equally as lodging and shop.

The incomes of craftsmen, like those of merchants, varied greatly. Although none were as wealthy as the richest merchandisers, skilled artisans—predominantly foreigners—could earn in excess of a thousand rubles annually. Yet by the end of Catherine's reign few artisans owned property in the central sections of town. Quite a few of them lived there, to be sure, renting accommodations from the owners. Most, however, resided in outlying districts, their lodgings often serving also as their places of business.[40]

The proportion of the city's population associated with the military remained constant throughout Catherine's reign at about one-fifth of the total.[41] As noted earlier in this chapter, the large military garrison contributed significantly to the preponderance of males over females in the city. Special guards units, composed of young noblemen, occupied individual *slobody* near the Fontanka. Several areas—

most notably Tsaritsa's Meadow, later to be called the Mars Field—were set aside as parade and drill grounds in summer for the four guards regiments. The units participated in ceremonial parades marking visits by foreign royalty and in the triumphal celebrations marking the departures and returns of the imperial court from extended sojourns outside the capital. Service in guards units introduced many provincial noblemen to the faster-paced life of St. Petersburg. Some, drawn by its delights, stayed in the capital after their release from service, either to accept positions in the civil bureaucracy or to partake of the variety of alternatives to provincial life offered by the city.

Regular army and navy units, officered by nobles, were composed in the main of peasants. Since Peter the Great's time they had been billeted not in barracks but with the city's civilian residents. Townsmen chafed under this obligation and long sought relief from it. Heeding their constant complaints, Police Chief N. A. Korff presented a plan late in 1763 for softening the burden.[42] As a result, householders gained by degrees the alternative of paying additional taxes in lieu of providing billets. The tax monies, in turn, partially financed construction of the large barracks that still stand in downtown areas of the city.

Like the young noblemen in guards regiments, peasant soldiers in regular army or navy units experienced city life for the first time while in military service. But for them the city was less inviting; most were without funds, single, far from home, and presumably bored by garrison life. It is not surprising, therefore, that soldiers, sailors, and marines often fell into the hands of the police, accused of brawling, drunkenness, theft, or murder.[43] The families of married soldiers could live with them except during wartime. They found housing only with difficulty, however, because the men had to live near unit headquarters but could not afford high rents. Therefore wives and even children often supplemented the family income by working as peddlers, milkmaids, and sellers of produce. Soldiers' wives—*soldatki*—were frequently equated in the popular mind with prostitutes, a role to which they were undoubtedly driven by economic necessity.[44]

Despite the city's high cost of living, many retired personnel remained there after separation from service. Some of the first public welfare programs in the city were designed to provide for these men and their widows and orphans, who otherwise could be expected to fare only slightly better than recently arrived unskilled peasants, since the majority of retired soldiers had no skills that could be practiced in peacetime.[45] They were given preferential hiring as watchmen and guards at state-owned buildings, but at salaries that never exceeded thirty rubles annually.

Peasants (including domestic serfs and servants) comprised the largest single social group in St. Petersburg, more than 35 percent of the total population. They could be found, scratching out their existence, in every corner of the city. In the better districts of town they served the wealthy homeowners, taking quarters in basements, attics, and outbuildings. Most of them, however, kept to outlying neighborhoods, particularly the impoverished and squalid *slobody* rising south of the Fontanka. Those fresh from the countryside frequently led lives of desperation, forced to accept any available work at proffered wages. Peasants who had been in the city longer and knew their way around, or who had skills or brought horses with them, gained better employment, whether as stevedores on the docks, as house servants, as steady laborers in construction, as teamsters, or in other occupations. Once newcomers obtained employment, life lost its sharpest edges, although few ever actually became men of means.[46] Rich or poor, manorial serfs continued to pay quitrent (*obrok*) to landlords in the interior of the country, state peasants sent their *obrok* to the state, and all paid the poll tax. These obligations remained in force even when peasants acquired urban legal status by registering in a merchant guild or an artisan *tsekh*. There are unverified accounts of shipping magnates worth hundreds of thousands of rubles who continued to remit annual feudal dues to their landlords on estates.

The above describes peasants who migrated legally, who had the necessary documents. What of those who came to the city illegally? Large numbers of serfs did so, despite the threat of severe punishment, including expulsion back to the estate, incarceration, or forced labor in the city. Despite repeated entreaties from the police (often through the Chancellery on Construction) to apprehend such people, the silence of the sources on this account indicates that the majority of peasants entering the city without passports avoided detection and arrest. Many even found employment on construction projects financed by the state. Others subsisted illegally, through theft and unregistered goods production.[47] Whether through the strong attraction of the city or because of a miserable plight in the village, peasants flocked to St. Petersburg by the thousands.

Whether nobles, civil servants, merchants, artisans, military personnel, or peasants, people living in St. Petersburg continued, of course, to live under Russian laws and customs. The legal and social structure governing the entire country maintained its power in a city where economic roles defined a different set of categories. Peasants in particular often lived in a state of de facto ambiguity regarding their legal status. The resultant tensions were not resolved during Catherine's reign or for decades thereafter. Even such a simple matter of who was eligible to participate in municipal self-administration, and to what degree, was not easy to resolve in a society where the nature of urban life was so at odds with the elemental legal and social structure of a far-flung agrarian society.[48]

Furthermore, the awareness of the relative status awarded by the state to the various legally defined estates continued to influence the habits and aspirations of St. Petersburgers. In a society that rewarded rank at least as much as wealth—and valued it more highly—it is not at all surprising that merchants schemed to gain nobiliary status.[49] In an ancien régime setting, there was a sense in which improved legal status was more important than increased wealth. An improvement in status carried with it a corresponding rise in rights and privileges. In the larger Russian picture, if not in St. Petersburg itself, wealth could serve as only a poor substitute for rank.

Population Dynamics

St. Petersburg attracted foreigners, Russians from the interior towns, and people from rural areas. Nearly every major nationality of Europe was represented in the capital. People of Asia—Turks, Persians, Tatars, Uzbeks, natives of the Transcaucasia, even a few Chinese—were likewise to be found. A small number of Africans, especially valued in Russia for their exoticism, were employed as servants. All of them together gave St. Petersburg an international flavor equal, according to Storch, to that of any city in the world.[50]

The social variegation raises questions of the extent to which people were emotionally and psychologically integrated into St. Petersburg. The majority of the population at any time was composed of people not born in the city, but who came to it at some stage in their lives. Was it difficult for these people to leave behind their former lives and assume a new identity in St. Petersburg? How well did newcomers from varied backgrounds assimilate into the city? To what extent did they consciously regard themselves as St. Petersburgers?

In considering these questions, it must be kept in mind that St. Petersburg belonged to the eighteenth century. It did not display the characteristics of "segmented" urban life as it developed after the transportation revolution in the nineteenth century. The sociological concept of segmented urban life is derived from the fact that many people in modern cities engage in different activities of their lives—eating and sleeping, working, playing, worshipping, and so forth—with completely different groups of people, often in differing geographical areas. Thus the people with whom a modern city dweller associates in one activity often know him or her only in that one role, without ever sharing or learning about the other facets of that person's life. This was not true of eighteenth-century St. Petersburg, where only the rare person had extensive contact with several parts of town. When people moved from one address to another, they normally did so within the same section of the city. Virtually all of the documented cases of artisans and unskilled workers show this to be the case. Furthermore, living accommodations were taken as close as possible to places of employment. Each district of the city contained enough stores, shops, and markets to satisfy the daily needs of the populace, giving little reason to venture into other quarters. Life was therefore concentrated for the most part in small neighborhoods. Indeed, the Neva's many channels and the several canals served further to distinguish the city's districts from each other. The sheer size of the city undoubtedly would have astonished many people who rarely ventured outside their own sections of town.

This pattern of living may seem to bear more similarity to the pattern of traditional village life than to that of the modern city, yet there were substantive differences. Moscow may have been an overgrown village, but St. Petersburg was not. In the first place, the city was new and, in its very form and substance, unfamiliar to Russians. Relationships in the village had developed over a period of a lifetime, and each villager knew his or her role and status. But it took some time to discover one's niche in the city. There were more people, from different backgrounds; psychological adjustment required time. The city offered a greater range of living arrangements than the village, where the number of buildings remained relatively constant and few people moved from house to house. One is struck when reading the supplement of advertisements to *Sanktpeterburgskie vedomosti,* the newspaper published by the Academy of Sciences, by the frequency with which the capital's well-to-do residents changed addresses. Some, at least, of those renting apartments moved as often as every six months. Houses changed ownership frequently. The newspaper from time to time contained personal notes by socially active people informing friends and acquaintances of the most recent change in address.[51] Such mobility was not characteristic of village life. In another sense, however, it is doubtful that the transposition from village to city had an immediate effect on relations between members of different legal estates. Artisans continued to associate primarily with artisans, merchants with merchants, peasants with peasants, and so on. In this respect the vast majority of inhabitants, never questioning their station in society, found little difference between town and country.

In many ways newcomers—particularly foreigners—clung to their former way of life. Non-Russians were isolated both by language and by custom. Some nationalities tended to preserve this isolation because of their relatively large numbers. John Parkinson was told by a French cleric in 1792 that there were a thousand Frenchmen in St. Petersburg and fifteen thousand Englishmen.[52] Foreign-born residents of the city did not tend to mix readily with Russians, establishing links upon arrival—if not prior to their departure from their homeland—with others of their nationality, not uncommonly renting apartments from them or actually living in the same rooms.[53] German-speaking, English, Swedish, Finnish, and Armenian St. Petersburgers had their own churches, which were usually therefore centers of social activity for those nationalities. German-speaking residents had their own newspaper from the 1770s, the *Sanktpeterburgisches Journal.* Its editors rarely printed Russian news, choosing to fill its pages with news items and stories from the various German principalities and about Germans. Once in a great while the newspaper ran notes concerning changes in laws governing commerce in Russia. The Germans had their own theater for a time, owned by Karl Knieper, where plays were also produced in English, French, and Italian. There was an English-language theater in a converted stable at the home of F. G. Wulf in the early 1770s producing mostly contemporary plays but also Shakespeare.[54] Virtually none of the English merchants confessed to an ability to speak Russian, including those who had been born and grew up in St. Petersburg. Instead they counted on the aptitude of Russians "above the condition of peasants" to speak German or French.[55] From 1770 the English Club was a gathering place for Englishmen in St. Petersburg as well as Anglophile Russians.[56] The municipal government after 1785 allowed segregation in artisan corporations (*tsekhi*), which foreigners dominated, not only by craft but also by subdivision into Russian and foreign organizations within the same handicraft.[57] Not totally at home in St. Petersburg, most foreigners hoped to accumulate small fortunes quickly in Russia's capital and return to their native lands. It never occurred to most of them to do otherwise. Even so, a few foreigners did forsake their nationalities and become Russian subjects, to the point of accepting baptism into the Orthodox Church and Russianizing their names.

Russians, who faced no linguistic or cultural barriers, would have encountered problems of a different sort in adjusting to life in St. Petersburg. Complete absorption into the urban milieu posed special difficulties for the part-time residents of the capital. Storch described their position well:

> A great part of the lower class of people can scarcely be reckoned among the inhabitants of the residence [city], from the constant flux and reflux of them. Throughout the summer many thousands are employed as carpenters, bricklayers, masons, paviours, house painters, etc., who return home at the approach of winter, and whose numbers are supplied by other thousands who gain their bread as cabmen, ice cutters, etc. Most of them therefore have no abiding city and no property except for the implements of their industry. They dwell chiefly in the outlying districts of the town, or in the surrounding villages, where they enter into artels or companies differently composed as to numbers, and defray the expenses of living out of a common chest. Many of them who have undertaken to erect a building or other job as bricklayers, carpenters or the like, never leave the place of their employment, but sleep in the open air among heaps of rubbish, in order to be the earlier at work in the morning. Great numbers live entirely all summer on board the barks and floats of timber that come to St. Petersburg under their conduct.[58]

These migratory habits, established in the Catherinian period and known in the historical literature as *otkhodnichestvo* (meaning "departure," as from the village), disrupted an earlier sedentary rural life and served as a transition between year-round life on the estate or in the village and a total adoption of St. Petersburg as home. Although a permanent move may have proven impossible, the psychological willingness to be uprooted from the past, evidenced during this period, helped give rise to the even greater growth rate of the city in the early nineteenth century. This pattern of partial break with the village and semiassimilation into the city continued to hold true of Russian peasants well into the period of industrialization.[59]

Russia in the eighteenth century was a society extremely aware of differences in rank, status, and place. Nowhere was this awareness more evident than in the new capital city, for it was there that the most extreme gradations could be found. It was impossible in that age not to be highly aware of social distinctions. Even clothing mirrored them. Virtually anyone appearing in city scenes painted at the time can be identified by station in life almost immediately by the educated observer. Status was not frozen; it was possible to move from one estate to another. N. I. Pavlenko has written about the efforts of some of the leading merchants to become ennobled.[60] As St. Petersburg expanded and peasants became urban residents, many found it possible to raise their status to another estate. Indeed, several of the more illustrious residents during this period started as poor men of no rank whatever and became extremely wealthy and honored. Best documented is the rise of Sava Iakovlev from street peddler to store keeper to tax farmer and manufacturer.[61] This way to success was not open to many, and extraordinary fortune contributed largely to the rise from such low estate to such high dignity, yet Storch cited the case of Iakovlev to illustrate that sometimes it was possible for the ambitious and lucky to acquire wealth and status in St. Petersburg.

Although figures for peasant registration in urban legal categories are incomplete, graph 2.3 shows that a steadily increasing number registered in artisan *tsekhi* and, even more markedly, in merchant guilds.[62] It was much more common for peasants becoming city residents to enter the merchant classification than the artisan, because the requirements for membership were much less exacting. Whether one actually engaged in commerce or not, as long as he could declare the minimum amount of capital, he could enter the appropriate merchant corporation. The artisan guilds, however, tested skills and were necessarily much more jealous of guarding entry. The vast majority of city residents undoubtedly never thought about engineering a change from one legal estate to another, although the evidence presented here suggests that the minority who did seek to advance in society could find openings to higher status.

Social and legal mobility was not without attendant social stress. In a society as status-conscious as eighteenth-century Russia, upward movement from the lower orders found opposition among those in the higher orders whose position would be, in their view, cheapened or threatened by those clambering up from below. The conflicts between merchants and nobility come quickly to mind. Catherine's ill-fated attempt to construct a "middle sort of people," an urban middle class, was intended at least in part to prevent conflict between those two groups by creating a new and honorable niche in society for townsmen. Balls and masquerades at court for nobles were frequently accompanied by similar entertainments for merchants and other respectable people, although the two estates never mixed, each being entertained in a different room of the palace. The Charter to the Towns helped realize the goal of upgrading the esteem of the merchant corporations. So great was the consciousness of place and status that within the merchant category itself there were sharp gradations of privilege, marked most dramatically by the regulations establishing the number of horses that could be used to draw the carriages of members of each guild as they rode about town.

But the pride of status was not the only cause of social stress in St. Petersburg. Economic disputes between local merchants and nonlocal peasants over commercial rights became a second source of friction. Closely related to it were the complaints of registered artisans and merchants against city residents not registered in commerce or industry yet practicing those trades. Laws guaranteeing the rights of

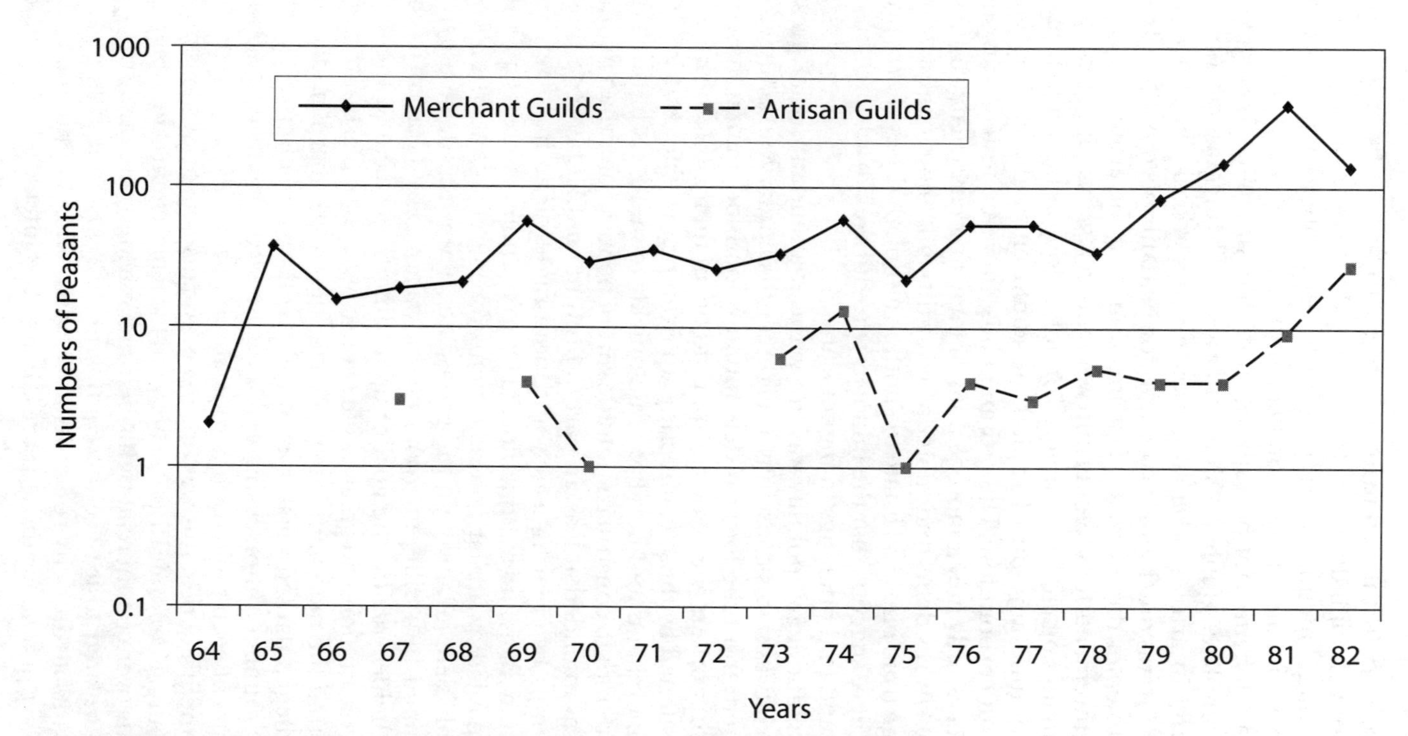

Graph 2.3. Peasants Registering in St. Petersburg Merchant and Artisan Guilds, 1764–82

merchants in the first case and of lawfully registered subjects in the second were expanded and amplified, but implementation of the edicts never effectively curbed illegal economic activities.[63] The issue was deeply seated and persisted as long as the state attempted to reserve certain economic activities to special social groups.

A third point of stress concerned relations between peasants, who comprised the largely unskilled day laborers (*chernye rabochie*), and their employers. Poor working conditions led to at least one effort by associations of construction laborers to appeal to higher authority, with some success.[64] But the undoubted exploitation of unskilled workers clearly represented a potential breeding ground for crime and riot by the end of the century, even if no outbreaks of violence actually occurred.

Quality of Life

Hygiene

In an age when few European cities could lay claim to excessive cleanliness, sanitary conditions in St. Petersburg were not high. Many factors contributed to the situation: streets befouled by horses, the lack of proper sewage facilities—with resultant use of canals and rivers for that purpose—water polluted from a variety of sources, and continually smoky chimneys.[65] But the principal cause of low hygienic standards was overly close living conditions. Although buildings in the central city were not noticeably crowded together, they were filled to capacity and then some. Construction had not kept pace with the expanding population, forcing overcrowded conditions in structures already standing. By the end of Catherine's reign, rooming houses had begun to characterize poorer districts, sometimes crowding ten or even twenty people into a single room.[66] A contemporary described the living conditions of workingmen:

> These people find quarters even in the best parts of town; and which are in such request that the cellars are often filled with lodgers, while the workmen are still employed in building the first and second stories of the house. Here numerous families live crowded together in one room; and not infrequently the population of the whole edifice is in the same proportion with that of the basement. The low situation, the narrow space, the short height of the room and the exhalations from the damp walls must doubtless occasion great havoc among the multitudes that inhabit these sonterains. . . . And whenever the contrary may occasionally happen,

yet there is even then a great want of that cleanliness, without which even the most sumptuous apartments are unhealthy.[67]

Communicable diseases spread quite rapidly in such conditions. The city fortunately survived the threat of plague that devastated Moscow in 1771. Although not dreaded to the same extent, another communicable illness, tuberculosis, together with unspecified stomach disorders, brought perhaps the greatest number of deaths in the city.[68] The stomach disorders did not exhibit the virulence or communicability of cholera or typhus. There is no evidence of epidemics of either of those diseases during this period. They struck St. Petersburg later, in the nineteenth century. It is impossible at present to diagnose the "stomach disorders" by modern pathology, however tempting it may be to attribute the symptoms to giardiasis. By the same token, apoplexy, frequently cited as the cause of sudden death, could have involved a stroke, a heart attack, or some other trauma. Smallpox epidemics raged periodically down to the 1760s and remained a threat thereafter despite well-publicized campaigns to inoculate the population. There were no reliable defenses against outbreaks of influenza, which hit the city hard in the latter 1780s.

Whether contributing to health problems or not, the disposal of human wastes revealed little concern for hygienic standards. One of the few sources on the subject, John Parkinson, noted that when entering the house of Vice Chancellor Count I. A. Osterman, he was "almost poisoned with the stench of the necessary." In fact, Parkinson never saw a commode, such as had become fashionable in England, in any Russian house in St. Petersburg—not even at the Winter Palace. The stench from Osterman's "necessary," which Parkinson noted in his diary each time he visited there, he supposed to have come from some common receptacle. In winter, "from being froze, the inconvenience is not conceived: but in Spring, particularly when it begins to thaw, the Nuisance is insufferable."[69] Sanitary conditions must have been much the worse among the lower orders of the population. Perhaps there were only the cold winters to thank for the absence of serious outbreaks of epizootic or viral disease.

With hygienic standards so lax generally, it is no wonder that still at the end of the century drinking water taken from the Neva continued to be regarded by natives to be "limpid and safe," especially if filtered at home. Water from the canals, however, was "cloudy, muddy, unhealthy, and of unpleasant taste," because of the filth thrown into them from the surrounding houses.[70] The Moika was the worst. People continued to use the water, though, after taking the precautions of boiling it and flavoring it with vinegar.

Medical Care

Notable advances were made during the period in providing facilities for the ill and infirm, beginning with Catherine's creation of the College of Medicine in 1763. The modern medical profession was still in its infancy at the time, yet a significant number and variety of medical facilities were created in St. Petersburg during Catherine's reign, and public health care extended relatively widely. Prior to 1770, however, only the military and naval hospitals on Vyborg Side were equipped to handle patients with even the simplest illnesses. Dating from the reign of Peter I, the infantry hospital contained a thousand beds and had a staff of nearly eighty professionals. Toward the end of Catherine's reign the hospital also made a place for several doctors serving in positions outside the regular staff. Known as "free" doctors, they were working toward full professional attestation.[71] The naval hospital, somewhat smaller, lay adjacent to the military hospital. Both hospitals treated only men in uniform; they were especially busy during times of war. Heinrich Storch recorded that in the war years of 1788–89, the naval hospital had between 7,900 and 8,800 patients.[72] According to Georgi, it took in more than 11,000 patients in 1790.[73] Neither was a "city hospital" in the strictest sense of the word, but with the city's military population numbering in the tens of thousands, they did service a sizable percentage of the people living in the capital.

In 1770 two specialized institutions were added for the general population. First, a quarantine house opened in case the plague threatened St. Petersburg. (Plague had broken out in the Russian army in Moldavia in 1768 and by 1770 had spread as far as Moscow.) The house remained in use for just two years, while the threat of plague lasted. A permanent quarantine house and smallpox inoculation center was established only in 1783. Its practice was to offer free inoculation to children in spring and fall, at the expense of the imperial court. The children remained under the house's care for two weeks, until the place of inoculation healed. Only about 1,600 children passed through the process during the first decade of operation, some 55 percent of them boys. Official statistics recorded only four deaths during this period.[74] Because the number of inoculated children obviously reflected only a small portion of all children in St. Petersburg, one suspects that only the more prosperous families, including especially those of western European background, availed themselves of this service.

Other children were served by the Foundling Hospital and orphanage which also opened in 1770, largely due to the patronage of Ivan Ivanovich Betskoi. Despite the good intentions of its backers, the hospital-orphanage managed to save few lives. From 1770 until 1798, over 80 percent of the infants and children in the trust of the orphanage died while in its custody, most of them in infancy.[75]

In 1779 the city's first public general hospital opened with sixty beds. Financed by the imperial treasury, the hospital was intended primarily for sick people who had no means of paying. Adjoining the hospital was a facility for the insane. Both institutions, located on the southern side of town on the Fontanka River, were overburdened from the beginning. Rapid expansion of the facilities was made possible by the construction of an imposing two-story masonry building in the mid-1780s with three hundred beds, although contemporary observations that four hundred could be squeezed in indicates that the facility only began to meet the city's need. In 1790 an additional 260 beds were made available for warm-weather use in unheated wooden barracks erected by the College of Medicine in the hospital's courtyard. For its time the hospital was modern and well run. Under the direction of the city staff surgeon Nilus, the hospital had a staff that included up to five other surgeons, in addition to a specialist who treated unfortunate patients with electricity—an experimental practice at the time that has long since, fortunately for patients, been abandoned. In 1791 the hospital was provided with hot and cold running water pumped into overhead reservoirs and from there by pipes throughout the building. In its standards of hygiene and treatment, the hospital compared favorably with medical facilities in other European cities. Incoming patients were all bathed and shorn and garbed in hospital-provided clothing. The sexes were totally segregated. Indigent patients were treated free of charge (those capable of performing various chores around the hospital did so in return), but artisans and those in government service paid four rubles monthly.[76] Heinrich Storch claimed at the end of Catherine's reign that the state spent in excess of 15,000 rubles annually operating the city hospital. Official statistics showing the number of patients admitted, discharged, and deceased indicates that the mortality rate through the 1780s slowly declined to a low of 14 percent in 1792.[77] The ward for the insane, attached at the rear of the hospital, was apparently the first attempt in Russia to hospitalize patients with mental illness. Those liable to become violent were bound with leather, not chains, and all patients were free during the daytime to roam the premises, which included a recreation garden. The ward could accommodate up to forty-four patients at a time.[78] That they were hospitalized and not merely placed in an asylum marks the experiment as especially enlightened.

Besides the city hospital, several other centers for treatment met particular needs. In 1783 a special hospital was established for patients with venereal diseases. It had only sixty beds, equally divided between the sexes. Because of the social opprobrium connected with syphilis and gonorrhea, the strictest secrecy was maintained regarding patients, and it was generally held that one could undergo treatment incognito. Popularly known as Kalinkin *Dom* (House) because of its location on the far side of the Fontanka at Kalinkin Bridge, the hospital was considered to be far smaller than it might have been, considering the need.[79]

A small medical-surgical school clinical hospital was opened toward the end of the century with room for eighty student surgeons. They practiced their art on indigent patients, of whom more than a hundred annually passed through the hospital's doors. Lutherans initiated a health service for indigent people at about the same time. Some twenty physicians cooperated in a joint program to provide these medical services. They apparently provided better treatment than the city hospital, for fewer than 10 percent of their patients died.[80] Finally, the deficiency in trained midwives (noted in the city's *nakaz* in 1767) was partially resolved by two "lying-in" clinics, one attached to the Foundling Hospital and the other at the medical-surgical clinical hospital. The latter institution maintained the strictest confidence regarding women who came to give birth, indicating an additional role it must have served to hide illegitimate births among the higher strata of society. Infants born in these lying-in rooms, if not claimed by their mothers, were sent to the Foundling Hospital's orphanage.[81]

The College of Medicine oversaw the city's apothecaries and ran the apothecary garden. Toward the end of Catherine's reign, there were two main state-owned apothecaries and five smaller outlets and an unknown number of privately operated apothecaries, each of which was inspected several times per year by a professional city *fizik*.[82]

Despite many shortcomings, these medical facilities and services represented the first efforts to establish public health services, with the city assuming some responsibility for its less-fortunate inhabitants. Funded by a combination of public subscription and tax monies, these hospitals offered health care to poor as well as to wealthy townsmen.

Cultural Life and Entertainments

The city's growth was accompanied not only by intensified health care but also by a proliferation of leisure-time activities, especially for the favored minority who were able to participate in the new features of cultural life that were as much European as Russian. Theatrical life flourished even by the end of Elizabeth's reign, as an increasingly knowledgeable clientele viewed comedy, drama, opera buffe, and ballet.[83] The theater's popularity continued to grow during Catherine's reign, together with its patrons' predilection to gossip and prattle during performances and the abuse they often heaped upon actor and author alike from front-row seats. Even considering these not-so-mild disturbances, by the end of the century, according to knowledgeable foreigners, St. Petersburg's audiences heard out the players with as much politeness and taste as English theatergoers.[84]

The nature of productions also changed during this period. At first presenting primarily translated works performed by foreign artists, the repertoire of city theaters slowly became more Russian, as works by A. P. Sumarokov, D. I. Fonvizin, and Catherine herself complemented those of foreign authorship, and Russian actors such as Petr Plavil'shchikov and Mikhail Shchepkin stepped into the shoes of Italians, Frenchmen, and Germans.

From the beginning of her reign Catherine sponsored plays that were produced in her palaces for the enjoyment of the social and economic elite, continuing the tradition begun by Elizabeth. A court theater and opera house operated in the Winter Palace from the 1760s, predating by more than two decades the construction of the Hermitage Theater. The growth in popularity of the theater was marked by the construction of the immense Great Stone (*Bol'shoi kamennyi*) Theater, which opened in 1783 and could accommodate more than a thousand spectators. Further demonstrating a growing capacity and appetite for theatrical productions, the Wooden Theater, home of Locatelli's opera buffe after opening in 1757, was taken over in 1776–77 by the wealthy Reval (Tallinn) merchant Karl Knieper to produce plays and operas in German. In 1783 it came under imperial management. Besides these public theaters, many of the city's magnates had plays produced in their own houses for their private entertainment.[85]

The club and society provided another form of diversion and entertainment for cultured St. Petersburgers. Masonic lodges led the way, following first the English and Scottish, and later the German and Swedish models. They attracted not only men of foreign birth but also many native Russians, of whom N. I. Novikov is merely the most celebrated.[86] Ostensibly the Freemasons were searching for truth and a deeper sense of moral duty, but they also inevitably took on the trappings of a pastime. Other clubs began to appear with the founding of the English Club in 1770, which, despite its name, had more Russian members than English.[87] Some societies merely formalized existing social relations; others united for a specific purpose or goal. Both types of clubs, as well as the Masonic lodges, involved only a small percentage of city residents—nobles, wealthy merchants (especially foreigners), and men in the professions.

Such organizations lay far beyond the experience of most of the people in St. Petersburg. "Leisure time" itself was a concept undoubtedly foreign to their experience of life. For much of the population, the group celebrations and festivities remained the same in St. Petersburg as they had been wherever people had come from. The Orthodox Church calendar provided for celebrations of the twelve great feast days and the days of saints of local importance. Some of those holidays were accompanied by processions, as for example the one that occurred every summer on August 15, the day of the Assumption of the Virgin Mary, marked by a massive procession from the church of the Mother of God of Kazan' to the Alexander Nevskii monastery.

In addition to religious processions, the common people enjoyed walking or promenading, activities embodied in the Russian words *shestvie* and *gulianie*. These were regularly occurring events when people walked along routes known to all participants, seeing and being seen, enjoying sideshow entertainments, taking rides on carousels, swings, and other forms of light physical entertainment, buying or selling small articles of seasonal significance. Shrovetide (*maslianitsa*) serves as an example, as does May Day, when people strolled and promenaded between the city's center and the park at Ekaterinhof, and midsummer (Ivana Kupala).[88] A traditional Russian holiday was "semik," the seventh Thursday following Easter or, to put it differently, the Thursday prior to Trinity Sunday or Pentecost. Traditionally people gathered on the banks of streams and ponds to wave garlands of wreaths and enjoy choir singing and folk dancing. The holiday was celebrated in St. Petersburg most of all at the church of the small monastery of St. John the Baptist in Moscow district where in particular merchants and petty townsmen gathered to celebrate in the traditional village manner. It is reported that Empress Catherine herself went there to celebrate this "national" holiday when the weather was pleasant.[89] To an extent, the celebrations on many of the religious and folk holidays were provided by the state or the court, such as the ice slides built on the frozen Neva for the Shrovetide festivities and the Easter week provision of swings constructed in public squares and parks, including Mars Field, and roving groups of comedians and actors entertaining the people.[90]

In St. Petersburg religious processions took second place to secular processions and parades. Surely those latter events through the center of town were intended as much to awe the general populace as for the court to interpret and celebrate itself for itself and those immediately dependent upon it.[91] In this regard, it is significant that the empress's secretaries, who left the formal record of such processions, usually noted as well the presence of innumerable onlookers who shouted their approval of the events and the court sponsoring them. The fanfare accompanying such events as the launching of naval vessels from the Admiralty shipyard each summer, the blessing of the waters of the Neva each January 6, the official moves between summer and winter palaces each spring and fall—all greeted by the booming salute of scores of guns from the Fortress of St. Peter and St. Paul and Admiralty, not to mention evening fireworks and illuminations—was designed at least secondarily to entertain the common people.[92]

On rare occasions the imperial court organized other public festivals-as-spectacle in celebration of itself. Two of the most memorable are mentioned here as examples, one in which the participants were the elite and the spectators the common people, and the other in which those roles were reversed, the common people participating and the elite watching. The first event took place in June and July 1766, centering on an enormous temporary wooden amphitheater built on Palace Square. Three days were set aside within that period, when lavishly costumed processions wound through nearby streets to the amphitheater, where various contests were staged as representations of earlier historical periods—jousts, horse races, footraces, and the like—in which all the participants, men and women, came from the social elite. The seated spectators included the empress herself. The common people crowded the streets, covered rooftops, and leaned out of windows and balconies to view the goings-on.[93] More than twenty years later the same large square was the scene of a different spectacle, celebrating the peace treaty with Sweden in 1792. Two circular platforms were each piled high with a veritable cornucopia of foodstuffs: cereals, fruits, vegetables, meats, crowned with a quarter section of beef. Each platform had the internal plumbing to permit the whole to become a fountain of wine, one red and the other white. As the well-born watched, the pressing crowd of common people were let loose, on a signal from Catherine herself, to plunge into the wine fountains, each seizing whatever he could of the goodies on display, a Rabelaisian sight giving delight to participants and observers alike.[94]

On a more traditional level of entertainment for a broad public, bearbaiting was provided by the empress every Sunday morning for popular delight at the park in Ekaterinhof southwest of the city.[95] Throughout most of the year, however, the common people provided their own, less-formalized, entertainment. John Parkinson recorded seeing a boxing match pitting teams of fifty on a side in a field outside the city on Sunday, December 30, 1792.[96] Popular entertainment and leisure at the neighborhood level centered around local taverns, nearly two hundred of which served the city's population. Most frequenters of taverns were the common people, and drinking houses often doubled as places of assignation, where women of the demimonde attracted customers, where thieves plotted their crimes, and where fights occasionally resulted in deaths. Several taverns, usually those also serving as inns, enjoyed better reputations; people of means came there to tipple and converse, and travelers without personal contacts stayed there while in the city. Apparently the coffeehouse, already a fixture in London, had yet to make an appearance. At the beginning of Catherine's reign only a few inns and hotels of quality existed. It is a mark of the developing city that by the 1790s a number of well-known hotels—the London, the Paris, the Royal, the Grodno, and the Württemberg, to name a few—provided safe and fairly comfortable lodgings for visitors.[97] The London was generally considered to be the finest.

Schools

During Catherine's reign a greater effort was made to provide formal education for the city's residents than in any earlier period. Not even a rudimentary system of public education existed when she came to the throne. The capital's only schools were four military academies, a school of dance, a parochial school run by the largest Lutheran church in town, St. Peter's, and a few privately run boarding schools known as "pansions." In conformity with her desire to be an enlightener, Catherine did more to foster learning than any other Russian monarch of the eighteenth century, setting up schools to provide general elementary education as well as institutes to teach trades and special skills.[98] In particular, she established the first formal schools in Russia for females, setting up two boarding schools for girls in the complex of buildings erected to be a female monastery on the riverbank at Smolnyi, one school for the daughters of the nobility and the other for girls of non-noble status.

At the empress's instigation, seven public schools offering two to four years of primary-level education were established in the capital in 1781. Prototypes for the general-education system set up in 1786 by Jankovic de Mirjevo, the schools initially enrolled some five hundred students. In 1786 a teachers' "seminary" was added to prepare instructors for primary schools planned in other cities. In the same year the "Statute on Public Schools" extended Mirjevo's educational system beyond the capital into provincial and some district capitals.

In spite of Catherine's good intentions, only a few parents in St. Petersburg sent their children to the new public schools. In order to expand the number of students, private Russian boarding schools were closed in 1786, providing an additional 159 children. Despite these measures to encourage participation, by the end of Catherine's reign only four thousand pupils (less than a quarter of those of school age) attended public schools in the capital, most of them apparently the children of merchants, townsmen, and soldiers.[99] Although the schools were intended to appeal to all social and legal estates, fewer than 20 percent of pupils came from the nobility. A slightly higher percentage was female.[100] Owing to the lack of public support for education, most pupils even when enrolled failed to complete the full course of instruction. Beyond rudimentary penmanship and simple arithmetic, many people at the time considered book-learning to be a waste of time; even to acquire a government post, only a bare smattering of education was necessary. Catherine's educational reform fared better in St. Petersburg than elsewhere, however, for the schools in the capital accounted for fully one-fourth of all public school pupils in Russia.

Complementing this rudimentary system of public schools, private boarding schools offered an alternative means to education for the children of foreigners residing in St. Petersburg. The best-supported school of this kind was established by the Lutheran congregation of the Church of St. Peter, on Nevskii Prospect, in 1762. Housed in a separate building on the church's land, the school was run on a nonprofit basis with salaried teachers. Children of both sexes and all religious faiths were invited to attend, although instruction apparently took place in German. The school was not inexpensive, charging from one hundred to two hundred rubles annually per child depending on which grade the child enrolled in. The stated intention when the school was founded was to become the equal of the best schools abroad, preparing boys for the university as well as for careers in the arts, commerce, and the trades.[101]

Efforts to establish private elementary schools for Russians in 1777 gained some support, but collapsed when N. I. Novikov, their founder, moved to Moscow two years later. The school-educated woman made her first appearance in Russia with the creation of the two girls' schools at Novodevich'e Convent (Smolnyi) in 1764, one for daughters of the nobility and the other for commoners.[102] Despite Catherine the Great's lofty intentions—and well-publicized pretensions—these institutions were in effect finishing schools, often enduring criticism for failure to achieve their goals, notwithstanding the imperial court's active support of them. When compared with other public and private schools, however, they did stand out as lively centers of intellect and wit.

Other schools were opened to provide training in particular skills or occupations. To the existing school of dance, five other specialized schools were added during Catherine's reign, including a merchant marine academy, a school for training porcelain makers, a mining institute, the medical-surgical school, and a drama school.[103] All were quite limited in both personnel and resources, yet produced a growing number of specialists.

Higher Education

Her inability to instill a high regard for education among the masses did not decrease Catherine's efforts to develop science and the arts. During her reign both the Academy of Sciences (founded 1725) and the Academy of Fine Arts (founded 1757) flourished as never before. From the former, expeditions were sent to all parts of the empire to study flora and fauna as well as the indigenous people. Peter Simon Pallas and Samuel Georg Gmelin in particular enriched knowledge about Asian Russia with their copious notes and sketches. Leonhard Euler contributed substantially to theoretical mechanics, optics, astronomy, acoustics, and other branches of physics. A. I. Leksel discovered the orbit of the planet Uranus. As the surnames indicate, a significant portion of scientists were foreigners, predominantly Germans, especially early in Catherine's reign. The Academy of Arts, although it turned out no artists of world renown, nurtured, under the leadership of Princess Ekaterina Romanovna Dashkova, Russia's first generation of formally trained sculptors, painters, and architects. The empress installed both academies in magnificent classical structures fronting the Neva, the Arts in 1788, and the Sciences in 1789.

The academies were joined by at least three other institutions for collecting and disseminating knowledge. In 1765 Russia's first learned society, the Imperial Free Economic Society, was founded. Intending initially to introduce techniques of scientific farming, it soon expanded to other economic interests as well, such as mining and manufacturing. Its *Works* (*Trudy*), first published in 1766, containing articles of practical and theoretical interest, eventually ran to 280 volumes over the next century and a half. The Russian Academy, devoted to the standardization of both written and spoken Russian, was founded in 1783 by Princess Dashkova and others.[104] Although it failed to accomplish its goal, it did begin work on a monumental *Dictionary of the Russian Language.* In the early 1790s, work was begun on an imperial public library. First suggested in 1766, the library opened only after Catherine's death, yet received its impetus during her reign.[105] It is crucial that these institutions were established in St. Petersburg; the capital city had clearly become the primary cultural as well as political center of Russia.

Summation

From all the evidence, St. Petersburg was becoming a thoroughly diverse city. The contention of T. P. Efimenko that the capital by the end of Catherine's reign had evolved into two distinct cities, rich and poor, is a gross oversimplification.[106] In one sense there were as many different cities as there were legal estates, for no two of them were equal in rights, privileges, and obligations. In another sense, however, St. Petersburg must be taken not as an artificial combination of estates, but as a vibrant organism much more than the sum of its parts. St. Petersburg was also a city of several distinct neighborhoods, distinguished in human terms by the differing sorts of people who lived in them and in geographical terms by the watercourses providing their boundaries. An evolving urban society such as St. Petersburg represented was new to Russia. It introduced activities and concerns identified specifically as urban: cultural enrichments, places of amusement and recreation, public welfare. It brought with it social flux, which induced a reordering of urban legal estates in the 1785 Charter to the Towns and other legislation. This social transformation more than any other single indicator provides the evidence of the capital's increasing urbanization.

3
"Such Beneficial Ordinances": The Structure of Urban Administration

THE RUSSIAN GOVERNMENT HAD LITTLE EXPERIENCE IN ADMINISTERING large cities. Prior to the eighteenth century, it devoted hardly any attention at all to governing towns. Russia was, need it be repeated, overwhelmingly rural. Only Moscow could be called a real city, yet the recurring references as late as the nineteenth century to Moscow as an overgrown village raise questions about the degree of even its urbanization. The Petrine reforms, which were the first in Russia to devise a distinct and separate municipal administration, found inspiration in the administrative structures of states where urban life remained on a small scale, states where no city had reached the size of a hundred thousand souls or more. The truly large cities of Europe, where problems were confronted that were comparable to those that arose in St. Petersburg in the 1700s, lay far beyond the boundaries even of Russia's immediate neighbors. No city nearer than Amsterdam or Venice boasted a population close to that of St. Petersburg or Moscow.

Before Catherine's reign all that the state hoped to do in its two large cities was to maintain public order, preserve power in the hands of those who held it amid a crowded and disparate population, and collect taxes from those making their living from the urban pursuits of commerce and production. Moscow could be administered, more or less, by following old patterns that had evolved there over centuries. St. Petersburg was a different case altogether. Yet for all that has been written about St. Petersburg's having been a thoroughly planned city, Russia's new capital did not have a logical, coherent administrative system imposed upon it. Instead, as though the city had come into existence before an administrative structure could be devised for it, its governance made do with whatever organs of town management as had already been developed in Russia. Working with institutions and a mental frame of reference far more suited to the stability of rural society than the ebb and flow of urban life, the Russian state attempted to find—somehow—an administrative organization and style suitable for its new capital, especially after its size began to swell in the mid-eighteenth century.

Besides its singularity as a planned city, St. Petersburg's role as imperial capital brought it more directly under the scrutiny of the central government than would have been the case for even a provincial capital. Thus the system of municipal administration developed for St. Petersburg bore certain unique features. Over the course of the reign of Catherine II, energies were brought to bear several times and in various ways upon the problem of developing a more coherent, systematic, and workable form of urban government.

In true enlightened fashion, the reformers attempted to create a single system applicable to the governance of towns both large and small. The most noteworthy legislation was issued in 1775, as part of the new "Institutions" of provincial government; in 1782, specifically relating to the policing of towns; and in 1785, in the Charter to the Towns that for the first time addressed towns as corporative bodies. The latter law wrought the greatest transformation of the structures of municipal government. It can be seen as the intended crowning achievement of Catherinian legislation for towns. Because Catherine herself regarded it as such, the Charter's promulgation will be used at least initially to divide the study of St. Petersburg's administration into pre- and post-1785 periods. In the preamble to the Charter, Catherine praised her predecessors for founding towns, claiming with false modesty that she sought only "to emulate such beneficial ordinances of our Ancestors" in fostering urban life.[1]

Before 1785

Prior to Catherine's reign the administration of Russia's towns was shared among many bureaus, offices, and chancelleries, generally yielding haphazard, ineffectual, and utterly confusing results. Although in the first years under Catherine towns continued to be administered much as they had been under her predecessors, the empress began almost immediately a process of rethinking the role of towns in the well-regulated state. J. Michael Hittle has called attention in *The Service City* to the increased importance placed on towns in the administration of government during Catherine's first years on the throne.[2] He notes that as early as 1763 a Commission on Towns grappled with the issues of how towns might be administered better and might be integrated more fully into the central state administration. Part of the quandary was that the term "town" (*gorod*) could be applied to a center of population of any size, large or small, yet not all population centers were administratively or legally considered to be towns. Following the work of A. A. Kizevetter, Hittle argues that what passed for town administration in the first half of the eighteenth century actually applied to no more than a fraction of the inhabitants of populated places, those people who were registered in the *posad*, or *posadskaia obshchina*.[3] This institution developed during the period from the late 1500s through the early 1700s, primarily for the purposes of defending the estate interests of the *posad* people and of collecting from them the taxes and services due the state.

As a new city, though, St. Petersburg could hardly be described as representing the full embodiment of the traditional Russian urban estate system. Its *posad* structure was at best artificially imposed. After all, Peter the Great from the first had in mind other administrative models for his pet project, derived largely from foreign sources.[4] Furthermore, Catherine was on the verge of abandoning the old *posad* structure. Because Peter's ideas regarding urban administration were only half thought out and had been poorly complemented by subsequent rulers, one can readily imagine the complexity and confusion in urban administration as St. Petersburg, with a population exceeding one hundred thousand in the 1760s, was governed by seven and more overlapping, contentious, and variously constituted bodies.

Organs of Central Government

In a state system that had been centralizing power for two centuries, it was perhaps inevitable that much of the burden of administering the capital city should have been shouldered by agencies of the central government. The empress herself assumed an active role. Not only did she contribute to the grand strategies for the city's future development and help design the legislation structuring its administrative hierarchy, she also intervened in mundane matters. Throughout her reign she asked that weekly reports be prepared for her perusal on "unusual occurrences" and on wholesale and retail prices of foodstuffs in the city's markets.[5] On occasion she cut through the bureaucracy to supervise personally the plans to construct hospitals and other institutions that saw to the health and welfare of residents. In 1770 she personally issued detailed instructions for digging the city's first sewer system.[6] St. Petersburg was important to her—she admitted her preference for it over Moscow—and her involvement in its administration followed not only from her awareness that she could best protect her own position by administering the seat of power efficiently, but also from her sense of proportion, harmony, balance, and good regulation.

Catherine took particular interest in the city's boundary marker to the south. From the late 1770s through most of the 1780s she personally directed that an earthen wall or berm be erected wide enough for riding horseback or promenading on foot "to open . . . on one side a good view of magnificent buildings and on the other the beauty of localities outside the city."[7] She directed that a ditch was to be dug alongside the wall, in subsequent years expanding its role to include an industrial function. "Deepen and widen the ditch," she instructed.[8] Water was supposed to flow through the ditch in both directions, toward the mouth of the Neva and toward a place upriver near the Alexander Nevskii Monastery. Up to fifteen watermills were to line the ditch. In the mid-1780s extensive plans were drawn up and technical specifications set, including precise estimates of the cost of the project (well in excess of three million rubles), but it is unclear whether construction on the industrial enterprises was ever begun.[9]

Emergency situations also summoned the empress's personal intervention. On May 23, 1771, a great fire broke out first on Vasil'evskii Island and then spread to the area near Kalinkin Bridge in the southwest of the city, then as winds shifted jumped to St. Petersburg Side. Terrified, Catherine sent her favorite, Gregory Orlov, into the city "with instructions not to return until the last spark was extinguished," as she wrote the following day to Nikita Panin. "He returned after four o'clock but sped off again after ten, for I think that Police Chief Chicherin's head was spinning from seeing so much misfortune."[10] The same day she dashed off the following lines to Ivan Chernyshev, who headed the Admiralty, "In the evening I was forced . . . to dispatch Count Orlov, fearing that the police chief was exhausted or incapable of turning to every side. I still don't know exactly what happened, for Count Orlov is still sleeping [she wrote in the evening], having returned from the city at five o'clock."[11]

Catherine frequently made known her will for the city through ukases issued to the Senate. Four of the six departments of the Catherinian Senate were located in St. Petersburg, and its members were called upon frequently to serve individually on commissions set up to deal with various problems that arose from the attempt to administer the capital city. Almost all major legislation dealing with the city passed through the Senate, which also sat as watchdog over other agencies with jurisdiction in the city. Lesser governmental bodies made their requests for monies through the Senate. By its powers of rejection the Senate was able to control capital outlays affecting the administration of St. Petersburg in numerous ways.[12] Thus the Senate's involvement may not have been visibly codified in law, but it continually appears in the papers and documents that survive as archival sources, the detritus of the living city. Far more than the laws would suggest, the Senate played a part in administering the city.

The peculiar historical pattern of development of St. Petersburg brought other agencies of the central government into the administration of the capital as well. In the city's first decades several of the governmental bodies needing a labor force organized their own *slobody*, or suburbs, in the city's outskirts, including the Admiralty, the Chancellery of Her Imperial Majesty's Houses and Gardens, and the Post Bureau. By the time of Catherine II these bodies continued to retain full jurisdictional powers over their *slobody* even though the city had grown to meet them and in some cases had almost enveloped them. They were like large villages within the city, and their administration, because it was not the primary function of the parent organization, undoubtedly suffered, particularly since the primary reason for their existence, to provide labor in a scarce market, was now outdated.

Various colleges and chancelleries had other responsibilities for administering or overseeing the city too. The Commerce College was charged with maintaining honesty and hygiene in marketplaces. The Admiralty had responsibility after the devastating flood of 1777 for warning the city of impending high water and for inspecting the privately owned bridges spanning the Neva. The War College maintained sentry booths on designated street corners throughout the central districts of the city. Until its liquidation in 1779, the Manufactures College, through the Manufactures Office, supervised all sorts of industrial activity (although not all industry) in the city.[13] Even the College of Medicine had certain duties in St. Petersburg, among them supervision of apothecaries, factories producing surgical instruments, hospitals, the medical school, inoculations, and the control of communicable diseases. Many of these duties, and others not offered here as examples, overlapped with the responsibilities of various local administrative organs, contributing to the chaotic state of affairs.

The military governor of St. Petersburg commanded the large garrison that could always be found there. Often referred to as the commandant, he was provided with quarters and offices in the Fortress of St. Peter and St. Paul. He had administrative authority over some of the most important industrial enterprises in the city (the mint, the artillery foundry), controlled much of its supply of foodstuffs, and commanded the troops who performed most of the ceremonial as well as the necessary guard duty in the city and its environs.

Even more important in overseeing the work of the city's local administrative organs were the civil governor and provincial board.

Before the provincial reform of 1775 the governor and his staff rarely participated in day-to-day business in the capital, although their offices were located there and St. Petersburg was the only city of any real size in the province. Yet their presence was felt in various ways. While defining the duties of the governors of St. Petersburg and Moscow provinces in 1765, Catherine reminded them that, although the capital cities were not under their direct control, they did have the authority to evaluate the quality and justice of the administration of the capitals and intervene when they deemed them inadequate. She also instructed them to coordinate affairs with the police chiefs at all times, taking care not to infringe upon police rights and duties.[14] The governor did have the power to arrest members of the city magistracy in the event of tax arrears from that body, and in effect could countermand virtually any action of the magistracy.

The 1775 reforms left no question that the governor now represented the final voice over the city's affairs. His new power extended to all functions of local city government, including the police. The governor, together with the provincial board, took seriously his power over St. Petersburg. After 1780, when the new St. Petersburg *guberniia* was actually instituted under the 1775 legislation, the provincial board was the body that represented the state in contracts for construction of public works projects. In its new dealings with the magistracy, the provincial board insisted upon punctuality, thoroughness, and responsiveness, generally exhibiting a persistence rare in Russia's administrative organs in the eighteenth century.[15]

Another task befell the provincial administration following the institution of the police board in 1782. Inevitable disputes between citizens and police could not all be handled by the Third Department of the Senate, responsible for public order and decency. When its docket was full it thereafter turned cases over to the province's court system for settlement.[16] In this way the provincial administration helped to define the limits of law in relations between the populace and the police.

The Commission for the Masonry Construction of St. Petersburg was an organ of the central government that stood outside the hierarchy of administration. Created a few months after Catherine came to power, the commission was concerned solely with town planning and future urban construction.[17] It existed from 1762 until 1796, with most of its activity coming before 1785. Indeed, the period of greatest planning for St. Petersburg was the mid-1760s.[18] After 1768 the commission was expanded to cover planning in every town of Russia. The commission co-opted architects, surveyors, draftsmen, and others to draw up plans, of which more than four hundred were completed and approved.[19] Only a small proportion of them dealt with St. Petersburg, but because both general guidelines for growth and such specific decisions as building size, construction codes, land use, and street patterns came from the commission, attention must be paid to it also as one of the agencies of the government competing to administer the capital city.

Local Organs of Administration

Magistrates

It is noteworthy that the primary organ of self-administration in Russian towns, the *posadskaia obshchina,* never took root in St. Petersburg. The reason, as stated earlier, is that the capital was founded too recently to have gone through the same stages of development as other, older towns. Furthermore, there was no real desire to transplant the *posad* into the soil of the Neva's delta. Peter I much preferred Swedish and German models of urban administrative structure, and the strong minority of foreigners whose participation in the capital's economy was essential to its continued health tended to argue against a traditional Russian pattern of administration. To be sure, the magistracy that Peter imposed on the city, in large measure to take the place of the *posadskaia obshchina,* was allowed to atrophy after his death. It was revived in 1743 under Empress Elizabeth.[20]

Like the *posad,* the magistracy had jurisdiction over only a part of the city's population, specifically the craftsmen, merchants, and other trading people. The members of the magistracy, who were elected by the people whose interests they served, consisted of a president, four burgomasters, and two councillors, all elected to three-year terms.[21] The magistracy, sometimes referred to as a kind of town council, actually had a somewhat different role and much less authority. Its principal tasks were to serve as a court of first instance (discussed below), to collect certain taxes, to oversee the registration of merchants and artisans in their corporate associations, the guilds, and to provide whatever information it could about commerce when asked to do so by higher agencies of the central government. The magistracy fulfilled one additional role, unique to the St. Petersburg magistracy. Both Peter I and Elizabeth, who revived it, made the St. Petersburg Magistracy a sort of supreme magistracy—its name was actually the St. Petersburg Main Magistracy—that served as supervisor and final adjudicator of appeals against the magistracies of all other towns in Russia.[22]

The provincial reform of 1775 altered the administrative role of the magistracy. Because a more comprehensive system of local administration was imposed on the countryside, tying together towns and rural areas, the Main Magistracy gradually lost its supervisory and appeals relationship with the empire's lesser urban magistracies. By 1782, according to Hittle, the St. Petersburg magistracy no longer fulfilled those functions.[23] The magistracy itself was likewise subordinated much more than before to the St. Petersburg provincial board. While retaining some judicial functions for its constituents in St. Petersburg (including those of the court of registry for deeds and contracts), it became after 1775 primarily an intermediary easing the relationship between the provincial administration and the merchants and artisans in St. Petersburg.[24] It retained a certain degree of jurisdiction over the establishment of industrial enterprises in the city. It could determine who might and who might not participate in commercial activity there.[25] It ran the private shipyard, so named because that was where private individuals could contract with shipwrights and purchase materials for constructing their own ships.[26] But basically it became the eyes and ears for other, higher organs that needed information to formulate policy. Thus in the early 1780s the provincial board turned to the magistracy several times to gain lists of prices in the city and their fluctuations. The magistracy also provided requested information about weights and measures used in the capital and population figures for merchants and artisans.[27]

Police

Perhaps more important than the magistracy, in a reign devoted to the creation of a *Rechtsstaat,* was the police. Whereas the magistracy was concerned almost exclusively with matters pertaining to the commercial and handicraft estates, the police circumscribed all estates, everyone living in the city. In a sense, it was the first local administrative organ to supersede estate boundaries, and thus the harbinger of a local administrative body to come later that would be concerned with the city as a whole. Marc Raeff, in his perceptive article devoted to central and eastern European roots of the idea of modernization, pointed out that police were set up, and the concept of the *Polizeistaat* developed, in order to enable princes to generate fuller use of resources by means of a governmental regulation of life.[28] It is indeed striking how many economic activities were given to the police to supervise. Nor should it be forgotten that professional police were introduced in St. Petersburg more than a century before they were in London.

Peter I introduced municipal police to St. Petersburg in 1718, charging them with specific responsibilities that remained largely unchanged until the reign of Catherine II.[29] Although the functions continued unaltered, the structure of police organization was modified several times. By 1762 the police possessed their own chancellery, responsible only to the provincial governor, the Senate, and the empress.[30] The head of the police also served as chief of police in Moscow and held indirect responsibility for police in other cities. The skeletal staffs under his command were supposed to perform all police duties, but most of them served in administrative posts. In fact, only in St. Petersburg and Moscow did the police come close to fulfilling the tasks they had been assigned.[31] Even in St. Petersburg few full-time policemen were "on the beat" by 1762, actually patrolling streets. Instead, the chancellery honored the long tradition of requiring inhabitants to do such work. For example, the responsibility for patrolling at night passed from house to house within each city block, with the owners of the houses accountable for ensuring the duty was met. As a scheme to save money the system worked fine, but the constant complaints about disorder in the streets testified to its failure as a police policy. Clearly the system of self-policing was inadequate.

Other police expenditures and responsibilities also were levied upon inhabitants. For example, under police supervision individual homeowners bore the expense and provided the labor for sweeping and repairing the streets fronting their property. Streetlamps were maintained by the police, but residents were taxed to pay for them. A small assessment on each stove paid the wages of chimney sweeps. Residents chose local police officials, responsible within their small areas of the city, from among their number. These representatives often expended considerable time and effort fulfilling their extra duties. Fires too were fought by people supplied from each household when the alarm was sounded. For the purpose of fighting fires, each residence was ordered to keep equipment handy for use at a moment's notice.[32]

It seems even from a cursory glance that the personnel and equipment provided to the police were unequal to the tasks confronting them. The police were faced with a burgeoning center of population, one that was growing virtually day by day; yet the police apparatus was inadequate, intended not for a briskly expanding city but for an established, stable, small town. It was out of necessity, therefore, that during the next twenty years police organization was reformed several times.

In 1763 a special dispatch office was created to deal with robbery, theft, and capital crimes. Its activity was to be closely supervised by the provincial board, an organ that came to have increasing dominance over the police.[33] That same year the unpopularity of a system requiring civilians to fulfill police duties came to the surface. The police chief, Baron N. A. Korff, reported to Catherine that the city's inhabitants had been complaining about unequal distribution of police duties among residents. In fact it was not so much their unfair allotment but the duties themselves that displeased people. Specifically unpopular were the obligations to serve as unpaid local police auxiliaries, to maintain night watchmen on the streets, to keep firefighting equipment at hand, and to billet soldiers. (This last obligation, while dissimilar from the preceding ones, was enforced and administered by the police.) Korff proposed alleviating the duty by permitting residents the alternative of paying an additional tax in lieu of providing various services.[34] Almost immediately some five hundred homeowners chose to pay an annual average of seventeen rubles each rather than endure billeting and other police obligations. Most of those who preferred to pay rather than serve were foreigners, merchants, craftsmen, and petty officials in the civil service. They were hit harder by service requirements than the court nobility because they did not possess large households with many superfluous servants, yet presumably had the means to pay, whereas householders of lesser wealth did not and were unavoidably stuck with the service obligation.[35]

The additional duties now falling to employees of the police, as well as the additional revenue in its budget, constrained Korff to propose a reorganization of the police staff in December 1763. In particular, the necessity of having a fire brigade led to the creation of an entirely new branch of the police. Thereafter the police had five offices: the chancery, with seventy-six employees; the housing office, with five employees, responsible for billeting troops; the technical section, with a staff of twenty-one to "look after buildings and make plans"; the fire brigade, with a headquarters of sixty-three people and about three hundred others in the various districts; and the "outdoor" police, those employees who were responsible for actually patrolling the streets and maintaining order, many of whom continued to be civilians supplied by homeowners or garrison troops from the city.[36] Although it gave the police a much larger staff, this reorganization provided few more of the means necessary to fulfill the tasks of policing the city. Nevertheless it did begin a process, from the top down, of enlarging the police so that it could deal effectively with its grand areas of responsibility. In particular, the creation of the fire brigade opened a new chapter in the police's work. Throughout Catherine's reign, this office received increasing attention.

Still, however, the police did not function well. They had to be reminded repeatedly during the 1760s and 1770s to perform specific tasks in areas over which the police had been given general responsibility, such as street cleaning, bridge repair, the rescuing of people who fell into the river or canals, and such like.[37] The police even allowed their own headquarters building to deteriorate miserably without making efforts to repair it, and when they finally turned to the Senate for funds, they took an additional five years to submit the plans for reconstruction and list of estimated expenses that the Senate had asked for.[38] Indeed, police reports to the governor and the empress through the 1760s and 1770s were increasingly concerned less with crimes and the maintenance of order and more with announcements of theatrical performances, special receptions at court, and similar affairs.[39] This was the case even as the police were being burdened with an ever wider scope of responsibilities, such as the instruction in 1778 from the Senate to develop regularized measures for dealing with mentally and emotionally retarded people found in the streets.[40]

Perhaps because the police chancery was not performing its duties adequately, the 1775 provincial reform included a provision placing city administration under the jurisdiction of provincial governors. The police remained the primary agent of city administration, but the change made possible closer supervision of the police chancery's activity. Mere supervision could not solve the police's problems, however.

In 1782 the police system was radically overhauled. In one of the major pieces of legislation of Catherine's reign, a new police organization, known discreetly as the Board of Decorum, was established for every town in Russia.[41] An attempt was made to recognize the differing needs of the large metropolises of St. Petersburg and Moscow and the several hundred small provincial and county towns. In the best Catherinian tradition the whole apparatus was made to look like a hierarchically constituted bureaucracy with the senior police chief of St. Petersburg at its head, but in fact it did not operate at all like a national police. At the head of the St. Petersburg police was the senior police chief. Although he was commander, his chief of staff, the police chief, had greater administrative responsibility. Both sat on the city police board, which also included two inspectors (one each for civil and criminal affairs) and two councillors from the city magistracy. For administrative purposes and to make law and order easier to maintain, the city's five police administrative districts were replaced by ten districts of two to seven hundred houses each.[42] The principal police official in each district was the police officer, who had to reside in the district he worked in. He had a staff of two clerks, a notary, and a head fireman. Wards, subdivisions of the districts, each contained from fifty to one hundred houses. The ten districts in St. Petersburg yielded a total of forty wards, each headed by a ward supervisor, who had under his command a lieutenant, a chimneysweep, and contractors to maintain the streets and streetlights.[43]

The police chief and officers were named by the Senate, ensuring continued Senate involvement in city government. Nominations were also approved pro forma by the provincial board. Ward supervisors were chosen by the police office but had to be acceptable to ward inhabitants. Aides of the supervisors, ward lieutenants (one per ward), were elected by ward residents every three years. Every district was supposed to have at least one oral court (*slovesnyi sud*) to handle misdemeanors; the judge in an oral court was elected by the district's inhabitants. Election of both the ward lieutenants and the judges of oral courts were subject to approval by the police chief. Thus local citizens retained a voice in the selection of police officials, but only at the lowest level.

The actual patrolling of the city fell more to the army than to the police. Military police subordinated to the board provided both foot patrols and dragoons to guard the roads leading into the city. In St. Petersburg they numbered several hundred officers and men. Furthermore, St. Petersburg normally garrisoned five battalions of soldiers, who were frequently used for guard duty, a service rotating monthly among the battalions.[44]

Although completely revising police organization, the reform of 1782 did not provide many changes in police duties. A few were strengthened immediately. Others were altered somewhat by decrees in later years. In one of its added powers the police gained control over courts handling misdemeanors, since oral courts came under the supervision of the police chief. No real solution was provided to the question of the composition of the fire brigade, but in 1784 a decree established the most reliable and least disagreeable fire brigade system to that time. Fifteen hundred houses were required to provide watchmen.[45] The year was divided into thirds, with five hundred households providing watchmen during each third of the year. When not responsible for supplying watchmen, households were compelled to have men ready to help extinguish fires should they start. In addition, some five hundred full-time firemen were hired, assigned to the various districts of the city proportionally to population and size. Their wages came from taxes paid by households that did not provide actual manpower to fulfill their police duties. Firemen's wages were very low, thirty-six rubles annually, plus at least fifty kopecks for each fire.[46]

Because of low wages, the police had considerable difficulty in hiring and keeping conscientious employees at lower levels. Before the end of Catherine's reign the police administration gave up its efforts to maintain moderate standards and accepted employees of any sort. This is evidenced by the fact that in 1792 there came an order to hire fire-wagon drivers and firemen from among the unskilled, idle, unemployed population (*prazdnoshataiushchiesia*).[47] The police had to take whatever sort of firemen it could find. Undoubtedly efficiency suffered: the measure could hardly have provided better or more motivated firemen than the system of self-protection practiced earlier in the century. Indeed, service was probably worse. In this as in other areas of police responsibility, the tasks continued throughout Catherine's reign to overmatch the resources assigned to them.

Other Officials

One of the new organs created by the provincial reform of 1775 was the Bureau of Public Charity. Although it was part of the provincial administration, not the city government, it nonetheless devoted most of its attention to matters in the capital. The bureau was composed of seven men: the governor and two members each elected from the *guberniia* magistracy, the superior land court (*verkhnii zemskii sud*), and the superior tribunal (*verkhniaia rasprava*).[48] As the number of public hospitals, charitable institutions, asylums, and schools in the city multiplied, the bureau's tasks of oversight increased commensurately.

St. Petersburg had few elected officials. Locally elected police officers were noted above. Members of the city magistracy were also elected. In addition to the magistracy, merchants and artisans each elected elders to represent them in legal and administrative matters. Prior to 1785, as after that date, the elders also contributed to the internal control of each group.

The law in 1767 calling a commission to codify laws provided for another elected official. Besides a delegate to the commission, a city head or mayor was chosen for the first time. Although the mayor was to be merely a figurehead with no power, the election was held in 1767 and biennially until 1772, after which year the mayoral election took place in conjunction with magistracy elections every three years.[49]

Courts

When Peter I set up the town magistracies, they were given administrative duties as well as the responsibility of adjudicating cases involving the urban population. The Main Magistracy in St. Petersburg, like all magistracies, was an "estate" court in that its jurisdiction extended only to trading people and craftsmen. Three parallel systems of lower and superior courts existed, one each for nobles, townsmen, and peasants. Theoretically all civil and criminal cases belonged naturally to the jurisdiction of one or another of them. But experience soon showed that at least in St. Petersburg and Moscow, a fourth parallel system was needed to cover those people who fell outside all three estates: city residents not owning real property, and those subordinated directly to the court, the military, or the civil service, frequently residents of *slobody*.[50] Called the *nadvornyi* (aulic) court, with lower and superior chambers, this institution existed only in the capital cities as a judicial body parallel to the magistracy. The Catherinian era also inherited the town orphan court, subordinated to the magistracy, likewise an estate-based court that dealt only with the mercantile and artisanal population. Finally, like other towns, St. Petersburg had oral courts, set up in 1727, to adjudicate civil suits with minimal formality and no permanent written records. Members of all these courts were drawn from the merchants, craftsmen, and others who were subject to them. Before 1775, the one judicial institution that spanned estate lines was the Criminal "Expedition" formed in 1763. As noted above, this special commission had the authority to investigate, bring to trial, and pass sentence upon anyone charged with a criminal violation. Copied from a similar commission set up in Moscow, it could be used to speed up the wheels of justice or to ensure the form of justice meted out in cases of special interest to the state. According to John LeDonne, most criminal court cases in St. Petersburg, regardless of the legal estate of the accused, were prosecuted within the Criminal "Expedition" between 1763 and 1780, when the commission ceased to function with the formal opening of the new provincial administration in St. Petersburg *guberniia* under the law of 1775.[51]

As a rule, appeals in either criminal or civil cases could be made from the magistracy and other courts to the College of Justice. The Third Department of the Senate served as the highest appeals court. This hierarchy of courts defines the system through which virtually all cases originating in St. Petersburg traveled. How well the system worked will be assessed in the next chapter.

Whether or not the municipal courts functioned efficiently in St. Petersburg after midcentury, the court system empirewide needed reform. Catherine sought to remedy the deficiencies in the judicial system with the provincial reform of 1775. Working largely with courts already in existence, the reform established a clearer hierarchy and parallelism of judicial bodies within the traditional framework of separate courts for the nobility, townspeople, and the peasantry. The revised court system took effect in St. Petersburg in 1780, the year when the new *guberniia* structure opened in that province. Under this setup, St. Petersburg became home to two magistracies. The old Main Magistracy lost its significance (although not formally abolished until 1785), replaced by the St. Petersburg city magistracy, with jurisdiction only over the townsmen registered in St. Petersburg, and the St. Petersburg *guberniia* magistracy, which stood as an appeals court between the various town magistracies in the *guberniia* and the criminal and civil court chambers of the *guberniia* board. The number of oral courts in the city was increased to ten, one for each of the police administrative districts of town. In addition, a court of conscience, or equity court, was instituted for the entire *guberniia*. Physically located in St. Petersburg city, this court could almost be considered a municipal court, since St. Petersburg was the only city of consequence in the *guberniia*. The court of conscience could hear cases involving people from any estate, because it had two judges each from nobles, townsmen, and peasants, who heard suits in which their own people were parties. Cases came to this court upon request or appeal of one of the parties; its purpose was to soften the harshness of the laws, according to the dictates of a good and healthy conscience, especially in cases against juvenile offenders or the insane.[52]

With such a large number of unrelated branches of government all attempting to govern St. Petersburg in whole or in part, it is a wonder that adequate measures to deal with the city's problems could be either enacted or enforced. Responsibilities overlapped, duties of particular organs were rarely clear-cut, and at any time duly instituted organs were subject to interference from above—or, for that matter, from either side. In summary, it may be said that the day-to-day administration of the city involved the following bodies. Most powerful was the police, which operated under the oversight of the provincial government. Elected officials had authorization only to carry out policies, not to make proposals or decisions. Advisory bodies included the Senate, various chanceries, and the planning commission. Certain of the colleges intruded into small sections of the outskirts where they alone had responsibility for administering their *slobody*. No municipal court system existed with jurisdiction over all cases arising in the city.

Revenues

The finances of St. Petersburg, as of other Russian towns, derived in part from the old practices of "collections" based on objects of use and production. Revenues were raised also by assessing fees for services, such as the twenty-five-ruble charge for hearing a suit in the city magistracy or, after 1780, sending an appeal to the *guberniia* magistracy.[53] The monies, although collected in part by the city magistracy, were allocated by the state treasury to finance particular services in the city. They were not expended by the city itself. Other than the magistracy, various farmers-general also collected these taxes.[54] Collection was turned over to farmers-general in Russia for the same reasons as in other European countries in the eighteenth century. The government thought it could save itself much time and trouble by contracting with individuals to pay a predetermined amount from that which they collected. Any revenue above that amount was, of course, the farmer-general's profit. Catherine permitted most of these monopolies over tax collection to lapse during the 1760s because the practice ran contrary to her fiscal and economic beliefs.

In addition to the collections there were special taxes to pay for particular needs, such as streetlamps, public safety, paving, bridges, street cleaning—but there was no unified city budget. And, of course, there was no "city government" as such into whose treasury various taxes and fees could be deposited. The state treasury often provided direct grants to finance construction projects such as embankments of rivers and canals, the reconstruction of merchants' shops following fires, the building of bazaars, and the raising of houses for postmen on Moscow Side. This income was always directed to specific projects and cannot be considered as part of the city's general income.[55]

Neither collections nor special taxes nor treasury grants were constant sources of general income. A few such sources did exist, however. First among these were taxes paid by craftsmen, merchants, and petty townsmen.[56] The amounts generated by these taxes were not large. Statistics for the entire province reveal that in 1784 only 12,664 rubles were collected from 2,342 merchants, while from 2,609 petty townsmen were gathered 3,193 rubles and from craftsmen 812 rubles.[57] A second constant source of income was a 2 percent share of customs duties collected in the capital. Finally, the police collected certain taxes on real estate. In certain inheritance disputes the police chief was empowered to decide who was rightful heir. In return 10 percent of the inheritance went to the police. Besides this, all real estate transactions were assessed a tax based on the area involved in the sale, as well as a stamp duty.[58]

The police had a separate budget. Revenues were derived from licenses of various types, police taxes, and assessments for particular services, such as driving cattle safely through part of the city. Police expenditures were irregular and ad hoc because constant and recurring expenses, such as salaries and equipment, were met by grants from the state treasury. For extraordinary expenditures requests were made through the Senate for special monies.[59]

Statements concerning city expenditures beyond the police budget must be general and tentative, for complete statistics have not survived —if indeed it was ever possible to compile them. It is clear that many of the city's expenses were not budgetary but were borne directly by the inhabitants. For example, because home owners were directly responsible for fighting fires and paving streets and were assessed specific amounts for streetlamps and guardhouses, a figure representing total expenditure for these purposes could never be compiled. We have noted the popular dissatisfaction with the duties, financial and service, borne by inhabitants. For this reason the government in 1785 began to use soldiers garrisoned in the city as night watchmen and sentries in order to decrease citizens' obligations.[60]

Thus much of the city's monetary income was budgeted for specific purposes. Direct grants from the state treasury certainly fit into this category. After 1784 the revenue derived from customs duties went to support and maintain the city-operated shipyard (before that year the private shipyard); any surplus monies had to defray the expense of operating a merchant marine school.[61] Otherwise, revenues were disbursed by the police.

Added to the jumbled financial picture is the fact that tax obligations were assessed on an entirely inequitable basis. Commercial and producing citizens paid an income tax of sorts, and commercial and productive turnovers were taxed, but much potential income remained untouched. In particular, the nobility—whose lifestyle was at times most ostentatious—was not directly taxed at all. Nor were there taxes on real estate per se, only on real estate transactions. The transient population, including wealthy foreign merchants who never registered in St. Petersburg, remained untaxed by the city (beyond import and export duties), although they benefited greatly from the city's need for goods and its shortage of labor. No reform in the eighteenth century enabled the city to tap these sources. In this sense the city's own interests suffered because of the central government's inability to comprehend the potential of the urban situation. Catherine and her advisors were keenly aware, at least, of the inadequacy of urban administration, because with much fanfare a new comprehensive statute was promulgated on the empress's fifty-sixth birthday.

After 1785: The Charter

The Charter to the Towns was issued on April 21, 1785, jointly with the Charter to the Nobility. For the first time all Russian towns were brought, at least in theory, under a coherent, unified system of administration. In its basic form the Charter remained in effect for nearly a century. Although the Charter was intended for all the towns in the empire, the following discussion focuses on its application to St. Petersburg, only summarizing its general provisions.[62]

Archival evidence strongly suggests that St. Petersburg was the conscious model for the new town corporations and revised municipal government in the Charter.[63] Such provisions as those granting foreigners equal representation in artisan corporations, when present in sufficient number, seem to have been designed expressly with St. Petersburg in mind. The heart of the Charter was apparently drafted first for St. Petersburg, then applied later to all Russian towns.

The Charter created several new organs of urban government. The broadest-based of them was the city-at-large (*obshchestvo gradskoe*).[64] Although most interpreters of Catherine's municipal legislation have treated the *obshchestvo gradskoe* as though it were an organization, it is perhaps better understood as the defining criterion within which all the organs of municipal government existed and operated. City government under the Charter took place within the bounds of the city-at-large; in order to participate in administrative affairs, residents had to belong to it. Through discriminatory membership restrictions, participation was possible only for wealthier inhabitants. The minimum age for membership was set at twenty-five; one also had to be worth at least five thousand rubles, proven from tax records. Poor people had only the empty privilege of attending the meeting.[65]

Members of the city-at-large, which can also be termed the urban corporation, elected the city magistracy and the judges who sat on lower-level courts, including courts of conscience, oral courts, and the city orphans court.[66] The only other duty of the city-at-large was to compile a complete list of city inhabitants (to be discussed later). The city-at-large was thus a periodic body assembled only triennially in order to perform these tasks; in other words, it met primarily to hold elections.

A second organ created by the Charter was the general city council (*duma*), made up of representatives from the six classifications of city dwellers defined in the Charter.[67] The first general council elected in St. Petersburg took office by February 1786. Composed of more than ninety men, the general city council was too bulky a body to handle the daily affairs of administration. Nor was it designed to fill that function. Its purpose was rather to select a six-man council from among its members, one person from each classification of city dweller. The general city council thus functioned primarily to guarantee indirect selection of the smaller council, the real organ of administration under the new system of urban government.

The assumption is frequently made that merchants controlled these three councils. Because qualification and selection to them followed varying guidelines, particularly for the general city council, the issue is worth exploring. Clearly the city-at-large was the domain of the wealthy, who therefore controlled elections to the city magistracy and the judges in the three courts under the city administration. With a minimum of five thousand rubles in capital necessary to become an elector, members of the third guild, most artisans, and all of the *posad* people would have been excluded. So, presumably, could have been some of the eminent citizens. In fact, the membership of the general city council was dominated numerically by artisans. Genuine city residents and *posad* people each had ten delegates, one from each police administrative district of the city. St. Petersburg merchants had only three representatives, one from each guild,[68] although home-owning merchants could add to their number if elected as genuine city residents. Foreign and out-of-town merchants could elect representatives from every town and state with at least five merchants working and living in St. Petersburg. Artisans, however, elected one delegate from each craft guild, or *tsekh,* giving them a huge majority in the council. Of the more than ninety members in 1786, between fifty and sixty probably were artisans.[69] In her study of the archival records of the St. Petersburg city council in the years 1788–91, Janet Hartley discovered that the artisan members of the council did not attend council sessions in the numbers allowed them. Often they sent only token representation in the person of the artisan head and a few others. Far more faithful in attendance and participation were the genuine city residents and the eminent citizens.[70] The group that could have dominated the council thus did not. The council could hardly be termed an instrument of estate interests. On the six-man council, each urban estate had one representative, chosen by the artisan-dominated city council and presumably not in conflict with their views. It was this group that had the greatest responsibility under the new law, because it met more frequently than the larger body and served as its "central committee."

In addition to laying out lines of administrative responsibility, the Charter introduced into city record-keeping two types of registers, which greatly facilitated administration. One, compiled by the city magistracy, contained full listings of the condition of all real estate in the city. Very detailed, the document was valuable both to prospective buyers or renters of property (who were able to get a true evaluation of the state and worth of the property) and to moneylenders (who could determine the actual amount of collateral a borrower had).[71] The second register, also innovative in its scope, consisted of a complete listing of all city inhabitants according to estate. It also included addresses and such basic personal data as marital status, identification of children, and length of time at that address. The register had at least three intended uses: it served as a basis for computing taxation, had legal authority in cases such as disputed station or heredity, and was used in compiling census figures.[72] It was this register of inhabitants that endowed people living in the city with legal rights to carry on commerce, industry, or crafts. As valuable a source for a social history of the city as this register would be, unfortunately no copies have survived from the eighteenth century.[73] The full register was not compiled during the first elective term of the new form of government, through 1788.[74] Preliminary registers were compiled, however. In fact, the committee responsible for compiling them was asked to go a step further than the Charter required. In October 1789 the six-man council sent the committee a recommendation from wealthy merchants who were disturbed that people who had not bothered to register in the city nevertheless carried on business there. The recommendation asked that people selling goods in stores, basements, and other places register the addresses of their shops, and identify the types of goods sold, in the register of city inhabitants.[75] Through this measure the merchants who conformed to the law hoped to identify those who sold goods illegally, either inducing them to register or, if they were peasants, forcing them out of business. The outcome of this request remains unknown but may be guessed at; businessmen who up to then had neglected (or refused) to register as merchants surely would have had no qualms about continuing to operate illegally.

The classification of city inhabitants according to their economic and social roles was a fundamental objective of the Charter. Merchants and artisans received particular attention. Those of both occupations who qualified for membership in the "guilds" won further improvement in status. Merchants who were first- and second-guild members were freed from corporal punishment and permitted to own finer carriages and livery than their less well-off neighbors. A provision allowing only first-guild merchants to engage in overseas trade (although intended to preserve a special "privilege" for them) protected overly ambitious traders with little capital from ruining themselves in risky ventures of that nature. Merchants from other cities and countries were assured freedom of religion, freedom of movement, and were given a share in local government.

Artisans received a comprehensive set of regulations of their own (*remeslennoe polozhenie*) governing mutual relations among craftsmen at the levels of apprentice, journeyman, and master. The regulations also sought to ensure high-quality work; to that end craft guilds, on the model of western European craft guilds, were established. The guilds were responsible in addition for the behavior of their members in society at large.[76]

The *posad* people, previously called the *meshchane,* made up at least one-fourth of the city's inhabitants. As delimited in the Charter, they were the unskilled laborers, day workers, workmen in manufactories, trading people without enough capital to qualify for membership in the third guild of merchants, peasants come to the city with passports granted by local authorities, and such like. After 1785 *posad* people continued to shoulder many of the same service and tax obligations, without gaining status or privileges to lighten their burdens.[77]

Conspicuous by their absence from the Charter's provisions were the nobility and the peasantry. The nobility received its own charter on the same day the Charter to the Towns was promulgated, but it dealt exclusively with the nobility as an estate of rural landowners, local administrators, and privileged subjects, not as urban dwellers. Yet large numbers of noblemen and gentry held town houses in St. Petersburg. The gentry were given no direct voice in city government as gentry. They had the right to participate in urban administration if they owned real property in town or were registered in the guilds, but otherwise the new organization of urban administration made no mention of the nobility.

Nothing in the Charter would have prevented the gentry from registering in the guilds. In the first few years after 1785, several attempts were made to do so in St. Petersburg. The guilds strongly opposed this, seeing it as an intrusion by the nobility into an area of activity Catherine had reserved exclusively for merchants. In 1790 Catherine gave substance to the merchants' contention by forbidding the gentry from joining merchant guilds.[78]

Peasants also appear to have gained nothing from the Charter. Indeed, the peasantry was not even considered to be a component of the city's population.[79] Instead, the Charter assumed that when they became urban residents, peasants changed their status, leaving behind their rural designations and assuming new roles, either as merchants—if they had sufficient capital, as artisans—if they possessed skills, or as *posad* people—if they did not fit into either of the former categories. In towns the traditional rural designations had no place; rural roles had to give way to urban ones.

Of administrative agencies in existence before 1785, the Charter said very little. On a number of points it made direct reference to specific articles in the 1775 provincial reform law, always doing so in the context of confirming previously assigned duties and functions.

It did not elaborate upon those instructions or rearrange the assignment of tasks in any way. The city magistracy continued to be subordinated to the provincial administration; its sphere of jurisdiction neither expanded nor contracted. The base of its composition was broadened though, at least in St. Petersburg, by the constitution of half its membership from the foreign citizens living in the city. The three new organizations—city-at-large, general city council, and six-man council—were conceived as no more than new, lower rungs on the ladder of administrative power. They were clearly subordinate to the governor and provincial organs of administration. The chain of authority remained the same at the top. The significance of the Charter is that it granted a bit more self-administration to St. Petersburg's populace at the bottom. The areas of authority ceded to the new organs did not diminish those of existing institutions. Instead, local self-rule was allocated primarily to commercial matters, which before 1785 were administered not at all well and by no unitary authority. The new administrative bodies were agents of the commercial population, either merchants or producers (craftsmen). The city for the first time received legal authority to build and own mills of any kind, taverns, inns, and bazaars. It was also supposed to guarantee that weights and measures were uniform and used honestly. Other provisions granted permission for residents from the surrounding rural district to trade in the city, defined the hours of commercial activity, and legalized foreign commerce by Russian merchants. To an extent these provisions only legalized the existing state of affairs. Unfortunately, every other city also had the right to establish its own weights and measures. It would have been immeasurably more helpful if one uniform system had been established for the whole country as was done for France by the Convention in 1793.[80]

Within the overall structure of government, the new bodies set to work with zeal and enthusiasm. It has been estimated, for example, that more than 12,500 people voted to elect the members of the first general city council in 1786, a figure that seems quite high in view of the severe suffrage restrictions.[81] As newly created bodies, however, they had flaws of design and operation, which could become apparent and be corrected only in the crucible of everyday affairs.

Many of the administrative functions given over to the six-man council were earlier carried out by the police. Despite the obvious overlapping of functions, the only mention of the latter in the Charter came in a reminder to the council that it should work in conjunction with the police. Nothing was said about the process by which the newer body should take over the administrative reins from the older. Indeed, the police were not wont to give up their authority, for they saw the council as invading activity heretofore under police supervision. Control over the maintenance of bridges and pavement, for example, was fully released to the council only in 1792.[82] In other cases the police simply refused to cooperate with the new body, yielding only when forced to do so by the courts. For two years the police even withheld city maps, without which the council could hardly begin serious work, releasing them only after repeated requests from the council.[83]

Resources

The Charter simplified financial arrangements, instituting a full range of provisions for revenues and expenditures by the new organs of administration. Income was now derived from several fixed sources. Because St. Petersburg was a port city, its coffers were enriched by more than sixty thousand rubles per year from its share of trade revenues.[84] Smaller amounts came from profits on the sale of alcoholic beverages in the city, from granting hunting and fishing privileges in the city and its environs, from taxes on merchants, artisans and *posad* people, and from public baths, stamps, fines, and penalties.[85]

The police continued to bear costs of paving streets, maintaining canals, sewers, and streetlights, and other urban tasks in their own budget, leaving the expenses of the new city administrative apparatus at a minimum. Those expenditures consisted almost exclusively of the salaries of elected officials, maintenance of the city hall, the city shipyard, and the public schools, rapidly growing but still few in number. The treasury surplus was invested in banks. Any other proposed expense had to win approval from the governor. He also received full annual account of the city's total debits and credits.[86] The earliest available complete city budget dates from 1797. The budget in that year amounted to a mere thirty-six thousand rubles. Yet a commission studying the finances of St. Petersburg estimated that total city expenditure, if police, council, and other accounts were combined, would total between four and five hundred thousand rubles, a much more realistic figure for what it cost to operate the city.[87] Seven years after Catherine's death, in 1803, the council finally gained control of the entire city financial system, realizing in actuality what had been instituted in potentiality by the Charter.

Thus the Charter to the Towns introduced a number of changes in the composition of St. Petersburg's administrative apparatus, financial structure, and economic relations. The impact and significance of the Charter can be summed up in four main points. The Charter introduced into Russia the concept of the city as a legal corporation, with an element of control over its own existence. The concept remained, to be sure, severely limited in scope, for "membership" in the city-at-large was open only to a small proportion of its residents. The realm of self-administration was generally restricted to the commercial sphere. Yet the important fact to remember is that the concept of "city" as a self-regulating, self-financing body had been introduced.

The two registers, one listing all real estate and the other containing the names of all inhabitants, helped to make concrete this wider conception of the city. Not only did the city become a legally recognized body, but its legitimization was further strengthened by the new methods of record-keeping. For the first time documents were to be kept for the city alone and relating to the city alone. On a more mundane level, the registers provided objective bases for taxation and administration.

One must also remember that the formulation of the Charter was more imposed from above than demanded from below. City residents had exerted pressure earlier in Catherine's reign for reforms of particular laws, mainly in the instructions to the delegate to the Legislative Commission in 1767, and many of their wishes were instituted in the Charter.[88] But Catherine's own interests, perceptions, and goals played the most important part in determining the content of the Charter. She stated her expectation that the urban population, heartened by the enactment of the Charter, would thereafter double its devotion to the welfare of Russia and to herself as sovereign.[89] Catherine sought to invigorate urban life by granting a limited amount of self-government and increasing the status of merchants and artisans, whom she considered to be important elements of the urban population.

But self-government covered only a limited sphere, which brings up the fourth point. The new bodies did not replace old ones. In a sense they had to shoulder their way into the existing hierarchy. Not surprisingly, in their earliest years they felt the hostility of the governmental organs whose functions they partially supplanted. In view of the ineffectiveness of earlier legislation to create viable institutions of town government, the wonder under the circumstances is that they managed to survive to function at all. Effectiveness of administration was only developed over a period of time. This fact was recognized by Kizevetter, a severe critic of the Charter, who otherwise misinterpreted its impact in the eighteenth century, ascribing the weakness of the new bodies in part to the inability of various estates to work together. Hartley, on the other hand, believes that the new institutions worked much better than one might have expected, especially in St. Petersburg.[90] As the members of the new bodies discovered both the limits and the potentialities inherent in local government, however, they expanded the roles of the new bodies. It is significant that after four years of experimentation with other schemes of urban government under Paul, Alexander I in 1801 reinstated the system introduced by his grandmother Catherine.[91] The council form of city government continued to serve St. Petersburg through various minor reforms. One of those reforms, in 1846, served particularly as a model for the government of other towns in the empire. Thus the general framework established by Catherine in 1785, designed particularly for St. Petersburg, continued in operation until the municipal reform of Alexander II in 1870.

4
"Incessant Labor and Solicitude": City Administration in Practice

THERE IS A LONG-STANDING DEBATE AMONG HISTORIANS OF RUSSIA over the role of the state in the history of Russian towns. One view, which seems to assume that western European relationships were uniform and normative, holds that the Russian state stifled the development of urban life through its overly rigorous regulation of society, by the too-heavy tax and service obligations placed on the urban population, by prohibiting the development and growth of indigenous and autonomous corporative bodies in the towns. Other historians point out that Russia differed from the West. The goals the state was pursuing were incompatible with fostering urban life on the pattern of western Europe. The backbone of the Russian state was the *dvoriane,* the landed gentry, whose interests lay elsewhere than in urban growth. This relationship between crown and landed estates therefore differed from that of western Europe, where the prince frequently was allied with townsmen in order to break the power of the gentry. A third view more recently espoused suggests that the state and towns related to each other in a pattern that may have been unique to Russia but not antithetically, each defending its interests and gaining whatever it could from the other.[1]

While these three points of view do not exhaust the treatment this issue has received, the debate raises the possibility that the state may have been developing policies and instituting measures that had countervailing effects. On the one hand, these policies stimulated the urban economy, aiding in the growth of the urban population and enhancing the various social and cultural patterns generally associated with cities. On the other hand, government policies through conscious design or unthinking neglect failed to provide a conducive climate for growth, perhaps even working toward goals antithetical to strong urban life. In Catherinian St. Petersburg the organs of administration had tasks covering a wide range of activities. By their nature some of these functions generated a climate more hospitable to urban growth, while others impeded the city's development. Given the conditions of overlapping structures through which these functions were carried out, discussed in the previous chapter, one wonders how it was possible for administrative bodies to fulfill any of their assigned tasks effectively.

Keeping the Peace

One of the first tasks of government is to preserve domestic peace and tranquillity. This was the major duty of the St. Petersburg police even under the concept of the *Rechtsstaat,* the "policed-state" that placed so many other responsibilities in the hands of the police as well. The frequent attempts to reconstitute and reorganize the police during these years indicates either a degree of dissatisfaction with its effectiveness or the realization that the city was constantly outgrowing the machinery set up to safeguard it. As seen in the previous chapter, the police had a much fuller administrative staff throughout Catherine's reign than it had patrolmen in the streets. Even so, we do not know the names or anything about most of these officials, making it impossible to gauge how well they functioned in their jobs. No bureaucracy is better than the people it attracts. Some indication of the quality of personnel on the police suggests itself through comparison of salaries paid to police with those paid to officials in the many other bureaucracies comprising Russia's central and local governments. The salaries of higher officials in the police appear not to have been out of line with those in other chancelleries and bureaus. At street level, however, wages were pitifully low early in Catherine's reign. Patrolmen, watchmen, and dogcatchers received only eighteen rubles annually, and chimney sweeps (young boys?) only a third of that.[2] This was far less than even a day laborer in construction could earn. In considering the degree of professionalism in the police, or how well they did their job, this information helps to explain the deficiencies and shortcomings of the force.

The Police

Judging by the biographies of the men whom the Senate named as police chief, it would appear that the police chancellery worked with mixed success. The first chief of police appointed by Catherine, N. I. Chicherin (1764–77), a career army officer, had had a distinguished pattern of service, serving immediately before as commander in chief of Kiev. His greatest accomplishment as St. Petersburg police chief was his leading role on the Commission for the Masonry Construction of St. Petersburg and Moscow. While police chief he became a senator (1766) and, after two promotions in rank, a four-star general (1773). But Chicherin was forced to retire in disgrace in 1777 following the disastrous September flood that killed "not just a thousand people," according to Catherine, who laid full blame for the police's lack of preparedness on Chicherin. The selection of the next chief of police, D. V. Volkov, would suggest Catherine's continued high regard for the post. A talented and mature civil servant, Volkov had drafted the 1762 statute emancipating the nobility and under Catherine had headed the Manufactures College and been governor of Smolensk province. He too became a senator while St. Petersburg police chief, but the following year, 1778, moved on to Orenburg as governor-general. His successor, P. V. Lopukhin, was an extremely young man, coming to the post at the age of twenty-six, two years after he had transferred from the army to the civil list. In fact, he was only confirmed in the post in 1780, two years after he began work. Like Volkov, he too was shortly transferred to a higher post. In 1782, after a brief stint in Tver', he became governor of Moscow for ten years. The other long-term police chief in the capital under Catherine, N. I. Ryleev (1784–97), seems to have been the least competent of the lot. Certainly his contemporaries held him in low regard. Catherine's secretary, A. V. Khrapovitskii, called him a fool. A. A. Bezborodko termed him a "scamp." A. M. Turgenev said he was known for his unsurpassed stupidity.[3] Thus, it would appear from a cursory glance at the top leadership of St. Petersburg's police that the reform measures to regularize and establish their activity were not always carried through in the appointment of effective police chiefs. The system may have been better designed than built.

From the beginning of her reign Catherine expressed her concern that the police make St. Petersburg's streets safe, especially at night.[4] Most patrolling was done at that time by civilian representatives of home owners, often servants, whose major task seems to have been to report violations to the police, not prevent them. This system may have worked well enough in those parts of town where neighborhoods were well established and home owners had sufficient manpower at their summons to provide patrol- and watchmen. But overall, particularly in outer sections of town, the system appears to have been unsatisfactory. Before the end of the 1760s the police began to resort to the use of garrisoned soldiers as watchmen, particularly on those occasions when fears of perceived increases in burglaries, murders, street muggings, and other violent crime demanded that something more be done.[5]

Although weekly police reports to the empress document occasional attacks even on policemen,[6] the evidence indicates that for a big city the rate of reported crime was quite low. For example, the annual murder rate reported to police hovered somewhere between seven and eight per hundred thousand population. On the other hand, between 2,400 and 4,000 per 100,000 could expect to be victimized by thieves each year.[7] Although the existence of a great gap between wealth and poverty and a social order that favors one group markedly over others may be inducements to crime, there is little to suggest that these factors operated significantly in St. Petersburg. Nevertheless, during Catherine's reign citizens began for the first time to lock their house doors and the gates into their yards. A greater number began keeping watchdogs in their yards, and some of the wealthy began to employ their own night watchmen in addition to the obligation to provide manpower for the police.[8] The court itself became concerned about theft and robbery from the Winter Palace as bands of robbers were discovered among workmen refurbishing its apartments.[9] Notices were posted in the newspapers offering rewards for information regarding such thefts and amnesty to those turning in property stolen from the palace.[10]

Undoubtedly the perception of increased crime can be attributed primarily to the growth in population. Even though the crime rate seems clearly to have remained lower in St. Petersburg throughout the century than in cities of similar size elsewhere in Europe, Catherine on occasion took pains to defuse western European newspaper accounts of crimes committed against foreigners in Russia's capital.[11] A reported conversation between N. I. Panin and I. G. Chernyshev leaves little doubt that they believed St. Petersburg to be safer than other European cities, noting that fences and latches in St. Petersburg were usually of wood, while in other cities private homes more closely resembled fortresses, with iron gates, locks, and bars.[12]

In addition to safeguarding against crime, Catherine's police were charged with maintaining decorum and preserving the proper appearance of a *Residenzstadt* in St. Petersburg's streets. Public drunkenness was not tolerated, and on occasions of great holidays, scores of drunken citizens might be taken into custody, frequently for their own protection from the weather as much as for their violations of decency.[13] Cabmen, whose loud whistles, abusive language, and frightening driving habits were constant points of concern, were finally licensed in order to place controls over both their numbers and their behavior.[14] During the 1780s taverns came under police scrutiny because of the gambling, fights, and open prostitution that repeatedly cropped up there, and severe laws were instituted to regulate them, although with debatable success. Public baths were strictly regulated as well, to reduce their reputations as centers of lascivious behavior.[15]

One of the features of eighteenth-century European cities that has attracted considerable attention from historians, the urban riot, seems hardly to have troubled St. Petersburg. One reason may have been the conscious effort made during Catherine's reign to keep out of the city all those people who did not have the right, recognized by the state, to be there. Peasants in particular could live and work in the city legally only if they had passports from their lord or village administrator giving them permission to go to St. Petersburg. Otherwise they ran the risk of being sent to forced labor if caught by the police.[16] Beggars were routinely picked up by the police and either deported from the city, early in Catherine's reign, or impressed into work on construction projects or other hard labor later in the reign.[17] For whatever reason, street riots must have been an uncommon occurrence in St. Petersburg, for extensive research has turned up only a few isolated instances of disorders or riots on the part of crowds.[18]

People held under arrest were housed in a jail adjacent to the police station on the Moika. When the English prison reformer John Howard visited St. Petersburg in 1781 as one of the first stops on his tour of European prisons, he was appalled by what he found. He later claimed that the use of the knout often resulted in the deaths of prisoners, and reported that the police chief (Lopukhin?) showed him, somewhat proudly, the various instruments for corporal punishment—breaking arms and legs, splitting nostrils, and branding. Irons, in some cases chained to logs, restricted even the simplest movements of prisoners.[19] Although there is not a great deal of documentation from which to judge, it would appear that the police frequently used high-handed methods in dealing with suspects. On at least one occasion a person unjustly arrested and detained won a settlement of 800 rubles from the police for the trouble and distress caused him.[20]

Conditions presumably improved when a new city jail, called Jail Castle, opened in 1787 at the confluence of the Moika and Nikol'skii canals, for the structure utilized several ideas that were being popularized by prison reformers. The new jail was pentagonal in shape, of two stories, and constructed around an open courtyard that was designed to let in fresh air and sunlight as well as serve as an exercise ground. Far more spacious than its predecessor, the jail had a built-in system of pipes running through the walls to serve as a sort of communications system that was frequently used in "broadcasting" religious services to prisoners as an integral part of the program of rehabilitation.[21]

More importantly, however, the new jail housed only those prisoners and alleged offenders charged with serious crimes, at least during the warm months of the year. In the years following 1783, in addition to the stockade on Vasil'evskii Island for more serious offenders, the police maintained during the summer two "workhouses," where people were confined and employed who had not committed grave crimes but who were either burdens on society or liable to become involved in crime: "lazy unskilled workers, people without passports, runaway serfs and servants, healthy indigents, drunkards, bullies, profligates, idlers, petty thieves, and their ilk."[22] Apparently the police satisfied themselves that they were keeping these sorts of people off the streets of the capital. By the middle of the 1780s an average of some 200–300 were being arrested under these charges each year.[23]

The Courts

Public tranquillity was not the province of the police alone. The judicial system shared the responsibility. Like the rest of the city's administration, the judicial system was complex. The police themselves adjudicated cases of theft and pilferage involving a valuation of less than twenty rubles. After the third appearance on such charges, a defendant was remanded to the appropriate court.[24] Court cases involving gentry were heard in the lower or superior land court. Cases dealing with peasants fell to the lower or superior tribunal. Most cases originating in St. Petersburg, though, ended up in the city magistracy.[25] The magistracy handled all civil suits among merchants and artisans. If the state was a party to the dispute, the magistracy as a lower court had to transfer the case to the Third Department of the Senate. Overcrowded dockets in town magistracies induced the creation of special courts to handle less important suits, the oral courts, and the courts of conscience.

Oral Courts

Oral courts existed from 1727. In the 1740s they were placed under the direction of the magistracy. This relationship was reaffirmed in the provincial reform law of 1775 and again in the Police Statute of 1782.[26] Oral courts operated without written briefs. Their judges, who were elected by the "company of citizens" in each district of town, were instructed to base their verdicts "on the substance of the suit, to wit: to satisfy plaintiffs by the power that is grounded in justice; for example, that people who borrow money return it; that what is promised be done. . . ."[27] Judges were to keep a daily notebook or journal describing each case and its disposition. All cases dealing with commerce except *vekseli* (letters of credit, promissory notes) fell into the province of the oral court. *Vekseli*, as written documents, were handled by the magistracy. Among the specific types of cases adjudicated by the oral courts were the following:

(1) nonpayment for goods received;
(2) problems with servants or people working for hire;
(3) rentals of horses;
(4) rentals of shops, houses, flats, corridors, corners, eating establishments, gardens, empty lots, and so on;
(5) problems with the terms of labor of artisans;
(6) disputes regarding contracts of people hired to teach and exercise the arts (professors of the sciences, teachers of languages, doctors, architects, painters, carvers, sculptors, etc.);
(7) deceptions in weights and measures for food items and other essentials;
(8) nonfulfillment of contracts by people indicated in (6);
(9) nonfulfillment of contract or damage done by artisans;
(10) day laborers and servants for nonfulfillment of work they had been paid for; and
(11) lessors causing troubles for tenants under (4) or renters under (3).

The oral courts worked closely with the police. When a plaintiff came to the court, notice was immediately sent to the police to locate the accused and bring him to court, after which a verdict was supposed to be reached within a day. Besides keeping the police district inspector informed about its work, the oral court reported to the provincial board weekly, forwarding a weekly journal to it. Other copies of weekly journals were to be bound together throughout the year, so that if frequent complaints came regarding the same person, the court would have a record and could make a more serious case against him before the magistracy.

It is significant that the oral court transcended estate boundaries. Its jurisdiction encompassed all people living within its district, "without regard to persons, for every court instituted by Her Imperial Majesty is a court of God, and before Him all dignities and ranks are equal." Although the oral court dealt with mundane issues, it was the first urban governmental organ to have jurisdiction over all ranks, estates, and people.

No requirement was made that the oral courts keep permanent records. After all, one of the purposes of establishing these courts was to reduce paperwork. Presumably the records sent to the provincial board were retained. They would comprise a fascinating and revealing source of information for the urban historian except for the disastrous fire in 1864 that burned much of the *guberniia* archives. Only incidental references to the way in which these courts worked survive.

Table 4.1. Cases in Oral Courts, 1785

District	# initiated	# resolved	% resolved
1st Admiralty	471	415	88.1
2nd Admiralty	657	632	96.2
3rd Admiralty	1,004	911	90.7
Foundry	378	350	92.6
Moscow Side	752	725	96.4
Rozhestvenskaia	237	237	100.0
Karetnaia	171	163	95.3
Vasil'evskii Island	368	302	82.1
Petersburg Side	419	371	88.5
Vyborg Side	42	42	100.0
TOTALS	4,517	4,148	91.8

Source: RGADA, *fond* 16, *delo* 521, *chast'* 1, *list* 200.

A list of the disposition of cases in the city's oral courts, by district, survives from 1785 (table 4.1). We do not know the decisions in these cases, who the parties were to them, or what bias the courts may have shown. What is clear is that people were using the courts and that the courts were resolving the vast majority of cases. Nearly 92 percent of all cases brought before the oral courts were resolved within the same year, and in two districts every case was decided. (In 1784, 79.9 percent of cases—2,933 of 3,672—were decided.) Where decisions were not reached, the reason usually given was that one of the parties to the suit could not be located.

Court of Conscience

The court of conscience, or equity court, which sat for the entire province, had a much lighter caseload as well as a higher rate of successful disposition of cases. Although the carryover of cases from one year to the next averaged 35 percent for the fifteen years from 1780–94, 96.2 percent of all cases were decided.[28] The business of the court of conscience was much simpler than that of the oral court, however.

The court of conscience had three functions: to examine cases arising from ignorance of the law or involuntary crimes, from crimes committed because of "youth or foolishness"; to arbitrate between two parties to a conflict when both parties agreed beforehand to abide by the court's decision; and to act on appeals from people who had been jailed for up to three days without being charged with a crime, either by releasing them or remanding them to jail.[29] Only

23.1 percent of all cases (546 of 2,362) handled came under the third category, but the percentage showed a slight increase during the period.[30] Both the oral court and the court of conscience need more study before conclusions can be drawn as to their effectiveness.

Magistracy

The St. Petersburg Main Magistracy did not work at all efficiently during the first years of Catherine's reign. This was a consequence in part of the magistracy's additional function as a court of appeals for all other town magistracies in the empire. Officially the magistracy served as a court for adjudicating civil suits involving commerce and handicraft production, but in practice it also handled petitions to enter the merchant corporations and handicraft guilds and collected information requested by organs of the central government and, after 1780, the provincial board. Before the provincial reform of 1775 it heard cases of protested *vekseli*.[31] Twice in the 1760s and early 1770s the vice president of the Main Magistracy Office brought reports to the Senate complaining that the magistracy was too overburdened with a backlog of cases to function well. In 1774, cases still remained unresolved dating from as early as 1732; approximately 3,500 awaited decision. There were another 50,000 or so cases that may or may not have been decided. No one knew because the bundles of materials in the magistracy's archive did not indicate whether these matters had been settled or not.[32] In 1764 this problem came to the Senate's attention, but nothing was done to resolve it. Following a second report a decade later, a temporary department was set up to deal with the backlog of cases, with Senate assurances that the forthcoming code of laws—presumably meaning the revision of the statutes governing the magistracy and the provincial reform of 1775—would solve the problem in the future.

The magistracy presumably was composed of the more capable and successful men to be found among St. Petersburg's merchants. We know the names of virtually all the burgomasters and councilmen from the triennial elections of 1774 through 1786. Seventeen of thirty-three men are known to have been merchants, and all but two of them to have owned more than one shop. At least seven owned more than ten shops each. A number of these merchants served later in higher elective positions. For example, of the six men on the magistracy in 1774, Nikita Puchkov was elected city mayor in 1780, councilman Vasilii Ol'khin was elected a burgomaster in 1783, and Fedor Iamshchikov and Ivan Kestner were elected to the provincial magistracy in 1783. A fifth member of the magistracy in 1774, Sava Iakovlev, was perhaps the richest and best known of all St. Petersburg's merchants in the eighteenth century. He is buried in a prominent place marked with a fine bronze monument in the cemetery of the Alexander Nevskii monastery. The evidence suggests that as time passed nonmerchants and less-prominent merchants became more numerous on the magistracy.

Despite the fact that the best men available may have been serving on the magistracy, it remained unable to exert a strong will of its own, either to formulate policy from general guidelines or to force merchants and craftsmen to carry out its instructions.[33] The magistracy was relieved of its responsibility over contested *vekseli* after the provincial reform, when that task fell to the *guberniia* magistracy.[34]

After 1785 the magistracy and the new city council organizations sometimes stepped on each other's toes. Lines of responsibility were not drawn clearly between them. Neither was obligated to report to the other, yet both of them were subordinated to the same higher bodies, and they handled similar matters. Catherine may well have assumed that a duplication of effort would ensure at least that jobs got done, but this was not always the result in St. Petersburg.[35]

Appeals Courts

The Third Department of the Ruling Senate served as an appellate court. There appear to have been no set criteria for determining what kinds of cases the Senate would hear, although in most instances a lower-level organ of government was party to the suit, usually as defendant. Many cases involved disputes over land ownership. On occasion the magistracy or other lower courts appealed to the Senate for guidance in making their own rulings. Judging from the records of these suits, the Third Department seems to have ruled as much as possible on the basis of precedent or statute. By no means did it settle all cases in the government's favor. Cases were frequently turned over to the *guberniia* board for further investigation and the compilation of all relevant documents and depositions. When decisions were handed down, often as decrees in the name of the empress, the statutes that comprised the legal basis for the judgment were as a rule cited.[36] The Senate inevitably heard many cases, since issues frequently arose for which no clear precedent existed. The Third Department of the Senate thus played a major role in establishing the legal traditions in Russia's towns and cities for the settlement of property disputes, questions of honor and privilege, living arrangements, and determination of socially acceptable behavior as these traditions began to assume shape and form in Catherinian St. Petersburg.

Regulatory Functions

The tsarist government traditionally concerned itself with every exchange of wealth and every money making proposition, as well as every violation of social norms. Following this tradition, the state sought to maintain strict controls over much of urban life. Given the government's attempt to exert control, its manner of doing so and its degree of success in regulating city life assume primary interest. The variety of controls extended to commercial activity and industrial production, of course.[37] Building codes were applied to construction throughout the city. Prices were closely watched and sometimes set by the government. Many such controls helped in administering the city.

Slightly different in conception and approach was another means by which government restricted life in the city—the control over people. It was not peculiar to St. Petersburg, but an inevitable corollary to Russia's social structure and the intention to preserve it. It assumes particular significance because it represented one of the fundamental differences between urban life in Russia and the pattern assumed to be the norm for Europe, where, beginning in late medieval times, "Stadtluft macht[e] frei," city air made one free.

The growth of St. Petersburg was marked by such excessive regulation of the population that much of the regulation could not realistically be enforced. Certain measures applied to all inhabitants of the city. All persons intending to leave the city were required to announce their impending departure in the newspaper three times, undoubtedly to prevent people from moving away from St. Petersburg in order to escape creditors or the police. But examination of the *Sanktpeterburgskie vedomosti* reveals that only a few people—exclusively foreigners, civil servants, and military officers—did so, and many even of them failed to comply with the law.[38] Furthermore, all residents had to possess passports or some other identification granting them permission to live and work in the city, with the exception of the nobility, who could live anywhere in the empire. One presumably could not legally gain quarters without offering this proof to the landlord, who in turn showed it to the police for verification.

Those caught without passports were invariably fined, and might be exiled from the city or imprisoned.[39] But so few police as there were could scarcely man the entire wall-and-ditch surrounding the city, and the law was easily circumvented. In the earlier years of Catherine's reign, the police expended much time and effort trying to apprehend unregistered inhabitants. The regulation against having anything to do with nonregistered residents was posted along with others on police bulletin boards at major intersections and on public houses.[40] The police circulated among employers lists of runaway serfs believed to be in the city. Contractors carrying out government-financed construction projects were repeatedly instructed to ferret out workers without passports and warned not to hire such people in the future.[41] Residents were liable to spot checks of documents in the streets or in public gathering places such as taverns.

In applying these prohibitions, the state certainly was defending the economic and legal interests of its traditional ally, the nobility, by restricting serfs to their villages. But more than that was at stake. The state also was revealing a preference for well-regulated cities of moderate size and a controlled rate of population increase. Eventually the police realized that they could not cut off illegal migration to the city and ceased their extensive efforts to capture all the runaway serfs, vagabond peasants, fugitive soldiers, and others, and return them to the places from which they came. Instead, when people without documents were arrested, they were put to work as obligated laborers on construction projects in the city, or if underage were apprenticed to craftsmen. As for runaway serfs, only when owners had notified the police of the identities of particular missing serfs did the police attempt to send runaways home.[42] Comprehending at last the extent of illegal migration to St. Petersburg, the government toward the end of Catherine's reign abandoned its pretense of stopping this flow of people.[43]

Urban Services

Keeping the peace and regulating economic activities and migration are tasks not exclusively urban in nature. The state attempted to carry out those duties in countryside, village, and city alike. But as St. Petersburg grew into a large city, its administration began assuming duties more identifiably urban in nature. Indeed, for life to be livable, city administration had to provide certain services. The introduction of the city's first sewer system serves as an example. When the city was smaller, the rivers and canals were able to handle wastes and ground runoff alike. With increasing population, however, the primitive practice of dumping liquid and solid wastes into the river became unacceptable. In the city's *nakaz,* drawn up in 1767 to instruct its delegate to the great legislative commission, the first article was devoted to the need for greater cleanliness in the city.[44] The earliest underground sewer system was dug in 1770 to carry off wastes from the main streets, depositing them in the Neva. Within a few years a main was dug that carried sewage nearly to the Gulf of Finland before emptying into the river, thereby reducing pollution in the city's water supply. Gutters on streets that did not have underground sewers also drained into the large sewer main.[45]

In the city's central areas in particular, the great population density and intensive use of the streets by horse-drawn traffic called for further measures. In 1778 a system was begun of placing thirty carts or wagons in the streets of First Admiralty district to collect horse droppings as well as household wastes. Hired contractors then carried the carts away. In 1779, however, the police tried to save some of the 5,735 rubles expended the previous year by requiring residents to dig pits or themselves provide baskets to collect waste material, then carry it to the city pasture themselves to dump, or give it to farmers or gardeners. Still, the police provided twenty wagons at a contracted price of 3,640 rubles. In 1780, finally, a special assessment of three and three-fourths kopecks per square *sazhen'* of land (forty-nine square feet) was laid on each home-owner in the district as a tax to defray the cost of removing garbage.[46]

Besides being kept clean, streets needed to be lit at night. Streetlighting not only provided a sense of security but also stood as a shining testimony to the glory of the sovereign who could successfully defy the dark of night. Special "illuminations" were occasional and expensive undertakings only provided in conjunction with great celebrations. The oil burned in streetlamps, which after all gave off only a severely limited amount of light, cost 1.50 rubles a *pud* (approximately 36.1 pounds) in 1770, up to 2.40 per *pud* by 1785, and each lamp burned about a *pud* per year. By 1770 the city had 1,257 streetlamps. The major problem with operating them lay not with the cost of oil but with the shortage of lamplighters and tenders. Early in Catherine's reign streetlamps were tended by police carters, whose other obligations frequently kept them from devoting as much time to this task as they should have. Furthermore, a man could care for only a limited number of lamps if they were all to be lit at approximately the same time. The twenty men who did the work tended the lamps only in the center of the city, leaving the rest of it in the dark. In 1770, a new arrangement diverted one hundred military recruits into the St. Petersburg police as lamplighters at a wage of eighteen rubles annually.[47] This allowed for the full use of all the lamps then standing. New streetlights were added slowly for the next fifteen years, to 1785, when Catherine ordered their number more than doubled, to a total of 3,100. An additional 155 lamplighters were hired.[48] Thus the city was adorned at night to the glory of its monarch, if not to the greater security of its citizens.

The condition of street surfaces was another object of attention. The paving of streets and bridges presented problems that were never fully resolved. First there was the matter of who was to be responsible for it, and second, there was the inability of eighteenth-century technology to develop a pavement surface that was both durable and economical in St. Petersburg's climate. The first problem was made more acute because of the second. Traditionally home owners were responsible for paving the streets fronting their property, but this, of course, had never been an effective way to keep the streets in good condition. The police carters were responsible for maintaining the road surfaces of the bridges spanning the canals and for the upkeep of pavement in front of government buildings. In the attempt to devise a form of paving that would last, skilled pavers were brought from Hamburg and other German cities, Holland, and England. None could resolve the problems of climate and geography.[49] By the end of the 1770s, the poor condition of streets even in the city center moved Police Chief Volkov to ask the empress to authorize massive paving projects to be undertaken under the direction of Col. F. V. Bauer, who was overseeing the embanking in granite of various canals and the Neva. With a grant of twenty thousand rubles Bauer paved the major thoroughfares in First and Second Admiralties.[50] But his failure to install a permanent surface was underscored by the competition sponsored in 1792 by the Free Economic Society to award twenty-five rubles to the person who could develop the best plan for paving the city's streets. The winner, P. E. Shreter, proposed a street surface made of three sizes of granite cobblestones in a ribbed box pattern. Early nineteenth-century paintings of street scenes often reveal this form of pavement.[51] But on the whole, the work of any paver, private home owner or government contractor, was doomed to early ruination within a season or two because of the severe climate.[52]

Finally, and most significantly, the embanking of canals in granite at state expense began and was largely completed under Catherine. Not only did this give the city an image of grace, harmony, and solidity, it also had significant economic consequences, permitting a much more intensive use of embankments as streets and for transloading of goods. The projects, lasting from the 1760s through the rest of Catherine's reign and into the early 1800s, provided employment for thousands of skilled and unskilled workers and went a long way toward solving problems of draining the low-lying, flat ground that characterizes the city's site.[53]

Generally speaking, these services and improvements were introduced first in the central quarters of the city, where wealthy people lived. In part this represented the ability of inhabitants of those sections to pay for the improvements. When paving was done by home owners, for example, it stands to reason that well-to-do residents were able to keep streets in better condition than could poor residents who had to struggle to earn their daily bread. But other improvements did stem from preferential treatment. Areas where important people lived received sewage systems, streetlights, granite embankments, "warming houses" and other improvements long before other parts of the city. By the end of Catherine's reign these new urban services had not yet totally penetrated into every sector of the city, illustrating again the two distinct Petersburgs that had begun to exist: the center, dominated by wealthy citizens, and the outskirts, home for poorer inhabitants. But to emphasize this aspect of change alone is to miss an even more significant development. In a whole range of municipal services the Catherinian period saw the failure of one method of providing needs and the gradual development of another. The relatively unsophisticated system of requiring home owners to provide services with their own labor and materials gave way to one in which home owners paid to have the same services provided by full-time employees. The resultant specialization of labor was an earmark of the early modern city and represented a significant change in the nature of urban life whenever it occurred.

Welfare

In the city the institutions that had developed in rural areas for caring for the infirm, the weak, and the helpless were slow in forming. In St. Petersburg's first few decades these tasks devolved upon the police and the church, but in general their capacity to deal with the scale of the problem remained very low. The nature of the problem can be illustrated by the case of the retired soldier Zav'ialov, who served in various military units from 1738 to May 1764. Upon retirement he was simply given a passport and told to find his own support. By his own statement he was old and sick, could hardly walk, had no property, and thus could not support himself through work. In his case, a petition for a place in the parish poorhouse of the Resurrection Church happily was granted, but many others were not so fortunate.[54] Parish almshouses were better equipped to care for the elderly than they were to take in infants and small children. The first institution to care for these unfortunates was the St. Petersburg branch of the Moscow Foundling Hospital, opened under the direction of I. I. Betskoi in

1770. Other orphanages and hospitals were subordinated to the Bureau of Public Charity created in 1775. The Bureau consisted of the governor of St. Petersburg province, two representatives from the superior land court, two from the *guberniia* magistracy, and two from the superior tribunal. It oversaw the operation of the Obukhov Hospital after it opened in the early 1780s, capable of handling over 200 patients at a time. Kalinkin House (the hospital for patients suffering from venereal diseases), a smallpox house, and an almshouse for the incurably ill (more than 200 beds) were all run by the Bureau. During the 1780s it opened an insane asylum and two poorhouses capable together of housing 1,800 people at a time.[55] After 1786 the public schools were placed under the Bureau's administration. It was charged with overseeing the operation of the *pansions,* privately run boarding schools, and instituting a qualifying examination for teachers, but opposition from the *pansions* prevented it from fulfilling either task. The Bureau was well endowed, having benefited from numerous large bequests when it was founded, and most of its day-to-day operations were covered by income generated through interest on loans.[56]

Mortality rates in most of the institutions administered by the Bureau were quite high, caused by the poor condition of patients when they were admitted, the generally severe climate, and inadequate care of patients. As the staffs became better trained, however, mortality rates steadily declined.[57] Despite the Bureau's healthy financial situation, one gets the impression that the institutions under its care remained small, chronically understaffed, and underfinanced. They did at least represent the beginnings of institutionalized public welfare practices in health and education in Russia's capital. As these organizations dealt with chronic social problems, other agencies were put in place to handle emergencies.

Response to Crises

Four different sorts of calamities—fire, flood, famine, and pestilence—confronted St. Petersburg's administrators during the Catherinian period. How well they responded gives a good indication of the degree of efficiency of government. In most cases, institutions were able to respond quickly and decisively to prevent sudden calamity from taking a dreadful toll. Controls were applied only when threats became very real or actually struck the city. Flexibility and creative policy-making on the part of those who governed allowed this success against each form of cataclysm.

Fire

Fires were everyday occurrences. The great conflagrations that gutted large areas of the city occurred rarely yet the threat was ever present that the smallest fire could roar out of control. The catastrophic fire of 1763 that swept through the southeastern part of Vasil'evskii Island, the worst fire in the city since 1736, precipitated a reorganization of firefighting capabilities. The city's fire brigade, subdivided along the lines of the police administrative districts, was supplemented by army troops and residents of each district. Firefighters held in reserve in other parts of town could be called upon when blazes were particularly bad. Only if fire struck the Winter Palace would all firemen converge on a single blaze. Not only did each house have to have a man standing ready for fire duty, but every address was supposed to maintain at its gate the common firefighting equipment: gaffs (to pull down houses in the way of rapidly spreading fires), buckets, axes, and mops.[58]

On May 23, 1771, another great fire flared up on Vasil'evskii Island. The variable and gusting winds carried the flames first to the area around Kalinkin Bridge and then in the opposite direction to Petersburg Side. Catherine said she "resembled Job: worse news with every hour."[59] In the end, as she informed Voltaire, the fire "destroyed 140 houses in all, by police accounting, among them 20 built of stone; the others were badly built wooden huts. . . . There is no doubt but that the vestiges of wind and heat soon will be effaced, for here we build more swiftly than in any other European country. A fire in 1762 twice as serious as this one consumed an entire great district consisting of wooden structures, but they were replaced with brick houses in less than two or three years."[60]

City planners were quick to draft guidelines to facilitate reconstruction in burned-out areas, designing building regulations to minimize the possibility of future fires. Of course, fires could not be completely prevented. Despite the regular and prescribed use of chimney sweeps, stove and chimney fires were an almost daily occurrence. Extensive and well-enforced regulations directed specifically toward averting fire in the hemp warehouses, applied from the summer of 1779, did not prevent a blaze from gutting the warehouses a year later.[61] But strictly observed measures did succeed in reducing the number of great fires.

Flood

Floods, or rather inundations, are a seasonal occurrence in St. Petersburg, presenting the greatest danger during the months of September through November, when rainfall is high and cyclones are liable to form over the Gulf of Finland, creating the conditions for an inundation. Centuries later, in the 1980s and 1990s, construction began on a massive flood-control dam to deal with the problem, which still troubled the city. It partially spans the Gulf of Finland and crosses the eastern end of Kotlin Island in the hope that, should a strong westerly wind blow, the waters of the gulf could be prevented from literally backing up at the mouth of the Neva as the river rose and spread over the outlying land.

During Catherine's reign only one flood damaged the city considerably, but it was a disaster. On September 10, 1777, the river suddenly rose during the night. The waters surged for almost a full day. Most of Vasil'evskii Island and St. Petersburg Side were totally inundated, with some sections under as much as fourteen feet of water. The police stockade near the sea disappeared entirely, taking with it nearly three hundred people. More than a hundred small houses in the southwestern quadrant of town were carried away. Shops and their wares were inundated. In the Winter Palace the rushing water broke basement windows around 2:00 AM, and a frantic empress fell on her knees and called for a priest to say a service.[62] Only Foundry district and Vyborg Side remained completely dry. Not having been warned, many people drowned in bed, while thousands of others were left homeless.[63]

Within two weeks measures were taken to ensure that the city would never again be caught unawares. Whenever water reached a certain height, cannon were to be fired, flares set off, and flags raised, and drummers were to range through the streets to ensure that everyone was awakened. The tocsin was to ring continuously as long as the threat continued. For rescuing stranded and drowning people, two large oared boats were kept in lower elevations of the city, ready for use. In addition, the police drew up a series of detailed maps to show the altitude of selected points of the city and which areas would be covered by floods of various heights.[64] These measures succeeded, for never again did a flood take the city by complete surprise. But those who had lost their homes—generally people whose residences were makeshift anyway—received no formal assistance in obtaining materials to reconstruct or clean up their dwellings. Government aid, sometimes given in event of fire, did not extend to this sort of disaster.

Famine

Famine never really threatened the city, but temporary grain shortages and steadily rising prices provided sufficient incentive to invoke government action on several occasions.[65] Until the late 1760s not only residents of the city but also those in rural areas of the province bought all their grain in the capital. Peasant dependence upon the city for seed corn, not uncommon in early modern Europe, could have caused the city serious problems. If peasants were unable one year to procure enough grain to plant, the subsequent low harvest could have created a far more dangerous situation the following year. Even in years of relative plenty, the practice of peasants from the countryside purchasing grain in St. Petersburg was seen as raising the price of grain in the city. Therefore in 1766 the city quartermaster general, Prince A. A. Viazemskii, forbade peasants to buy grain in the city.[66] His fundamental concern was to induce them to become self-sufficient, thereby ensuring adequate grain supply throughout the province. By 1776 this policy allowed grain prices, previously controlled, to be released to be determined by the market. Thereafter the state intervened only rarely, as in 1786, when poor crops nationwide caused a temporary shortage.

Pestilence

A fourth potential natural calamity was epidemic disease. In late 1769 and early 1770 detachments of the Russian occupation army in Moldavia and Wallachia contracted bubonic plague. Swiftly the disease spread up from the south to Kiev, by late summer, and on to Moscow before the end of 1770. The severe economic dislocation, extensive loss of life, and violent "Plague Riot" in Moscow took place despite the government's concerted effort to eradicate the plague.[67] Its strict measures had much greater success in preventing the plague from striking the capital on the Neva.

Reports from late July and August 1771 of suspected cases of plague near Pskov and Novgorod aroused fears in the capital. At any time the multitude of government personnel moving in and out of the capital, the thousands of migrating workers, or the tons of goods from Russia's interior intended for export or consumption in the city could harbor the infection and cause as severe a catastrophe in St. Petersburg as was occurring in Moscow. By the third week of September active measures to protect the capital were put into practice. Attention focused at first on the movement of money, mail, and people, reflecting the widespread belief that personal contact spread the disease. Provisions were made to disinfect goods with fire, smoke, and vinegar, and to quarantine people entering the capital.[68] In early October police checkpoints were erected on all roads entering the city and people living in the city were required to comply with a series of detailed precautions regarding the movement of goods and people. The scare lasted through October, when the plague's dissipation calmed fears for the capital. Quarantine measures remained in effect for nearly a year.[69] Whether these measures had any real effect on limiting the spread of plague is open to question. The most detailed study of the episode concludes that St. Petersburg's northern location, its distance from Moscow and the onset of winter were what really saved the capital.[70]

Public measures were also taken against smallpox. Although smallpox may have been less virulent in St. Petersburg than in other European cities (in 1764, eight people died of it there, but 187 in London and 99 in Berlin),[71] it was still feared both for its mortality and its likelihood of permanently disfiguring people who survived it. Catherine's own husband, the unfortunate Peter III, bore its scars in his post-adolescent years. Medical advances made possible inoculation against smallpox during the eighteenth century, and as early as the 1750s the *Ezhemesiachnye sochineniia* lauded the novel treatment as a possible means for guaranteeing an increase in Russia's population by lowering mortality rates. Catherine herself became interested in inoculation for the imperial family, and so it was that in 1768 she decided to undergo the treatment.

The physician chosen to inoculate the empress was Dr. Thomas Dimsdale from Hertfordshire, England, a graduate of Aberdeen University medical school. His primary credential was that he had written a popular book on smallpox inoculation in 1767. In fact, he was not a major practitioner. Nevertheless, he arrived in St. Petersburg in October 1768 and set up an inoculation hospital in the home of a former English merchant. Dimsdale's first two subjects were cadets from a guards regiment, followed by the empress on October 12 and Tsarevich Paul three weeks later. Because this was inoculation and not vaccination, those taking the treatment assumed some risk of catching a serious case of the pox. When all went well in these first cases, however, the members of Russia's leading houses (and the patriciate of St. Petersburg) decided to hazard the treatment. Dimsdale successfully inoculated more than 140 people before returning to England with rich rewards and a barony.

Before the year's end, Catherine had established a public house to extend inoculation to all social levels, including the poor. For their encouragement she promised gifts to all who volunteered for the treatment. The initial success of the enterprise remains uncertain. There were suggestions at the time that many were inoculated, but Catherine noted later that the "common folk" did not "present themselves with much eagerness."[72] As long as the number of cases of smallpox remained small, the authorities did not press the matter of forced inoculation. Little public concern was voiced even when authorities discovered that isolated deaths from smallpox were hidden from them and the corpses buried secretly.[73] But an increased outbreak in 1778 raised fears sufficiently that certain churches were designated as smallpox treatment centers and a quarantine house was constructed on an island in the gulf as a compulsory port of call for all ships coming from Turkish areas. Even apparently healthy crews and merchandise were quarantined for six weeks. When someone on an incoming ship was sick, the period increased to ninety days, and only metal goods could be unloaded in the city.[74] Dr. Dimsdale returned in 1781 to inoculate Catherine's two oldest grandsons, Alexander and Constantine.[75]

Governmental responses to all four types of catastrophe were sufficient to contain the dangers. Fires, of course, continued to occur, but they caused much less damage after implementation of the fire-fighting and building codes. Despite the peculiar supply problems of the city, well-planned storage measures staved off famine. Following the one severe flood, procedures were taken to reduce future loss of life. And the plague was turned back from the city at least in part because of a series of precise measures to counter it. A proportionate and timely response to crises kept the city from decimation by any of these calamities.

City Planning

To respond to crises is one thing; to govern with vision is quite another. In the first months of her reign, Catherine decided that giving her reign the character she wanted it to have would involve her personally in guiding and directing the future growth of St. Petersburg as a visible symbol of that reign. Not only was St. Petersburg the imperial residence, it was also more malleable than Russia's older towns. As a new city, St. Petersburg was not bound by the city walls that discouraged outward expansion in other cities. Indeed, on three sides St. Petersburg had no natural boundaries to limit spatial expansion, so that as a consequence fringe areas often came into use before land closer to the center was fully built up. St. Petersburg suffered from uncontrolled urban sprawl. Besides seeking to control expansion, Catherine wanted to clean up the city's appearance, to dispose of the refuse, garbage, and dirt that had accumulated everywhere. She wanted protection from fires. And the absence of a symmetrical street pattern contradicted the image of well-regulated life. Therefore Catherine formed a commission to plan future growth and to devise solutions to these and other problems.[76]

The Planning Commission

An ukase on December 11, 1762, established the Commission for the Masonry Construction of St. Petersburg and Moscow, placing it under the supervision of the Senate.[77] Although its name implies that the commission was concerned with only a small part of the science of city planning, it covered a much broader range of topics than simply architecture. The commission's tasks were, in general terms, to determine the limits of St. Petersburg, to define where suburbs started, and to maintain the city at a size not too cumbersome to be governed. A specific duty before the commission, crucial in reducing the difference between mere planning and the implementation of planning in construction, involved the finances of reconstruction. Two motives lay behind the decision to rebuild St. Petersburg in brick and stone. First, masonry was obviously more durable and less susceptible to fire than wood. But equally important, the supply of lumber was felt to be decreasing. Therefore the commission was ordered to make readily available the materials necessary for masonry building. Costs of building timber and masonry houses of the same sizes were to be computed. Because stone was more expensive, the difference in cost was to be made up to anyone constructing a masonry house.[78]

Members of the commission, men of proven ability—Z. G. Chernyshev, I. I. Betskoi, and Prince M.-K. I. Dashkov—were empowered to select a staff, including architects.[79] All records of past planning were opened to them and all existing maps made available. Other agencies of government were requested to cooperate in any consultations that the commission felt necessary.[80]

The commission set to work slowly. The first architect, A. V. Kvasov, joined the staff only in 1764. His selection followed a competition, open to architects from any country, to compose a plan for the future construction of the city. Plans were supposed to focus on two problems: first, how best to improve living conditions and architectural symmetry in the city center without destroying buildings already in existence; and second, how to define and lend elegance to fringe areas, the outskirts, and suburbs of the city.[81] There is no clear evidence that Kvasov won the competition. He was the brother of the architect of the original Catherine Palace at Tsarskoe Selo.[82] The following year the commission broadened its staff with the addition of draftsmen to draw the necessary maps, charts, and plans. Because maps could not be drawn accurately without careful land surveys, ten laborers were hired to carry measuring chains and other paraphernalia used by staff architects and draftsmen.[83]

During the next seven years detailed plans were molded and presented for approval as the commission worked carefully and thoroughly.[84] In 1768 the scope of its activity expanded beyond the capitals to include all cities in Russia. Before it was dissolved by Emperor Paul late in 1796, the commission turned out 416 approved plans for various Russian cities.[85] Almost all of the commission's activities in the 1760s and early 1770s dealt with St. Petersburg, but by 1773, planning for the capital was completed and attention permanently diverted elsewhere. The only city planning for St. Petersburg to emerge during the latter part of the eighteenth century was contained in the proposals submitted during this period by the commission on masonry construction.

Initial Plans

The first report of the commission was given to the Senate for approval in 1764. It attempted to formulate principles for limiting urban sprawl while permitting consistent population growth. Having decided earlier to consider the city in sections, offering its proposals district by district, the commission limited its first plan to the part of Admiralty Side bounded by the Neva and Moika, in the center of town. Admitting that the area was quite small and that its selection precluded any possibility of a proposal to curtail growth at the city's edge, the commission defended its choice of the center by affirming that the primary goal of ending construction beyond the city limits could be realized by putting the center of town in order. Planned, orderly construction downtown would allow the center to absorb many more inhabitants.[86] The report assured the Senate that unnecessary changes or overly expensive projects would not be forthcoming. Proposals would be practical and keep costs to a minimum. Wherever possible, houses built of stone would be left standing, altered only by embellishments to exterior facades, which home owners would be encouraged to construct. Streets would be joined wherever possible to facilitate communication. Affirming its responsibility to point out areas from which junk and discarded materials should be removed, the commission noted that large rubbish piles near the church of St. Isaac ought to be cleaned up. The tone of the request was apologetic, as if the commission were not yet sure of its place in the administrative structure. Later reports lost that note of uncertainty as the commission assumed greater authority.

Two principles of city planning recognized in the commission's first report guaranteed that its work would not remain a pipe dream but lead to real changes in the city's shape and form. First, the commission realized that planning must involve the entire city. Simply to place regulations over the outskirts would solve nothing if growth then had no guidelines in the center. And second, the commission did not attempt too much, did not overplan. It recognized that planning must leave the living tissue of neighborhoods intact, not raze whole areas of the city and reconstruct them artificially. The recognition of these principles indicates that the commission understood fiscal and physical realities far better than many later planners.

The detailed plan for the area bordered by the Neva and Moika was approved and became law in February 1765. All buildings constructed thereafter in that area, as well as major reconstruction of houses already standing, were to comply with its building code. The commission left unchanged the existing street pattern and all buildings already completed. In the future, however, all buildings were to be constructed on line, presenting one front along the length of a street. The commission expressed its desire that all houses fronting a street be built to the same height, but this was not required. New houses could be built only of stone and the walls between adjoining buildings had to be built to the standards of firewalls. Roofs were to be of sheet iron when owners could afford it, but cheaper roofing tiles were also acceptable. Residents were to submit plans for their houses' external facades to staff architects, but internal construction was left entirely to their own tastes. Besides enhancing the comeliness and safety of the city, the plan was intended to make it possible for more people to live in the city center. By filling in open areas and raising all houses to uniform height, the city would not have to expand as fast at the fringes. The building code adopted for this central section of the city was eventually applied to nearly all other districts. Although not requiring immediate transformation, the regulations established the process by which the city could become stone as remaining wooden houses were either torn down, burned, or rebuilt.

The planning commission recognized its role as one dealing with more than just buildings, for good construction alone does not make a grandiose city. There also had to be attention to cleanliness, order, and safety. For these reasons the commission ordered the police to patrol the Admiralty district more vigilantly and approved the installation of streetlamps—more as a safety measure than to beautify the city. The plan gave responsibility for maintaining streets to homeowners whose lots fronted them. Owners of empty lots, whether private people or the state, were exempt from this duty. Concerned that proposed changes not cost too much, the commission requested to be notified of the cost of these changes during the first year.[87] This first detailed plan was the simplest, because few of the difficulties present in other quarters of the city existed in Admiralty Quarter, already the most splendid in town, containing a great number of stone houses, broad streets, and fine buildings.

The second plan submitted by the commission, covering the area between the Moika and the Fontanka, grappled with a greater number of problems. Differentiation in buildings by size and material and in land-use intensity was much greater here than in the first area, making line building impractical without wholesale demolition of existing structures. Other problems posed by the large commercial sector and, in the center of the area, a swampy, sluggish stream emitting an "evil vapor" demanded individual attention.

Looking beyond the fact that results would not become apparent for many years, the commission recommended that henceforth all new houses be built of stone and on line. It sought to achieve integration of existing off-line buildings into this scheme by constructing fences to straighten the frontage of lots. Areas along the Fontanka and Moika, occupied for the most part by huge estates, were to be broken up into small plots. To this end the proposal empowered police to strip owners of their land if after five years they had not intensified their use of it. This concept was another of the ideas introduced by the commission to have great influence in increasing land-use density in inner-city areas.

Because river and canal embankments were desirable locations for commerce, the plan sought to set aside a section along the Fontanka for that purpose. With a canal lapping against one front of their buildings and a street running past the other, merchants could do business both by water and by land, with the conveniences of both means of transportation close at hand. But to implement the plan, merchants would have to abandon their shops at some distance from the canal, where they already had extensive operations. On paper an excellent idea, this transfer of commercial activity from one site to another, apparently more fitting, never came about. One reason is that magnates did not surrender the land along the Fontanka. When estates were subdivided, the rearward property, away from the canal, was sold. Second, merchants chose not to move their businesses at the mere behest of government planners. The patterns of activity built up through years of operation in the commercial sector of the city, which was, after all, only a block or two from the canal, could not easily be altered. This part of the commission's proposal strayed from the earlier realization that old neighborhoods, with their vibrant complexity of life, could not be instantaneously duplicated by planners. All other elements of the plan were adopted in whole or in part, but this one not at all, for it failed to take into consideration the people of the city as well as its buildings.

The commission farsightedly decided to widen, deepen, and lengthen the stream in the center of the quarter. As a canal, it would provide a transportation route, improve the appearance of the city, and facilitate distribution of land and the placement of new streets. A number of houses had to be moved, but the government intended to ease the financial strain on inhabitants by assuming part of the cost. Large barracks for troops garrisoned in the city were included in the plan, placed just to the south of the new canal. To pay for them, inhabitants were assessed a tax, but on the other hand, they were also freed from billeting obligations. This provision gained acceptance with the commission because of dissatisfaction among the populace with the obligation to house soldiers. Its inclusion reflects the intention of the commission to keep inhabitants' preferences in mind in its planning. A special chancellery was created to build the canal. When it came to the houses standing in the way, it simply evicted the residents without providing services or money to ease the burden of moving. The canal was given Catherine's name.

Few large squares or plazas had been provided for as the area between the Moika and the Fontanka had grown up. Thinking them desirable, the commission ordered several to be laid out.[88] The squares would provide areas where residents could mingle together. Trees and shrubs could provide welcome natural greenery among man-made structures. Sunlight and fresh air would reach into them, making for a more healthful situation. Monuments to heroes whose service had glorified the state could be erected in the squares. All these benefits were recognized in the plan.

The Senate for some time debated these strong proposals: measures to break up large inner-city estates; a plan to dig a major canal; construction of squares; and the transfer of commercial interests from one area to another. They finally became law in January 1766.[89]

The plan for a third area was ready by the following May. It dealt with outlying areas of the city, defining two kinds of suburbs: *predmest'ia,* suburbs outside or beyond the city proper; and *slobody,* the geographically small areas within the city housing the families of men who worked for particular government agencies, chancelleries, or offices. The boundaries of the *slobody* had shown clearly in earlier years, but as the city grew up around them, the *slobody* had lost their distinction. The report proposed that several *slobody* be totally disbanded. On the other hand, *predmest'ia* were more prominent. Three now covered the entire area on the left bank of the Fontanka. Beyond the *predmest'ia* lay the city pastureland. To avoid infringement on it by urban sprawl, the plan proposed a wide ditch to separate grazing lands from those given over to construction. Slobody were likewise differentiated from *predmest'ia* by ditches. Because *slobody* were administered by subordinates of the governor (land commissars) but *predmest'ia* remained, like the remainder of the city, under the police, ditches served to outline distinctly the areas of authority.

While only making recommendations concerning construction in most areas, the report included specific building instructions for frontage along the Neva and Fontanka. In those areas houses were to be at least two stories high, built on line, and constructed exclusively of masonry. It was clear that the commission intended eventually to require stone and brick buildings elsewhere also, because all wooden houses in the future had to have stone foundations. It would not be difficult at all to pull down the wooden superstructures at a later date and build in masonry in their stead.[90] River and canal frontages in particular were supposed to have a clean, prosperous, regular appearance.

Through the completion of the third plan, the work of the commission had progressed steadily with new reports in May and December of each year. The fourth report, submitted in December 1766, was the last to follow this pattern, largely because the Senate took until April 1767 to approve the plan. Only as each plan was accepted could the commission turn its attention to the next task. The Senate hesitated over the report because it treated a wide area. Rather than dealing with one district of the city, like earlier reports, it proposed changes in two of the oldest and most problematic areas, Vasil'evskii Island and St. Petersburg Side. For the first time, the commission related the past course of construction in the area it was treating, described the present situation, and offered plans for future building. Much more at ease in its role as city planner than it had been in earlier reports, the commission included historical details to support its suggestions.

The proposal related briefly that Peter I and Catherine I had intended Vasil'evskii Island to be the city's center. Using Amsterdam as a model, they built several miles of bulwarks and bastions and, according to the commission's own calculations, dug well over one hundred miles of canals and basins. But because the palace and Admiralty were built elsewhere, the area was soon reduced to suburb status. Reminding the Senate that many government offices, the cadet academies, the bourse, and other buildings were located on the island, the commission recommended inclusion in the city proper of the entire area east of Thirteenth Line. Thus the commission recognized that the eastern half of the island was functionally a part of the central city. The report kept building regulations simple. Only row houses built of stone could henceforth appear on both river embankments, Bol'shoi Prospect, and First Line. Elsewhere people might build with wood, as long as the structures included stone foundations and maintained the line concept. Special provisions ensured the survival of city pastureland on the western half of the island. People living on the pasture were to be evicted in five years if they did not move sooner. Two nonagricultural establishments were allowed to remain, a poorhouse and the cemeteries along Black Creek (*Chernaia rechka*).[91] Conversion of the plan into reality offered few perplexities. Of all the sections of the city, Vasil'evskii Island was laid out most geometrically, already possessing many characteristics that had to be fabricated in other districts.

St. Petersburg Side contained far greater difficulties for the commission. In the past, gardens and poorer sorts of housing had occupied its islands, which remained boggy marshlands, unsuitable for building. The commission proposed to dig a deep and wide ditch to demarcate the city limit, spreading the dredged earth to elevate building sites, making land more suitable for housing and the air fresher for breathing. In establishing building restrictions, the Fortress of St. Peter and St. Paul received primary consideration. Not recognizing that the Fortress was no longer a strategically functional defense base, the commission stipulated that there should continue to be no masonry buildings in its vicinity. To make the regulation easy to enforce, it refrained from demanding that all future buildings on St. Petersburg Side be of masonry. All foundations were to be made of brick or stone, however, because of the low-lying land. In this report the commission for the first time failed to regulate the size of buildings or to realign the street pattern. It had no other choice if it intended to continue in its subscription to the principle that its plans be as easy to comply with as possible. To apply the same building code on St. Petersburg Side as in other districts would have involved a wholesale razing of existing structures and redrawing of streets. The commission wisely chose not to press such a radical scheme. But wooden buildings required greater safety precautions. Therefore the gunpowder factory was moved away from inhabited places to the outer extremity of the quarter. The hemp and flax warehouses, however, were left in their location at the juncture of the Neva and Small Neva rivers across the water from the customhouse, because of their commodious and advantageous situation for commercial products. The plan recommended that wooden warehouse buildings be replaced by masonry ones as soon as possible.

Later Plans and Revisions

The plans for Vasil'evskii Island and St. Petersburg Side marked an end to the commission's district-by-district proposals for future growth in St. Petersburg. The commission was satisfied that it had completed the plan for Russia's capital. But developments soon forced the commission to meet again and present wholly new plans as well as revisions of old ones.

The first revision affected city pastureland. Grazing areas for livestock were important to urban inhabitants, who often supplemented their living by keeping a milk cow or goat. Not entirely urbanized, many city dwellers continued, as in the village, to own livestock. Obviously not everyone could pasture his animals in the city's center (although some clearly did so until late in the century). Instead commons, or city pastureland, were created in areas adjacent to the city. If the city's population had remained relatively constant, the amount of land devoted both to construction and to pasturage would have sufficed. With such rapid and sustained growth as St. Petersburg experienced, however, new construction infringed upon city pastureland and conflict developed between longtime residents, who owned the livestock, and newly arrived squatters, who inhabited the grazing land.

This conflict, which occurred particularly in St. Petersburg but in other large towns as well, was one of the reasons for the promulgation of the surveying instruction of 1766, which ordered cities to survey and set aside in perpetuity areas approximately one and one-third miles wide outside their boundaries as city pastureland. The law was issued without sufficient research into existing situations in towns, for it rapidly became clear that the actual consequences of the law limited the amount of land under pasturage, since almost every town already used more land than the law allowed.[92] Furthermore, it absolutely prevented any further outward growth by towns. Dissatisfaction with the instruction was voiced by town delegates to the commission to codify laws, elected the following year. These developments led to a proposal by the planning commission that appeared in May 1768. It was quite clear and decisive in its recommendations. First, all wooden houses in the pastureland were to be removed or destroyed and their inhabitants moved into *predmest'ia.* The law was to be applied leniently at first, until the ditches surrounding the suburbs and delimiting them from the pasture were completed. After that those who had not yet moved would be evicted forcibly. Because the few masonry houses in the pastureland were more difficult to move, they were to be left if their owners chose to remain. To demarcate them from the pasture, however, they were to be surrounded by fence and moat.[93]

For the second time the commission made a proposal that was inadvisable, by placing more emphasis on achieving clearly defined city limits than on considering the welfare of city inhabitants. Other governmental agencies and the people who were to be affected raised an immediate outcry against the decisive and categorical recommendation. Catherine ordered the commission to present a variant plan, one that might be carried out with less effort and expense. She pointed out that many people in the prohibited area lived in *slobody* maintained by governmental bodies that could find no other suitable places to house all their residents together. Faced by her opposition, the commission relented. *Slobody* could stay if ditches were dug to separate them from city pastureland. However, only people employed by the agencies administering the *slobody* could move into them in the future. All those not thus employed but presently living there had to move out. In this way the commission hoped to keep the *slobody* at a constant size, to prevent further expansion onto grazing lands. The new city limit was drawn carefully, especially on the south side of the city where violation of it by migrating newcomers was more apt to occur. The commission argued that in making these exceptions it had not solved the fundamental problem of insufficient pastureland. After all, city inhabitants owned over twenty thousand head of cattle, not to mention other types of animals. Insufficient grazing areas even forced some to rent land from surrounding farms at high prices. The continuing need for more land justified a decision to appropriate landholdings of state factories, former monastery lands, the outer edges of remaining *slobody*, and Ekaterinhof, a court property, as pasture. State peasants living in the near vicinity and not tied to the city economy were forcibly moved from their lands, which also became part of the city pasture.[94] This substitute plan was satisfactory, for no more complaints about insufficient pastureland were voiced. Orders to dig the ditches—actually canals—came in July 1769, and the issue was settled.[95]

The primary tasks of the commission, to limit outward growth and to guarantee the orderly development and aggrandizement of the existing city, ended with this plan. The commission now turned from St. Petersburg to other cities. Drastic changes wrought by fires forced the redirection of planning energies once again, however, resulting in revisions of earlier guidelines for development.

More Revisions

In May 1771 a fire burned an area from the Small Neva to Bol'shoi Prospect on Vasil'evskii Island. Without calling upon the commission, busy with other work, Catherine applied the building code it had adopted for Admiralty Side to Vasil'evskii Island. Henceforth only stone houses could be built. Catherine went one step beyond the commission by ordering that remaining wooden houses be razed and replaced by stone ones. Roofing materials could be only sheet iron or roofing tiles. There were to be no exceptions.[96] Because the embankments, First Line, and Bol'shoi Prospect were already under these regulations, nothing was changed for them.[97] Special exceptions made for Vasil'evskii Island in the commission's first plan were thus removed, and the same building code applied as was in effect on the Neva's left bank. Only St. Petersburg Side now had differing provisions. In spite of Catherine's stipulation, however, the remaining wooden houses on Vasil'evskii Island were not razed. In actuality the code was applied here, as elsewhere, only to future construction.

In 1773 other fires brought the commission back to work on St. Petersburg. A series of blazes in the Moscow district postmen's *sloboda* burned a number of houses and stables. The commission was designated to learn how such fires might be averted in the future. As in many small areas on the fringe of the city, houses were built too closely together. There was no regular street pattern, but houses and outbuildings were thrown together indiscriminately and totally without plan. The conclusion of the report was not unexpected. It proposed that each house have its own yard, that more space be left between houses, and that more streets traverse the neighborhood. It is ironic that besides attempting to fill open spaces in much of the city, the commission had to decrease density in several other areas. Yet these dichotomous situations serve to illustrate how complex St. Petersburg was, as well as the conflicting problems administrative agencies had to face.

The specific suggestion made by the commission was simple. Streets should be laid in grid pattern. Houses, built of brick, were individually to occupy small plots of land so that none of the houses touched. The plan involved total eradication of the old community's physical identity and creation of a new "subdivision." In this case it was justified, for the old buildings had been largely destroyed. The neighborhood would continue to house the same people, but in finer and more durable structures. Construction began immediately and by 1782 nearly 170 houses were built at a cost of just over 90,000 rubles.[98] A consequence of the reconstruction was to set a precedent for eradicating the *sloboda* building pattern from the city, integrating the area formerly occupied by the *sloboda* into the surrounding city.

In the same year, 1773, the commission issued its last proposal for St. Petersburg, suggesting the construction of grand gates for the city, where highways crossed the new boundary canal, and the construction of fireplaces in city streets so that watchmen and passersby might have small warming houses in winter. The former merely represented an attempt to adorn the city and lend it grandeur, but the second suggestion was extremely practical and was utilized extensively in later years. An engraving of the Great Stone Theater reveals four warming houses in nearby streets.[99] That the commission ended its plans for St. Petersburg with two proposals so different in motivation was entirely appropriate, for each represented one of the principal concerns behind the commission's work: the aesthetic and the practical.

The Legislative Commission

No organ other than the planning commission—and direct intervention by Catherine—contributed substantially to city planning for St. Petersburg. But the legislative commission called into being in 1767 played a minor role in formulating principles to guide city growth. Each town in the empire elected a delegate to the commission and a committee to draw up instructions to aid him in representing the city.[100] Several articles in the instruction (*nakaz*) from St. Petersburg reflected concern for an improvement of living conditions in the city.[101]

The legislative commission contributed to planning for St. Petersburg in at least two ways. First, the instructions revealed problems bothering the populace. A number of them—the requests for increased pasturage and the replacement of wooden houses by masonry ones to name only two—were later incorporated in plans adopted by the commission for stone construction. The instructions thus provided government for a brief time with a forum in which city inhabitants voiced their needs, which were taken into consideration in future planning. Second, the work of one of the standing committees of the legislative commission, the Committee on Towns, later served as a vital source of the Charter to the Towns. The committee collected documents and requested information about various aspects of urban life from Russian towns. Unfortunately, it chose not to use a questionnaire composed by a committee member. Among information asked for were vital social and economic statistics about city inhabitants.[102] Ideas gathered by the legislative commission, although not in the form of plans drawn up by that body, were used in planning for St. Petersburg.

In summary, it is clear that plans for late eighteenth-century St. Petersburg were realistic and often carried to fruition. The building code was not applied in its strictest forms—wooden houses throughout the city were not immediately pulled down and replaced by masonry ones —but the government constructed new buildings only when it could certify that the blueprints fit the regulations made by the planning commission.[103] Because only masonry houses were to be constructed in the future, at least in central city areas, it was only a matter of time before they came to predominate. The plans recognized fundamental limitations of finances and expendable effort. They kept changes to a realistic minimum, while at the same time upholding principles of order, beauty, and safety. The commission did not seek primarily to change what already existed, but to control the shape and size of future development. Thus the commission called for few changes on St. Petersburg Side, where change would have been hardest to bring about, demonstrating that it adapted its conclusions to the situation. By restraining itself to practical proposals, the commission showed that its thinking was pragmatic. It did not attempt to reshape the city to meet preconceived notions or to conform to outdated needs. Rather it sought through a minimum of interference to facilitate the new sort of urban life by requiring safe buildings, sufficient routes of communication, and high aesthetic standards.

Three efforts by the planning commission stand out from today's perspective as its most long-lasting and farsighted. First was the deliberation everywhere to foster the construction of masonry houses. The effort succeeded only partially; to be sure, isolated wooden structures still exist in quarters where they were prohibited more than two hundred years ago. But the measures did change the basic complexion of the capital from wood to stone. In this respect St. Petersburg at least until World War II stood alone among Russian cities. Even Moscow remained predominantly wooden, containing many wooden buildings near its center well into the 1970s, whereas in St. Petersburg wooden structures ceased long ago to be a common sight.

The attempt to beautify the city has contributed in no small way to the reputation of St. Petersburg—under whatever name—as the most regular and harmonious of Russian cities. Careful prescription of building size and shape and the insistence from an early date that house plans be approved by city architects were factors introduced by the planning commission that contributed to the city's overall elegance.

The commission adopted the principle that city property owners had to put their lands in use by constructing buildings on them. The consequences of this affirmation hastened the breakdown of huge estates in the city before the end of Catherine's reign and increased the intensity of land use. Without such coercion to use land more intensively, St. Petersburg soon thereafter might have become one of the first cities in the world to have to deal with truly large-scale urban sprawl.

The Charter to the Towns

The broadest criticism made of urban administration in Catherine's Russia is that the grand system she created in 1785 did not work, at least not in her lifetime. This conclusion, developed by I. I. Ditiatin in his history of the first hundred years of the St. Petersburg municipal corporation, and repeated by A. A. Kizevetter, P. N. Miliukov, and many other historians since, claims that the newly created organs remained weak, insufficiently funded, and incapable of doing anything of genuine importance. Ditiatin found virtually no archival evidence testifying to the activity of the various new elective bodies during the last decade of Catherine's rule. He could not even determine when the new urban institutions were founded. St. Petersburg's budget was inordinately small for such a large city, only 36,000 rubles in 1797, the first year for which Ditiatin found a complete budget.

While much of what Ditiatin said about the weakness of the new system is true, he exaggerated its extent. The reason he could not find the exact date for the establishment of several of the new organs is that they were not new at all.[104] The guild structure, court system, and mayoralty, for example, already existed. Elections to both new and old bodies, supervised by General N. Saltykov, took place in mid-January 1786. Thus within a year of the publication of the Charter its provisions were put into effect in the capital city. By way of contrast, St. Petersburg *guberniia* was not officially opened until five years after the provincial reform legislation was issued. To ensure that the city of St. Petersburg had complied fully with the charter's instructions, Saltykov reported the elections by listing them opposite the appropriate article from the Charter.[105] He reported that the city register was completed on January 20, 1786.[106] It did not list the names of everyone in the city, but only of those who fell under the six categories defined as comprising the urban population. In accordance with the Artisan Regulation, sixty-one craft guilds were established and the artisan board selected with a tailor as its president.[107] In fact, there were two artisan heads, one for the foreign (mostly German) organizations —Jakob Viems—and one for the Russians—Stepan Elizarov.[108]

Two years later senators Prince Mikhail Dolgorukii and Sergei Akchurin were assigned to inspect St. Petersburg province. The third point of their report read as follows: "The articles of the Municipal Regulation have been implemented in the councils . . ., with concomitant benefit for the citizens; above all, here in the capital city, under the special inspection of the Governor, the order to be constituted among the various artisan guilds deserves attention, and one hopes that this aspect too will be brought to completion in the near future. In this regard, we venture to draw to Your Majesty's attention the Head [mayor] of the local city council, Semen Kalashnikov, who in the exercise of his calling renders incessant labor and solicitude."[109] For the senators to go out of their way to mention the way Kalashnikov was performing his task, the new system must have been functioning better than Ditiatin later imagined.

The City Councils

Indeed, the analysis of the performance of the city council for the years 1788–91 undertaken by Janet Hartley found that most members of the council attended its meetings regularly. The artisans apparently did not take full advantage of the number of councilmen allotted to them, often sending only token representation. But eminent citizens and genuine town residents seem to have participated fully. The council met on average more than once a month, far more frequently than called for in the charter. Hartley also found that people not on the council frequently attended its meetings, especially members of the city magistracy.[110]

The charges to the new city council organizations duplicated various administrative functions already in the hands of the magistracy. A close relationship developed between the two. Within a few years the city magistracy often drew its burgomasters and aldermen from among men who had sat on the city council. Rather than neglecting some of the areas of responsibility assigned to it, the council seems to have stepped beyond them into areas that did not fall specifically under its instructions.[111]

The six-man council set about its work immediately in 1786, assuming control over the city shipyard, street lighting, bridge maintenance, and tax collection, among other things. It took seriously the charge to fulfill its assigned tasks and was willing to employ severe measures to implement its will. In that first summer of 1786, it had thirty-three merchants jailed for nonpayment of the 1 percent tax on their capital, and it kept the merchants in custody until their forced labor retired the amount of back taxes they owed.[112] The six-man council established a working relationship with the city magistracy, although on occasion it held in its own hands matters that it technically should have turned over to the magistracy, as, for example, its examination of a large number of protested bills of exchange in 1793.[113] And by locating its offices adjacent to the city's busiest commercial district, the bazaar, the council consciously sought to make itself available to the merchants, artisans, and others under its jurisdiction who carried on their livelihood there.

The activities of the six-man council extended beyond purely administrative and tax-gathering concerns. It also sought to protect and safeguard public morals. Its authority in this sphere was clearly set forth in the Charter: "forbid everything that is contrary to good order and decorum."[114] Particularly at issue were the city's taverns and drinking houses. Popular gathering places for the common folk, taverns had long been associated with vice and debauchery. Boisterous games of card and dice often ended in fights, injuries, and sometimes deaths. Prostitutes openly enticed clients among the patrons of drinking houses. In 1790 the council proposed a reform of public drinking houses, limiting ownership to people whose trustworthiness and honesty could be relied upon and prescribing the beverages that could be sold in each type of tavern. What became obvious about the crackdown on this particular manifestation of loose morals is that it was directed against peasants, who were specifically barred from owning taverns. Thus in one fell swoop the council was able to prescribe more orderly behavior and to procure a monopoly over tavern ownership for merchants and petty townsmen at peasant expense.[115]

Finances

Ditiatin's claim that the city had virtually no money at its disposal also needs to be clarified. Ditiatin based this judgment upon a budget he found for 1797, indicating that the city administration had only 36,000 rubles at its disposal. In reality the budget was much larger. According to an ukase of September 22, 1782, 2 percent of export duties and 1 percent of import duties collected at St. Petersburg were to go to the city. This decree was confirmed both in Article 146 of the Municipal Regulation and in a special ukase to St. Petersburg governor Konovnitsyn on November 9, 1786.[116] The same law drew a sum of 115,511 rubles from the state treasury for the council to use in running the city's schools, the city shipyard, and the maritime school. In addition to this, the city had a number of other sources of revenue in 1789. The municipal government collected rents from merchants leasing stalls in the various bazaars as well as from those using city-owned warehouses to store hemp and salt. Together these fees amounted to just over forty thousand rubles annually. Another seven to eight thousand came from assessments on horse collars belonging to cabmen. For opening the pontoon bridges spanning the Neva, in order to allow craft to pass through, the city government received a ruble per vessel. This generated more than four thousand rubles annually.[117] Taken together, these sums indicate an annual city budget in excess of 250,000 rubles.[118]

In addition, many taxes collected and expended in the city, as, for example, the so-called *kvadratnye den'gi* spent on police salaries, remained outside the council's budget.[119] The amount of money expended in the city's administration represented a much greater ruble figure than Ditiatin realized. When a unitary city budget was finally introduced in 1804 under Alexander I by bringing into one list all the expenses to run the city, the initial budget ran to more than a million rubles.

The city was unable to protect its treasury from depradations by other governmental agencies. On June 29, 1790, A. A. Bezborodko, the most active member of Catherine's advisory council, ordered Governor-general Ia. A. Brius in Catherine's name to take 3,000 rubles from the city's income to pay salaries of hired skippers and others in the Lake Ladoga flotilla.[120] Even within the city, the city's funds were sometimes spent by people other than those authorized to do so by law. From 1788–91 Bezborodko several times ordered expenditures "from the local city's revenues" for various purposes: 520 rubles for landing points on the Neva (December 1788); 1,000 rubles for bridge maintenance and 500 rubles to outfit and man three cutters (April 1789); another 5,000 rubles to repair bridges and pavement (May 1789); another 1,585 rubles for bridge repair and 508 rubles for a landing (November 1789); 2,000 rubles for bridge maintenance and 5,000 for pavements (February 1790); 6,000 rubles to clean up various state-owned buildings in the towns of the St. Petersburg region (August 1790); and 5,569 rubles to repair firefighting equipment (May 1791).[121]

These external claims upon the city's resources would indicate either that the six-man council was failing to do its duty or that it was powerless to intervene. In either case, these examples support the thesis that the financial basis of the new form of urban government was shaky at best, and raise questions of how well the council could operate even with the best of intentions, when it did not have final control over purse strings.

Evaluation of Municipal Administration

An evaluation of the administration of Catherinian St. Petersburg must first accept that administration on its own terms. It would be anachronistic to criticize governmental institutions for not dealing with problems not recognized at the time as belonging to the sphere of urban administration. Evaluation must consider the milieu of the eighteenth century and determine how efficient and capable city government was in its time.

For this reason one must not criticize the governmental structure, as did Ditiatin and Kizevetter, for its lack of democratic ideals. Popularly elected officials were few and had little authority. But the goal of urban government was not democracy, notwithstanding the criticisms of nineteenth-century liberal historians on that account.[122] If one takes responsiveness to stated needs as a better instrument for evaluating St. Petersburg's government, it must be admitted that administrative bodies responded surprisingly well in attempting to solve problems. Planning was realistic and took into consideration actual grievances by inhabitants. The government dealt successfully with the four types of crisis faced by the city. Problems of sanitation received much consideration, and the solutions reveal a genuine concern to raise the quality of life. Hazardous and polluting industries were relocated to sites less populous. Pavement and lamps were added to more and more streets. A sewage system was introduced. In the realm of welfare, public education was adopted in principle. Hospitals operated by the city and state provided services to the poor as well as the wealthy. In almost every case, though, planning was the product of crisis. Planning was undertaken to solve a problem rather than to create something new out of nothing.

Criticism of St. Petersburg's government is directed most often at the utter complexity of the administrative structure. There was no one city government, but rather many different offices, departments, chancelleries, commissions, and boards with authority over various segments of life. To be sure, this characteristic was unique neither to St. Petersburg nor to Russia, but typified early modern administration throughout Europe. Here as elsewhere Catherine's legislative attempts, instead of reducing the number of agencies and integrating them, only added new bodies with limited authority over small areas. Complexity of organization led to uncertainty as to where the exact authority of various bodies lay. General areas of responsibility remained quite clear, but it was inevitable that many specific instances arose over which several organs claimed authority. Nevertheless it must be underlined that in everyday affairs the police was the body most involved in running the city. Citizens came in contact with the police more often and in more ways than with any other agency.

Legislative changes affecting the city often were introduced as belated attempts to keep the laws in step with altered conditions. Even as the government moved slowly to give legal recognition to one state of affairs, that set of circumstances was being eroded and replaced by another in the vigorously growing city. This phenomenon is noted most clearly with regard to restrictions over commercial activity. During times when the establishment of new factories was strictly forbidden in the city, a number of them were set up, offering employment to hundreds of workers. Peasants were not allowed to trade in the city, but gross violation of this law forced its relaxation. And one of the most far-reaching legal failures—with positive results for the development of the city—concerned the futile attempt to register all city inhabitants, which would have forced runaway peasants out of the city. Despite measures intended to impede natural development, the city continued to gain in strength and numbers through its powers of attraction.

An anecdote purporting to date from Catherine's reign offers its own criticism of the effectiveness of urban administration. Once during an evening conversation in the Hermitage Catherine praised the impartiality of the city's police, crediting in particular the publication of the Charter to the Towns and the Police Statute of 1782. She claimed that notables and ordinary people were treated alike.

Lev Naryshkin, a cousin of the Romanovs and one of the city's best known wits, responded, "Well hardly, Little Mother—I'm not so sure."

"I tell you, Lev Aleksandrovich, it is so," persisted Catherine. "Were even you to violate the law or disobey the police, you would not receive special treatment."

"I'll see about that tomorrow, Little Mother, and report to you by evening."

Early the next day, as soon as it was light, Naryshkin put on a rich caftan covered with his medals and orders but on top of it donned a frayed old frock coat belonging to one of his furnace stokers. Completing his costume with a hole-filled hat, Naryshkin set out on foot for a street market selling meats of all sorts. "Good honorable merchant," he said to the first purveyor of chickens he came upon, "how much for young pullets?"

"For live ones a ruble and for slaughtered, fifty copecks a pair," shot back the seller, eyeing the shabbily dressed Naryshkin.

"Fine. Slaughter two pairs of live ones for me."

The poultryman immediately set to work. He cut off their heads, plucked them, wrapped them in paper and placed them in a bag. Meanwhile Naryshkin laboriously counted out a ruble in small copper coins.

"Do you really think that's enough, my good sir? That'll be *two* rubles."

"And for what, my dear?" sweetly asked Naryshkin.

"For what? For two pairs of live pullets! I told you, live ones cost a ruble a pair."

"Fine, my good man. But since these chickens aren't alive, why should you demand more?"

"But they *were* alive!"

"And the ones you sell for half a ruble a pair were alive too, so I'll pay the price you quoted for slaughtered pullets."

"Why, you shyster, you trickster!" the infuriated seller shouted. "Give me another ruble or I'll summon the policemen standing over there!"

"Why the racket?" asked the policemen, who at that moment strolled up.

"Here, your excellency, decide between us," said Naryshkin calmly. "This good merchant is selling live pullets for a ruble and slaughtered ones for half a ruble the pair. As a poor man wanting to save money, I asked him to kill them so I could get two for fifty copecks."

The policeman started in on the side of the poultryman, agreeing that the chickens had indeed been alive and badgering Naryshkin to pay a ruble a pair, or would he rather see Siberia? Naryshkin bowed low and asked for a more merciful consideration, but the policeman insisted. "Give him another ruble or it's off to Siberia!"

At that moment Naryshkin threw off the frock coat and appeared before the poultryman and the policeman resplendent in his dress. Immediately the policeman began berating the seller, "You shyster! You said yourself that live ones go for a ruble and a pair of dead ones for half that, and here you are trying to collect for dead chickens as though they were alive. Do you know what I can do to you, you thief? Say the word, Your Excellency, and I'll haul him off right now. This rascal will learn how to treat gentlemen properly and not demand a price for dead chickens as though they were alive!"

Having proven his point Naryshkin paid the poultryman fourfold and thanked the policeman for his good judgment. That evening at the Hermitage he related the entire tale to the empress as only he could, acting out the role of each in turn. Everyone howled with laughter except the empress. . . .[123]

In conclusion, notwithstanding the evidence that the city's administration may not have functioned as perfectly as Catherine imagined, the city's governing performed its greatest service by preparing St. Petersburg for future physical expansion. Planners and police forced intensified use of land. By public works projects, building codes, and control of natural calamities, the government made the city more inhabitable. It fostered the development of a communications and transportation network through intensified use of river and canal embankments made possible when they were lined with granite. The provision of services from waste removal to firefighting was turned over to full-time workers rather than being left to inhabitants to perform. And the city government felt the first twinges of a social conscience, with commensurate actions to benefit victims of society. Administration thus worked responsibly, under whatever restraints, to encourage and ease the city's development.

5

"All Sorts of Commodities in the World": Sustaining the City's Needs and Wants

UNLIKE MOST PREINDUSTRIAL CITIES, ST. PETERSBURG COULD NOT depend primarily upon the surrounding countryside for its necessities. Although it was located on the coastline, most of its supplies were not brought from across the sea, as was the case with ancient Athens. Instead, it drew from the distant reaches of the Russian interior the goods and produce necessary to sustain its life. Within twenty years of the city's founding, its residents were forced to look well inland, far beyond the immediate outlying territory, for sustenance. As the city steadily expanded, it devoted an ever-larger share of human resources to its logistical needs. In addition to the city's own inhabitants, many people elsewhere in Russia helped to supply the capital. Indeed, the provisioning of St. Petersburg provided a major stimulus to the Russian economy by the end of the eighteenth century.

FOODSTUFFS

Consider, for example, the impact of the solution to the food problem alone. Because the soil in St. Petersburg province is sandy and clayey, the growing season short, and weather inhospitable, local agriculture could not feed the fast-growing city unaided. The geographical and climatic conditions go a long way toward explaining why there was so little agriculture in the area before the city was founded. Peter the Great was the first to wrestle with the predicament. He decided to improve the system of supply by constructing of a network of canals to connect St. Petersburg with the agriculturally rich black soil region and the Ukraine.[1] Empress Elizabeth's decision later in the century to abolish internal tolls on trade was in part motivated by a desire to remove artificial hindrances to low-cost provisioning of the new capital. These measures had far greater impact than merely to facilitate food supply to St. Petersburg, for other commercial wares followed the same canal and river routes to the capital. The Soviet historian

Iu. R. Klokman estimated that as many as seventy to eighty thousand people traveled to St. Petersburg annually in the 1770s as workers on river and canal boats.[2] The entire Russian economy benefited from the effort to supply St. Petersburg.

The market for produce in St. Petersburg in the latter third of the century was enormous. In a single year the court alone consumed many tons of beef, poultry, and game animals, and over half a million fish and eggs.[3] The city annually required tens of thousands of bushels of wheat, barley, oats, rye, semolina, fresh and dried fruits and vegetables, nuts, large quantities of beef, mutton and pork, over three and a half million pounds of butter, and from five to fourteen million eggs.[4] A small percentage of foodstuffs, particularly fresh produce, came from St. Petersburg and nearby Novgorod provinces, but most provisions originated much farther away. Cattle arrived on the hoof from the Ukraine and the lower Volga valley. By boat, barge, and raft came caviar, sturgeon, beer, rye, fruits, and vegetables from the far south and the Ural region. Seasonal changes from summer to winter only altered the primary mode of transport from rivers and canals to roads, for "the speedy and easy conveyance on the snow . . . brings fresh provisions to market a thousand English miles by land, as those can witness who have often eat [*sic*] in St. Petersburg the beef of Archangel."[5] Grain was the primary staple, bread and soups the mainstay of most diets. Potatoes were as yet unknown to most people.

Merely to provide enough produce for the city to survive necessitated a high level of activity. To appeal to the capital's palate required care, efficiency, and timeliness. The fact that delicacies were made available in sufficient quantity for those who could afford them provides ample proof that after midcentury the supply system was capable of functioning well. Most delicacies were shipped to Russia from western Europe. Apples and pears came from German and French ports. Oysters were shipped from London and Flensburg in Holstein. Holland and Prussia supplied cheeses and butter. Bacon and ham came from Hamburg.[6] The advertisements section of the newspaper *Sanktpeterburgskie vedomosti* often offered for sale imported luxury foods and beverages. In February 1764, for example, a Hungarian merchant, having rented a shop from the Miliutin family, announced the arrival of Hungarian and Tokai wines. In the same issue was a notice for people wishing to purchase the remaining tea from a Chinese caravan to come to the Commerce College.[7] To be sure, one had to pay premium prices for gourmet items, particularly when they were out of season. Naturally, merchants selling such rarities as freshly imported lemons, apples, and pears in midwinter demanded luxury prices at that time of year when fresh fruits were so rare.[8]

Skippers and crewmen on ships bringing various wares and products in their holds engaged in retail trade in foodstuffs. Depending on what was available in their most recent ports of call, they provided numerous items of food, each man engaging in his own retail trade, by the barrel, half-barrel, crate, box, bag, jar, and pot. On ships coming from Danzig, Stettin, Lübeck, Rostock, and other Pomeranian ports, they brought fresh and dried vegetables, coffee, chocolate, cracked grains, hams, geese, sausages, gingerbread, and dried fish, as well as earthenware, clay pots, and various sorts of housewares. From Holstein and Danish, Swedish, and Norwegian ports, they imported the same goods plus oysters, mussels, salted fish including herring, lemons, wild oranges, porcelain dishes from the East Indies, paper napkins, leather gloves, and small amounts of wine and fresh butter. On ships coming from greater distances, such as from Hamburg, Holland, England, France, Spain, and the Mediterranean, they brought lemons, oranges, wild oranges, dried candies, anchovies, capers, olive oil in glass jars and metal steins, chocolate, cheese, Dutch herring in little barrels, salted and dried fish, English beer, wines, curative waters, almonds, chestnuts, raisins, and other foods.[9]

The forgoing examples and figures illustrate effectively that St. Petersburg drew its food from a vast Russian hinterland as well as parts of Europe. But the role of the city's immediate surroundings must not be underestimated either. Nearby villagers produced most of the capital's dairy products, garden vegetables, berries, and mushrooms, and a small portion of its grain. Fishermen living in the city and its environs supplied varying if less than substantial amounts of seafood. Women in Okhta and Galley Haven supplemented the family income by selling milk in the city. Finally, many residents maintained kitchen gardens for their own use, sometimes trading part of the produce in the city's markets.[10]

Local peasants did not gain the right to trade in the city easily. Throughout the eighteenth century, the city's merchants and local peasants vied with each other over commercial rights in the city.[11] The merchants sought to be middlemen in all exchanges, but peasants wanted to sell directly to consumers. Early in the century merchants clearly had the upper hand, but peasant protests and changed circumstances resulted in a law in 1755 permitting local peasants to sell agricultural products at retail prices, but at restricted hours. This provision was underlined and strengthened by later inclusion in the Charter to the Towns.[12] Peasants from outside the local district also quickly seized the opportunity to trade in the city. Consequently a law intended to open commerce to a small number of local peasants attracted direct trade from much greater distances. Merchants, of course, protested vehemently against this violation of what they felt to be their traditional estate privilege to control trade, resulting in 1776 in a tightening of restrictions on peasant commerce. A new law forbade peasants from coming on any form of watercraft or by cart to sell products in city markets.[13] This abruptly curtailed peasant schemes to transport large quantities of goods over long distances. Unfortunately it also limited substantially the amount of trade local peasants could initiate and drove up food prices in the city, since now middlemen were involved in most goods exchange.

For the most part, merchants from Russia's interior were responsible for the vast amounts of foodstuffs traversing the water communications system en route to St. Petersburg. Partial statistics for vessels passing through Vyshnii Volochek Canal from the Volga toward St. Petersburg exist from 1775 through the 1780s, when annual passage in the number of vessels was as follows:

Barks	from 2,000 to 3,600
Half-barks	from 600 to 1,000
Small barks	from 450 to 800
Flatboats	from 900 to 1,200 and more

According to the statistician, perhaps half of the freight represented food for St. Petersburg.[14]

The transporting process was long and involved. Most grains originated in provinces along the middle Volga system. Buyers transported the grain to Rybinsk (Rybnaia Sloboda), where it was transferred to smaller boats and often sold to the merchants who would actually convey the foodstuffs to St. Petersburg. From Rybinsk each craft could carry up to 115 tons of grain. Cost of transport included the use of at least ten men and approximately twenty horses to guide each craft through the river and canal system. Transportation costs for only one 325-pound sack totaled nearly two and one half rubles.[15] The rates of loss and spoilage en route were high, results of poor packaging and carelessness in transport; between one and two sacks of every ten never completed the trip downstream.[16] Yet this process brought vast amounts of grain and other food to market in St. Petersburg. Despite its length and intricacy, this supply route continued to meet the demands imposed on it by a growing market at its northern end. Because it existed, St. Petersburg was able to develop quickly.

While the food supply was normally adequate in quantity, few people ate well year-round. The distance between source and market considerably shortened the time of year when fresh fruits could be found at prices people could afford. To a lesser extent the same was true of vegetables. Other foods varied in price from season to season. The wealthy could purchase most foods at any season of the year. Indeed, at times it was easier to provide luxuries for the rich than it was to make accessible necessities for the poor.

Not all poor people and workingmen bought food in shops and markets for preparation at home. With a predominantly male population, there was a need for communal eating places where workingmen could fill their stomachs at small cost. Expensive, more exclusive restaurants existed (one established in 1786 was still in operation in 1900), but workingmen frequented far less pretentious establishments known as *kharchevye,* inexpensive eateries that might be termed "grub houses." Histories of the city largely have ignored the existence of such establishments, which met a continual need in feeding the men of the city. One of the few published references to *kharchevye* was an advertisement in the *Sanktpeterburgskie vedomosti* in 1764 offering to rent land to anyone wishing to establish such an eating-house.[17] *Kharchevye* were rarely large establishments. The majority were housed in one room or basements of buildings used in main for some other purpose and owned by merchants, civil servants, military officers, or the state. Most *kharchevye* operators were peasants, followed by merchants, a few of whom operated a chain of such grub houses. More than half of these eateries were located in the oldest sections of town—First and Second Admiralty sections and, predominantly, Vasil'evskii Island. Poor people living in these areas often rented living quarters in the basements or garrets of the large houses of the wealthy. Their rented space rarely included eating facilities, making it necessary to eat elsewhere. In outlying areas, where many workers owned their own small wooden houses, there was much less need for *kharchevye.*[18] Finally, the staff of life, bread, could be purchased from street vendors.

Other Necessities

Besides the people who made their living supplying the capital with food, many found employment filling local needs for clothing, housing, hardware, furniture, transportation, and other goods and services. Comprehensive figures showing the number of persons thus employed cannot be compiled, but partial figures provide clues. At the end of 1789, for instance, registration figures for artisans (master craftsmen, journeymen, and apprentices) contained the names of 838 Russian and 210 foreign tailors. Nearly 1,200 Russians registered as cobblers. There were 149 commercial barbers and 64 hairdressers. One estimate indicated the presence of 4,600 cabmen.[19] These figures give some idea of the volume of work involved in providing goods and services for the city. Better than 10 percent of the city's inhabitants made their living supplying these daily needs. The variety of occupational specializations continually increased in order to meet the city's needs, whether by street hawkers offering food products, cabinetmakers and joiners, barbers and wigmakers, metalsmiths and tobacconists, or the myriad of other skills practiced in a large city.

Contractors supplied much of the material and labor necessary to provide firewood, building materials, cross-city transportation of goods, and other necessities. Although the efforts of peasants to provide goods for the city were severely restricted, there were few regulations against peasants offering their own services, commonly done through contractors. Again, no reliable figures show the number of men thus employed, although these people surely comprised at least one-fifth of the capital's laborers.[20]

The majority of private, as well as much state-financed, building was carried out by these semitransient peasant construction workers. Because the weather severely shortened the season in which construction could reasonably be undertaken, work had to be well organized and take advantage of whatever daylight and good weather were available. Early every spring workers swarmed into the city from many areas of Russia, the men from the same region specializing in similar tasks.[21] This tendency to job specialization within geographical areas extended beyond the construction industry. Men from a particular district were noted as tailors, fishermen, or butchers, while from other regions came waiters, bakers, and other specialists. One can conclude that workers were often organized into groups (artels) before arriving in the city. From year to year their work became known, thereby making it less difficult to find work with each succeeding year. In dividing their lives between the native village and St. Petersburg, furthermore, maximizing the economic potential of each, these men, for the most part state peasants, showed remarkable adaptability to the possibilities offered them by the city. This ease in moving from country to city and back again with the changing seasons set in motion the process that often ended at some point in a permanent break with the village and the affirmation of St. Petersburg as home.[22]

The men who banded together in artels in their villages before setting out on their seasonal migration to St. Petersburg generally found employment in their chosen field of work. Matters were not so easy for those who sought work individually, even when they brought highly developed skills. A labor market developed but slowly. Individuals often advertised for employment in the *Sanktpeterburgskie vedomosti.* Men with skill and experience found work most quickly of all, unless—as with translators—supply exceeded demand. People without particular talent often sold their services door-to-door. They could hope to gain positions as domestics or house servants, or, if literate, as record-keepers, in both cases at wages that provided little more than room and board.[23] Merchants often contracted with public and private institutions to supply certain everyday needs, as is illustrated by three brief examples. Merchant Egor Volkov supplied firewood for the imperial tapestry manufactory in the early 1760s and was paid according to volume; one year he also contracted to provide lemon juice and soap. Another merchant, Ivan (Johann) Stark, bought foodstuffs from several sources and by contract supplied them to the state orphanage. He was one of many to provide goods by contract to that institution. Third, in 1793 the State Assignat Bank placed a notice in the *Sanktpeterburgskie vedomosti* seeking someone to provide janitorial services for a contracted sum less than that already offered, indicating that custodial services in government buildings were sometimes let out to private individuals.[24]

Western Europeans—particularly Frenchmen—proved adept salesmen of their services as tutors, house managers, barbers, and so on. One French barber procured an annual salary of two hundred rubles—equal to the wage of a minor government official—plus clothing, board, and equipage, from a Russian gentleman.[25] Indeed, wealthy Russians were so taken with the idea of employing Frenchmen to supply some real or imagined service that pointed barbs became widespread about the ways in which French servants and employees took advantage of them. Nikolai Novikov's satirical journal *Truten'* (The Drone) printed the following "announcement":

> KRONSHTADT: Several days ago a ship from Bordeaux arrived in this port; aboard it, besides the most stylish wares, came twenty-four Frenchmen, chatting about themselves, making it known that they are all barons, chevaliers, marquises and counts who, being unhappy in their native land, were carried to such extremities that they had to come to Russia to acquire gold. In their stories they lie very little: to be sure, they are all Frenchmen who, it is proven, exercise various trades and duties of the third estate; many of them have had major quarrels with the Paris police, who asked that they be deported from the city. Because of this they have arrived here and are prepared to enter into service as teachers and governors of the young noble-born.[26]

The ultimate goal of many foreign rogues surfaces in the following conversation, almost certainly apocryphal. The son of a French craftsman, posing as Chevalier de Monsange and receiving five hundred rubles per year plus servants and carriage, was questioned by a skeptical German.

German: Tell me, what do you teach your charges? Just between us, you know nothing besides the French language, and *any* French bumpkin knows that as well as you!

Frenchman: My dear fellow! I do not intend to earn wages, but to receive money as a gift. The parents have done a silly thing—they put me in charge of their children's education; but I, on the other hand, am acting very wisely. . . . For I did not enter into service to teach my charges, but to save money. By accumulating money and going around with young people, I can be both teacher and merchant. I will order French wares and try to get them duty-free. Consider how cheaply I will acquire them: duty not paid; a shop for them not rented; I will not pay merchants' taxes and will bear no overhead. I will be able to sell the goods to the young people who are my friends, and if I get in debt, then I'll be able to register in the accounts and get a letter of credit. In five years I will have several thousand rubles and return to my own country. In the end, quite ironically, I will be cursed as a barbarian and an ignoramus by the very people whom I have used as tools for my enrichment.[27]

By no means did all foreign immigrants take such blatant advantage of their Russian hosts, but those whose scheme it was to accumulate instant wealth and disappear came to St. Petersburg as to any other city.

Shops and Markets

We saw earlier that bazaars, or *gostinye dvory,* operated in all central sections of the capital. They formed the largest agglomerations of shops and markets in the city. The first bazaar appeared on Vasil'evskii Island in 1721 or 1722. It consisted of a large building forming a perimeter around an open square courtyard. Permanent shops occupied the building, whereas the central, open-air area was reserved for merchants (later including peasants also), who sold goods there only periodically. This huge market burned down in 1763. Following the fire, the building was enlarged and rebuilt in masonry. Two-story and arcaded, it had shops on the first floor and warehouses above. To reduce the danger of fire, no permanent structures of any kind were allowed in the open square. Initially the only large market on the island, the bazaar offered for sale every sort of necessity from ribbon to firewood, from groats to hay.[28]

Because of its central location and because it was the largest collection of shops in the city, the bazaar on Nevskii Prospect between the Catherine Canal and the Fontanka was by far the best known one in St. Petersburg. (Even today, Gostinyi Dvor, occupying the same building, remains one of the largest shopping complexes in the central city.) It first appeared on that site in 1736. In its earliest years it achieved such importance that a foreign visitor left the following description of it.

> In the southernmost [*sic*] part of the city is the marketplace, where all sorts of goods, both home and foreign, are kept to be sold. It is a very large square with four entries, on each side whereof is a range of shops, both within and without. There are covered galleries built quite around the square, both on the out and inside, that people may be defended from rain. A stranger need not, as in other places, hunt through this great city for what he wants to buy: a pleasant walk in these galleries will give him an opportunity of seeing many of the best people in St. Petersburgh, and all sorts of commodities in the world. The younger merchants and their servants guard it during the night, and in it great order and decency are always observed.[29]

The shops were arranged in "rows" according to the sort of goods sold. Thus all the shops dealing in cloth stretched along one passage, as did those offering furniture, china, shoes, iron goods, candles, hats, and so forth. Foodstuffs, including vegetables, sugar, and coffee, were sold in the Admiralty Side bazaar during its early years, but when reconstruction of the wooden building into brick began in the years immediately preceding Catherine's reign, they were banished into other areas of the city because of the messy conditions and stench that often accompanied them.[30]

The new masonry *gostinyi dvor* opened in stages as construction was completed. Despite the law setting rents at five rubles annually, merchants purchased shops at prices reflective of the value of their location. Two merchants who wanted to buy a large corner shop agreed in 1783 to pay 43,200 rubles for the space before learning that two stairways to the second floor and a passageway into the inner courtyard were to be carved out of the area they had purchased. The two buyers were among the wealthiest Russian merchants in town, but so were the men from whom the space was bought. The purchasers filed suit to block the construction of the stairways and passage, on the grounds that they had not been informed beforehand about the construction plans. After an investigation by the Commerce Commission, which had responsibility for oversight over the *gostinyi dvor*, the buyers lost their case. In the end one of them agreed to accept his share (for 15,700 rubles) of the now much smaller shop and the other exchanged his part of the purchase for another space elsewhere in the complex.[31] The purchase price was quite high compared to costs of doing business elsewhere. For example, the annual rent at that time for a shop at the bazaar adjacent to the bourse at the eastern point of Vasil'evskii Island was only 100 rubles.[32]

The big *gostinyi dvor* on Nevskii Prospect expanded into neighboring areas as business boomed. Immediately to the west sprang up Tolkuchii (Secondhand) Market, where, as the name indicates, secondhand goods, especially clothing, were sold. In 1787 it was incorporated into the larger bazaar as its wooden buildings were replaced by masonry ones. But shops continued to spill over into other buildings. Some located across Nevskii Prospect in the Catholic church of St. Catherine (ten shops there belonged to foreign merchants from Italy, Switzerland, and Nuremberg). Further commercial activity spread into an alleyway between Great Garden Street and the Fontanka. Called "Hunt" or "Bird" Row (*Okhotnyi, ptichii riad*), it displayed meat of all kinds. Peasants sold berries and other fruits of the forest, including mushrooms, in a nearby vacant lot.[33] The building of the city council itself was overrun with shops. The entire first floor of the two-story structure was devoted to commercial activity and only the second floor to city administrative offices. If an item was on sale anywhere in the city, chances were it could be found in the vicinity of the Admiralty district bazaar.

These two bazaars or "merchant yards" (the literal translation of *gostinyi dvor*) served as prototypes for new bazaars built in designated places in every district of the city. Demand was such in some sections of town that merchants had to reserve space for shops in the new markets before they were built. If too many signed up, either they drew lots to see who would receive the space, or the market was expanded to include every merchant desiring a shop. In the bazaar near the bourse, if more than one merchant spoke for a space that came open, it was assigned to the one who had the largest inventory of goods.[34] Despite the vitality of commercial life in the city's center, insufficient merchant response precluded the construction of merchant yards in the more outlying Rozhestvenskaia, Karetnaia, and Vyborg quarters.

Bazaars were permanent structures providing space for relatively established merchants. Shopping for everyday needs occurred more commonly in neighborhood markets (*rynki*) typified by more transitory small-scale dealers whose stalls were often dismantled at the end of the day. Their places of business were not so much shops as benches, tables, bins, chests, trunks, or cupboards, often sheltered from the elements by awnings. Markets brought together a wide variety of people from various locations and social backgrounds. A list of those renting space in Morskoi (Sailors' or Sea) Market in 1780 yields nearly three hundred names (see table 5.1).[35] Morskoi Market was located on Nevskii Prospect at the head of the two Morskaia streets, Large and Small. Most striking is that fewer than half of the renters had permanent legal ties to St. Petersburg. Only forty of the stall-holders were legally registered as residents of St. Petersburg, nineteen merchants and twenty-one petty townsmen. Five of those merchants rented multiple stalls in the market; three merchants rented two each and two merchants each rented four stalls. Nearby towns were also represented minimally. Within St. Petersburg *guberniia* only the town of Sofiia, the modern city of Pushkin (also called Tsarskoe Selo), was represented by either merchants or petty townsmen.

Virtually none of the renters of stalls from beyond the immediate vicinity of St. Petersburg were merchants from significant towns. There were none from *guberniia* capitals other than Olonets in the north and Kaluga beyond Moscow. Merchants from more significant towns undoubtedly found it not worth their while to conduct business on the small scale found in markets. On the other hand, almost as many peasants (133) as townsmen (140) rented stalls. Fifty-nine of the peasants were serfs, more than half of them coming from Iaroslavl' *guberniia*. The largest number of serfs came from estates owned by Gregory Orlov (16), Countess Kurakina (9), P. B. Sheremet'ev (7), and from the Ukraine, lords unknown (6). Despite the regulations noted earlier to discourage peasants from coming great distances to sell wares or produce in St. Petersburg, they obviously continued to do so. Among the trivial details discovered in the list is that two renters of stalls were women, one was a "free man," one a Polish subject, and four were postmen. Business must have been brisk because only one space or stall in the entire market was reported as unrented. The evidence from Morskoi market indicates that many of the daily necessities of life were provided to city residents by people who themselves had no legal rights in the city yet who traveled great distances to engage in livelihood there.

Shops selling highly flammable goods—wool, rags, woodenware, beds, carts, bast shoes, and so on—were limited to only two markets. As a further fire prevention measure, shops were given in perpetuity only to merchants who built their shops of brick.[36] Further restrictions prevented merchants from selling meat and fish in shops located in private homes, for reasons of hygiene and public comfort. Fish could be sold in gardens along the rivers and meat in regular

Table 5.1. Social Origins of Renters of Stalls, Morskoi Market, 1780

Guberniia/ Town/District	Merchant	Petty Townsman	State Peasant	Economic Peasant	Serf
St. Petersburg					
St. Petersburg	19	21			
Kamennyi Nos			1		
Kopor'e			1		3
Krasnoe Selo					1
Sofiia	12	2			
Olonets					
Olonets	2	8	12		
Petrozavodsk	2	1	2		
Vytegra	1	7	2		
Novgorod					
Staraia Rusa		1			
Iaroslavl'					
Borisoglebsk					1
Danilov	4		4		2
Iaroslavl'				1	
Liubim	7	6	4	5	20
Mologa			2		
Myshkin	1	1			
Poshekhon'e	1	3	3		
Romanov			1	1	12
Rostov		2			
Uglich				3	
Tver'					
Tver'		1			
Kashin	3	10			1
Novotorzhok		1			
Moscow					
Moscow					
Vereia	1				
Kostroma					
Chukhloma	1				3
Galich	2	8		1	4
Kostroma			1	5	
Sol' Galitskaia	1	4			1
Kaluga					
Kaluga	1				
Vologda					
Vologda			1		
Riga					
Dvinsk (Daugavpils)					1
None Given	2	3	20	4	10
TOTALS	60	80	54	20	59

Source: RGADA, *fond* 16, *delo* 504, *chast'* 1, *listy* 79ff.

markets.[37] The largest fish market was on the shores of Kamennyi (Rock) Island, where people could purchase their choice of freshly caught fish, clean, cook, and eat them on the spot or in sheds along a nearby boardwalk.[38]

As new sections of the city developed, necessary commercial establishments sprang up also. For instance, Nevskii Prospect in Rozhestvenskaia section (from Ligovo Canal to the Alexander Nevskii Monastery) was built up wholly during Catherine's reign. The following establishments lined the street by the 1780s: (1) a long line of warehouses offering carriages, lorries, and their equipages; (2) a privately owned market selling foodstuffs; (3) a branch of the customhouse, which also contained a number of shops; (4) twenty long wooden buildings selling housewares, food, hardware, and the like to people living in the neighborhood; and (5) a field where slaughtered and frozen meat was sold during winter.[39]

The primary building materials could be bought in several places in the city. Unlike many goods consumed there, almost all building materials came from relatively local areas. Clay and sand were abundant in the vicinity, and local brickyards, both state- and privately owned, ably met the city's needs. The village of Putilovo on a low ridge along the southernmost shore of Lake Ladoga provided cut limestone for building foundations. Sawmills and lumberyards were located in at least five convenient places around the city's edge by the beginning of Catherine's reign.[40] Glass, roofing tiles, and other finishing materials were manufactured in the city. Labor was supplied by the groups of peasants who came to the capital from the interior in the warmer months.

St. Petersburg was the first Russian city to demonstrate a high demand for rental housing, enough to permit a small group of people to make much of their living providing it. During Catherine's reign a number of individuals purchased or built rooming houses, letting apartments, rooms, or just portions of rooms to people of varying means. From the Catherinian period on, the majority of inhabitants rented quarters instead of owning their own homes. This increasing practice led to legislation governing contracts between landlords and tenants, beginning in the 1760s.[41]

In most eighteenth-century towns and cities, shop owners lived in upper stories over their shops, which occupied the first (street) floors of structures. This pattern did not establish itself in St. Petersburg, in part because of the concentration of commercial activity in the grand bazaars. The government made it legal for merchants to live in their shops, but few chose to do so.[42]

Home Ownership

It has been estimated that no more than 3 to 4 percent of residents in St. Petersburg owned the houses in which they lived.[43] The Charter to the Towns called for the compilation of a book of city inhabitants, which was to list everyone eligible to register under one of the six classifications. One of the classifications was "genuine city resident," those who owned real estate. Each registrant was supposed to provide specific information about the property, including in whose name it was registered, how it was acquired (whether built, inherited, purchased, or received in dowry), and its location. "Property" was meant to include dwellings, shops, or vacant land. No complete book of city inhabitants survives from Catherine's reign, but from the fragmentary evidence it can be estimated that up to seven thousand people owned real estate. One would expect that high-level government functionaries, both civil and military, would be well represented among home owners. They did indeed own more than a fifth of all privately owned houses as extrapolated from the surviving evidence. When other employees of the civil and military service are added to their number, including those retired from service, the percentage of ownership by people directly dependent upon the government, court, and military for their livelihood rises to more than 50 percent. Merchants owned nearly a quarter of all privately owned houses and craftsmen and artisans accounted for slightly under a tenth.

A few merchants each owned several houses, generally registering them individually to family members, perhaps to hide wealth in case of severe financial reversal. Usually wives were the first beneficiaries of this practice, then sons, and finally daughters. Through this measure and more frequently through inheritance, women came to own several hundred houses of various sizes. Even more numerous were the women who testified that they purchased their houses or had them built—nearly half of the home-owning women in the sample. Michelle Marrese has drawn attention to the expanding role in the eighteenth century of noblewomen who controlled property,[44] but the evidence of St. Petersburg is that women of other backgrounds were also involved. Slightly more than a quarter of the privately owned real estate in St. Petersburg had come to be in the hands of women by the late 1780s. A number of women testified in the questionnaire for the book of city inhabitants that they derived their living in whole or in part from renting part of all of their houses as apartments, shops, or both. Joint ownership of real estate, male or female, seems to have been extremely rare but not unheard of.

Transport

In a city as large as St. Petersburg there was obviously a need for public transportation. Conveyance at a price was provided by cabmen, who carried not only people but also freight. Peasants spending a few months at a time in the city swelled the number of cabbies even before Catherine's reign. As early as 1757, a fodder shortage persuaded the authorities to limit the number of cabmen who could be registered in the city to two thousand. Increasing needs and wholesale violations of the law resulted in the repeal of the limit only two years later, and the number of cabmen rose steadily throughout Catherine's reign, reaching five thousand before the end of the century.[45]

Cabmen were ubiquitous in central squares and streets, each sitting astride or behind his single horse, which was hitched in summer to a yellow single-axled chaise and in winter to a yellow sleigh. Prices depended on the competition for passengers. If several haggled over a fare, the price would be quite low and agreed upon in advance. When only one cab was available, however, the inexperienced passenger might not settle the fare until reaching his destination, when he might find the charge to be quite high. Cabmen were not noted for their honesty or propriety. Laws were promulgated from time to time to limit their unchecked racing through the streets, slinging around corners, threatening to run down any pedestrians in their way.[46] Cabmen were compelled to register annually with the police, at which time they were issued written instructions and small slates on which were inscribed their names, numbers, and addresses for a two-ruble licensing fee. The measure was introduced ostensibly to provide a complete list of cabmen so that they could be mobilized to aid fire victims, at which times they were expected to convey both people and furnishings without charge. But cabmen were also linked in the public mind with petty crime, and this measure provided some degree of control and identification. Clearly there was an oversupply of cabmen; it should not be surprising that some turned to crime in order to survive.[47]

The owners of ferries provided transportation for a fee across the Neva, Small Neva, and Large Nevka. Rates were determined by weight. It might cost as much as two rubles to cross in a fully liveried carriage, while a man on foot would pay as little as two kopecks.[48]

Public Storehouses

On a few occasions, breakdowns and bottlenecks in the service industry presented challenges to the government because of the implied threat to the social order stemming from even a temporary collapse in the system supplying St. Petersburg with its necessities. Although they were surmounted, these challenges reveal the level of awareness on the part of the tsarist government that the city's needs had to be met and illustrate what the central government was willing to do to avoid catastrophe.

Granaries

The most obvious example has to do with the supply of grain. A shortfall was potentially disastrous for the city. St. Petersburg never faced outright famine, but there were shortages in several years, with resultant high prices and, on occasion, a restive population. Almost five hundred bread shops were scattered throughout the city, certainly enough retail outlets to meet the city's needs.[49] Many citizens did not have to buy their bread in stores, obtaining what they needed through other sources, either private shipments or unmarketed governmental supply systems.[50] But for many of the poorer people in the city, high prices in times of shortage made it difficult to buy enough to eat. To provide for them, the idea of public granaries took root, from which bread and flour could be sold at a low price.

Such warehouses were mandated by law as early as 1718, but functioned unsatisfactorily if at all. Unless stocks of grain were replenished periodically, which evidently was not done, the supply in storage spoiled and became unusable within a few years. A poor harvest in 1766 renewed interest in a public storehouse and once again one was instituted.[51] At first its administrators had no method for deciding when to release grain for sale. In 1767 most of the forty-six million bushels in the storehouse were sold in only four weeks. The government decided that such rapid emptying of stocks was dangerous. Rather than regularly testing the sufficiency of the granary's reserves, early-season shipment of grain to the capital would be encouraged. Catherine posted an award of six hundred rubles to the first individual to import grain to the capital in May (after the ice had passed downstream), and a thousand rubles to the man who imported the most during the course of that month. Other rewards were offered for importation in June and July. In this manner the empress sought to stimulate timely movement of grain into the capital.[52]

The empress further guaranteed a profit for all shipments from the interior. This provision gave a number of merchants the idea to attempt to deceive the warehouse administration by falsely declaring prices paid at distant points of origin or by packing bags with substances other than grain or meal. Such violations led to a set of instructions in 1782 clearly establishing the process by which merchants could supply grain to the St. Petersburg warehouses. Written contracts were to be made in advance, outlining both the price for which grain was to be delivered and the time of delivery. In order to discourage deception, merchants were carefully warned to "turn over flour which is good, fresh, not damp and milky, with no sand or ashes or any other kind of grain mixed in with it: in general a food fit for humans; and groats also in good quantity; and oats of the best, fresh sort of food, without any kind of deception or flour in it: groats in two and oats in one heavy bast sack."[53] Few such contracts survive. One that does, however, comes from Iaroslavl', where one of the major grain-buying merchants from St. Petersburg, Ivan Khlebnikov, had an agent. The contract specifies clearly what is to be delivered and how, although the only price it mentions is the amount paid to Efim Ukropov, the Iaroslavl' merchant who transported the shipment.

> On 23 April 1786 Iaroslavl third guild merchant Efim Vasil'evich Ukropov gave this contract letter to Iaroslavl' townsman Petr Vasil'evich Erykalov, the agent of Saint Petersburg second guild merchant Ivan Lukianov Khlebnikov, to the effect that I contracted with him Erykalov to deliver from Iaroslavl' to St. Petersburg on my own bark various groats; to wit, of oat groats forty four *chetverti,* of barley eight *chetverti,* of wheat two *chetverti,* in total in number of bags, fifty-four *chetverti;* of these groats each *chetvert'* will consist in two new *kuli* made of matting; of barley twenty small *kuli* (fifty *puds*), of dried oat meal twenty-five small *kuli,* two *puds* in each (fifty *puds*), of starch one wooden barrel (fifteen *puds* seventeen *funty*), and in total of the entire lading the weight of five hundred twenty *puds,* which amount having been taken by me on my next journey I am to preserve from every danger, both above from the coursing of water and below from dampness; which lading upon arrival in St. Petersburg I am supposed to give in its entirety to the aforementioned Khlebnikov. And if something appears by my carelessness to be damaged or dampened or lost, then I am to pay Khlebnikov the actual price without dispute. And for the above described lading I Ukropov contracted with him Erykalov for delivery to the denoted Saint Petersburg for each *pud* nine copecks, which contract money I Upropov am to receive from the aforenamed merchant Khlebnikov upon delivery in St. Petersburg of that lading in its entirety of which in declaration I sign the original contract letter by hand, writing thus. . . .[54]

Ukropov was illiterate, so two people had to sign for him, one of whom was his twenty-one-year-old son. The entire load weighed nine and a third tons, less than one-sixteenth of what a large bark could hold. Ukropov stood to earn less than fifty rubles from the execution of the contract.

The greatest single challenge to the supply system came in the year of Ukropov's contract, 1786. Grain prices rose dramatically during the first months of that year, forcing Catherine to name a commission to investigate the causes.[55] In the course of its probe, the commission discovered gross deficiencies in the management of the public granaries, concluding that their better administration might have avoided the crisis altogether. St. Petersburg's public granaries were placed directly under the empress's control. The vice governor was instructed to report regularly to her on their activities. The size of reserve stocks was increased by 25 percent. Detailed instructions spelled out the process for purchasing grain for the granaries. In order to ensure both adequate supply and low prices, the grain was to be purchased by contractors or special agents as close to the producer as possible. The honesty of the operation was to be cross-checked by lists of grain prices in the cereal-producing provinces provided through independent means.[56] Under this system, warehouse administration became increasingly efficient. Thereafter it was able to maintain supplies while keeping prices within reasonable control.

It is noteworthy that the idea of a public storehouse for alcoholic beverages gained currency at least as early as that for grain warehouses. In 1765 we hear of an insufficiency of spirits of high quality. Promises were made that "storehouses convenient and reliable . . . both here on Admiralty and on Vasil'evskii, as in other leading cities, will soon be built from our treasury."[57] Normally the alcoholic beverage (vodka, wine, mead, beer) concession was granted to merchants, usually for periods of four years. Every phase of operation from production to consumption theoretically was under police supervision.[58] Retail establishments selling alcoholic beverages for on-premise consumption were especially problematic. It has been noted above more than once that drinking establishments frequently had poor reputations. After 1785 the city council took up this issue. On May 20, 1790, the second elected council passed a statute on taverns and inns stipulating that all persons wanting to own a tavern or inn must get permission from the committee responsible for the city inhabitants book. Tavern owners had to be registered in the city in one of the six categories of town inhabitant, they had to be debt-free, and they had to be people of good reputation. When they filed application for ownership, the petition had to be countersigned by at least two people willing to vouch for them as meeting at least the third qualification.

Two hundred twenty-nine names of applicants to own and operate taverns and inns were sent in the name of the empress to the main commander of police, Governor-general Iakov Aleksandrovich Brius on November 9, 1790.[59] Virtually all of the applicants were men registered as merchants or petty townsmen. Approximately a fifth of them reported that they were registered in more than one category, the second category in all but one case the first section in the city inhabitants book, as an owner of immovable property. A third of the applicants noted the number of years they had lived in St. Petersburg. Only one indicated that he had been a resident of the city for more than ten years (he claimed to have moved there in 1768), with half of the remainder citing residence for more than five years. Judging from surnames, the vast majority were Russian. If all were licensed, there was one tavern in the city for every 950 people or so.

Firewood

Besides bread and drink, the authorities had to concern themselves with the supply of fuel, needed for heating, cooking, and industrial purposes. The demand intensified during the period under consideration. The particular necessity of supplying sufficient fuel to last through the long, bitter Russian winter is obvious. To meet the need, Russians traditionally turned to wood.[60] As forests around St. Petersburg were cleared, the source of firewood moved ever farther from the city. As early as 1755, decrees were issued to restrict the number of factories in St. Petersburg that made intensive use of wood fuel in their manufacturing processes.[61] The government farsightedly attempted to preserve some nearby forests, but this meant that logs had to be brought still farther to the fireplaces, stoves, hearths, and ovens of the capital. The problem of fuel supply therefore became more intense in two distinct ways. With an ever-larger city, demand increased steadily, as it did for other items like food and building materials. But whereas the source of supply for other goods remained fairly stable geographically, firewood had to be brought over increasing distances. The combination of both factors served to push the price up as well as produce doubt about the sufficiency of supply in future years.

Once this situation became clear, the government interposed itself in case private commerce might not meet the city's needs. It is not known when the first firewood warehouse appeared, but by the 1780s such a depot existed in Second Admiralty along the Moika.[62] In November 1783, to stem an apparent shortage of fuel, it began to sell wood at a low price to the poor, limiting purchase to a precisely defined small quantity. Alarmed by the particular shortage that year, but also because the problem had been developing over several years, Catherine named a commission to discover why firewood was so expensive, why shortages occurred, and to propose a solution. The commission's findings shed much light on the process of fuel supply and hint at the process of supply of other goods.

The commission first sought to determine whether, in fact, shortages existed. It discovered that most people by November purchased sufficient firewood to last the winter and that enough remained on sale in some quarters to fill the needs of sections where supply was exhausted. In addition, smaller amounts of wood continued to trickle into the city during early winter. For these reasons commission members as well as merchants dealing in firewood felt that there could be no insurmountable shortage, at least not in 1783.

Still, prices had risen. The commission investigated the reasons, examining in detail every aspect of the industry. It learned that merchants often forced upriver peasants to sell firewood at disadvantageous prices by reminding them of the restrictions on peasant commerce in the capital. Many merchants thus had permanent suppliers or owned land and hired their own workers to do the timbering. A small number of merchants, almost exclusively from Novgorod and Novaia Ladoga—the largest towns in the timbering area—controlled the business, mutually agreeing to keep prices high in order to maximize profits.

This explained generally why prices continued to rise, but there were other problems. There was no suitable, convenient, inexpensive place in the city to unload and store firewood until it was sold. Instead, merchants leased land along the riverbanks for two or three hundred rubles, receiving part of the outlay in rebate as the wood was sold. In addition to this expense, the privately run pontoon bridge across the river charged excessively high rates to allow vessels loaded with wood to pass. A final problem was that in 1783 the use of short logs was proscribed, but not until most wood had been timbered and was on its way to the city. Thus much available fuel could not be sold legally.

To correct these deficiencies the commission proposed specific changes to encourage both peasants and merchants to trade in firewood, to establish a firewood market, and to enlarge the warehouse. To ensure proper cutting, it strongly recommended that wooded lands in the Ladoga and Onega areas be parceled out and surveyed.[63]

Throughout the century firewood supply barely kept up with demand. Indeed, boats and barges utilized to convey goods to the city were often chopped up and sold for fuel rather than pulled back upstream. But through the implementation of the commission's proposals, the firewood supply achieved some measure of stability, even if rising prices could not be completely stemmed.[64]

Government Actions

Government increasingly assumed responsibility for guaranteeing adequate provisions of essential products—food, fuel, and building materials—throughout Catherine's reign. As the city expanded and its supply problems became more complex, the establishment of warehouses under governmental direction helped ward off disasters that, without comprehensive and farsighted planning, might befall a city in St. Petersburg's geographical situation. By assuming control over supply only during crises, the government left private commerce free to provision the city at all other times. This is not to say, however, that in every instance administrative bodies acted wisely or responsibly.

Through the police, the state maintained a keen interest in the city's price structure. Insufficient evidence remains to draw exact price relationships for the period under consideration, but there is enough to warrant a fairly accurate generalization. Through the latter third of the century, food prices rose steadily. The amount of bread that ten kopecks would buy in 1768 was approximately half what it had been in 1764.[65] From 1767 to 1775 prices on selected foodstuffs increased an average of 25 percent; one or two items went up as much as 100 percent.[66] Part of the increase was due to inflation and the ongoing war with Turkey, but food costs as a percentage of the cost of living also increased during this period. So that a close watch could be maintained over food prices (an index for determining whether supply continued to be adequate), the police chief supplied Catherine with a semiweekly register listing prices of all produce sold in the capital. The government actually determined retail prices of foodstuffs, requiring shops to sell comestibles for 10 percent above their wholesale price.

The rise in prices over a number of years did not mean that there were exaggerated fluctuations from season to season. On the contrary, there was surprising uniformity in prices at all times of the year—officially, at least. Some items became noticeably more dear in late winter, but prices usually fluctuated no more than 20 percent, maintaining the same ratio between wholesale and retail prices. Even in late winter luxury items could still be found: lemons, olives, coffee and tea, anchovies, imported cheeses, and Rhine wines among them.[67] A member of the Academy of Sciences remarked with some irritation that, despite great stores and warehouses filled with goods, it was difficult at any time to procure retail amounts of small but essential items such as coffee, tea, sugar, vinegar, string and thread, sealing wax, nails, writing paper, and candles. With considerable effort one might find a small shop, probably hidden in a basement somewhere, in which the proprietor offered such items, charging unreasonably high prices for the goods.[68]

On the other hand, there is evidence incidental to a case involving a protested *veksel'* in 1791–92 indicating the ease with which luxury food items could be gotten, and in plentiful quantity. Ivan Kalitin, a St. Petersburg merchant involved in the litigation, regularly bought coffee, tea, sugar, and other items from Mokei Undozerov, who was subletting Kalitin's shop in the great bazaar on Nevskii Prospect, charging his purchases to his account:

November 28, 1791: a "head" of sugar; 5 pounds coffee;
December 5: 14 pounds of "head" sugar; 1 pound black tea; 5 pounds coffee;
December 9: half a pud of sugar; 1 pound black tea; 5 pounds coffee;
December 11: 10 pounds of sugar; 5 pounds [wig] powder; 4 jars pomade.
December 17: 20 pounds of sugar;
December 22: 14 pounds of "head" sugar; 1 pound black tea; 5 pounds coffee;
December 24: 3 pounds of wood oil; a pitcher of sweet clover;
December 31: a pud of sugar; 8 pounds coffee; 1 pound each black and green tea; 5 pounds [wig] powder; 4 jars French pomade;
January 4, 1792: a pud of refined sugar;
January 25: half a pud of sugar; 10 pounds of "only the best sort" of coffee;
January 31: the same quantities of both items;
February 8: 30 pounds of "the best" sugar; 5 pounds coffee, 1 pound green tea;
February 10: 11 pounds of "head" sugar;
February 21: 10 pounds of sugar; 10 pounds coffee;
March 2: a pud of sugar; 15 pounds green tea; 2 pounds black tea; 8 pounds powder; 4 jars pomade; 1000 sheets of No. 1 paper;
March 12: 12 pounds of "head" sugar.[69]

This rather long list provides evidence both of the availability of luxury items throughout the winter and of the degree to which an "average" merchant household consumed them. Over the course of less than four months more than 250 pounds of sugar were purchased, 63 pounds of coffee, 6 pounds of black tea and 17 pounds of green tea, plus 13 pounds of wig powder, and 12 jars of pomade and other products. All this for the household of a Russian merchant!

Prices of clothing, furniture and furnishings, and building materials were not watched as closely as food costs. Consequently fewer documents record these prices. The relationship of wholesale to retail prices remained the same—a 10 percent markup.[70] Inflation drove all prices upward throughout the period under consideration. This rise in prices was not limited to St. Petersburg. The same phenomenon occurred throughout the country. Real prices of goods in great demand in the city—building materials, firewood, and hay, for example—rose to a greater extent. In spite of the fact that everyday necessities cost more at the end of the period than at the beginning, the processes of supply functioned more efficiently.

By the end of the century the viability of St. Petersburg could not be doubted. Despite the fact that most of life's necessities were much more expensive there than in the interior of the country and that prices tended to rise ever higher, the goods necessary for the day-to-day existence of the city clearly could be—and were—supplied, sometimes across vast distances. Merchants from the interior had realized that profits might be earned by transporting essential products to the capital. In so doing they established trading routes that could be used for moving other sorts of goods, too—such as wares intended for exportation, which will be discussed in the next chapter. The synchronized and well-developed supply system of life's necessities lay at the root of a new, independent stage in the city's life. Daily needs were provided to a great extent by the market. Hired labor carried out much of the work of transport, supply, and sales. Where a need was perceived to exist, someone attempted to meet it. Prices were controlled within certain limits, although there is some evidence to argue that price limits were only official. What was reported to the authorities and what was actually done may not always have coincided. If this was true for the commerce to meet the city's daily needs, it was also true for the commercial activity on a grander scale, the import and export of goods.

6
"The Empire's Most Principal Emporium": Commerce

St. Petersburg's role as a center of commercial activity antedated its selection as Russia's capital. For all that has been written about the area's hostile climate and nature's resistance to human habitation there, a limited amount of trade took place there well before Peter the Great set foot on the Neva's delta. In the days of Lord Novgorod the Great, Hanseatic ships plied the river. In the seventeenth century the Swedes built a small fort, Nienshants (in Swedish Nyenskans), at the confluence of the Okhta and the Neva, and by the 1690s more than a hundred merchant ships per year visited the small port.[1] Peter's new city fell heir to this trade, beginning with the celebrated Dutch ship in 1703 that braved the war in northern waters. Thus from the start St. Petersburg had a commercial side, and the city played a major role in giving new life to the mercantile population in Russia.

Historically, merchants had not fared well in Russia. The nobility did not like them and the Church did not trust the acquisitive spirit that they embodied. The state saw the urban population, and especially merchants, as sources of revenue. Merchants often were deputized to collect taxes and then held personally liable when shortfalls occurred, as they always did sooner or later. The merchants had no corporate organization to represent their interests; many of those registered for tax purposes as *kuptsy* (merchants) in fact made their living by agriculture and handicraft production.[2] Prior to the founding of St. Petersburg, only Moscow and Arkhangel'sk differed significantly from this pattern, the former because of its dominant position in the politics and geography of the central productive region of Russia, and the latter because of the influx of foreign merchants in the seventeenth century.

By the time of Catherine II, St. Petersburg had far surpassed Arkhangel'sk in commercial turnover and, although its role was quite different, could almost challenge Moscow in mercantile significance.

Unlike Moscow, St. Petersburg drew much of its commercial strength from the import-export trade. While the presence of court and government assured the continued existence of St. Petersburg, they characterized only a *Residenzstadt,* not a metropolis. It was the city's extensive commerce that guaranteed a continuing, sustained urbanization beyond the "subsistence level" of simply meeting the city's own needs and desires.[3] The trade necessary to maintain the economic viability of the city, discussed in the previous chapter, represented an essential segment of the total commercial activity in St. Petersburg. But the role of the port city, the increasing importance of the capital's commercial turnover for the Russian economy, and the city's visible role in European maritime commerce must be seen as an important aspect in the city's life and development. J. G. Georgi, the author of the most complete book about St. Petersburg published in the eighteenth century, used the superlative form of the adjective *glavnyi* (principal, chief, main) to describe the city's commercial role in Russia. St. Petersburg was not simply the "chief" or "principle" center of trade in the empire, it was the *glavneishii,* the most important, emporium.

The Place of Commerce

The primary sites for wholesale trade are already familiar to the reader: the area around the bourse and customhouse at the easternmost point of Vasil'evskii Island, Kronshtadt, the Admiralty Side bazaar, and the wide expanse of riverbank near Smolnyi where goods from the interior were unloaded, sorted, and transferred. To the casual observer, it seemed that most activity took place at Vasil'evskii Island's wharves. A contemporary engraving shows boxes, casks, bales, and assorted hardware—anchors, rope, lumber—stacked or strewn about on the pier. Here and there men push loaded wheelbarrows or strain to move the bulky containers of goods. Merchants immersed in conversation stroll along the wharf, oblivious to the yapping dogs racing this way and that. Merchant ships, anchored close together and lying low in the water, disgorge their wares into dories shuttling back and forth to the dock.[4] Well-dressed ladies at the edge of the landing peer into a ship's hold as if to ascertain the latest Parisian style. Meanwhile a longshoreman, heavy sacks pressing down on his shoulders, can be seen furtively relieving himself behind a column of the arcaded warehouse.[5]

The engraving illustrates the two-tiered trade that took place at the wharves. Ships' manifests listed the bulk commodities and wares being imported. In addition to those wholesale goods, skippers and sailors imported items for sale in small quantities or lots, items on which customs duties were paid separately from those on the ship's bill of lading. The way this trade in imported goods operated was revealed in some considerations made by Court Councillor Farber in 1778 for the Commission on Commerce.[6] He presented his commentary somewhat self-consciously, noting that what he had to say was probably known to everyone already. Ships' captains and crews brought barrels, boxes, pots, and packages of foodstuffs and household items that varied with their ports of origin and distance from St. Petersburg. During the time while a ship's hold was being emptied of its wares and following the ship's repositioning to the warehouse wharves for loading prior to departure, a period of time lasting altogether up to fifteen days, the captains and crew members sold the items they had brought personally. If they had not sold everything by the time they sailed, they unloaded whatever remained at low prices to poorer townspeople, including soldiers' and sailors' wives, for them to sell in the city at whatever price they could get. Farber spoke in defense of this form of importation, legal under Article 47 of the maritime tariff regulation, because it helped provide a living for poorer townspeople as well as for those not officially registered in the city but still needing to earn a living.

By the end of the 1770s the wharves were so crowded that ships sometimes stood three and four deep, complicating the loading and unloading of wares. Storage facilities were so overcrowded that there was virtually no place to warehouse all of the bar iron and hemp, two major items of export, and consideration was given to renting basements in private dwellings and various buildings in the neighborhood housing other government offices as a temporary solution. Projects calling for an extension of the wharves downstream on the Neva toward the buildings housing the Kunstkamera and the Academy of Sciences were approved in 1780 but never brought to fruition.[7] The other commercial sites bustled with similar activity. They too were centers of large-scale trade, wholesale as well as retail.

Commercial enterprise extended well beyond these few areas, of course. Individual merchants and artisans living throughout the city sold wares from their homes or rented quarters, accounting for a large proportion of the city's overall commerce.[8] Before 1763 they were prohibited on some of the better streets from putting up signs to mark their shops, but Catherine did away with this restriction. Some traders had no permanent location from which to sell goods. Known as *raznoshchiki*, they walked the streets hawking their wares. The turnover of each street peddler was quite small, of course, yet taken together such traders accounted for considerable turnover of goods.

Wares coming from the Russian interior invariably followed river and canal routes downstream to the city. Those returning to the interior of the empire traveled by road or, in winter, by sledge up the frozen rivers. A particular mode of transport was selected out of consideration of cost and convenience. These land and water routes were heavily traveled. By the midpoint of Catherine's reign more than twelve thousand river craft, carrying virtually all the goods coming to the capital from distant areas of Russia, passed annually through Vyshnii Volochek canal en route to St. Petersburg. Couriers were sent overland to St. Petersburg, which they could easily reach in a week, to inform the capital city of the imminent arrival within two more weeks of the flotillas of goods-carrying boats and barges. The information helped keep prices stable, as merchants in the capital were informed through the pages of the newspaper published by the Academy of Sciences, *Sanktpeterburgskie vedomosti,* of the number of vessels and the points of origin. The reports were longer and provided more details when the traffic came from unusually distant places—Orenburg, Nizhnii Novgorod, or Astrakhan, for instance—and caravans were especially large.[9]

The commercial process relied heavily upon merchants from the interior, who provided goods both for export and for use in the city. For the most part these merchants operated on a small scale, frequently maintaining a loose relationship with a firm in St. Petersburg to represent them in their absence. They themselves or their contractors made annual journeys to St. Petersburg to deliver wares already under contract and conclude agreements for future delivery. An example can be seen in the business of the merchant from the town of Dmitrov, Ivan Alekseevich Tolchenov, analyzed by David Ransel.[10] Contracts for goods to be exported were invariably made with the foreign merchants who controlled overseas commerce.

Because the Russian merchants from towns in the interior of the empire provided the non-Russian trading companies with their access to exportable merchandise, the foreign merchants in St. Petersburg proved willing to provide them with credit, most frequently through the use of promissory notes.[11] A unique archival holding from 1773 provides a glimpse into the workings of this mechanism. The source consists of a list of all negotiable notes "protested" in St. Petersburg in that year.[12] A note was "protested" before a notary public by the person holding it when no one would redeem the note for cash or accept it in payment. This usually occurred because potential "accepters" doubted the debt could eventually be recouped from the "payer" designated in the note.[13] In 1773 notes were protested in St. Petersburg by or against Russian merchants from more than a hundred towns throughout the empire. These were not simply random occurrences. Ten notes or more were protested against merchants in nearly forty of those towns. If these "protests" can be taken as a measure of which Russian merchants from the interior were trading in St. Petersburg, an interesting pattern emerges (see map 5). Merchants from such nearby towns and cities as Riga, Reval, Vyborg, Novgorod, Pskov, Narva, Novaia Ladoga, and Olonets came to St. Petersburg to trade, but so did those from a parade of towns on the Volga, including Ostashkov, Rzhev, Staritsa, and Tver' on its upper reaches; Kashin, Uglich, Mologa, Rybinsk (Rybnaia Sloboda), Romanov, Borisoglebsk, Iaroslavl', Kostroma, Kineshma, Iurevets, Nizhnii Novgorod, and Kazan' in the middle course of the river; and Simbirsk, Syzran', Saratov, and Astrakhan on the lower portion of the river. Besides the middle Volga, the provinces of Moscow (Moscow, Zvenigorod, Volokolamsk, Dmitrov, Kolomna, Serpukhov, Mozhaisk), Kaluga (Kaluga, Vereia, Borovsk, Peremyshl', Kozel'sk, Meshchovsk, Mosal'sk), and Orel (Orel, Briansk, Karachev, Bolkhov, Mtsensk, Elets, Trubchevsk) were well represented by itinerant merchants. Others came from the northern and northeastern towns of Kargopol'e, Kholmogory, Arkhangel'sk, Vologda, Sol' Galitskaia, Sol'vychegodsk, Velikii Ustiug, and Slobodskoi. Two merchants from faraway Irkutsk appear on the list. Virtually none came from the Ukraine, however, with Poltava the sole exception. None of the towns on the Dnepr, not excepting Smolensk and Kiev, seems to have been involved in trade with St. Petersburg, except for Dorogobuzh, far upstream near the portage to other river systems. None of the newer towns south of Kursk, Voronezh, and Tambov seem to have had much trade with St. Petersburg. The list of protested notes reveals only those cases in which a transaction went sour; one can only guess at the amount of trade successfully negotiated through this simple means of providing credit.

Few other credit facilities existed. No differentiation had yet emerged between banker and merchant, at least in the realm of commercial credit. Despite the fact that the wealthiest native-Russian merchants in St. Petersburg were themselves able occasionally to act as bankers, credit was generally advanced by agents in St. Petersburg for commercial firms with their home offices abroad. Lacking its own exchange facilities, St. Petersburg was dependent for negotiating contracts in foreign trade upon bourses and discount houses elsewhere in Europe. Most of this business continued throughout Catherine's reign to go to Amsterdam, frequently through intermediaries in Warsaw, Vienna, and Frankfurt.

Even though the total value of goods bought and sold in St. Petersburg was enormous, the technological level of the city's commercial

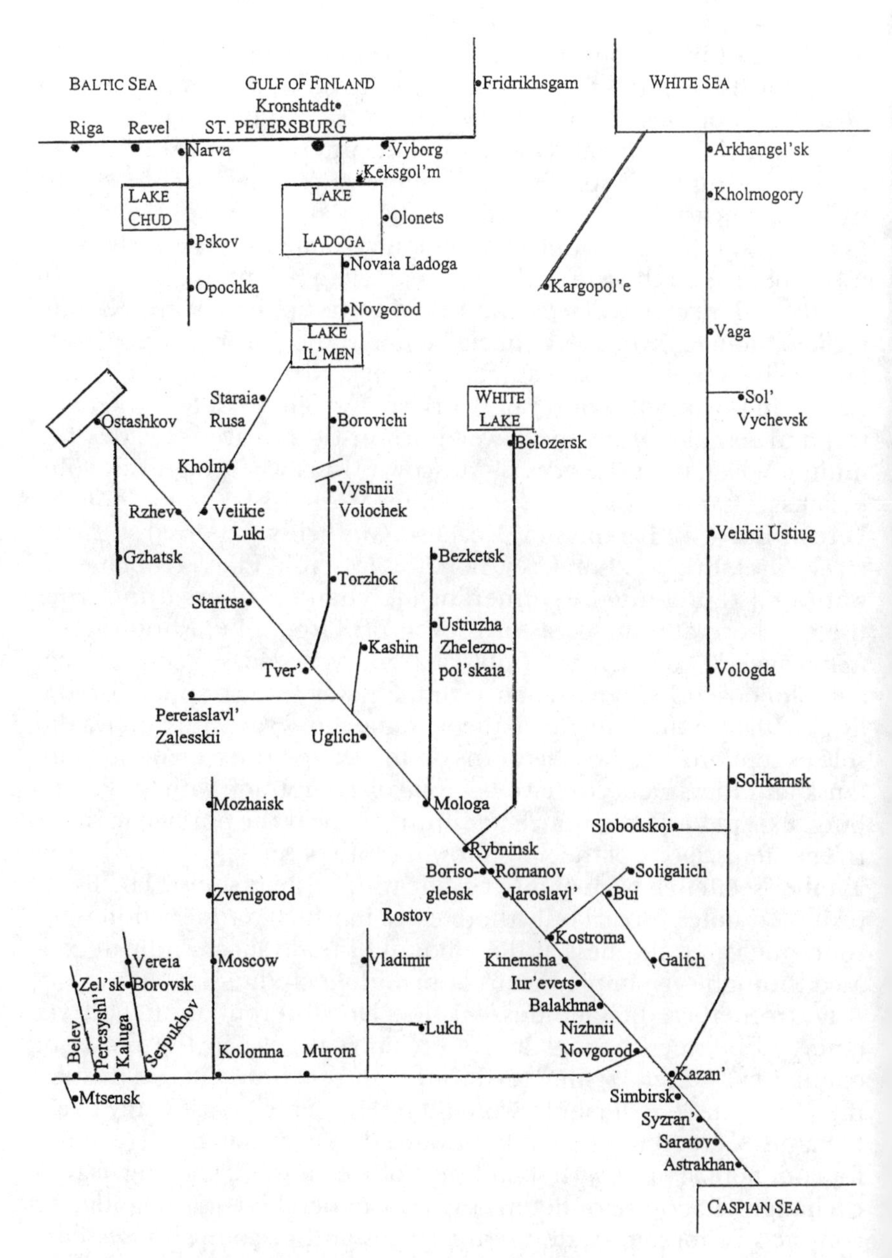

Schematic map: Trade connections with St. Petersburg.

relations remained remarkably simple. In most instances, the retail merchants from the interior received partial payment prior to their delivery of wares to the capital. At times they received full value for goods on no more substantial grounds than their promise to deliver. Contracts were registered in court, although the value of this procedure in constraining merchants from the interior was uncertain. Foreign agents in the city did not like to pay for goods before receiving them, but could do little to change the situation since they could not legally undertake retail trade in the interior of the country. Foreign merchants often complained that the Russians used their position advantageously, accusing them of being quite cunning, adept at eliciting favorable prices and gaining unfair advantage from their business deals, although they rarely kept ledgers, performing most calculations either on the abacus or mentally.[14] These complaints were voiced, it should be noted, by merchants who continued to do business in St. Petersburg for a number of years, and who must have been turning a fair profit themselves. On occasion, of course, merchants from the interior who had been paid in advance did fail to deliver the contracted goods to St. Petersburg.[15] In general, however, the wares appeared after a few months, having successfully negotiated the water route (except for a few goods of high value relative to bulk, such as Russia leather, which might come overland). Licensed brackers or sorters in St. Petersburg examined the goods to ensure that quality was commensurate with contractual stipulations. The Russian merchants then received whatever money the foreign agents still owed them for the goods.[16]

The merchants from the interior next arranged to dispose of the craft on which they had transported their wares. These rafts or barges were flat-bottomed, built of good fir. With gunwales some four feet high and drafts of twenty to thirty inches, they were not small craft. Although it cost from one to three hundred rubles to construct a raft, each one only made a single run to the city, for two reasons. First, it was difficult to renegotiate the water system going upstream, and second, there was a ready use for rafts in the capital.[17] If no one expressed interest in utilizing rafts for transporting wares within the city, merchants could realize from twenty to fifty rubles from each by selling them as fuel because of the high price of firewood in the capital.[18]

As noted above, the arrangements between Russian merchants from the interior and foreign export houses in St. Petersburg compensated for the weakness or outright absence of financial institutions in Russia's capital. By contracting prior to delivery, Russian merchants escaped the burden of financial risk in shipping their goods, receiving enough money in advance to purchase and transport the merchandise, and making their profit at the end of the operation. Not all business was conducted in this manner, however. A few merchants did have the means to bring exportable goods to market without contracts, either selling their wares at the market price or stockpiling them, awaiting more favorable prices. In the former case, the merchandise was sold at the docks near Smolnyi before being unloaded. Unsold goods were put in temporary storehouses or simply spread under mats, boats, overturned rafts, or some other protective material. At least one merchant from each flotilla of rafts remained in the city to sell the remaining cargo.[19] The ability of such merchants both to ship goods at their own expense and to wait for a favorable price change indicates that they may have operated on a larger scale than most merchants from the interior. Prior to the great fire that consumed them in 1780, the hemp and flax warehouses on an island in the Small Neva provided storage facilities for those primary goods of Russian export. The accounting made following the fire indicates a substantial number of Russian merchants from the interior trading on their own accounts.[20]

Imported goods were distributed throughout Russia in the reverse of the pattern just described. Russian merchants from the interior bargained for and received imported goods, taking wares on credit for three, six, nine, or even twelve months. Interest rates on promissory notes were limited by law to 6 percent, but the shortage of credit and vicissitudes of trade forced the rate much higher unofficially. It seems to have hovered around 20 percent, yet Russians preferred—or were compelled by circumstances—to do business this way. Again, they at times bilked their foreign counterparts in the capital by taking goods on credit but never reappearing to pay for them, leaving the latter no effective legal recourse.

The extent of foreign trade can be measured roughly by counting the number of ships calling at Kronshtadt each year. Statistics compiled by one merchant showed that the number of ships increased markedly during Catherine's reign. In the early 1760s, from 288 to 387 ships called at St. Petersburg annually.[21] By the mid-1770s more than seven hundred vessels came each year. The figure swung upward until 1790, when more than a thousand ships took on or let off cargo. This activity was crowded into seven months of the year, since the port was open only from late April to mid-November.[22] A few annual fluctuations were evident, however, especially during the diplomatic crisis of 1780, brought about by the American War of Independence.[23] No interruption in the expansion of commercial turnover lasted more than a year.

One of the characteristics of St. Petersburg's foreign trade was that many ships arrived in ballast and left laden with wares. In selected years for which there are data, some 45 percent of ships arriving at the port reported carrying only ballast. Of those with lading, only about two-thirds reported that they were fully loaded. On the other hand, virtually all ships left St. Petersburg fully laden.[24] In 1786 an order was issued that ships passing through the Danish Sound at Elsinore bound for Kronshtadt take on rock and stone as ballast, materials that could be used later for construction in Kronshtadt and St. Petersburg. British skippers in particular were accused of evading this regulation, preferring to load sand as ballast before leaving England in order to avoid the charges for off-loading the rock and stone. Kronshtadt's harbor master complained that skippers dumped the sand just before arriving at the roads in Kronshtadt. He warned of the danger of the harbor's mouth silting up, claiming in 1791 that the water already was not as deep as in earlier years and that ships once freed of ballast had difficulty maneuvering in the harbor under their own sail power.[25]

Statistics indicating the total value of imports and exports are by no means complete, but those that do exist permit several generalizations (see graph 6.1).[26] During Catherine's reign, not only was there a constant rise in foreign trade through St. Petersburg, but the increase over twenty-five years amounted to more than 300 percent. Furthermore, according to official figures, the total value of imports exceeded that of exports in only two years for which statistics exist. Undoubtedly St. Petersburg, home to the court and the wealthiest nobility, had a larger appetite for imported goods than anyplace else in Russia. In 1783, one of the two years noted above, the value of imports exceeded that of exports by more than a million and a half rubles (11.67 million to 10.1 million). In the same year Riga, Russia's second port in terms of volume and value of goods, imported 1.45 million rubles worth of goods and exported 5.86 million rubles in value.[27]

The ratio of imports to exports may have been altered considerably by smuggling, since government officials assumed that far more was smuggled in than out. Judging from the policies implemented in the late 1780s to limit smuggling, policy makers attributed the problem much more to overland border points than to St. Petersburg itself. A prohibition on importation through border points, implemented in 1789, was intended to funnel imported goods primarily through St. Petersburg. The president of the Commerce Commission and the Commerce College, Count Alexander R. Vorontsov, assured Catherine that St. Petersburg and Riga were diligent in collecting customs duties, yet at the same time estimated that more than a million rubles worth of goods were smuggled into Russia through St. Petersburg in 1783, nearly a tenth of the volume of goods on which duties were paid.[28] It

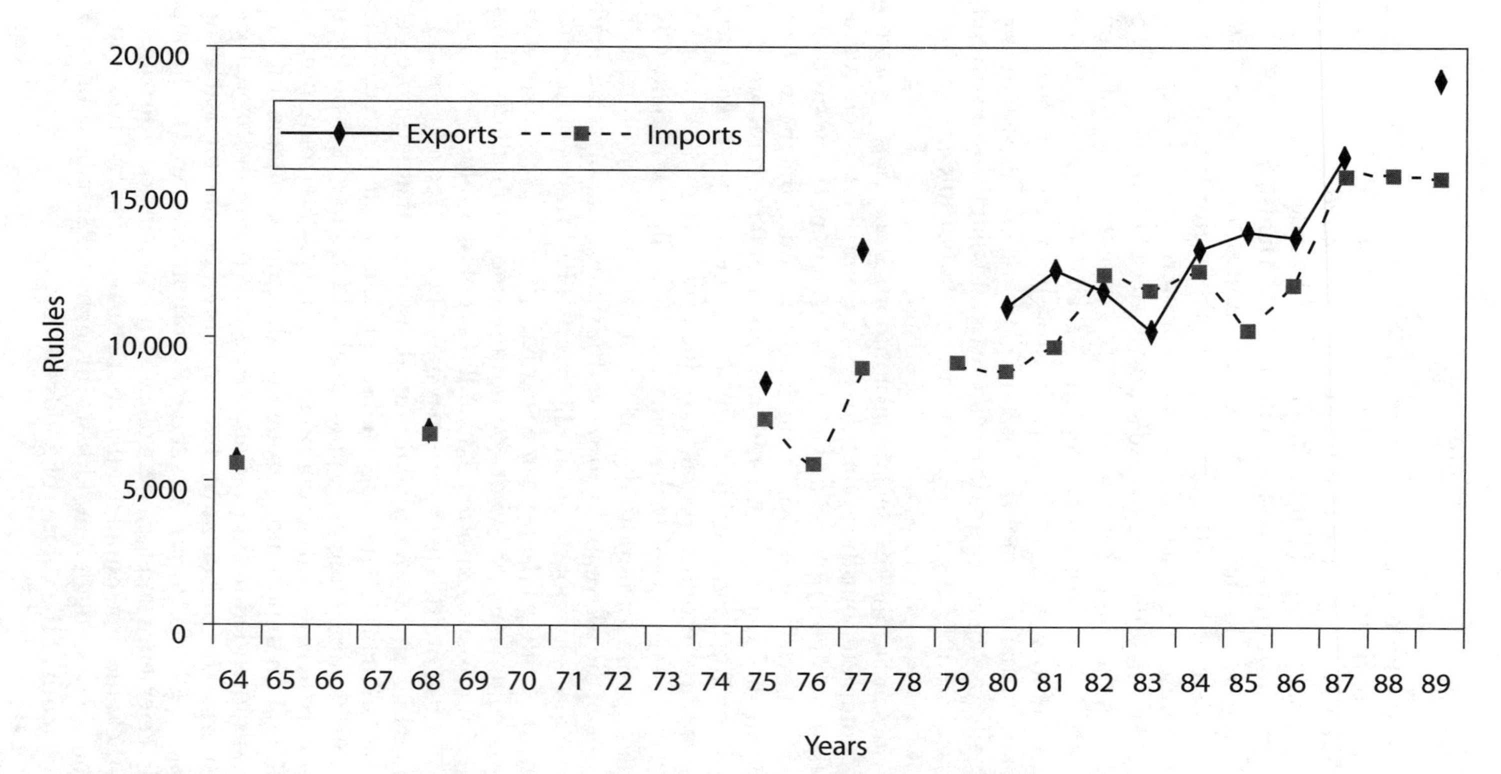

Graph 6.1. Value of Imports and Exports Passing through St. Petersburg, 1764–89 (thousands of rubles)

Table 6.1. Percentage of Russia's Foreign Trade Handled Through St. Petersburg

Year	Percentage	Year	Percentage
1762	40.6	1780	55.6
1763	45.9	1781	52.2
1764	51.3	1782	54.5
1765	52.7	1783	43.0
1766	49.6	1784	49.0
1767	53.4	1785	53.1
1768	50.8	1786	58.5
1769	52.4	1787	61.7
1770	50.1	1788	70.7
1771	52.0	1789	69.8
1772	41.0	1790	66.1
1773	49.2	1791	58.3
1774	54.0	1792	54.5
1775	44.6	1793	54.1
1776	49.7	1794	56.2
1777	54.1	1795	58.3
1778	53.1	1796	54.8
1779	59.6		

Source: Kahan, *The Plow, the Hammer, and the Knout,* table 4.1, 164.

is impossible, of course, to gauge the extent of smuggling, but its implied existence should instill caution in attempting to make too much of official figures, which whatever one may make of them do at least give baseline figures for both imports and exports.

A third measure of overseas commerce in St. Petersburg can be found in the figures showing St. Petersburg's role in Russia's aggregate foreign trade. Table 6.1, based on the current ruble value of exports, demonstrates that St. Petersburg's importance increased during Catherine's reign, during the last third of which nearly three-fifths of all Russian external trade passed through that one port city.[29]

Kronshtadt was developed into an excellent port. Safe from the most severe storms, it was able to accommodate as many as three hundred ships at once.[30] Goods were transferred there from ships to galleys for transportation to docks in the city itself. The larger vessels could not pass sandbars in the Neva's mouth while fully loaded. The families living in Galley Haven at the southwestern extremity of Vasil'evskii Island manned the oared boats that made up for an obvious deficiency in the city's harbor system. By the end of the 1780s merchants registered in St. Petersburg and other Russian towns owned

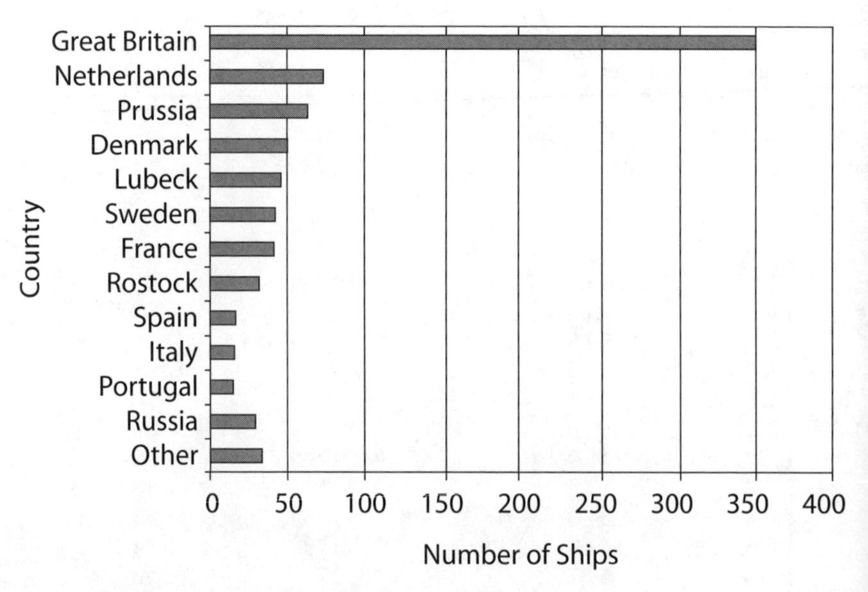

Graph 6.2. Flags of Ships Trading in St. Petersburg, 1775–90

nearly three hundred boats involved in the carrying trade between St. Petersburg and Kronshtadt, with a capacity of almost twenty thousand lasts.[31]

Nearly all the ships plying maritime trade flew foreign flags, just under half of them (43.7 percent) British.[32] Graph 6.2 shows the distribution of ownership of these ships. More than half the maritime trade was in the hands of the two states that dominated shipping in the eighteenth century, Great Britain, and the United Provinces. Three Baltic Sea states and France also owned more ships calling on St. Petersburg than did Russia. For the most part, the trade had a regional quality, for it centered in the areas of the Baltic (34.7 percent) and North (53.9 percent) seas (together, 88.6 percent). An annual average of only thirty-three ships plying international trade routes flew the Russian colors, vividly illustrating the extent to which foreigners dominated international shipping. The government encouraged Russians to enter more actively into international commerce by granting favorable excise duties for goods carried in Russian bottoms and providing credit facilities, yet for various reasons these efforts failed.

Earlier in the century, one foreigner explained that Russians lacked the skills to run ships, pointing out that many of the ships that Russians put to sea were soon wrecked.[33] Count Alexander Vorontsov, who had greater responsibility for Russia's commercial policy than anyone else in Catherine's reign, remarked in an undated memorandum on ways to improve commerce in St. Petersburg that "it is known that Russian ships are built to accurate rules of architecture and are as seaworthy as those of other nations; but as to skippers, navigators, pilots, and ship's officers, they unquestionably must be provided from other lands and used until such time as Russians possessing a greater inclination to seafaring and navigation acquire the appropriate knowledge."[34]

Count Vorontsov's point is well taken. With no maritime tradition, few Russians had the requisite knowledge, skill, or desire to enter foreign commerce. Likewise, few had sufficient fluid capital to outfit and operate merchant ships. But with the emergence of St. Petersburg, these limitations began to disappear. During Catherine's reign the absolute dominance of foreigners in the capital's maritime commercial sphere began to diminish as increasing numbers of Russian merchants gained the experience, wealth, and technical competence to venture into international trade. Russians began to handle foreign trade themselves, in Russian ships.[35] Far more of them became importers than exporters. Foreigners continued to control trade leaving the city, while slowly making way for Russian participation in the import business. Not only the wares shipped but the ships themselves, insurance, and brokerage were for the most part in foreign hands. Russians thus proved unable to take full advantage of their government's favorable excise duties on goods shipped by native merchants.[36] Despite the campaign in the mid-1780s to persuade foreign skippers to gain the same advantages as Russians by becoming Russian subjects, a strong "Russian" merchant marine was not created.[37]

Merchants

It is clear from the preceding pages that foreign merchants, Russian traders from the interior, and native Russians in St. Petersburg all participated in the city's trade. But who exactly were these merchants? How large was their number? How did they live? What were their values?

To be considered merchants by the law, traders had to be registered in one of three guilds (two before 1775). This applied to Russians and foreigners alike, and in 1789, more than two thousand individuals were so registered in the capital. The number was constantly in flux. The committee that was assigned the task of compiling the city inhabitants book after the promulgation of the Charter to the Towns in 1785 prepared a list of all those newly registering as St. Petersburg

Table 6.2. Social origins of newly registered merchants in St. Petersburg, 1786

Merchants		42
Russian	29	
Foreign	13	
Petty Townsmen		17
Peasants		54
State	20	
Economic	25	
Freed serfs	9	
Other		6
TOTAL		119

Source: Arkhiv SPbF IRI RAN, *fond* 36, *opis'* 2, *delo* 9, *listy* 51–56.

merchants in the first ten months of 1786 (table 6.2).[38] They registered as individuals but also as family groups including as many as five people. Thus the 119 registrants comprised a total of 186 individuals. Of those 119 registrants, twenty-nine were merchants from other Russian towns and thirteen merchants from other states. An additional seventeen were petty townsmen from various Russian towns (only one from St. Petersburg) whose declared capital now permitted them to register in the wealthier category of merchant. Other registrants included a master artisan, a postman, "free men," and a "Jew converted to the Greek faith." Nearly half of the registrants (45.4 percent) came from the peasantry, including freed serfs (9, one-sixth of the total number of peasants), state peasants (20), and economic peasants (25), that is, those coming from villages formerly belonging to monasteries. The large number of peasants registering as merchants underlines the point made earlier in chapter 2 that the formal legal categories for subjects of the Russian Empire underwent transformations in the matrix of St. Petersburg. Seven of the new registrants were women, for the most part widows. With one exception, all of the Russians registered in the third, or least wealthy, guild, most of them declaring capital in the range between 1,005 (thirty cases) and 1,050 (eleven cases) rubles. A freed serf registered in the second guild. Seven of the foreigners registered in the third guild, one in the second, and five in the first. The St. Petersburg merchants were a diverse group.

Large numbers of people involved in commercial activities seemingly neglected or avoided registering as merchants, including some foreign factors whose business was quite considerable. The large transient population, estimated by Alexander N. Radishchev in the 1780s at thirty thousand, was in part composed of men not registered as merchants who nevertheless came to the city for a brief time each year to buy or sell goods for import, export, or urban use.[39]

Registered merchants sought to limit the commercial activity open to nonregistered people. Agreeing that commerce should be the exclusive domain of merchants, Catherine II issued laws permitting peasants to sell only certain types of produce in the city. When nonregistered traders were discovered selling wares, merchants in guilds complained to such authorities as the city council. On a recommendation by a first-guild representative, the city council in 1789 required the committee preparing the register of city inhabitants to compile a separate register of people engaged in trade and commerce, along with their places of business, whether home, shop, or basement. Legal merchants hoped that this would make it easier to limit the large numbers of "unregistered foreigners" and Russian traders not in guilds.[40] Like earlier attempts to eradicate unlawful commercial activity, the law was insufficiently enforced. Wealthy foreign agents as well as Russian part-time merchants, the transient residents of the city, continued to trade both in markets and on the streets.

Numerous merchants registered in other Russian cities lived in St. Petersburg at least part of each year. The exact number of such merchants can only be estimated. Extant statistics do indicate that among traders in the capital the proportion of merchants commercially active in St. Petersburg but registered in other cities was very high.[41]

Consider the merchants involved in the export of flax and hemp. Following the 1780 fire in the hemp and flax warehouses, the Commerce College carefully recorded the names and addresses of the 113 merchants who lost goods in the blaze. Only seventeen of those merchants were registered in St. Petersburg. Two merchants came from Tver', nineteen from Kaluga, six from Serpukhov, eighteen from Rzhev, five from Staraia Rusa, three from Moscow, and forty-three others from different areas. Thus, fewer than one-fifth of the affected merchants were local residents.[42] Merchants from other areas lost far more goods than St. Petersburg merchants, who owned only a negligible percentage of the hemp, flax, and tobacco destroyed.[43] The minor role of St. Petersburg merchants is further demonstrated by the fact that none of the twenty-one merchants on duty in the warehouse on the day it burned were registered in St. Petersburg.[44] The hemp and flax markets were among the most important of all markets, for together with iron they were Russia's primary exports during this period. Goods from the interior destined for export passed directly from the hands of merchants from provincial towns to the care of foreign factors. St.

Petersburg was the depot, but its merchants shared insignificantly in the transaction. Presumably this was also true of such other exported wares as iron, isinglass, grain, and timber.

Local merchants rented shops in bazaars or markets or sold goods from other permanent locations. The law limited each shop to a narrow range of items. Merchants who wished to diversify had to maintain shops in different areas. Wives, brothers, sons, nephews, in-laws, and business partners helped to run these enterprises. Besides selling wares, merchants of means served as moneylenders.[45]

Merchants, whether registered or not, frequently tried to turn a profit in violation of the many laws and regulations. A law curtailing the variety of goods that could be sold in each shop was motivated by a concern to halt trade in stolen goods, including items belonging to the court.[46] Smuggling, particularly involving alcoholic beverages, was reduced to tolerable limits only in the 1770s if at all. Indeed, a stereotype of merchants as dishonest and money-grubbing was widespread, indicating that many city residents believed that they were dealing with merchants of questionable honesty. The archetype of such merchants was the character Ferapont Pafnut'evich Skvalygin in Mikhail Matinskii's opera, "Sanktpeterburgskii gostinyi dvor," first produced in 1779 and revived in 1792.[47] Skvalygin, whose name means "miser," charged excessively high interest rates, sold goods of poor domestic manufacture as the finest imported quality, offered his guests stale food so that they would eat less, was unfeeling toward debtors (but pleaded for mercy before his own creditors), and altered or destroyed promissory notes to escape paying his debts. His credo was:

> A merchant striving for profit . . . is supposed to get rich any way he can. . . . Good will is no more than an evil habit, and whoever pays attention to it will remain all his life without dignity and in poverty; but whoever has only a certain regard for good will shall be called a brilliant and honest man and shall live well. . . . Here are my unwavering rules: (1) besides yourself, do good to no one; (2) get what you can for yourself, though it may be harmful to others; (3) use others in whatever way necessary, whether it be by giving them bread or by cutting them to the quick. Here are the bases of true merchant-hood which have made me wealthy. Note them down and you too can be rich.[48]

Several Russian merchant families made large fortunes in St. Petersburg. Among the wealthiest were the Popov, Tuchkov, Iamshchikov, Ol'khin, Shemiakin, Lukin, Pokhodiashin, Loginov, Gorokhov, and Iakovlev families. The easiest fortune to trace is that of the Iakovlevs. The founder of the family's wealth was Sava Iakovlev, whose original surname was Sobakin (dog). As a young peasant hawking meat pies on St. Petersburg's streets, his pleasant voice caught the attention of Empress Elizabeth, who granted him the right thereafter to supply all the meat pies needed by the court. Diligently using this favor to his advantage, Sava Iakovlev opened a shop where he sold various wares. He lent part of his profits at high interest rates to other merchants, much like Skvalygin in the opera. Amassing wealth through these practices, Iakovlev opened more shops, plowing profits back into his business. Eventually he became an importer and exporter, even owning his own factories both locally and in Iaroslavl'. He also won a contract to sell alcoholic drinks in St. Petersburg. In 1758 he asked to be freed from the soul tax. In the same year he and his descendants were made hereditary nobles.

Iakovlev got off to a poor start with Catherine following her coup in 1762, refusing to provide free vodka to the public as instructed. As the story was related by the cultural historian M. I. Pyliaev, the outraged public raised a hue and cry and there was rioting in the streets. To punish Iakovlev Catherine made him wear a cast-iron medal weighing a *pud,* just over thirty-six pounds, on holidays. He managed to restore himself to the empress's good graces by reconstructing a dilapidated church she noticed while traveling to Moscow for her coronation a few months later. She intended to see to the church's repair herself, asking to be reminded about the building on the return trip to St. Petersburg. Iakovlev deduced her intentions and had the building repaired at his own expense. When Catherine visited the church on her return trip, she happened upon a procession of the cross with church bells pealing. Inquiring how the building came to be repaired so quickly and so elegantly, she was told that Iakovlev was responsible. Catherine shortly promoted him to collegiate assessor, which carried with it hereditary nobility.

By the time of his death, Sava Iakovlev was one of the most envied men in St. Petersburg, honored in death by burial among nobles in the cemetery of Alexander Nevskii monastery. After his death the family continued to expand its interests, becoming major landlords and real estate brokers by the end of the century.[49] One of his grandsons, for example, Sava Mikhailovich Iakovlev, was able to register as an eminent citizen as a twenty-one-year-old bachelor in 1791, claiming to have capital worth seventy thousand rubles and owning, besides his own house covering two lots on Vasil'evskii Island, a masonry house in Third Admiralty and a wooden house near Semenovskii bridge, besides two shops and an empty lot.[50] The Iakovlev story was well known in St. Petersburg and was often cited as evidence that hardworking newcomers could build large fortunes in the capital through commerce.

Much more diverse in background were foreign merchants, who first came to St. Petersburg shortly after its founding. As early as 1714 merchants from eastern areas including Armenia, Persia, Turkey, Tartary, China, and India were resident in the city, not to speak of Europeans.[51] After another fifty years foreign merchants were well entrenched indeed. Among them the British were preeminent.[52] The role of foreign merchants can partly be deduced from lists of merchants operating in St. Petersburg prepared for the Commerce Commission in 1773 and 1774. In the former year the list included the names of twenty-seven Dutch firms, twenty-seven French firms, fourteen from Spain and Italy, eleven from the Holy Roman Empire, sixteen from the city of Lübeck, fourteen from Hamburg, three from Rostock, eight from Switzerland, eight from Armenia, six from the kingdom of Saxony, four from Prussia, four from Denmark, and sixty-five from other, unspecified states. In 1774 the list included fifty-six "English" merchant firms from the United Kingdom. The 263 foreign firms listed in the two years nearly doubled the 140 Russians engaged in foreign trade through St. Petersburg.[53] Somewhat later, a different measure can be seen from the number of foreign merchants registered in St. Petersburg in 1790 not in business for themselves, but as agents of firms owned outside the city: twenty-eight "Englishmen," seven Germans, six Dutchmen, four Frenchmen, four Danes, two Swiss, two Portuguese, one Spaniard, one Italian, and several Prussians. In addition, twelve foreigners were eminent citizens and 106 listed as merchants of the first guild.[54] The reputation of foreign merchants outshone that of Russians. The foreigners were generally serious, cultured, and respectable. Yet from time to time their image was tarnished by foreigners not registered in the merchant guilds who nevertheless traded illegally.[55]

Regulation of Commerce

Government interest in and supervision of commercial activity resulted foremost from a concern for the welfare of the state's finances, dependent in turn upon a flourishing economy. This interest was outwardly expressed by the creation in 1764 of a Commerce Commission subordinated directly to the empress. Working in conjunction with the Commerce College, it was charged with discovering ways to improve commercial activity in Russia generally and in St. Petersburg particularly. To this end prominent merchants, including Sava Iakovlev, Fedor Iamshchikov, and Ivan Chirkin, were asked to provide information to the commission, together with government officials whose work touched on commerce, especially those in the Commerce College. Over the course of several years the commission offered proposals designed to increase commerce in the capital.

Perhaps the most important contribution of the commission was a plan designed to make it easier for merchants to borrow money from the Commercial Bank. According to the proposal, merchants in St. Petersburg could borrow as much as ten thousand rubles for terms up to a year at only 6 percent interest simply by submitting lists showing the goods they proposed to buy, their cost, and the period of time for which they wanted the loans. After investigating the statements and attaining letters of credit, the bank would grant promissory notes that merchants could use to buy goods. Such promissory notes could be redeemed only at the customhouse.[56] By effectively becoming guarantor of their debts, the state intended to remove Russian merchants from excessive dependence upon private lenders of capital and to encourage them to enter into maritime commerce (which would, not incidentally, come at the expense of foreign merchants in St. Petersburg). Had it been implemented fully, the measure might have contributed to a growing proportionate share of maritime trade conducted by Russians. As matters turned out, it was underfunded, quickly overwhelmed by demand, and had little real impact.

No issues assumed greater importance than those regarding credit and finance. Nowhere in Russia were there banks of deposit. The sole lending bank in existence at the start of Catherine's reign, established in 1754, was intended to aid indigent nobles. (The Commercial Bank founded the same year had already lent its entire supply of capital and lay dormant.) Catherine supplemented its original capitalization of 750,000 rubles with another six million during the first twenty-five years of her reign. Because it was a Lending Bank for Nobles, this institution provided minimal assistance for commerce. Loans were made for the improvement of landed estates, not the marketing of wares. The founding of the State Assignat Bank by a decree of December 1768 did address mercantile problems. In Catherine's own words, it was established "to give more opportunities for the universal circulation of money" and to obtain "the highest degree of general credit."[57] Finally, the continuing need for credit led Catherine to establish the Imperial Loan Bank in St. Petersburg in 1787, placing twenty-two million rubles at the disposal of the nobility and eleven million for "the towns." Townsmen were able to borrow sums at 4 percent interest, with an additional 3 percent due upon repayment of the principal, for terms of twenty-two years.[58]

Tariffs were a particular means used to bolster the state's fiscal welfare, as Catherine employed them primarily to produce revenue.[59]

(State monopolies in the salt and vodka trade served the same purpose.) To facilitate collection of duties, all products intended for both import and export were required to pass through the customhouse on Vasil'evskii Island. Wares from incoming ships were, in fact, unloaded there. Shippers paid duties on their own valuation of the goods they carried. When customs agents determined that goods were undervalued, the wares were liable to an additional 20 percent assessment. Numerous fines offer the best evidence that the threat of additional assessment did not effectively discourage violation of the law.[60]

Others attempted to smuggle goods through the port, paying no duties at all. It was commonly believed that the treasury lost considerable potential revenue in this way, especially from alcoholic beverages. In 1766 a special command of dragoons was created to intercept liquor smugglers. The command was increased in size in 1771 and given the means to intercept runners at sea as well as on land. All these government measures proved ineffective, because smugglers often bribed the patrols to allow the illegal trade to continue. Indeed, results were so dismal that the tax receipts from spirits actually declined. Finally, an entirely new force was created, its agents paid in part from the fines they collected. These last regulations, enacted in 1776, seem to have been much more successful in curtailing smuggling.[61] The episode demonstrates that at least on occasion a small degree of governmental flexibility could be summoned forth when necessary to deal with an important matter. Excise duties provided significant income both for the municipal administration and for the central government's treasury. To ensure their collection the government adopted several different measures before hitting upon a logical solution: to pay agents a percentage of the value of goods intercepted.

Tariff tables were designed to discourage the importation of goods that could be identified as luxury items as part of a conscious policy to place limits on ostentatious living. The nobility, not to mention Catherine's own court, greatly increased its demand for luxury goods during the latter third of the century.[62] The principal market for these wares was located in St. Petersburg. To offset this demand, the tariff of 1766 eased restrictions on imported necessities but heavily taxed luxury goods.[63] A good Cameralist, Catherine used economic policy to regulate the morals of society.

In the 1780s the concern over smuggling and unpaid tariff duties took on new urgency as the central government became increasingly concerned about the long, slow decline in the value of the ruble relative to other currencies, particularly the Dutch guilder. That concern was compounded by developments in foreign policy necessitating large expenditure of government funds abroad. Wars with Turkey and Sweden and the garrisoning of a large number of army troops in Poland forced the government to seek long-term loans abroad. In the process of determining what policies to adopt to address these fiscal problems, the proposal was made to ban the importation from abroad not just of sumptuary goods but of all wares. After considerable discussion within the Commerce Commission and Commerce College, the decision was made to ban the importation of all foreign wares through overland border points, channeling them exclusively through the ports, where presumably customs officials were more honest and thorough in assessing duties on imports. At the same time, a decree was issued to inspect all bazaars and other stores and shops, including those located in people's houses, to ensure that all wares of foreign origin bore the stamp and seal of the customs office, certifying that import duties had been paid.[64]

The decree aroused a storm of protest from merchants, particularly those in St. Petersburg. Their main point was that most wares in retail establishments had been taken out of their original packing and the customs stamp had come off, worn off, been discarded, or otherwise could no longer be found, especially in the case of wares that had been imported months before. Sixty-one of the leading merchants and "eminent citizens" trading in the main bazaar of the "capital and *guberniia* city of St. Peter," including the city's mayor, signed a petition addressed to the president of the Commerce College, Alexander Vorontsov, protesting the decree.[65]

A third impetus for government involvement in commercial life was the desire to preserve and protect health and safety. Regulatory measures dealt with three specific problems of this nature. Chapter 4 discusses the response to threats of plague and famine. In the former case the movement of goods from affected areas was carefully controlled. Trade was maintained as normally as possible while the danger lasted. To avoid famine, the export of grain from the city was at times totally forbidden or made dependent upon price, with the stipulation that if the price rose above a certain level, export was to be forbidden.[66] These measures were temporary in nature, designed to permit as much commercial freedom as possible while guaranteeing full provisioning for the city. For example, in 1795 Catherine ordered a cessation of wheat shipments so temporary that merchants could continue to load grain aboard ships.[67]

Fourth, measures were adopted to protect commercial interests against fire. Increasingly complex regulations in 1767, 1771–73, and 1779 were designed to prevent fire in the hemp warehouses. But only as a consequence of a blaze there in 1780 did the Commerce College, which ran the warehouses, begin to enforce the regulations strictly. No more than two barges could unload at once, the others remaining at the docks near Smolnyi. No ship laden with hemp or flax was permitted to carry any form of oil as cargo. Merchants, contractors, and laborers were forbidden to light fires or to smoke in the vicinity of warehouses and barges. Finally, since the cause of the 1780 fire was never determined, no laborers considered dangerous or not possessing passports were to be hired. The College wanted to keep potential arsonists away.[68]

Sometimes shops were moved from, or not permitted to locate in, thickly populated and densely used areas if danger from fire was considered great. Among the most carefully watched shops were those selling wares made from leather and leather products.[69] The growing awareness of the necessity of complex fire prevention measures illustrates the government's recognition of the importance of St. Petersburg's commercial activity in raising revenues for the state.

Other regulations ensured that merchants used true weights and measures (the police supervised standardization of weights and measures during Catherine's reign), guaranteed order and decorum in the marketplace, and generally enhanced the reputation and status of lives spent in commercial endeavor.

Significance of Commercial Activity

The vast majority of goods exported through St. Petersburg were products of agriculture or mining. In some cases materials were reworked in St. Petersburg, but by and large the capital acted only as a depot. Agricultural produce exported in great quantity included hemp, flax, linseed, tobacco, rhubarb (esteemed for pharmacological qualities), grain, and derivatives of livestock, such as horsehair, pig bristles, and hides. Hundreds of tons of pig iron, saltpeter, tar, potash, and talc from Russia's mines passed through St. Petersburg. From plentiful natural resources came honey, wax, furs, masts, planks, lumber, and caviar. Not all products exported in sizable quantities were nonindustrial, however. There was a large market in Europe for Russian sailcloth, linen, cordage, candles, bast mats, and leather goods (including Russia leather).[70] Most exported manufactured wares were bulky. With the exception of leather goods, furs and pelts, caviar, masts, and a few other products, exported items had low value relative to their bulk. Thus ships fully loaded with Russian iron, for example, did not carry as valuable a lading as ships sailing to St. Petersburg with half a load of French wines.

The fact that exports consisted largely of raw materials should not necessarily imply that imports were limited solely to finished and manufactured articles. Import lists indicate that the opposite was often true; many imports were agricultural products: coffee, sugar, indigo, fruits, and dyewoods. Others, such as tin, lead, pewter, and steel, were metals in a semifinished state. Nor can beaverskins, broadcloth, and brass wire be considered finished products. Russia imported wines and liquors, it is true, but it also exported caviar and brandy. One can conclude that much of the exchange resulted from specialization in goods qualitatively the same, that is, raw materials and semifinished products.[71] This runs counter to the general assumption that St. Petersburg's exports in the eighteenth century consisted almost exclusively of raw products and imports just as predominantly of manufactured articles. This general assumption, true for the nineteenth century, has been applied inappropriately to the eighteenth.

Russia did, however, import luxury goods—from France and England in particular—including silk material, mirrors, clocks, English glazed china, and other products. Nor did Russia manufacture her own musical instruments, fine clothes, scientific instruments, and high-quality furniture.[72] But St. Petersburg was beginning to develop domestic production to offset importation of luxury goods. Great stimulus came from foreign craftsmen living and working in St. Petersburg. Storch (himself a German) claimed that foreign influence had so developed a domestic luxury goods industry toward the end of the century that certain items did not have to be imported at all, including embroidered cloth, millinery, coaches and carriages, furniture, stoves, porcelain, glassware, tapestries, and jewelry.[73]

As stated above, the value of exports exceeded that of imports in almost every year. It is difficult to assess the significance of this fact. In the first place, the figures for both imports and exports do not include the value of goods smuggled into or out of the capital. Most contemporary observers did believe, however, that the trade balance remained in Russia's favor even when smuggled goods were included, albeit by a much smaller margin than official statistics indicated.

The most likely explanation for the favorable balance is that the Russian market simply was not large enough to handle as great a value of goods as western Europe was prepared to buy from Russia. St. Petersburg provided necessary items for maritime nations: masts, iron, and hemp. Not even luxury imports offset the value of these exports, for the number of conspicuous consumers in the Russian Empire, even taking into consideration the existence of an opulent court, was quite limited.

An important role in facilitating commerce was played by the advertisements supplement to the capital's largest newspaper, the *Sankt-peterburgskie vedomosti,* published by the Academy of Sciences. Chapter 9 treats the significance of this medium for Russia. For the moment discussion is limited to St. Petersburg. The advertisements supplement to the semiweekly newspaper grew steadily during the latter third of the century, so that by the end of Catherine's reign its size overwhelmed the regular news section of the paper. The supplements served to bring buyers and sellers together. They were the only available form of advertisement other than word of mouth and simple signboards.

The discussion of commerce in St. Petersburg would be incomplete without an evaluation of the technological level of trade in the city: the degree of sophistication; the use of modern methods of banking, finance, and record-keeping; and the cast of permanence. Such an evaluation must be couched in the eighteenth-century context, with conclusions keeping that milieu in mind. As a judgment on the quality of commercial life in Russia's capital city, this examination brings together several observations made earlier about trade in St. Petersburg that merit reemphasis.

In the first place, it is doubtful that a single system of weights and measures was used at the start of Catherine's reign by either Russians or foreigners from various countries. Instructions to the police told them merely to supervise honesty in weights and measures, not to guarantee sameness. Before the midpoint of the reign, however, uniformity was established. Early in 1780, in response to a request from the Senate, the city magistracy reported that all enterprises selling like wares used the same weights and measures; the system was fully standardized. That the Senate should frame the question suggests that standardization had not obtained for long.[74] In short, standardization of weights and measures, an important prerequisite for the development of modern commerce, was achieved in Catherine's reign.

A second prerequisite is the efficient utilization of capital for investment. This aspect of commercial activity was not very advanced, especially among native Russian merchants. Foreign observers noted that there was not a strong propensity to invest among Russians. A few did use their proceeds in this way, of course, but the vast majority showed little interest in large-scale investment. One commentator earlier in the century thought that Russians commonly buried money because they distrusted others, and then died without revealing the location of their assets, "so that it is reckoned there is in Russia much more money under ground than above."[75] A much more likely explanation of Russians' hesitation to invest is that they feared the possibility of losing their assets because of unwise investment or the unsmiling face of chance.

Furthermore, it was hard to procure loans. Although in 1754 a Commercial Bank was set up in St. Petersburg to lend money to merchants using the port city, it soon ran out of funds, and in 1782, never having realized its potential, it was merged with the State Bank for the Nobility, losing its uniqueness as a bank solely for merchants. Merchandisers who borrowed from the bank when it did have funds to lend were often unable to repay loans by the specified dates. As might be expected when this happened, their holdings were sold at public auction to make good their bank debts. With little capital to lend, it did not really matter that interest rates were lowered to 6 percent early in Catherine's reign.

Another state agency, the Foundling Home, made large loans during this period. Not as restrictive as state-run banks, it lent to gentry and merchants, Russians and foreigners. Collateral was mandatory; terms required payment of a thousand rubles per year, plus interest.[76] Even when the interest rate was low, such rapid retirement of the principal often proved impossible. Many borrowers were forced to ask for extensions of several months in repaying loans. A few private bankers in St. Petersburg, usually foreigners, also lent large sums, and it was quite easy to find pawnbrokers in any part of town for the purpose of eliciting small loans. Interest rates soared under private bankers, who charged as much as 10 percent per month.[77] Russian merchants in St. Petersburg could hardly be blamed therefore for a reluctance to take out large loans to capitalize their business ventures.

Beyond the measures already discussed, the government did little to establish credit facilities or to encourage greater capital investment in commerce. The Commercial Bank had been set up at merchants' urgings and the Imperial Loan Bank upon Catherine's initiative, but otherwise the state devised no consistent policy to make sums of money available to merchants. Upon occasion, however, the government did respond to individual requests by granting monopoly or initial capital outlay to merchants. In 1763 in a case involving nearly a hundred merchants, the state provided funds to rebuild a market on Vasil'evskii Island's Fifth Line that had burned down. The merchants had proposed a government grant of eighty thousand copper rubles to be repaid without interest in ten years in silver coin. Approved by the Senate, the plan permitted merchants to reestablish their businesses quickly.[78]

On the positive side, communication about commercial activity was generally good. As indicated earlier, newspapers regularly published advertisements and news about the arrival of caravans from the interior.

The city's commercial enterprises lacked permanence. Few existed longer than one generation, sometimes two. Often sons were not interested in continuing their fathers' businesses and sold them. Widows continued to operate their husbands' shops only to have them sold after their deaths. Because most businesses were small and dealt in a limited selection of goods, it was simple to disband operations if heirs so chose.

Another telling characteristic of the level of commercial development is that the Russian merchants were held in low esteem. Russians themselves spoke often of the dishonesty of their merchants. Two of the three possible causes of the fire in the hemp warehouses in 1780 reported by Alexander Vorontsov, following his investigation, reveal a suspicion of merchants. According to one, a merchant with many debts was trying to escape from his creditors by burning out everyone. According to the other, a merchant contractor sought to hide his misdeeds.[79] Vorontsov heard these opinions from merchants who had lost goods in the fire.

Foreign merchants at the hemp warehouses constantly complained to the Commerce College that Russians short-weighted them or sold one grade while pretending to sell another. Foreign travelers likewise held low opinions of Russian merchants. Russians themselves understood the stereotype created in Matinskii's comic opera. Finally Aleksandr Radishchev in his *Journey from St. Petersburg to Moscow* categorized Russian traders as dishonest—a fault Radishchev as head of the customhouse in St. Petersburg knew all too well.[80]

The general conclusion is that commercial activity in St. Petersburg during the latter third of the eighteenth century, although enormous in volume, remained at a much lower level technologically than in the principal western European maritime ports. Russian merchants were still unable fully to utilize developments in banking, finance, and record-keeping, unless they were among the very few whose scale of operations was large enough to permit them to maintain accounts in Amsterdam or some smaller foreign trading center.[81] Nor were they noted for their sophistication. Yet St. Petersburg led all other Russian cities in volume of commerce, accounting at the time of Catherine's death for fully one-half of Russia's maritime trade.[82] The obvious quantitative increase in commerce came about despite the technological backwardness, as possibilities for expansion evident at the beginning of the reign were realized.

7
"Diligence and the Means of Livelihood . . .": Industry

MOST HISTORICAL WORKS EXAMINING THE ROLE OF ST. PETERSBURG as a major manufacturing center begin their study in detail with the nineteenth century, for it was in the years following 1800 that the modern factory began to make its appearance in Russia.[1] While historians agree that there was industrial activity in eighteenth-century St. Petersburg, they cannot agree on its extent. Even more problematical is the matter of whether the industrial activity of St. Petersburg can be tied in any way to the coming of the Industrial Revolution.[2] Part of the difficulty results from terminological imprecision. In the eighteenth century, productive activity (*promyshlennost'*) could be undertaken in three kinds of establishments, the *zavod, fabrika,* and *manufaktura,* all of which can be translated loosely, if somewhat inaccurately, as "factory." The debate over the precise meaning of each term, and what sorts of activities it circumscribed, began in the eighteenth century and continues today.[3]

Generally speaking the *zavod* was the most capital-intensive of the three and usually involved the greatest transformation between raw material and finished product, often through chemical processes or the application of extreme heat. Sugar refineries, breweries, distilleries, glassmaking establishments, brickyards, tanneries, and extractive enterprises were all called *zavody.* The Latin-rooted *fabrika* (at least one contemporary source stated that the only difference between the words was that the latter had a foreign derivation) referred to places making passementerie (or galloons), hats, most textiles, processed foodstuffs, cordage, and tobacco and paper products, among others.[4] The *manufaktura* was the smallest of the three in scope of operation. Little technology was involved in the productive process, and the workplace was usually manned by master artisans and their subordinates. Clocks and tapestries were turned out by *manufaktury.* For our purposes, all three types of productive enterprises will be considered as having been part of the city's industrial establishment.

The "factory" in eighteenth-century St. Petersburg may not yet have been the nineteenth-century industrial factory, but the preindustrial work setting was beginning to see subtle changes that would eventually give way to the industrialized mode. The organization of the workplace, the tempo of labor, the composition of the workforce, and the goal of production began to undergo transformations. These changes did not constitute an industrial revolution—far from it. Yet the accommodation of production to meet new demands and provide for a changing market helped establish the preconditions of future growth. This does not suggest that one should study the city's productive life by looking solely for signs of a new industrial age or evaluate it in terms of how far toward industrialization the city advanced during Catherine's reign. It is far more fruitful to examine the nature of goods production on the era's own terms, giving greatest consideration to its role in the city's economic life in its own day. Fedor Sukin, vice president of the Manufactures College, wrote in 1765 that the work done in *fabriki* and *manufaktury* could be distinguished from that done in the workshop of the artisan as "the trade which, to be brought into complete use, requires separate buildings, diverse raw materials, different skills and instruments—in short, the joining of many hands and complicated machines."[5] But in eighteenth-century St. Petersburg the artisan's workshop and protofactory both played important roles.

Factory Production

A complete list of the *manufaktury, fabriki,* and *zavody* in St. Petersburg in Catherine's reign was never made. The counts taken were known to be inaccurate even at the time because many enterprises were never registered with the authorities.[6] Indeed, there was no single administrative body responsible for keeping track of all of them. Until its dissolution at the end of the 1770s, the Manufactures College had oversight over most privately owned industrial concerns in the city, but its jurisdiction did not extend to such enterprises as breweries and distilleries, nor did it cover the small workshops run by individual craftsmen.[7] The lists of enterprises overseen by the College that survive, from 1775 and 1779, provide the fullest information at our disposal as to location, ownership, scale of production, and dates of operation, yet provide only partial information on the changes these enterprises underwent over time.[8] Fortunately, these lists and other available information do make it possible to differentiate several distinct types of productive concerns that met the needs of various markets.

Long before Catherine's reign, the first industrial enterprises to appear in the city were founded by the state to produce goods for its own use. In keeping with the city's early military significance, the first industries supplied munitions, arms, and equipment for the army and navy.[9] Several such enterprises, including the Admiralty shipyard and the arsenal and cannon foundry, dated from the reign of Peter I. It is noteworthy that the names Admiralty and Foundry were later used to identify administrative districts of town. Other state-owned manufactories produced the coin and paper for the nation's currency. Still others provided chancellery materials for the use of the growing bureaucracy. Included in this classification were the gold and silver smelting works, the mint, a bronze factory, a sealing-wax factory, and a paper mill producing the parchment on which assignats were printed after their introduction in 1769.[10] Several governmental agencies even operated lumber mills and brickyards to supply needs for construction materials. In all these factories production was geared first to fill the needs of the governmental apparatus. Surplus production could then sometimes be sold to private individuals.

Another group of state-owned enterprises produced goods not for state use, but to provide luxuries for the court and privileged people. Porcelain, faience, glass, crystal, china, mirrors, tapestries, clocks, and cut and polished precious stones were turned out by these concerns.[11] As indicated below, private manufactories turned out such wares in large amounts only later. The government had begun to produce luxury goods primarily because the few private factories earlier in the century had not been able to meet the demand for their consumption.

State-operated production was not intended to provide manufactured wares for the mass of the city's population or even the products for the daily consumption of the privileged people. This was left entirely to private entrepreneurs. Their food-processing plants supplied the capital with such products as sugar, pasta, and chocolate. They owned the distilleries and breweries and tobacco-processing plants.[12] Their tanneries tooled suede and Russia-, patent, and Moroccan leather. Dye-making plants and the first textile (cotton and linen) and woolens mills aided clothing production. Other privately owned manufactories turned out such household wares as soap, candles, wallpaper, waxes, pottery, cast-iron ware, and paper for books.[13]

Following the example set by the state-owned factories producing luxury goods for the court, private industrialists founded enterprises that turned out silk and semisilk goods, stockings, passementerie, playing cards, and silver and gold worked into plate, leaf, and braid.[14] Such enterprises were small, characterized by a more intensive use of labor than capital. The high incidence of manufactories making items for luxury use testifies not only to a pattern of production that made a capital city different from other towns but also indicates the uses made of wealth by those who had it. Under the value system prevalent there, conspicuous consumption was to be preferred over the accumulation of capital.

Capital-forming industries did have their place in St. Petersburg. In addition to the state-operated plants already mentioned, privately owned brickyards, sawmills, and clay and gravel pits produced building materials on a large scale.[15] Merchant ships were constructed on Vyborg Side in the private shipyard, put under the jurisdiction of the city magistracy in 1781.[16] Smaller shipyards in other locations built a limited number of vessels.[17] The first metalworking enterprises appeared during this period. The largest one, owned and operated by the English merchant Charles Baird, cast the tools used by many artisans in producing light industrial commodities. It also turned out cast-iron goods needed in the home.[18]

These factories produced goods for the most part under contract. Only a few, most notably those providing foodstuffs and household items, produced for the market. Despite the existence among them of several enterprises each employing scores of workers, the scale of manufacturing remained small. Machines were few and just coming into use, providing minimal assistance in the productive process. In most manufactories a small number of workers and a labor-intensive process of production remained the norm. The mode of production was clearly preindustrial.

Geographical Location of Enterprises

Each section of town contained some industrial activity throughout Catherine's reign. Location was not purely a matter of chance, and by the end of the period a tendency toward geographical differentiation of industries was becoming apparent. The Soviet scholar V. V. Pokshishevskii, analyzing the pattern of industrial location, decided that the primary factor affecting site location for industrial concerns was proximity to market.[19] Thus factories producing luxury goods and other products for the wealthy and the court predominated in the central city, where the wealthiest people lived. Enterprises catering to the general public were distributed throughout town. Concerns providing construction materials were located in a circular pattern between the inner city and the outer suburbs where they would be convenient to all sections of town. The evidence bears out that the greatest number of industrial establishments could be found in precisely that circular area.

Pokshishevskii's analysis of factory location has much to credit it, but factors besides proximity to market also determined their location. His explanation emphasizes the consumer as the primary determinant, yet it is equally important to examine the role played by the unique demands of production, at least for certain industries. For example, tanneries and leatherworking establishments were still scattered throughout the city as late as the mid-1770s, with a small knot of them located where the cattle drives to the capital ended, adjacent to the slaughterhouses in Moscow district. Two decades later, however, none were to be found next to the abattoirs. The necessity for large quantities of fresh water in the tanning process, as well as the noisome by-products of the trade, had forced their relocation almost entirely to one or another of the riverbanks, downstream from the places where the city was likely to draw its water. Thus the tanneries were clustered on the banks of the Great or Small Neva or on the Nevka.[20]

Other industrial concerns were located, or sites chosen initially, for similar reasons. Factories making use of extreme heat were relegated to fringe areas where the danger of fire would be lessened. They were also close to waterways, so that large quantities of firewood could be supplied to them cheaply and easily. The gunpowder plant was removed to a more remote end of St. Petersburg Side when the area around its old site became built up with houses. The glass factory was relocated above the city on the Neva at a site where there were no nearby buildings to catch fire. Somewhat earlier, the consideration of fuel supply and cost had led Empress Elizabeth in 1759 to ban the future construction of factories in or near St. Petersburg. Her decision was based on the report that timber, virtually the sole source of fuel for factories, was becoming scarce in the city's environs. She feared that increasing the industrial usage of firewood might totally destroy the remaining forests and raise the cost of firewood for household consumption. The problem was considered so grave that some existing factories were to be removed from the capital, although there is no evidence that this was actually done, and the law remained a dead letter.[21]

Industrial concerns did, however, begin to vacate the central core of the city, where land values demanded the most intensive use of space. The new playing card manufactories permitted to open in the 1770s did locate there, as did other productive enterprises in which goods of high value relative to bulk were produced, or which required small amounts of space. But the ropewalks were displaced to sites where there were far fewer competing demands for use, primarily to the Vyborg Side.[22] New enterprises were opened primarily outside the central city. As a result of this tendency, the proportion of concerns in the city center declined, despite an increase in real terms, as the greatest growth took place in the outskirts. By 1789 the three Admiralty districts together held only seventeen factories in a list compiled by the city government. By comparison Foundry district had thirteen, Moscow district thirty, Vasil'evskii Island twenty-nine, and Vyborg Side fifteen.[23] Thus the amount of space needed for production, the degree of investment involved, the impact of the production process on the environment, and the level of technology that was utilized all played a part in site selection for factories. Industrial concerns clearly owed their location to more than market considerations.[24]

Except for the tendencies observed above, there was little differentiation of industrial from nonindustrial districts in the city. Certainly there was no concerted policy to segregate all industrial growth into certain zones or areas. Enterprises were permitted to locate virtually at will, and in only a few obvious cases were restrictions placed on freedom of site selection. What is clear is that the number of enterprises, wherever their location, sharply increased. When the factory lists of 1775 and 1794 are compared, and the various kinds of factories (breweries, distilleries, chandleries, etc.) not found on the earlier list

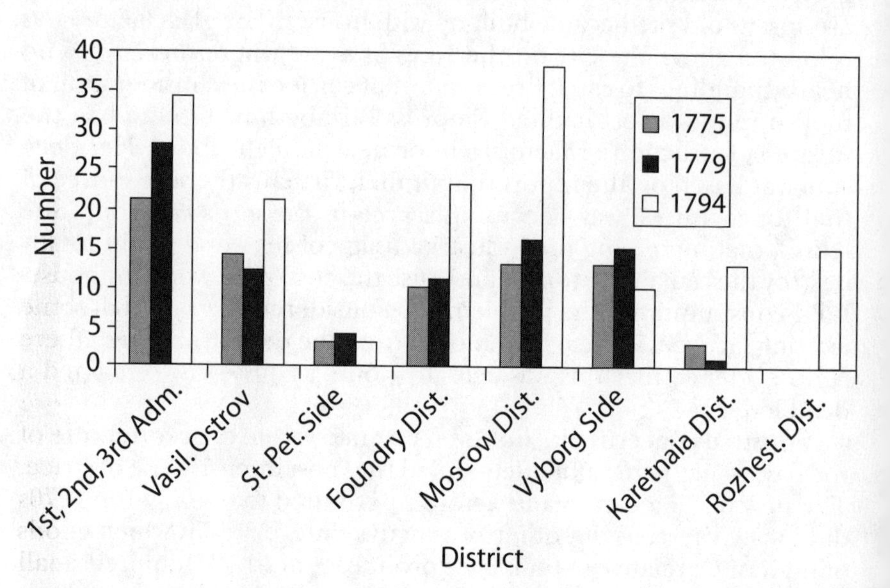

Graph 7.1. Number of Factories in St. Petersburg by District, 1775, 1779, and 1794
Source: See note 25 of this chapter.

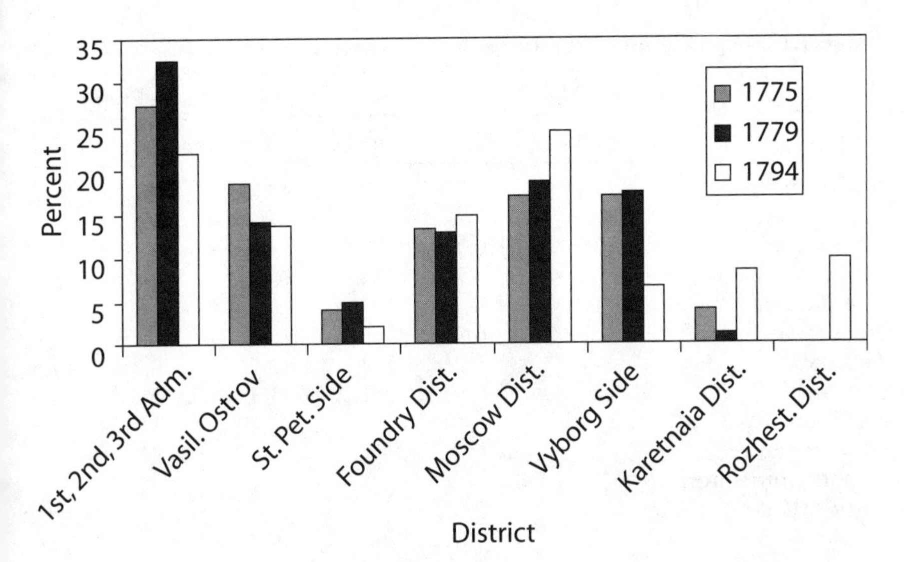

Graph 7.2. Factories in St. Petersburg, Percentage by District, 1775, 1779, and 1794
Source: See note 25 of this chapter.

deleted from the later one, there is still an increase from sixty-four (fifty-eight known to have been working in 1775) to ninety, a significant change for only two decades. The increase occurred in every part of town except Vyborg Side (see graph 7.1). The geographic distribution of enterprises remained surprisingly proportional, particularly in St. Petersburg Side and Foundry district, and the relative growth was greatest along the southern perimeter of the city, where one might have expected it, in the area closest to the heart of the empire (graph 7.2). The only area to exhibit a decrease in the number of industrial enterprises during this period was Vyborg Side, where a natural attrition brought about by the deaths or bankruptcies of owners was not offset by an influx of new concerns.[25]

Factory Owners

Even though the state established the first industrial enterprises in St. Petersburg, by the time Catherine ruled Russia, government-owned and operated firms comprised a minority of all manufactories, if not of all industrial workers. Among factory owners could be found a wide variety of people, both native born and foreigners. Just as merchants attempted to restrict commercial activity to themselves alone,

Table 7.1. Social Composition of Factory Owners in St. Petersburg, 1775–94

	1775		1779		1794	
Group	Number	%	Number	%	Number	%
St. Petersburg merchants	35	43.2	39	43.3	68	40.2
Foreigners	33	40.7	39	43.3	47	27.8
Other Russian merchants	5	6.2	3	3.3	11	6.5
Russian artisans	5	6.2	2	2.2	23	13.6
Gentry	1	1.2	2	2.2	8	4.7
Peasants			1	1.1	6	3.6
Civil servants					3	1.8
St. Petersburg petty townsmen*					3	1.8
Other/Unknown	2	2.5	4	4.4		
TOTALS	81	100.0	90	99.8	169	100.0

*The category of petty townsman (*meshchanin*) was new in 1794. There were more factory owners than factories in each year because of a few cases of multiple ownership.
Source: See note 25 of this chapter.

so the owners of larger factories sought to limit factory ownership to certain groups. At their instigation an article was placed in the St. Petersburg *nakaz* in 1767 asking that peasants, *raznochintsy,* foreign tutors, and domestic servants be prohibited from owning factories.[26] No legislation was enacted however, although measures were instituted to regulate factory ownership by peasants. To open a factory, a peasant had to possess a valid passport and to demonstrate that he owned sufficient capital to finance the undertaking. When these conditions were met, permission was normally granted to begin manufacturing. As table 7.1 indicates, owners of manufactories came from a variety of social backgrounds. St. Petersburg merchants throughout the period comprised just over two-fifths of all factory owners. Foreign entrepreneurs suffered a sharp proportional decrease over the period even though their number continued to rise. The greatest increase came among Russian craftsmen, who by the end of Catherine's reign were concentrated in the production of braid, tobacco, hats, leather, and furs. Very few gentry owned factories in the city, and those who did were distributed among almost as many industries, turning out china, potash, playing cards, sugar, silk goods, beer, and brandy. The St. Petersburg experience thus presented no challenge to the generalization that in Russia industrial enterprises owned by the gentry were usually located on their estates, not in the cities.

The role of foreigners in developing the city's early industry is particularly interesting. They were concentrated in those areas where skilled labor was necessary, such as passementerie, the production of gold and silver braid, hatmaking, clock and watch production, and the rope and cable industry. Foreigners also owned a disproportionate number of the heavy industrial concerns, the ironworks opened by Charles Baird in the early 1790s providing the best example. In a number of specialties foreign entrepreneurs opened the first enterprises, to be followed in later years by Russians after the original factories had demonstrated that the market could support production. This was especially true of products relatively new to Russia. For example, the first sugar refineries were established by foreigners in 1718 and 1752, but Russian merchants opened other refineries in 1756 and 1770. The first cotton mills were foreign-owned, as were the first playing card manufactories, but Russians owned the earliest, and the majority, of galloon manufactories and ropewalks and tanneries. The impact of foreigners was clearly felt in industry as well as commerce.

The Characteristics of Industrial Concerns

To speak of all these enterprises equally as factories obscures the obvious differences among them. Could glassblowing establishments and braid-making enterprises, ropewalks and soap-producing plants really have been comparable in number of workers and value of goods produced? How enduring were these plants? Were they so small in scale that the death of the owner meant the end of the enterprise? What sort of labor did they use, freely hired workers or forced labor, either as serfs, ascribed peasants, or military recruits?

In considering these questions, several points need to be kept in mind. The first is that these establishments made far more extensive use of labor power than machine power. Labor was relatively cheap and industrial technology, where it existed, all but prohibitively expensive. More hands were employed in most enterprises than would have been in an economy more attuned to productive efficiency and maximization of profit. Most of the workers performed unskilled labor in support of the master craftsmen and specialists in each form of production. Furthermore, whatever distinctions we might make among the several types of factories, contemporaries were certain that these establishments were all qualitatively different from the workshop of the artisan. They frequently made use of machines as well as tools. They used labor from outside the proprietor's household. They also exercised division of labor in the productive process.

It is extremely difficult to trace factory ownership over time. One might conclude from the names of owners in 1775 and 1794 that only ten of 161, or one-sixteenth (6.2 percent) of factories survived for as long as two decades, because only ten factories appear on both lists as owned by people with the same surname. These included three sugar refineries, two tanneries, two ropewalks, two galloon manufactories, and one cloak and gold- and silver-wire drawing factory. A brief look at the history of these enterprises is instructive. Two of the sugar refineries belonged in 1794 to John Cavanaugh (Ivan Kavanakh), an English merchant and member of the Russia Company. His factory on Vasil'evskii Island was licensed to his father, Nicholas Cavanaugh, in 1752, so had been in the family for nearly half a century by the 1790s. The other sugar refinery, on Vyborg Side, was begun in 1718 by a merchant of Dutch descent named Paul Westhof. In 1732 it passed to Councillor Hewitt (Giuvit), and in 1747 to the English merchants John Meux (Ivan Mei) and Thomas Stephens (Tomas Shtifens).[27] Meux died in 1764, and in 1767 Stephens sold the enterprise to John Cavanaugh's father. Thus the refinery passed through six owners in seventy-six years. The third refinery, in the Karetnaia district, was founded in 1756 by Tula merchant Fedor Volodimerov. Upon his death it passed to his son, Ivan, and belonged apparently to Ivan's son (Fedor's grandson), a lieutenant colonel, in 1794.

The tanneries, on Vasil'evskii Island and the adjoining Golidai Island, were founded respectively in 1760 by the Saxon native Georg Gesseler (Egor Gesler), and in 1767 by St. Petersburg merchants Lev Manuilov and Boris Popov. Gesseler still owned his in 1794, but when Popov died sometime prior to 1775, Manuilov assumed ownership of the entire business. Manuilov's widow, Zinov'ia Grigor'evna, held it in 1794.

On Vyborg Side were the two ropewalks, one owned by the English merchant Francis Gardner and the other by the St. Petersburg merchant Aleksei Ovchinnikov. Gardner's apparently was founded in 1751 by St. Petersburg merchant Vasilii Desiatil'nikov, whose widow and children held it in 1775 and sold it to Gardner, whose father had owned another St. Petersburg ropewalk from 1733 until his death prior to 1761, when his widow sold it. Ovchinnikov's ropewalk was opened by his father Grigorii in 1733.

Galloon manufactories also had a long history. Nikolai and Petr Rogovikov inherited one in Foundry district from their father, Semen. The enterprise actually began operations in 1736 under the ownership of two men from Saxony, Miller and Richter, passing upon their deaths in 1745 to Miller's brother, Werner, and his partner, Alexander Gon (or Gan). In 1754, after Werner Miller's death, it was acquired

Table 7.2. Founding Dates of St. Petersburg Factories Operating in 1775

Year of Founding	Number of Factories
Prior to 1720	2
1721–25	2
1726–30	0
1731–35	2
1736–40	3
1741–45	1
1746–50	6
1751–55	11
1756–60	14
1761–65	14
1766–70	16
1771–75	20

by the brothers Semen and Ivan Rogovikov (Ivan died the next year). The second galloon factory, owned in 1794 by the cousins Aleksei and Ivan Kokushkin, was founded in 1755 by a foreigner named Rheinhart and taken over from him two years later by the fathers of the 1794 owners, the brothers Petr and Ivan Kokushkin. Finally, the cape and gold- and silver-wire drawing factory owned by Christopher Friedrich Bomgart (Baumgart, Bomgarten, Baumgarten) in Foundry district was opened by him in 1770 and remained in his possession in 1794.

From the examples of these ten firms it is clear that productive enterprises did survive occasional changes in ownership. Four of the ten had been sold (or, more properly, reregistered with the Manufactures College) at least once. The sugar refinery established in 1718 had passed through five different sets of owners. Six enterprises had changed ownership through inheritance. Two of those had also been sold at least once. Only two of the ten, founded in 1760 and 1770, were still owned by their founders in 1794.

These ten factories were not all that exceptional. Just as one-sixteenth (10 of 161) of the factories in 1794 were owned by the same families that held them in 1775, so were one-sixteenth (5 of 80) in 1775 still owned by the families that held them in 1755. Table 7.2 shows the founding dates of factories still in existence in 1775. Of course, one would not expect many concerns to date from before the 1730s, when St. Petersburg was still being built primarily by government fiat. Indeed, the period of 1726–30, when the capital was temporarily removed again to Moscow, seems to have been devoid of industrial

Table 7.3. Factories Changing Ownership Before 1775 (and Still Operating in that Year)

	Decade of Change					
Number of times changed	1726–35	1736–45	1746–55	1756–65	1766–75	(Number of firms)
once		1	1	5	3	(10)
twice	1			2	1	(2)
three times	1		1		1	(1)
four times		1	1	1	1	(1)
Number of transactions	2	2	3	8	6	(14)

growth. But every five years thereafter, with the exception of 1751–55, showed a growth in the number of industrial establishments still operating in 1775, the sharpest increase coming after midcentury. (The 1759 ban on factory construction, reconfirmed in 1762, seems to have had little impact.) Of these concerns, fourteen had changed ownership at least once (see table 7.3) and seventeen had passed through inheritance. Three factories had been inherited twice.

The continuity of operations can also be viewed another way. All but five of the factories established before 1755 (twenty-seven in all) were owned by someone other than their founder in 1775, but of those started after 1755, only eleven of fifty-one had changed ownership or been inherited. This evidence indicates that the average span of ownership of an industrial enterprise lasted from fifteen to twenty years, and that the enterprise frequently outlasted its owner, surviving not only the vicissitudes of business but also the repeated shocks of turnover of ownership.

Several factories were jointly owned, a practice not limited to either Russians or foreigners. As was seen in the examples of the ten factories examined in detail, it was not unusual for Russians to follow foreigners as owners, but in only two cases (a ropewalk and a tannery) did a foreigner purchase an operation from a Russian. Nor was it unusual for women to operate factories. No cases were found of women establishing factories, but there were at least eight instances of a widow continuing to run her husband's business after his death. In fact, it was more common for a widow to retain possession of a factory than for sons, which may also be indicative of the age of children when the father died.

Some indication of the size of St. Petersburg's eighteenth-century factories was given by the Soviet scholar A. V. Safonova, whose selec-

Table 7.4. Number of Workers in St. Petersburg Factories

Type of Factory	Number of Factories	Number of Workers	Workers per Factory
Galloon/passementerie	10	162	16.2
Ropewalk	7	185	26.4
Linen weaving	2	67	33.5
Silk weaving	3	194	64.7
Sugar refineries	3	117	39.0
Glass bloweries	4	66	16.5
Cotton weaving	2	287	143.5
Tanneries	21	166	7.9
Paper	3	160	53.3
Dyeing plant	1	70	70.0
Bleaching plant	1	74	74.0
Clocks and steel (metal)	2	49	24.5
Playing cards	3	9	3.0
Hatmaking	1	10	10.0
Soap producing	1	3	3.0
TOTAL	64	1,619	25.3

Source: See note 28 of this chapter.

tion did not include all enterprises but is suggestive of their scale.[28] Her data are given in table 7.4, and include factories outside St. Petersburg but within twelve miles of the city. Although there was a wide variation in the number of employees, the average of 25.3 for all industries marks these enterprises as having been rather substantial.

When examined more closely, Safonova's evidence indicates that one-third of the factories employed almost seven-eighths of the workers, or slightly more than sixty-two each. The remaining two-thirds of the enterprises hired, on an average, slightly more than five persons each.[29] Several of the state-operated enterprises were significantly larger than any of the privately owned factories. The Admiralty shipyard regularly employed about four thousand people.[30] By the end of the century some two hundred worked at the imperial porcelain factory. The Okhta gunpowder works employed approximately three hundred during Catherine's reign.[31]

Although both private and state-owned establishments brought a relatively large number of people to work in a single place, they were not yet factories as we would understand the term, but rather transitional workplaces between the workshop and the nineteenth-century full-fledged factory. More will be said below about the workplace and the men and women who filled it.

Table 7.5. Capital Investment in St. Petersburg Factories, 1775 (in Rubles)

Factory type	to 250	251–500	501–750	751–1000	1001–5000	5001–10,000	10,001–20,000	20,001–50,000	over 50,000
Hosiery, silk							1		
Paper; groats							1		
Sugar								1	2
Passementerie				1	2			1	1
Cloak and wire		1		3	1				
Leather	1	3		4	3	2	1	1	
Rope	2	1			1	2	1		
Hat		1		2					
Sealing wax				1					
Soap	1								
Playing cards					3				
Silk					2				
Dye printing					1				
Dye and bleach								1	
Waxed paper						1			
Wall paper						1			
Locksmith/mechanic					1				
TOTAL	4	6	0	11	14	6	4	4	3

Source: See note 32.

One gauge of the scale of operation is the number of employees; another is the owner's capital investment. Fortunately we know something about the amount of capital tied up in many of St. Petersburg's factories because this information was included in the list of factories under the oversight of the Manufactures Bureau for 1775 published by E. I. Indova.[32] Table 7.5 summarizes this information for the fifty-four factories that submitted the report (67.5 percent of the registered factories). What is most apparent is that there was a wide variation in investment, ranging from 100 rubles for the smallest (a tannery owned by the widow of a foreigner) to 80,000 rubles for the largest (the sugar refinery of St. Petersburg merchant Kirila Popov). The median amount of capital investment lay between 1,000 and 5,000 rubles.

Within the same industry there could be a wide variation in factory size. The fifteen tanneries showed a range of investment from 100 to 50,000 rubles (the largest one owned by Sava Iakovlev); the seven ropewalks, a range from 150 (spinning master Stepan Klishin) to 14,474.40 (foreign merchant Iurii Pfliug). In a few cases, for those factories employing serfs, it is possible to correlate investment and the number of workers. In each case the minimal amount of capital investment per worker was about 100 rubles.[33] Presumably the ratio was at least as high in those factories employing hired labor.

A few years later, in 1789, the St. Petersburg *guberniia* governor Peter Petrovich Konovnitsyn made a verbal request of the city's mayor for a list of all factories (*fabriki* and *zavody*) in the city, and to whom they were registered. He specifically wanted to know the number of factories in each section of town. The mayor turned the task over to the deputies responsible for compiling and updating the city inhabitants book. Within four months the answer was provided to Konovnitsyn. The list identified the type of factory, the district of town where it was located, the owner's name, whether the owner was listed as a St. Petersburg merchant or one from another town or country, the amount of capital investment in the factory as declared by the owner, and whether the owner was registered in the city inhabitants book. Of 111 factories, only 57 (51.4 percent) indicated their amount of capital (table 7.6). The list varies from the one showing investment in 1775. Breweries do not appear on the earlier list, yet there were seven of them in 1789. Tallow-producing plants are not listed for 1775 but there are eight in 1789. Several types of factories included in small numbers in the 1775 list are absent from the one for 1789. What is most noticeable in comparing the two lists is that the amount of invested capital is much higher in the later list. No factory indicated an investment lower than 1,010 rubles, and the median was between 5,000 and 10,000 rubles.[34]

Table 7.6. Capital Investment in St. Petersburg Factories, 1789 (in Rubles)

Factory type	to 250	251–500	501–750	751–1000	1001–5000	5001–10,000	10,001–20,000	20,001–50,000	over 50,000
Tobacco					1				
Brewery					7	1	1		
Sugar							4	1	
Passementerie				1	2			1	1
Vodka							1		
Cloak and wire					1				
Foil (metal)					1		1		
Leather					3	7	4		1
Rope					2		2		
Hat					1				
Tallow and tallow candle					4	1	1	1	1
Playing cards					3				
Cast iron					1		1		
TOTAL				1	26	9	15	3	3 (57)

Source: TsGIA SPb, *fond* 781, *opis'* 2, *delo* 550.

Going Out of Business

There were, of course, failures. Before the Manufactures College gave a license to a business, the proprietor had to give evidence that he had the capital to sustain production. There were no sophisticated ways to test the market before beginning production, however, and numerous factories failed. Of those registered and not reporting or not working in 1775, the reason for closing was cited in twenty of twenty-six cases. In five cases the owner was in debt or had even been jailed for not satisfying contested *vekseli.* In three others the police would not permit work to continue because buildings were too dilapidated. The owners apparently could not afford either to repair the establishment or move to a new site. Two factories had burned and not been rebuilt. In three cases a large inventory could not be sold, halting production, and another two factories had closed because raw materials had not been supplied. Four proprietors had simply closed up shop: two became involved in other businesses, the third left town with no forwarding address, and the last one took employment in another factory producing similar goods. A soap factory closed because the only master of the productive process had left to open his own soapmaking plant.

Failure to turn a profit thus claimed numerous factories. This stemmed in part from the limited market for goods. The city produced by and large for its own consumption. Although wares manufactured in St. Petersburg were shipped elsewhere, the majority of goods were put into use in the city. These industrial enterprises were not well prepared or situated either to supply massive quantities of goods to the interior of Russia or to export finished products abroad. As Roger Portal and others have pointed out, the distance of St. Petersburg from both the supply of raw materials and the potential market of consumers hampered the rise of extensive industrial growth in the capital. The development of the city's latent productive power awaited a more efficient means of transporting raw materials to St. Petersburg and finished goods into the interior.

Furthermore, Russian-made products were regarded as of poor quality. Even brickyards came under regular government scrutiny to ensure adequate quality.[35] The Medical Chancellery, when ordering surgical instruments, specified that the steel be English or German, not Russian.[36] German and French master craftsmen were in great demand in factories. It was simply assumed that foreign products and producers were superior to Russian.[37]

Government-owned factories, not as bound to laws of profit and loss as private industry, rarely closed up shop. Their primary function—to supply goods to the state as the state needed them—required frequent subsidies to undergird operations. The fiscal problems that troubled Catherine's entire reign, particularly its later years, forced the government to try to operate its factories at a profit even though this was not always possible.

The Sestroretsk gun works outside the city suffered from endemic problems of shortfall in raw materials and poor quality of production, and the number of employees allocated to the factory by its written regulations slowly decreased throughout the period.[38] Alternatively, the Imperial Bronze Factory (est. 1778) imposed a 10 percent surcharge on all orders in order to meet production costs. However, since only two work orders were received by the factory in its first ten years of existence, state subsidies, however reluctantly awarded, made up the annual deficits.[39]

Some state-owned enterprises did show profits. One of the most efficiently run—and most prosperous—was the Imperial Tapestry Manufactory. Profitability came on the heels of an extensive reorganization in the early 1760s. The factory's managers issued monthly financial reports. Assuming that there was a direct relation between cost-consciousness and profitability, other state enterprises adopted the same idea by the 1790s, submitting regular reports closely patterned in format and style on the tapestry factory's reports.[40]

Laissez-Faire

Catherine had no greater panegyrist than collegiate assessor Petr Kolotov, whose six-volume work *The Deeds of Catherine the Great* summarizes the empress's activities chronologically.[41] In the last volume, after discussing her death and burial, Kolotov reprises the late empress's life, lavishing praise for more than thirty pages on deeds of all sorts. Near the end he praises Catherine's reign for reviving town life, not just commercial relations but also productive enterprises, for "dispensing diligence and the means of livelihood."[42] The truth of the matter is, other than owning factories, the state showed little interest in manufacturing. It granted monopolies on occasion. At least twice the state treasury lent sums in excess of 25,000 rubles to fabricants to aid them in setting up shop.[43] But the state regulated industry much less than it did commerce. The police, used extensively to regulate commercial activity, had no similar control over the quality of production or the treatment and wages of workers. For the most part government left factories alone.

Entrepreneurs often ignored the few regulations that the state placed over factory development, such as the law early in Catherine's reign forbidding factory construction in the capital. In most cases such violations went unpunished even when clearly pointed out to authorities.[44] Although factory owners were not allowed to sell their goods in the city's retail markets, a right reserved for merchants, some blatantly violated this law, which gave factory owners outlets for their products only at their factories unless they were also merchants.[45]

From all these statements, it would seem that the government adopted a different attitude toward privately owned industry than toward private commerce. The latter was closely regulated, with the state decreeing who could participate, what commerce could take place, how business was to be conducted, and so forth. Manufacturing was limited by many fewer regulations, and the regulatory measures that existed were enforced only halfheartedly.

The relative nonregulation of manufacturing is explained by the fact that factories were new to Russia. Indeed, even the artisan guilds were not indigenous, but transplanted from Germany by Peter the Great. Apparently the government had not yet decided how to fit the exercise of factory manufacturing into the estate and taxation systems. Or, having recognized the value of industry for the nation's economy, the government had yet to adopt a regulatory policy that would both foster further production and create additional income for the treasury.

In summary, factory production was in its infancy. Most privately owned enterprises remained relatively small, representing a moderate capital outlay and producing in small quantity. There was a moderate degree of durability among factories, but few lasted in the same family's hands for more than a short generation. Heavy industry had not yet assumed a leading role. Indeed, no one industry stood out above the others. Overall production was geared to satisfy local needs, and although some finished products were shipped overland to other parts of Russia or overseas, industry was clearly oriented to the demands of a bureaucratic and aristocratic capital city. If this was true of factories, it was all the more characteristic of the productive trades.

Handicrafts

Peter the Great called Russia's first artisan guilds (*tsekhi*) into existence, but he did not make membership in them obligatory for craftsmen. Because craft guilds were not indigenous to Russia, many artisans neglected to join, and the guilds soon fell generally into disuse.[46] St. Petersburg proved an exception to this rule, in part because the government's will to institute guilds could be carried out more easily in the capital city than in provincial towns, and also because of the high number of foreign-born artisans there, who for the most part joined guilds both because the guild structure had a stronger tradition in western Europe and because they believed that registration in a guild gave them definite status in the social order, with the privileges of that status.

Even so, the 1,127 people listed in the craft guild register on the eve of Catherine's reign totaled less than half the number registered at the end of Peter I's reign, when the city was much smaller. They were concentrated in a few trades. There were 216 cobblers, 179 tailors, and 126 grinders, for example, together comprising nearly half the total of registered artisans.[47] Several guilds had only one or two members, and in some cases several guilds existed within a single specialty.[48]

The number of artisans increased dramatically during Catherine's reign. Craftsmen registered in guilds totaled more than seven thousand by the end of the period, six times more than in 1761.[49] Undoubtedly the number of unregistered artisans multiplied also, although this expansion cannot be measured. The numbers of foreign craftsmen increased at about the same rate as those of Russian artisans, primarily because agents of the Russian government in western Europe were able to persuade Germans, Swedes, Frenchmen, Dutchmen, Swiss, and Englishmen to migrate to St. Petersburg.[50] Some of these foreign craftsmen came expressly to enter factory service. Not infrequently both private factory owners and state factory managers understood little about the manufacturing process and were heavily dependent upon the expertise of craftsmen, who in such cases received high wages. The number of Russian artisans increased primarily because these foreign master craftsmen were willing—at a supplement in wages, to be sure—to take on large numbers of Russian apprentices.[51]

Artisans lived in every sector of the city, generally renting quarters that served them as both workshop and residence. Until Catherine's reign their place in the city's social hierarchy had remained uncertain. On the one hand, the services they offered were indispensable, and the taxes they paid, like those of all taxpaying city dwellers, were welcomed into the government's coffers; but on the other hand, the residence city of the Russian emperors was too grand to permit an open display of the presence of lowly handicraft production.

For this reason, in order not to detract from the city's harmonious vistas, artisans' signboards were banned until 1770, when Catherine allowed them to be hung, albeit with strict regulations regarding size and appearance.[52] Prior to this craftsmen had been dependent upon word of mouth to provide their business. Scattered throughout the city, they did not even have the advantage of some merchants in St. Petersburg, that of having their businesses located adjacent to those of their fellow specialists, a situation frequently enjoyed by artisans in other cities. Some few artisans did advertise their work irregularly through the pages of St. Petersburg's newspaper, the *Sanktpeterburgskie vedomosti,* but the wares advertised in this manner tended to be those luxury goods of interest to a wealthy and educated clientele, and more than likely represented above-average skill and quality.

Measures to Improve the Condition of Artisans

Catherine took many steps to improve the legal and social status of craftsmen. Her efforts were bolstered by an increase in the number of foreign artisans, frequently more adept at their trade, better educated, and more attuned to Catherine's worldview than Russian craftsmen. In 1766, St. Petersburg's foreign-born craftsmen, predominantly Germans, petitioned the Ruling Senate to have their own guild organization, segregated from those for Russians. There were in fact already thirty-four guilds with no Russians in them (some of these had only a single master craftsman). The foreigners preferred to follow the regulations applied to Prussian craft guilds in 1719 rather than Petrine legislation.[53]

Their petition, which was granted, indicates the polarization between foreign and Russian artisans in the capital. Not only were there the obvious linguistic differences, but there was also the foreigners' belief that they were far better masters of their trades than the Russians, and masters of trades requiring superior training and skill. By granting their request, the Catherinian administration confirmed this opinion, reasoning that the new arrangements would be more beneficial to the artisans. Foreigners then set up 53 artisan guilds totaling 777 master craftsmen; Russians had 35 guilds with 562 masters.[54]

Beginning in 1770, Catherine permitted artisans to live on Millionnaia Street and on the Moika near the Winter Palace, a privilege they had lost nearly twenty years before.[55] In this residential area lived the wealthiest and most powerful people in the city. Artisans had been excluded because they did not fit in socially, but Catherine signaled her interest in raising up a new urban middle class by this significant gesture.[56] By the latter years of the century, Georgi could compare St. Petersburg's artisans favorably with those in other European cities. Those in St. Petersburg seemed more courteous, wealthier, more cultured, and more self-assured. Only in England, thought Georgi, did craftsmen live better.[57] To this extent Catherine's efforts to improve the status of artisans had proved successful.

But there were also artisans whose skills in and practice of their trade left much to be desired. The city's delegate to the Legislative Commission in 1767 was asked to support regularized inspections of craftsmen's work and the establishment of self-regulating bodies for all trades. The request said that artisans pretended to have skills that they did not possess. They often received pay from customers in advance, then produced nothing. In these cases, deceived customers had no further recourse.[58] The low quality of artisans' work forced the Court Intendant Office (responsible for the interior design and repair of the empress's palaces), to stop hiring craftsmen and give contracts to peasants instead, even though this was illegal.[59] Many other cases could be cited to demonstrate that some form of control was needed over production.

Russia had no strong tradition of craft guilds as guarantors of high standards of workmanship, and when Catherine granted the right to anyone registered in a town to sell wares he had made himself, all sorts of possibilities for fraud and shoddy workmanship appeared.[60] Furthermore, a different set of rules applied to the foreign artisans, who under their regulations adopted in 1766 had to belong to guilds. When they did not join, as was the case of some saddle makers dealt with by the city magistracy, they had to pay a fine of ten rubles and suffer the confiscation of the tools of their trade.[61]

The Artisan Regulation

Here as in so many other areas, Catherine's solution to a problem was sweeping legislation. The legislation redefining artisan guilds, an adjunct to the Municipal Charter of 1785, stemmed both from Catherine's intention to enhance the social and legal position of artisans and from pure necessity to control the quality of production.[62] The legislation also dealt with problems caused by the increasing number of foreigners and the growing complexity in relationships among artisans.

Without undertaking a detailed investigation into the Artisan Regulation, an exercise long overdue but for which this is not the place, its provisions can be laid out briefly.[63] Each specialty in which there were at least five master craftsmen working in St. Petersburg had the right to organize itself as a corporation. Every craft corporation, or artisan guild, elected three officials, the guild foreman and two assistants. All the guild foremen together made up the artisan board, which was chaired by a head chosen by all the members of the guilds. Each guild also had a secretary (literally a sworn broker—*prisiazhnii makler*) who handled the written business and kept accounts. He was the only official who could be paid for his service to the guild or board. The foremen of the several guilds sat on the general city council, and the board head represented the artisans on the six-man city council.

These officials had general oversight over all matters pertaining to the public's confidence in the crafts; the quality of production; the relationships among masters, journeymen, and apprentices; and the care of dependents, widows, and orphans of men in the trades. Foremen and their assistants also rendered oral decisions in legal suits and damages involving members of craft guilds, up to the amount of twenty-five rubles. The city magistracy handled cases in which more than twenty-five rubles was at issue. In a sharp departure from the standard practice of craft guilds in western Europe, the masters' boards did not have the right to establish prices for specific jobs or pieces of work. Within each craft there was also to be a board of journeymen to handle matters originating with journeymen and apprentices.

A master craftsman in one city was accepted as one in any other city in the empire, and attestations were also supposed to be accepted from foreign cities. This eased considerably the difficulties of moving to St. Petersburg and setting up business there. When there were questions about competence, however, the board in each craft was empowered to examine the work of the one in question.

The regulations outlined mutual relations between master craftsmen and their journeymen and apprentices, thoroughly subordinating the latter to the former but providing a means of appeal against an overbearing master. The standard period for apprenticeship was set at three to five years, with three years the norm for journeymen, who were expected to be at least twenty-four years of age when they became masters. Provisions were made for state and crown peasants to become artisans if they received passports to live in town.

The men who controlled the St. Petersburg city council were dissatisfied with the Artisan Regulations, however, feeling that the ordinance did not properly address the nature of handicrafts or give artisans a status appropriate to them. They expressed this view in a remarkable document, the "Opinion of the St. Petersburg City Council about putting the trades into better condition and order," dating from several years after the Artisan Regulation went into effect.[64]

The premise of the "Opinion," which was signed at several intervals by ten men,[65] was that the crafts (*remesla*) remained insufficiently understood and protected in Russia. The evidence that foreign imports were both less expensive and of higher quality than domestically produced goods substantiated their assertion, as did the unemployment in St. Petersburg. The document expressed the conviction that Peter the Great understood the crafts and would have seen to it that trades were properly developed had he lived longer. His successors proved incapable of properly encouraging the crafts. Even the Artisan Regulation of 1785 placed severe strictures on the proper development of crafts.

What the "Opinion" called for was a three-tiered system of craft guilds. It treated *remeslo* (craft, occupation), *khudozhestvo* (applied art), and *masterstvo* (trade, handicraft) as all belonging in this category. The first level was to be made up of those trades that required the most skill, practice, or perfection. It should include architects, painters, sculptors, mechanics, chemists, engravers, teachers, gardeners, druggists, metalworkers, jewelers, and those working with both precious metals and gems, doctors, and experts in maritime navigation. They were to be indistinguishable in status and rights from first-guild merchants.

At the second level were to be those trades that had to be learned well: clock and watchmakers, makers of instruments, gunsmiths, welders, gold and silversmiths who did not work with gems, coppersmiths, porcelain makers, potters, hatmakers, galloon makers, woodworkers, woodcarvers, makers of wooden and stone figures, candy makers, dentists and others besides doctors who treated the sick, interior decorators, engravers not included in the previous group, and people who sewed thread of precious metals. Their status was to be the same as that of third-guild merchants.

The third category, which according to the "Opinion" did not necessitate formal training (*nauka*), included the likes of bookbinders and smithies, cobblers and saddlers, barbers and bakers.[66] Their legal status was supposed to be equivalent to that of the *posad* people.

This stratification of artisans, clearly intended to relegate most of them, whether Russian or foreign, to the lowest level, must have been inspired by merchants fearful that their rights and privileges would have to be shared too broadly. It may well have taken into consideration the income level of most artisans, however, and placed them in a category with people at the same level but who derived their income in other occupations. This "Opinion" would have had the effect of sharply reducing the representation of artisans on the general city council, where they predominated according to the 1785 charter. It would have taken fifteen masters in the first category to form a guild, thirty in the second, and fifty in the third. No distinction was made between foreigners and Russians. All would have to belong to the same guild. Of course, only the most widely spread trades would have had enough practitioners to form a guild, but when there was an insufficient number, closely related trades could have joined together to form a single guild.

Serfs (*gospodskie liudi*) would have been able to join the crafts guilds, but their mobility would have been limited under the terms of their passports. They could not have become masters or have journeymen working under them, nor could they have had any apprentices under them save serfs of their common lord. Foreign masters would also have been placed under certain restrictions. No one who was not registered in the appropriate guild could have practiced that trade or called himself a city craftsman. All artisans would have had to swear an oath to support their system of administration. They would have been put under further control by the prohibition against collective price-fixing and against introducing any new machine or tool designed to make the work of that craft easier or to improve it significantly, unless first receiving permission from the city council and the elected artisan leadership.

That leadership would have consisted of two or three elders elected from each trade, the equivalent of judges in the oral courts for merchants. These elders were to choose the members of the artisan board and its president, in addition to the head, who would have sat on the six-man city council. The head was to stand in the same relationship to artisans as the burgomaster to merchants. The board members and president were to be comparable to the merchants' aldermen. Elders were to have general charge over the operation of the craft, and the board over the trades.[67]

There is no evidence that the "Opinion" was ever taken seriously by higher officials, much less put into effect. Nevertheless, the very fact that merchants felt so keenly the need to undercut the status of artisans demonstrates that Catherine's Artisan Regulation gave artisans a higher place than they had enjoyed before. The merchants were willing to grant this status to those in what we would term today the professions, but insisted on a delineation of privilege and status that would place those practicing the professions above the majority of craftsmen. Relations between merchants and artisans were not entirely peaceful.

Social stress also manifested itself among artisans, primarily in the relations between native Russians and foreigners. The latter predominated in crafts requiring the most skilled labor. For example, fully half of the owners of weaving looms were non-Russians, with Frenchmen most numerous.[68] Because of their higher levels of skill and culture, foreigners continued to feel themselves superior to Russian craftsmen, as expressed in their 1766 request to be granted privileges beyond those given to Russian artisans. Although the Artisan Regulation of 1785 seemed to call for an integration of all artisans in a trade, regardless of their nationality, in a single guild (Article 64: "If any artisan from another city or a foreign country wishes to be registered in the Board, he must present either a written certificate from the Board of the other city or the work of his own skill, as is specified in Article 60."), foreigners continued to maintain their own artisan board, parallel to the one overseeing Russian artisans.

Undoubtedly the inability of Russians and foreigners to cooperate in the corporative structure stemmed from cultural as well as economic differences. With neither side willing to relinquish direction of artisan affairs, complete integration of the two corporate structures failed, and two orders of craftsmen continued to operate side by side in the same city.

Labor

Reliable figures showing the composition of the labor force have yet to be compiled, but six groups of people who comprised it can be identified. They include: (1) state peasants assigned to various enterprises, most of them state-owned; (2) military recruits diverted to the city for various kinds of work in the construction battalions and in state-owned factories; (3) serfs and other peasants working in the city on quitrent, or *obrok*;[69] (4) foreigners, most of them skilled laborers but a few of them unskilled; (5) people from smaller towns who were still registered there but who actually lived and worked much of the year in St. Petersburg; and (6) vagabond peasants who, lacking passports, could not legally find work, but were frequently hired anyway. The first two groups worked under obligation, as did those *obrok* serfs sent to St. Petersburg under contract; the others were hired.

Obligated Workers and Hired Workers

During this period of time, labor relationships in St. Petersburg underwent a shift that was to be followed by other areas of Russia during later decades. Obligated labor gave way to a freely hired labor market.[70] This was particularly so in industries having a strong tradition of small-scale peasant production, where new workers could easily be fit into the manufacturing process. It was also generally true for those enterprises producing for a large market, not by contract.[71]

Soviet historians working on this issue identified three specific tendencies among privately owned factories in St. Petersburg. First there were factories where hired labor predominated throughout the period, growing even stronger toward its end (those producing leather, rope, sugar, soap, hats, and playing cards). Second were those factories that shifted from a majority of obligated workers in midcentury to a preponderance of hired workers by the end of Catherine's reign (silk, bleaching, galloon, haberdashery, glass, and metallurgical manufactories). And finally, in a small number of plants obligated labor remained the norm (papermaking, cotton cloth, and dyeing establishments).[72]

The same tendency toward a labor market could be seen in a number of state-owned productive enterprises as well. The Admiralty increasingly used contractors who hired workers to build naval ships. All the workers at the city-owned shipyard were hired. The imperial porcelain works increasingly hired its workers rather than having them assigned. Virtually all of the six hundred workers in the state-owned brickyards were hired, because obligated labor apparently had shown itself to be untenable by midcentury in that large an enterprise.[73]

As early as the 1760s, well over half the workers in all factories were hired (63.5 percent in 1769–72 according to one study),[74] and the figure increased thereafter. In fact, the size and influence of the labor market in St. Petersburg was beginning to blur the lines defining the traditional social and legal categories of population. As perhaps the largest single labor market in Russia, St. Petersburg attracted workers who were serfs on *obrok* or peasants on passports when considered from the standpoint of the village, but who were workers hiring themselves out, frequently in self-administered artels, when in the city.[75] In the view of V. M. Paneiakh, they could be seen as a "preproletariat."[76]

Working Conditions

As the workers came to the city's factories or construction industry, the impact of this muted challenge to the accepted order was felt far from St. Petersburg. Without a large population nearby to draw from, St. Petersburg attracted people from much of Novgorod *guberniia,* especially Olonets district on the far side of Lake Ladoga. Other workers came from the areas around Arkhangel'sk and Vologda, Kostroma and Iaroslavl', and from Moscow *guberniia.*[77] Frequently these workers came from locales noted for their specialization in a particular craft, and found employment in the same or a closely related industry in St. Petersburg.

Living essentially in two worlds, bound to the village or estate and hired in the city, they found their commitment to the second world limited by the length of time granted them there by the first. Most passports issued to peasants on quitrent expired within one year, necessitating an annual pilgrimage home for renewal. More rarely the period was set at two or three years. This practice of short-term passports necessarily affected labor practices in St. Petersburg. Few employees drawn from the passport-bearing population could sign on for long-term employment. More than half the workers hired in St. Petersburg's privately owned manufactories were peasants. Three-fifths of these were state and economic peasants, who generally had passports of longer duration than landlord serfs.

The evidence put together by N. N. Dmitriev for the cotton textile plant owned by Christian Lehman (Lieman) at Shlisselburg may show an extreme. He found that of seventy-six people hired as short-term laborers in one thirteen-month period, nine worked less than a fortnight. Eleven more stayed for a period of less than a month, forty-four from one to three months, ten from three to six months, and only two longer than six months.[78] In a study covering many factories, S. I. Kolotilova found that hired workers under contract also stayed for relatively brief periods: 62 percent had contracts for up to a year, 30 percent for a period from one to five years, and only 8 percent for longer than five years.[79] Elsewhere Kolotilova argued that statistical evidence of the hiring of peasants from St. Petersburg *guberniia* is difficult to find in archival sources precisely because "local" peasants were hired only as day labor or, at most, on a week-to-week basis.[80]

The contracts themselves demonstrate the nature of relationships between employers and employees. The duties of workers were specified, as were their wages and any penalties that could be levied against them for misbehavior. For example, Christian Lehman and Vasilii Antipov were parties to a contract at Lehman's Shlisselburg cotton cloth factory in which Antipov agreed to work five years at a wage of forty-eight rubles the first year, sixty the second, and another raise in the last three years if he worked hard and performed his job well. He promised not to get drunk or play cards or gamble at dice. He was to be fined twice his daily wage for every day of work he missed through his own truancy, and would have to pay a fine of fifty rubles if he ever broke the contract by leaving.[81]

Bogdan Khakhberdov, an Armenian merchant who owned a silk factory on Vasil'evskii Island, made a contract with one of his master workers, the serf Petr Ivanov, in which Ivanov agreed to work every day except holidays and Sundays for two years, at a wage of eighty-five rubles a year. He was to comport himself well, not get drunk, and pay a fine of fifty kopecks for each day's work he missed. As the master worker, he was also responsible for keeping the looms in a good state of repair and for showing the other workers how to operate them.[82]

In occupations requiring substantial training, laborers often entered into employment at an early age. For example, when Benjamin Müller opened his silk stocking factory (soon to be sold to Count Iaguzhinskii), he sought to persuade parents to apprentice their children to the factory so that they could learn the silk stocking trade. Other factories placed advertisements in the newspaper inviting parents to do the same thing. Following their training, children had to remain in the factories for a few years. State- as well as privately owned enterprises practiced child apprenticeship in this way, often using orphans as apprentices in shops or factories when they were about ten years of age.[83] In fact, Catherine intended for most of the young males reared in the Foundling Home to receive their training for an occupation in this way.

Because of the apprentice system of labor, employees received wages on two different levels. As a rule, workers who knew their trade received wages on which one could live quite easily. Laborers with undeveloped skills, however, received but a fraction of what skilled workers earned, and could hardly have maintained their own households. A comparison of wage levels at the imperial tapestry works illustrates the point (see table 7.7). Unlike the modern factory, the tapestry works did not give highest salaries to managers. In fact, their wages were not too out of line with their percentage of the total workforce. The same was true of the journeymen.

The real divergencies lay in wages paid to master craftsmen and to apprentices. The former, only 3.2 percent of the workforce, received 42.1 percent of the wages. (The foreign masters, 2.2 percent of the workforce, received 34.0 percent of the wages.) At the other extreme, apprentices comprised 64.6 percent of the workforce, but were paid only 22.7 percent of wages.[84] On the average each master thus earned thirty-six times as much as each apprentice. This extreme difference in salaries bears far greater similarity to early modern craft guild pay schedules than to wage scales of nineteenth-century factories.

Skilled craftsmen quickly found work at good wages, for their labor was in great demand.[85] As Russian artisans developed their skills, wages rose accordingly, although not to foreigners' wage levels. Advancement was slow, requiring many years of service and assiduous practice. Once again, to cite an example from the imperial tapestry works: the first Russian apprentice there, who began work in 1735,

Table 7.7. Wage Levels at the Imperial Tapestry Works

Position	Number	Wages (rubles)	Average per worker	Percentage of workers	Percentage of wages
Managerial	10	1,592	159.20	5.5	8.6
Master craftsmen	6*	7,800	1,300.00	3.2	42.1
Foreign	4	6,300	1,575.00	2.2	34.0
Russian	1	300	300.00	0.5	1.6
Journeymen	40	3,700	92.50	22.1	20.0
Untermastera	14	2,050	146.43	7.7	11.1
Podmastera	26	1,650	63.46	14.4	8.9
Apprentices	117	4,212	36.00	64.6	22.7
Other	8	1,206	150.75	4.5	6.5

*The nationality of one master craftsman is not known. *Source:* See note 82 of this chapter.

became a master weaver only in 1763, after twenty-eight years of service. His salary, two hundred rubles annually, was only an eighth of what his mentor, a Frenchman, had earned.[86] The discrepancy is understandable. Foreigners had more experience, they trained Russian apprentices, and they drew much larger initial salaries because they could not be induced to migrate to Russia for less.

Wages for short-term employment varied greatly from season to season. Information compiled by A. I. Kopanev indicates that wages averaged from one-third to two-thirds higher in summer than in winter, even though far more workers were available in summer.[87] The working day in summer was longer than in winter, but not enough longer to account for all the difference. If one were a part-time resident of the city, it was best to reside there in summer. During the colder months of the year when work was not available, one could live much more cheaply in the countryside. For this reason temporary residents left their families at home They did so not only because of the difficulty in moving households, but also because summer working hours were so long no leisure time remained to spend with families, relatives, and peers.[88]

Worker Discontent

Low pay for unskilled hired workers and obligated employees led to labor problems. Usually workers protested poor conditions simply by disappearing. Even workers at the upper end of the pay scale ran away. The serf master craftsman Petr Ivanov, whose contract with factory owner Khakhberdov was outlined above, ran away from work in the first year after agreeing to his contract. Apprehended, he ran away again five years later while still working in the factory.[89] This was the only real form of protest the individual worker had.

Although obligated workers seem to have run away more frequently than those who were hired, the latter also escaped the workplace through flight. In 1766 alone, forty-eight workers ran away from Vasilii Ol'khin's paper mill on Vyborg Side. Among the Okhta carpenters flight was so common that in 1796 a full 20 percent of them, 118 men, were fugitives.[90] Runaways usually moved into other areas of the city and found employment in other enterprises.[91] Aware of this pattern of behavior, government agencies warned contractors not to hire runaways; detailed instructions were distributed to this end.[92] Nevertheless flight continued to be an oft-used and reliable method of escaping harsh conditions.

A second expression of discontent was the formal protest. From the 1770s on, workers began to seek changes in their working conditions by making formal protests. For example, in 1771 a spinner named Shibkov at the ropewalk on Vasil'evskii Island owned by the Englishman Robert Kramp (Cramp) was sent to the Manufactures Office with the complaint that he worked poorly and incited others to do the same. Another ten workers lay down their tools and went with him, not only to defend him but to object to the quality of raw materials given them, which decreased productivity and in turn meant lower wages.[93] Although the resolution of this case is not known, in most other cases the workers lost and were returned to their employers for punishment.

The result was different, however, in the best documented case of collective protest in Catherinian St. Petersburg. In 1787 a large number of state peasants working for a man named Dolgov, a subcontractor on the project to erect granite embankments on the Catherine Canal, walked off the job in the last week of July. The state, wanting the task completed before the onset of winter, sought to mediate in the case, but the workmen refused to return to work, choosing rather to seek a hearing of their grievances in court. Despite urgings from various officials, the workers remained on strike into the first week of August.

These developments took place while Catherine was returning from her extensive tour of southern Russia. After her return on August 7, the workers determined to take their case directly to her for mediation. Four hundred representatives, one-tenth of the strikers, marched to Palace Square opposite the Winter Palace. They refused to speak with lesser officials, insisting on an appointment with the empress herself. The demonstration remained orderly and respectful. Every time a woman appeared at a window of the palace the crowd, thinking her to be Catherine, raised a cheer. But the empress refused to listen to querulous peasants, and finally ordered the guards to disperse the group. Using force and arresting seventeen people, the troops quickly scattered the men.

Now the state faced two problems: how to bring the work on the canal embankment to completion, and what to do with the arrested workers. The lower aulic court at first sentenced thirty workers to be whipped, with the five ringleaders sent to hard labor after having their nostrils clipped. The superior aulic court, in consultation with the city magistracy, lightened the terms upon appeal to whippings for sixteen men, with the five leaders sent for a month at hard labor. The criminal chamber of the provincial board ratified this, but Catherine then interfered, sending the case to the court of conscience, where the arbitrators chosen on the workers' behalf were the provincial procurator and solicitor of financial affairs. Here the men were found guilty only of "impertinence and stubbornness."[94] Throughout the period, while the case was being decided, the remaining laborers steadfastly refused to heed warnings from the police chief or anyone else to return to work. The deadlock continued through August and September without resolution. Finally on October 1, realizing that every day lost meant greater probability that the work could not be completed until another season, the government decided to satisfy the workers' demands (which never were recorded in detail) and drop charges against the men who had been arrested.[95] In this instance, from all indications the largest protest of its kind in eighteenth-century St. Petersburg, workers won a clear victory as the government met their demands and pledged to improve working conditions.

Criminal court cases involving obligated laborers show how miserable their lives often were. They began work at an early age, frequently at nine years and younger. Poor treatment by their masters caused many to flee again and again. Often they were driven to steal in order to supplement their meager wages. Many never completed their apprenticeships. Unskilled, they turned to crime to earn their livelihood.[96]

Hired laborers, on the other hand, were able to gain more favorable working conditions. Often they banded together and sought employment collectively, forming artels that could contain up to sixty men. In the purest form of artel, the men elected their foremen. Groups of workers brought together by contractors resembled artels but properly speaking were not. Artels assumed collective responsibility for the actions of their individual members. Prospective members paid a small sum to join.[97]

In addition to artels, peasant contractors often hired other peasants to work for them on public projects under government contract. Contractors learned of these tasks through advertisements in *Sankt-peterburgskie vedomosti.* Terms of contracts usually stated that the agency wanting the work done would supply everything except workers. Sometimes contractors were responsible for supplying tools, but only rarely did they provide materials also.[98] The embanking of canal and riverbanks with granite, a landmark improvement dating from Catherine's reign, was accomplished through contracted peasant labor. The Admiralty increasingly contracted the building of naval vessels as well. The extensive work done to prepare the house where Prussia's Prince Henry was to live in the early 1770s was carried out largely by peasant contractors. The separate contracts varied in value from twenty-five to more than seventeen hundred rubles. Among those contracting to do the work were seven estate peasants from Iaroslavl' district and one from near Kostroma, a monastery peasant from Iaroslavl' district, two craftsmen of German origin, an ironmonger from Kholmogory, two journeymen, and numerous others less clearly identified.[99]

In sum, although factories made up a substantial portion of manufacturing enterprises in St. Petersburg, handiwork shops owned by individual craftsmen also contributed to goods production, particularly in products intended for domestic use. Neither type of enterprise was large-scale. Most factories and shops over a period of thirty-five years either changed hands or disappeared.

Technology was not as advanced as elsewhere in Europe at the same time. In the assessment of N. A. Rozhkov, "not only did the Russian cottage-industry laborer work with his hands, with the aid of the most primitive tools—it was the same even in factories. In essence, the factory in the eighteenth century did not deserve this awesome title; it was a manufactory, it carried on without machines, by hand labor, which allowed the possibility of competition with it on the part of cottage industry, which was from the standpoint of technology, thus, no less a factory. It is sufficient to say that even such a simple and uncomplicated machine as the spinning jenny was unknown to Russian industry in the eighteenth century."[100]

Foreigners played an important role in industrial activity, especially at skilled and managerial levels. Russians who were not from the capital or who had been there only a short while predominated in unskilled jobs. In spite of the unmistakable premodern cast of goods production in late eighteenth-century St. Petersburg, it was then and there that Russian workers, managers, factory owners, and craftsmen developed the technological expertise and managerial acumen necessary to run the larger enterprises that began to appear in the first years of the nineteenth century. This early development of industrial activity—especially as it involved foreign specialists and peasants from the Russian hinterland—contributed significantly to the urbanization of St. Petersburg.

8
". . . and I Shall leave Petersburg dressed in Marble": St. Petersburg in 1796

WE RETURN AT LAST TO CATHERINE'S QUIP THAT SHE FOUND ST. Petersburg built of wood and would leave it dressed in marble. It comes from a letter she wrote Frau Johanna Dorothea Bielcke in July 1770. Giving credit to the originator of the saying, she wrote, "Augustus said that he found Rome built of brick and would leave it built of marble; I say that I found Petersburg virtually wooden and will leave its buildings dressed in marble."[1] To what extent was it true? What changes had been wrought in St. Petersburg during the thirty-four-year reign of Catherine II? Perhaps the best initial vantage point from which to examine this question is through an overview of the capital at the end of her reign, when the city of 1762 was still recognizable, but bore the clear stamp of the intervening third of a century.[2]

TOPOGRAPHICAL CHANGES

Most startling was the city's change in size. The outer limits of the city in 1762 fell well within the built-up area of 1796. St. Petersburg seemed huge to A. T. Bolotov when he rode his horse across it at the beginning of Catherine's reign. Had he returned near the end of her rule he would have recognized a few streets and buildings, but little else. The steady outward expansion of construction drew official concern as early as the mid-1760s, especially along the southern and southeastern perimeter of town, where new arrivals most naturally settled. As the land set aside for pasturing livestock inexorably gave way to the ax, the hammer, and the saw, the authorities sensed the need to place limits on spatial expansion, yet their efforts to do so proved futile. By the end of the century the city proper measured nearly five miles wide in any direction. The area within which construction was permitted had a circumference of nearly sixteen miles.[3]

A much higher value accrued to land near the center of town than in the outskirts. Many of the new buildings at the edges of the city resembled those in the center a third of a century earlier, while in the center much grander edifices had been erected and the open spaces between buildings was disappearing. People of limited means who wanted to build their own houses had to construct them near the city's edge, where they constantly encroached on the remaining city pastureland. Toward the end of the century a broad and shallow ditch was dug to outline the limits of the area in which construction was permissible. It was deliberately placed far enough out to leave space for expansion, while still preserving some pastureland.[4] That open space for grazing, originally intended to be an area about two miles wide, had shrunk considerably because of outward growth. When Jean-François Georgel, the bishop of Strassbourg, entered St. Petersburg in 1799 on the Tsarskoe Selo road, he noted that the gate to the city, in the form of a triumphal arch, and the city limit ditch lay only one-third to one-half mile beyond the farthest developed area of the city.[5]

Along some of the principal transportation arteries, the city expanded even beyond the ditch. Outside the city gate, the road to Peterhof became early in Catherine's reign a popular place for the wealthy and powerful to build their dachas, the summer homes that sometimes were quite large. Already well developed by 1779, the highway was lined with the villas of counts, generals, and court councillors, with nearly a hundred dachas lining the road, most of them facing the highway and the Gulf of Finland. There were also inns and at least one monastery. The fact that the empress frequently traveled the road to and from Peterhof hardly diminished the area's popularity.[6] The city also spilled beyond its officially defined border on the right bank of the Neva upstream from the city, toward the Okhta settlements. Although these neighborhoods were still not included within the city limits at the end of Catherine's reign, economically and socially—if not administratively—they had to be considered part of St. Petersburg. Many industrial concerns had sprung up around Okhta, stretching some distance up the meandering Okhta River by this time.[7] The banks of the Neva itself were a third area of sprawling urban growth. Commercial and industrial establishments in particular located farther and farther upstream with each passing year. The enterprises providing building materials were concentrated especially thickly in this area, which could also be considered part of the city.[8] Without its brickyards, sawmills, and tile-producing works, the construction industry in the city would have been considerably hampered.

The St. Petersburg of 1762 was divided into five administrative districts. By 1796 there were ten. Outward expansion accounted for two of the new districts as well as the enlarged boundaries of others. But the remaining three new districts were created by dividing Admiralty

Side into First, Second, Third, and Fourth admiralties. This subdivision into much smaller districts geographically testifies to the much denser utilization of land and concentration of population within the old city.

Despite the enormous growth overall, in some sectors of the city there had been little or no outward expansion. The districts closest to the sea, Vasil'evskii Island and St. Petersburg Side, retained their semiurban, semirural character. Virtually no construction appeared in the western half of Vasil'evskii Island and the northern portion of St. Petersburg Side. Those areas were low-lying and poorly drained, more subject to periodic flooding than most other districts, and thus inhospitable for habitation. But their protection from construction was also intentional, for several large parcels of land in those areas were designated for agricultural use as garden plots and pasturage (the apothecary garden of the College of Medicine lay in St. Petersburg Side), or as cemeteries. Vasil'evskii Island in particular seemed to embody each stage of urban development from primitive nature to fully developed city. The eastern end of the island housed the city's wholesale commercial establishments, larger and more sophisticated than in 1762. Major institutions of learning were there, too, including the Academy of Sciences, Academy of Fine Arts, and Mining Institute, all given splendid new buildings during Catherine's reign. In the island's better districts, wealthy merchants and men of letters lived in fashionable masonry houses. Expensive churches of some architectural note had been built. Toward the center of the island, the lines were typified by smaller wooden houses that became poorer as one moved west. Near the outer limits of the built-up area, the few inhabitants lived as if in the countryside.[9]

As the example of the island demonstrates, not all physical changes during Catherine's reign resulted from spatial expansion; many changes likewise took place within older parts of town. To contemporary observers, one of the most evident transformations involved the system of water transportation, the rivers and canals. As noted earlier, when Catherine came to the throne, river and canal embankments remained quite primitive. At best they were lined with wooden posts at the water's edge to protect and preserve the sandy banks. With time these pilings rotted and erosion again became a problem. In order to prevent this and give embankments permanence, stability, and an appearance becoming to a *Residenzstadt,* Catherine issued an edict in the first month of her reign directing that the banks of the Neva River be constructed with granite, beginning with the southern embankment.[10]

Seven years later similar work began on the canals. In the worst state of repair was the swampy, garbage-choked stream between the

Moika and the Fontanka. Using it as an example, we can see the process by which canals were improved. Planning actually began in 1764, but in the first few years no more was done than to rename the stream Ekaterininskii (Catherine) Canal. Construction of granite embankments, contracted to be done in sections, commenced in 1769. Four sections were completed by 1777, when there was a slowdown in the work.[11] In 1780 the project was infused with increased funding and given greater scope. The decision was made to straighten the remaining portion of the canal somewhat, dig it deeper, and connect its eastern end to the Moika. This work was completed in 1788.[12] As one of the great urban public works projects in eighteenth-century Russia, the construction of embankments on the canals and the river deserves its own full-scale study.

By the end of Catherine's reign the Neva, Fontanka, and Catherine Canals were quayed with granite, bordered by broad streets, and lined with many magnificent houses. Only the Moika remained undressed in granite. As the innermost of the three concentric canals, it was narrower and had more twists and turns than the others. Even though its banks had not undergone reconstruction and the adjacent streets were narrower and less imposing, the properties abutting the Moika were in great demand. Among others, foreigners were competing to purchase the stately houses lining the canal.[13]

The granite embankments of the Neva, Catherine Canal, and Fontanka contributed greatly to the architectural dignity and grandeur of St. Petersburg. With their decorative wrought-iron railings they comprise one of Europe's most picturesque vistas of urban waterways. Two other reasons for their construction, not to be forgotten, were to prevent erosion of soil into rivers and canals, and to prevent the waterways—an effective system for cleansing the city of its wastes—from becoming clogged. Furthermore, by strengthening shorelines the embankments facilitated the discharging and taking on of goods from boat to shore, and boat landings included for that purpose frequently mark the quays. In this way, the renovation of the embankments made its own impact on the economic life of the city.[14]

Less pretentious canals also took shape during Catherine's reign. Built near the edges of the city, their purpose was not to facilitate the exchange of goods and encourage water traffic, but rather to drain swampy land, to provide periodic flood control, and to serve as borders for the city or its police administrative divisions.[15] The Ligovo and Obvodnyi canals were two such waterways at least partially dredged in Catherine's time.

Catherine's claim to have found St. Petersburg built of wood and left it dressed in marble applies even to the city's bridges. In 1762, the rivers and canals of St. Petersburg were bridged almost exclusively with wood, which Catherine sought to replace with others constructed of stone. Included among her noteworthy successes were eight granite vaulted bridges over the Fontanka, two of which still stand in a form closely reminiscent of the original.[16] But not every plan was successfully carried out. Kharlamskii Bridge over the Catherine Canal, for example, was allowed to fall into such disrepair through bureaucratic negligence and the failure to appropriate funds for construction that it was eventually closed and rotted away.[17] Nor were engineers of that era able to construct a permanent stone bridge across the Neva. Instead, money was provided to maintain the pontoon bridges, which continued to span the river throughout much of the year as the weather permitted. At least one man claimed to have developed a workable plan for a single-span wooden arched bridge across the Neva. I. P. Kulibin, a craftsman and inventor from Nizhnii-Novgorod whose clocks and microscopes appealed to Catherine, drew up plans and even built a model of such a bridge in the 1770s. The plan is now on display in the State Hermitage. Interesting as a curiosity, his project apparently did not receive serious consideration.[18] Although the Neva's main channel remained unspanned, permanent bridges did stretch across the Small Neva from Vasil'evskii Island to St. Petersburg Side and from there across the Nevka to Vyborg Side. Consequently the city was separated into no more than two parts during those times when temporary bridges could not be used, facilitating greater access and enabling a greater degree of day-to-day interaction than had been possible at the beginning of Catherine's reign.[19]

St. Petersburg's physical appearance improved in other ways during the reign of Catherine II. The city lost the rough-and-ready appearance of a frontier town and became a multifaceted city. Inhospitable land was made hospitable, roadways were improved, streets were lit at night, the primary building material—at least in the center—became masonry rather than wood. Indeed, wooden areas of the city seemingly had metamorphosed into masonry by the end of the century. An anecdote related at the time to A. T. Bolotov, living far from the city on his estates, indicates that these changes may have surprised Catherine herself on occasion. While riding one day with her master of the hunt, V. I. Levashov, she is supposed to have arrived at a spot where she knew there had been some squalid little huts, only to find two huge masonry houses of good architecture standing side by side. Catherine reportedly exclaimed, "Good Gracious! There is so much building going on here! And what good construction it is! Decaying shacks stood here not that long ago, and now houses are already in place."[20] Whatever one makes of Catherine's evident surprise, St.

Petersburg was transformed during the third of a century she reigned. Although exact figures are difficult to come by (and those that do exist often disagree among themselves), it has been estimated that in 1765 the city contained 460 masonry houses and over 4,000 houses of wood. Thirty years later masonry houses numbered approximately 1,800. The number of wooden houses increased only to 4,300, the increase primarily coming in new areas of town.[21]

This change from wood to brick and stone came about because of the desire to avoid the frequent and severe conflagrations that swept wooden quarters of the city. Weekly police precinct reports reveal that fires broke out somewhere with almost daily regularity. Usually they were contained, but once every four or five years the winds fanned them out of control or they reached highly combustible materials. On those occasions fire destroyed large numbers of homes, shops, and warehouses, as firefighters worked more to limit a fire's spread than to extinguish it. In these infernos it was not unusual for a hundred buildings or more to be destroyed. Of one such fire in May 1771, N. G. Kurganov wrote, "A strong eastern wind aided the flames; from this fire burned almost half of [Vasil'evskii] island from 7th to 20th lines, including the building of the Naval Corpus. Numerous houses burned completely down, of others only the walls remained. The Corpus property, chancellery papers, cadet ammunition—everything was destroyed."[22]

As a consequence of the first destructive fire in Catherine's reign, in 1763, a comprehensive building code was put into effect that closely regulated the types and sizes of buildings and the materials to be used in the reconstruction of houses. Because of this building code, there were virtually no wooden homes in either First or Second Admiralty by the end of Catherine's reign. Catherine's boast of metamorphosing wood into stone had a certain basis in reality, if only in the central city.

The Dynamics of Center and Outskirts

The distinctions between the city's central and suburban areas became more pronounced during Catherine's reign than earlier in the century. Indeed, the tendency toward differentiation between them was affirmed in the measures taken by the city's various governing bodies. The city's planners concentrated on the central districts, consciously gracing them with structures that were as much architectural statement as functional building. The austere rationality of classicism was expressed not only in the buildings of the two academies, sciences, and the fine arts, but also in the merchants' bazaars and other trading establishments, to be copied on smaller scale in the better private houses, the masonry homes of gentry and merchants. The government's own offices and chanceries were concentrated in the several central districts, and those individuals with any social or political ambition at all knew to seek residency only in neighborhoods at the center, to a greater degree in 1796 than in 1762. Relegated to outer districts and the suburbs were industrial works and the nondescript wooden houses of laborers, shop workers, and new arrivals from rural Russia. During Catherine's reign there developed more clearly than ever before two distinct Petersburgs. The first had masonry houses, paved and lighted streets, canals with stone banks, and stately bridges. In it lived the nobility, the wealthier townsfolk, officialdom. In the other Petersburg were evil-smelling, befouled streets, ramshackle wooden houses, and muddy riverbanks, the inhabitants decidedly less affluent.[23]

One must be careful, nonetheless, not to interpret the contrast as absolute. The view from the street in the centermost quarters of the city may not have betrayed their presence, but a glance into the courtyard or through basement windows would have revealed many people of few means—those usually associated with the outskirts—living in the rich downtown houses. Even in the best houses the number of inhabitants per room remained surprisingly high, as the well-to-do maintained large staffs of live-in servants, and frequently rented ground-level and basement living space to those who could not afford to buy houses or even rent entire flats. The poor could easily be found in the city's center, but the wealthy rarely so in the outskirts. The few large, lavishly furnished houses in the outskirts were summer houses, rarely in close proximity to poorer neighborhoods or industrial works.

As has already been indicated, growth on Vasil'evskii Island and St. Petersburg Side extended no further throughout the period under study than the streets already laid out at the beginning of the period. On the other hand, Vyborg Side grew to such an extent that by 1777 it was no longer included as a part of St. Petersburg Side but became a separate administrative quarter.[24] The greatest changes took place on the left bank of the Neva, with the division of Admiralty district into four administrative divisions and Moscow Side into three. Another district, Rozhestvenskaia, was created upstream from Foundry district where, in 1762, the city had not reached at all. It was natural that the left bank area should have developed most extensively; not only was it closest to the remainder of Russia, whence came new citizens, but also it was situated on the highest, best drained land in the city.[25]

By the end of Catherine's reign the central sector, the city proper, expanded to include parts of Rozhestvenskaia, Moscow Side, Karetnaia, and perhaps Narva district in addition to the areas already in the center. Vyborg Side remained purely outskirt; despite its growth it was still the most rural of the city's districts. The northern sections of St. Petersburg Side, the western half of Vasil'evskii Island, and all remaining lands southwest of the Fontanka Canal also remained suburban.[26]

Land in the central parts of the city acquired ever more intensive usage. Open areas were gradually filled in. For example, in accordance with the guidelines for development issued in the late 1760s by the planning commission, the huge nobiliary and crown estates along the Moika and Fontanka canals were being broken up. The police sold lots that stood vacant for some time at low prices to people who agreed to build houses on them; if properties continued to stand unimproved after a specified period of time, the purchase contracts were considered broken and the land resold to others.[27] Despite such official and other informal pressures to bring land in the center of town into fuller use, some areas in the center of the city still remained open and unused. In most cases they were owned by the crown, a governmental agency, or a private citizen powerful enough to resist public constraints against vacant tracts of land. The desire to foster the subdevelopment, if necessary, of large open areas partially explains a decree in 1783 broadening the base of land ownership by making it legal for merchants and lesser townsmen to buy land from private owners.[28] With this measure legal pressure was added to the economic impulse to utilize central areas more intensively, leaving open spaces to the outskirts.

Land Use

The tale of outward expansion of the city's built-up area provides only part of the story of the physical changes that occurred during Catherine's reign. They establish quantitative change, but say less about the qualitative shifts in the patterns of land use during those decades. As the city's population increased and its spatial limits expanded, a tendency toward geographical differentiation of neighborhoods by social or economic function became increasingly more pronounced. This transformation was accomplished in two ways.

First, enterprises, institutions, and other entities similar in nature or function tended to cluster together. Where older businesses of a certain type were located, the newer ones tended to be founded as well. The same tendency for like to seek out like characterized the city's housing patterns, as foreigners of various nationalities settled near each other and people who had come to live in St. Petersburg from the same region of the empire congregated together. Similarly, residential neighborhoods became differentiated by wealth and status and even occupation as the city's size increased. Even governmental institutions followed the pattern. This has been a common pattern in the European model of urbanization. Segregation by function has been used as one measure of the degree of urbanization in a center of population.

Second, public policy contributed to the functional segregation of land use. Governmental agencies and officials pursued the same ends toward which trends were leading naturally, not only through the broad concepts enacted in the late 1760s and early 1770s, but also in frequent decisions regarding individual issues. The effort to remove unwanted industrial works from the city's central areas provides an example of this policy, as does, in its own way, the endeavor to create craft corporations.

As the areas devoted to specific kinds of activities become distinctly identifiable, it becomes possible to measure and compare the relative importance of the various space-using elements that comprised the city, because land was meted out on a scale and by a value system deemed appropriate by those in power at the time. Counterbalancing this intent, however, was an "invisible hand" of market force and population pressure, frequently at odds with official policy. The result of the struggle between these forces was the pattern of land use that actually existed at any given time.

Several shifts in the type and intensity of land use have already been noted. One of the most obvious concerns the size of buildings and density of construction. Several contemporaries who knew the city well over much of Catherine's reign could not help but note the displacement of small, unprepossessing dwellings by larger ones and the continuing encroachment on vacant land between buildings by new construction. No one described this process better than the anonymous observer who wrote: "It is impossible not to marvel at the variegation and contrasts; from a magnificent block you suddenly cross into a wild and damp forest; next to huge palaces and opulent gardens you find ruins, or ashes, wooden cabins, or deserted areas; but most startling is this: after several months these same places are impossible to recognize. Sometimes whole rows of wooden houses suddenly disappear, and in their stead appear palaces, masonry houses, not yet complete but already occupied. In this way several parts of the city change so much that after a few years it is not possible to recognize them."[29]

Increasingly intensified use of land in residential neighborhoods, and the filling in of "deserted areas" noted in the preceding quotation, did not take place solely through individual initiative. To a great degree they were goals pursued by the government, particularly manifested in the breakup of large estates on canals, which the nobles wanted as garden and open space around palaces, but which were the objects of even greater demand for other, more intensive uses appropriate to a city.

By the end of the century, several sections of the city had begun to take on the particular features that were to characterize them for some time thereafter. These distinguishing marks resulted from the concentration of activities, or the associations of a particular way of life, or the confluence of people with similar background or occupational ties. Through various processes, St. Petersburg was becoming divisible into neighborhoods recognizable among other things for the roles they played in the city's economy and society. Heinrich Storch, the noted statistician and academician, drew these contrasts more vividly than any other writer. He saw Vasil'evskii Island as the concentration point for international commerce. By the end of Catherine's reign an imposing new stock exchange was under construction, to be completed under a different architect in the reign of Alexander I, where the point of the island parted the Neva into its two branches. Near the bourse sat the customhouse. Both were surrounded by two- and three-storied warehouses for tobacco, flax, and hemp, the latter an extremely valuable product for maritime nations and one of St. Petersburg's most important exports. The island was also the educational center of the city, for located there were the academies of sciences and of fine arts, the Mining Institute, a military academy, a naval academy, and a small number of private schools.[30]

Storch compared First Admiralty to the Quartier du Palais Royal in Paris. It was the heart of the city, the home of luxury and wealth, the center of amusement and business, the resort of pleasure and fashion. This was reflected in rents, which were up to 50 percent higher in this section than anywhere else in the city. Provisions were most expensive here, because of the demands for instant consumption in great quantity.[31]

If First Admiralty seemed thoroughly aristocratic, Second and Third Admiralties were to the same extent bourgeois, peopled by the trading classes. As Storch wrote, "Here are the greatest number of mercantile houses and shops, the banks, and the government tribunals. If therefore we here meet with fewer palaces and brilliant equipages, on the other hand the crowd of busy people is so much the greater."[32] This retail commercial activity was most visible on Nevskii Prospect, by far the busiest street in the city, with the majority of hotels and many shops located on it. First among them was the two-story arcaded bazaar, the *gostinyi dvor.* The bazaar first appeared on the corner of Nevskii and Great Garden Street as a wooden structure in 1736. Its reconstruction in masonry began in 1755 and lasted until 1785. Although immense, the building housed only a part of the shops in the area; they spilled outside the walls of the bazaar and enveloped several blocks behind it toward the southwest.[33]

Foundry district, less commercial than industrial, was quieter than any of the admiralty sections. It was more densely built up, yet its buildings were more modest. Much of the district had at one time been composed of military *slobody,* quarters for the workers in the cannon and armaments factories, which neighborhoods were still identifiable in shape and extent by the street pattern and buildings. Storch saw the quarter's inhabitants as "laborious artificers, peaceful consumers, and soldiers."[34]

These graphic characterizations by Storch, faithfully detailed and accurately representative insofar as they go, nevertheless leave the reader with an incomplete picture because Storch limited himself to describing only the city's center. Taking for example his depiction of commercial activity, it is indeed true that its wholesale exercise and import-export operations were limited to a very few places in the city. But by describing only the innermost districts of town, Storch omitted at least one highly significant locus of commercial activity that developed extensively during Catherine's reign: the goods depot on the elbow of land behind Smolnyi Convent, where the Neva changes its course from northerly to westerly. Early in the reign of Catherine there was no designated place for merchants arriving in the city by the Neva to unload their cargo and turn it over to retailers. Some such site was obviously needed, as the future clearly belonged to river transport. This location, low-lying and previously unused, was selected by the government and rapidly became a bustling center of economic activity.[35]

Retail commercial outlets were spread throughout the city, enabling shoppers to purchase most items of everyday household use without having to frequent the large wholesale markets. Even at the beginning of Catherine's reign most sections of the city—particularly the central quarters—were independent of others in shopping for items of everyday use, each with its own markets. In order to provide large shopping facilities in each quarter, a decree in 1782 provided for the establishment of full-scale markets in every part of town, on sites to be selected by the police.[36] The implementation of this law undoubtedly served to strengthen a sense of neighborhood and certainly made life easier for shoppers. Undoubtedly also it alleviated confusion and crowds at the city's large central markets.

By the end of the century St. Petersburg was devoting a larger share of land to industrial establishments than it had earlier. Moscow, Tula, and other cities had bigger industrial plants throughout most of the eighteenth century, but by its end St. Petersburg surpassed all but Moscow in number of enterprises and quantity of production, establishing a position of leadership in industrial development, which it held throughout the nineteenth century. By the end of Catherine's reign, the changing location and function of industry make several generalizations possible.

Relocation from Center to Periphery

A great variety of productive enterprises operated in St. Petersburg, but few industrial concerns remained in the inner city. Many were forced to move because of pressures in the central districts to use land more intensively. Rents there were the highest in Russia, a circumstance that encouraged even state institutions to find less costly sites for the productive enterprises under their jurisdiction. Space in the city's center could be used more profitably in other pursuits. For example, the Admiralty's rope factory, long housed in a long and narrow masonry structure extending from the Admiralty to Kriukov Canal, was moved to Kronshtadt in 1792 and the land sold for residential use.[37] The private shipyard, although established not many years before, was forced in the 1780s to move from the left bank of the Fontanka to Vyborg Side. The few enterprises that remained downtown were those producing goods of high value and requiring little working area. Generally these were small operations, employing only a few craftsmen. They tended to satisfy primarily a demand for luxury items, such as gold and silver braid for uniforms, or lace, and to a great extent served the social and political elite who lived in the same neighborhoods. Moving outward from the center of town, one could find ever-increasing numbers of industrial concerns, utilizing both labor and land more extensively.

Other considerations besides the purely economic also drove industry out of the inner city. Relocation at times was forced by hygienic concerns. The danger and discomfort caused by certain industries were all too apparent. St. Petersburg's tanneries serve as an excellent example. They were set up initially on rivers and canals in numerous locations throughout the city, wherever their owners had suitable sites for them. As the population increased, so did demands upon the water supply, which meant that wells alone could not provide enough water. The river itself became a direct source of water, yet at the same time industrial wastes from tanneries were also increasing, fouling the Neva and the canals. For this reason leatherworking enterprises were moved downstream from the city. As a result of other health concerns, the comprehensive plan for the development of St. Petersburg Side, published in 1767, called for the gunpowder factory to be relocated in an uninhabited spot, in order that possible explosions not kill or maim nearby residents.[38] Both economic and safety considerations contributed to the eventual relocation of the state-owned glass and mirror factory. Relocation was first suggested in 1766 from an essentially central site to a spot south of the built-up region and much nearer the gulf. In 1767 Catherine approved the plan; she also implemented the construction of houses for artisans on the vacated site. In the new location the factory provided little threat to the city in case of fire, whereas at the old site the wind might have fanned flames directly into some of the better parts of town.[39]

As these two considerations of more intensive land use and the public's health constrained industrial activity to move out of the heart of the city and into outlying areas, it would seem that the workers employed in these industrial enterprises were also compelled to move in order to live near the workplace. They were not ordered out of the center but moved for the sake of convenience. The fact that workers did move to sites adjoining the enterprises employing them tended to maintain the differentiation of neighborhoods and apply brakes to countervailing trends toward greater spatial integration of the various aspects of urban life.

In certain outlying areas, land was used less for manufacturing (in the eighteenth-century meaning of the term) than for agriculture. The city there resembled not so much a metropolis as a large village, where "houses, as a rule, were wooden and single-storied, roofed with boards and thatch; the layout of the streets was chaotic, the water system primitive; lighting and cleaning of streets and squares hardly existed. . . . There was generally a lot of land, but by far the smaller part of it was occupied, that is, used as living quarters; there was a considerable amount of tilled land, which was given with rights of property or rented to the urban lower middle classes, who used it for agriculture."[40]

Workers usually found housing near their place of employment. Many industrial concerns included housing as a portion of their employees' wages. Earlier in the century, whole neighborhoods were built by large employers, especially governmental agencies such as the Admiralty. These housing complexes, the traditional *slobody* found in older Russian towns, gave St. Petersburg for a time a housing pattern segregated by occupation or place of work. There were *slobody* for almost every category of worker from court servant to shipbuilder to gardener.[41] Such settlements were often self-contained, and before Catherine's reign, when space was plentiful, often did not even touch each other's boundaries. As the city expanded and vacant lots were utilized, however, *slobody* slowly lost their identity. In some cases the administering agency ended its control over them, they were torn down, and their inhabitants were permitted to scatter throughout the city. Other *slobody,* such as Okhta, shrank because the inhabitants individually found better housing elsewhere.[42] Most were simply absorbed into the city, their identities blurred as people with other employers and occupations moved in.

The empress personally provided direction for an industrial district that was planned in detail for more than a decade yet apparently never came to fruition. The plan was to link a series of mills to the moat and wall that marked the city's southern boundary. From the late 1770s to the late 1780s the project was developed in detail to channel water from the Duderhof hills south of the city to a point from which it would flow through the moat (fifty-six feet wide on the surface, thirty-seven feet wide at the bottom, and slightly more than eleven feet deep) in two directions to the Neva both up- and downstream from the city.[43] Interspersed periodically along the moat there were to be millponds and races to supply water reliably to no fewer than fifteen undershot water mills. Envisioned were a flatting mill, a turning mill for iron, a hammer mill, a mill for cutting granite and marble, a mill for cracking grain, a flour mill, a sawmill, a wire-drawing mill, a paper mill, a boring mill, a crushing mill for preparing cement, a polishing mill, a grinding mill for various instruments, and a turning mill for large wooden objects.[44] The projected cost ran into the millions of rubles. Even spread over a ten-year span, as the project proposed, the sum was too large at a time when Russia found itself at war with both Turkey and Sweden, and the project was abandoned.

From Wood to Stone

As noted earlier, Catherine herself considered the transition from wood to masonry (stone and brick) construction to be one measure of the degree to which St. Petersburg had become a true city. Indeed, this is a gauge that has often been used.[45] Unfortunately, there are no accurate figures contrasting the locations of masonry and wooden houses at the end of the century; the disposition of the two types can

Table 8.1. Numbers of wooden and masonry houses in St. Petersburg in 1778

District	Masonry	Wooden	Total
First Admiralty	216	0	216
Second Admiralty	194	551	745
Foundry	56	426	482
Moscow District	46	278	324
Karetnaia and Iamskaia	6	76	82
Vasil'evskii Island	107	382	489
Vyborg Side	5	898	903
Rozhestvenskaia	0	167	167
St. Petersburg Side	3	389	392
TOTALS	633	3167	3800

Note: These figures do not include Third Admiralty, nor do they count state-owned buildings, reconstructed buildings, or ruins. *Source:* RNB, Manuscripts Department, Ermitazhnoe sobranie, no. 286.

only be approximated. Figures do exist for 1778, when more than a third of the masonry residences in the city were located in the small area between the Neva and the Moika. Almost two-thirds of all masonry houses in the city were found between the Neva and Catherine Canal (table 8.1). At that point, halfway through Catherine's reign, five times as many wooden buildings as masonry still existed in the city. St. Petersburg Side, Vyborg Side, Rozhestvenskaia, and Karetnaia each contained fewer than 1 percent of all masonry houses in the city. Construction in masonry intensified in the 1780s, but the balance of masonry to wooden buildings was altered only in central areas (table 8.2). As late as 1806 four times as much square footage in both Foundry district and Rozhestvenskaia was under wooden houses as under masonry. Because masonry houses were considerably larger than most wooden ones, the ratio of wooden to masonry houses remained much higher than four to one in those districts a decade after Catherine's death.[46]

Moscow district in particular showed a marked increase in the number of masonry houses before the end of the century; this appreciation was due almost entirely to a single government building project. In 1773, the Commission on Masonry Construction proposed that the *sloboda* for postmen be rebuilt in brick. The project was proposed in the wake of fires in 1772 and 1773 caused by overly dense construction of wooden buildings without sufficient space for yards or streets. When all plans had been approved, construction began; by 1782 more than 160 brick houses had been finished.[47]

Table 8.2. Estimated number of wooden and masonry houses in St. Petersburg in various years

	1762	1775	1783	1787	1791	1798
Masonry	460	573	1094	1291	n.a.	1834
Wooden	4094	3126	2734	2140	n.a.	4238
TOTAL	4454	3699	3828	3431	4554	6072

Source: Vasil'ev, "K istorii planirovki," *Arkhitekturnoe nasledstvo,* no. 4 (1953): 24.

Quite obviously, had the population of the city remained constant, the amount of new masonry construction would have allowed the number of wooden houses in the city to decline markedly. But newcomers built wooden abodes of various descriptions—bungalows, cottages, cabins, shacks, hovels, and so forth—in newer sections of the city, thereby keeping the number of wooden houses approximately the same at the end of the period as at the beginning.

Open Spaces

From first glance it is clear that construction in 1796 was more dense than in 1762. Indeed, the population had more than doubled, whereas the amount of land in the city had increased much less significantly. Nevertheless, in relation to the other major cities of Europe, population density in St. Petersburg remained light. In part this is explained by geography. Broad rivers and canals represented much of the total area of the city. Other wetlands, although not river or canal, were low-lying and swampy. Until 1780, the left bank of the Fontanka remained a morass in which building lots had to be readied first by preparing mounds of earth on which to build. As late as 1765, the middle of the area between the Catherine Canal and the Fontanka was a swamp. And the space between the Winter Palace and Nevskii Prospect, still used as grazing grounds for imperial cows, continued to be low, marshy, and poorly drained even in the 1780s. Building patterns also contributed to the low population density. Even at the end of Catherine's reign, a third of the structures in the Russian capital had only one story. And the size of lots owned by wealthy citizens contributed to low population density. In an extreme case, the wealthy merchant Nikita Teplov owned a house that sat on a lot over four acres in size. By the end of the century few other individual properties remained that large, but the palaces of wealthy citizens continued to be surrounded by gardens and park areas.[48] Particularly in the outskirts, whole neighborhoods of vacant spaces remained between buildings.

Quite surprisingly, areas that one would think were thoroughly developed in fact stood bare past the beginning of the nineteenth century. The well-known English artist John A. Atkinson painted four scenes from the roof of the Kunstkamera in 1801, depicting the entire panorama, dedicating the whole to Emperor Alexander I. A description of one of these paintings demonstrates the point most clearly. The view to the north shows the building housing the twelve colleges on the left and the bourse on the right. A grassy meadow with a pond fills the broad expanse between the two buildings. Cattle and horses graze in the meadow. Near the pond, slightly to one side, hunch several ramshackle log cabins, as though leaning on each other for mutual support. A small number of men are bathing in the pond. It is incredible that this essentially rural scene could be depicted a mere stone's throw from the commercial center of the city.[49] Yet as late as the 1830s, the number of vacant lots amazed visitors, particularly in view of the fact that rents were so high in the same districts.[50] Ironically, the high cost of land in the center during Catherine's reign did much to create the situation. Because lots in more remote places could be purchased less expensively, they were sooner built upon by people of lesser means.

The problem was not that no one owned the open land in the center of the city; it was rather that owners did not maximize the use of every square *sazhen'* of their property.[51] One intriguing case concerned Prince Andrei Nikolaevich Shcherbatov's attempt to clear all construction off his property by evicting people who lived on it. Five months after purchasing the land in 1778, the prince discovered that two registered merchants were already living on the property, each residing in his own wooden house. Although the two had lived there under three previous owners, having contracted with the first of them to have residence there in perpetuity, Shcherbatov went to the police in 1779 to have them evicted from his property and their houses destroyed.[52] The nature of large estates owned by the imperial court and by aristocrats was clearly "un-urban" in this regard. Educational institutions such as the schools for girls at Smolnyi and the Infantry Cadet Academy also controlled large tracts of land that remained relatively free from construction. Finally, military units were situated on properties largely unused save for the drilling of troops. All these factors contributed to the persistence of low population density even in the city center and a relatively inefficient utilization of land.

As urban as the city had become, much in it remained purely rural. Many residents kept parts of their residential lots for agricultural purposes. Even in the 1830s it was estimated that a full one-seventh of the land area within the city was devoted to kitchen gardens. In the 1760s, the Commission on Masonry Construction estimated that twenty thousand cows were kept in the city by its inhabitants. Livestock grazed in small numbers even in the better residential districts of the city.[53] Besides this, St. Petersburg stabled tens of thousands of horses. Despite the fact that they were kept indoors for the most part, they added to the rural atmosphere that ever surrounded the cityscape. Even in a city as large as St. Petersburg, the land used for agricultural purposes, as well as numerous private parks and gardens, assured a continuing and inescapable juxtaposition between rural and urban.

As has been seen, the government certainly did attempt to increase land-use intensity by forcing landowners to construct buildings on lots standing vacant. Those who refused to build on their land were subject to its possible confiscation; the land would then be offered for sale by the police to the highest bidder. The new owner would then have to agree to meet three conditions: (1) at the end of one year plans for construction had to be completed; (2) construction actually had to start before the end of the second year; and (3) the work had to be finished within five years. If any of the conditions were not met, the police might again confiscate the land and sell it at auction, giving the proceeds to the unhappy former owner.[54] As the following example illustrates, the law was put into practice.

In 1781 Petr Chir'ev, a merchant, bought a piece of property along the Fontanka at Nevskii Prospect under the aforementioned conditions. His land had been used as a storage point for materials necessary to build the granite embankments of the Fontanka. He went to the overseer of the work on the embankment and to the governor in attempts to get the land cleared, but unsuccessfully. Then in 1786—before five calendar years were completed—the police confiscated the land because Chir'ev had not built anything on it, and sold it to the aristocratic civil servant and poet Gavriil Romanovich Derzhavin. Chir'ev, outraged, took the case to court in an attempt to win back his land. After two years of gathering information, the Senate honored Chir'ev's claim and returned the land to him.[55] Only because he proved that he had not been able to build due to the supply stores on his land did Chir'ev regain his property. In numerous other instances the previous owner's pleas were of no avail.

One final comment must be made concerning the density of land use. When compared with western European cities, use in St. Petersburg was less dense; when compared with other Russian cities, however, St. Petersburg's utilization of land was considerably denser, primarily because houses were much larger there and could provide space for more people. This is a significant point, for in its more intentional utilization of space, St. Petersburg reflected the European city and was a harbinger of future urban development for Russia's other towns.

Imperial Architecture

The historical image of St. Petersburg began to emerge during Catherine's reign as the city increasingly assumed the appearance that would be recognized in many respects even today. Before her reign the buildings housing official St. Petersburg followed the baroque style. Following the era of Peter the Great they had inclined to increasingly lavish detail, culminating in Bartolomeo Rastrelli's Winter Palace and cathedral at Smol'nyi Convent and S. I. Chevakinskii's five-domed St. Nicholas Cathedral. But Rastrelli was in his early sixties when Catherine came to the throne and Chevakinskii almost fifty. She rejected their ornate decorative motifs for the much more severe classical style then gaining popularity throughout Europe. She brought about this change first by using architects who were already working in Russia, but eventually by importing others from abroad. Catherine financed two periods of construction of public buildings, in the 1760s centering around the Winter Palace and nearby areas, and in the 1780s in several places on an even more ambitious scale. Her projects begun in the 1760s may be taken to indicate what she wanted in those years to symbolize her reign: the Small Hermitage (1764–7) attached to the Winter Palace, the Neva embankments in the vicinity of the Winter Palace (1763–80) with their simply designed wrought-iron railings, the elegantly harmonious Academy of Fine Arts (1764–88) facing the Neva, and on the opposite bank the Bronze Horseman statue of Peter the Great (1766–82).[56] Her principal architects during this period were the Frenchman J.-B. M. Vallin-de la Mothe and A. F. Kokorinov, both of whom she inherited from the previous reign, when Vallin-de la Mothe began his masonry reconstruction of the columned and arcaded Gostinyi Dvor (1761–85) and Kokorinov was the first native Russian to be designated an architect in the Academy of Sciences. Catherine also announced in the 1760s her intention of improving the physical appearance of the entire city by establishing a special commission to oversee her intended transformation of St. Petersburg from wood to masonry, the work of which is discussed in chapter 4.

Her war with Turkey and the suppression of the insurrection led by Emelian Pugachev diverted Catherine's attention and soaked up tax revenues during the 1770s, during which time the empress began only two major building projects in St. Petersburg: the pilastered Marble Palace (1768–85) by the Italian Antonio Rinaldi and the Large Hermitage (1771–84) by I. M. Fel'ten along the Neva embankment between the Small Hermitage and the Winter Canal. These buildings from the 1760s and 1770s began to give St. Petersburg its classical architectural lines. But it was in the 1780s that the works were commissioned, which swung the scale clearly away from the baroque to the classical.

In 1779, Catherine brought Giacomo Quarenghi to Russia from Italy. His commissions, while including the Hermitage Theater (1783–87), the fourth of the five buildings in the Winter Palace–Hermitage complex, dealt less with palaces than with buildings erected as monuments to the power of governmental institutions. Thus he designed the severely classical Academy of Sciences (1783–89), the State Assignat Bank (1783–90) with its semicircular wings, and the ill-fated bourse (1790s, but demolished in the early 1800s to prepare the way for Thomas de Thomon's bourse, which still stands). Under the same stately classical and Palladian influence, N. A. L'vov designed the Main Post Office (1782–89) and I. E. Starov built the Tauride Palace (1783–89) and the Trinity Cathedral at the Alexander Nevskii monastery (1778–90). At the end of Catherine's reign E. T. Sokolov's designs were approved for the corner building of the State Public Library at Great Garden Street and Nevskii Prospect (1796–1801). Even churches began to assume a classical appearance, and among the more noteworthy were Fel'ten's church of St. Catherine on Vasil'evskii Island (1768–71), Vallin-de la Mothe's Catholic church of St. Catherine on Nevskii Prospect (1763–83), and Rinaldi's Church of St. Isaac, later pulled down to make room for the much more majestic St. Isaac's Cathedral.

Following the lead of official opinion, several private people had magnificent houses designed for themselves following classical or quasi-classical lines, among them Count I. G. Chernyshev's palace (1766–68) done by Vallin-de la Mothe, G. R. Derzhavin's house on the Fontanka (1790s, by N. A. L'vov); the Iusupov palace on the Moika (1770s–90s); the Sheremet'ev palace on the Fontanka; and others. With these buildings the city clearly began to take on the architectural appearance it has retained. When the students of these Catherinian architects continued to develop classicism into what is widely known as the Empire style in the first half of the nineteenth century, the formative influence of the Catherinian period was firmly established. One must disagree with Stolpianskii's judgment that the city as it is now only began to exist in the reign of Alexander I. Much assumed its present form under Catherine II.[57]

The Urban Environment

In First Admiralty the radial street pattern was determined in the 1730s. By 1796 the entire layout of streets was nearly established.[58] The same can be said for most of Second and Third Admiralty quarters. On Vasil'evskii Island the street pattern was complete by 1796. In other sections of the city the main streets were laid out in their permanent configuration. More than two hundred streets existed in the city, the vast majority of which are still identifiable. An important aid in establishing streets in their permanent location was the practice of "line building," first employed in Catherine's reign. "Line building" embodied a principle of harmony and order typical of Enlightenment thinking regarding town planning, by seeing to it that all houses were built at the same distance from the center of the street, thereby creating a unified facade on either side that clearly delineated the thoroughfare.

Building codes implemented to control housing construction did much to preserve intact large sections of the city. According to the code adopted in the 1760s, houses were for the most part to be built of masonry. In a few areas wood was a permissible substitute, but in such cases houses had to have masonry foundations. Roofs had to be built either of sheet-iron or of tiles. Where wooden houses existed, firewalls were required between lots.[59] Safety was not the only motivation behind the building code, however. Regularity and order were to be achieved by placing houses on line, creating single fronts along streets. Where houses were already set back in yards, owners were to construct either masonry or iron lattice fences along streets to preserve the formal appearance. Thus line building was officially adopted as an element of future construction. A minimum height for houses and fences was established in some areas.[60]

As the city became more completely developed, so did the average building increase noticeably in size. Three- and four-story structures became common in the center and two- and three-story ones in the outskirts. Available information about the architecturally unremarkable houses that have long since been demolished suggests that perpendicular wings were added to the ends of rectangular structures in stages until they eventually attained the shape of "well" houses, that is, buildings with four rectangular wings touching at the ends, forming squares with courtyards (the "wells") in the center. In such large houses the space not used for living was rented as shops or apartments.[61]

Further evidence that St. Petersburg was assuming its permanent form is provided by the fact that identifiable sections of the city had already developed, which retained the same flavor, character, and function over the years. For example, Gostinyi Dvor remains the largest department store in present-day St. Petersburg. With the introduction of huge freighters the eastern end of Vasil'evskii Island lost much of its commercial significance, yet until the revolutionary year of 1917 the bourse and customs office were located there. Vasil'evskii Island, already the educational center of the city by the end of the eighteenth century, further enlarged this role in the nineteenth century, as the university was founded in and around the former Twelve Colleges Building. The Great Stone Theater, built in the eighteenth century, was reconstructed in 1875–95 and is now the core of the Conservatory.[62] And the tanneries moved to the southwest corner of Vasil'evskii Island during Catherine's reign have direct descendants in the leather-working factories still in the same location.

A final indication of the capital city's metamorphosis into its relatively permanent form—the historical city core of post-Soviet St. Petersburg—can be seen in the increasing attention paid to those improvements in the urban environment that reduced problems specifically caused by density of population. To speed transportation, streets were paved. The government attempted to ensure that nearly all streets in the center of the city, as well as the principal arteries in suburban areas, received hard surfaces. Property owners were held responsible for paving the length of street fronting their land, and the police assumed responsibility elsewhere.[63] Few home owners performed the work themselves, preferring to hire laborers from among the peasants who came to the city each summer to work. Such peasants were never wanting for work, because most forms of pavement required annual repairs—the average life span for a section of pavement was only three to five years.[64] Any improvement was deemed preferable to the alternative of no pavement at all, however, when streets became virtually impassable in the slushes of spring and fall and during rainy weather in summer.

Meteorological conditions in St. Petersburg brought frequent fogs. The addition of smoke from several thousands of chimneys and odors from such industrial operations as tanneries could hardly have helped the pulmonary condition of citizens. Attempts were made to improve the quality of air by relocating factories into less populous areas. In 1778, *Sanktpeterburgskii vestnik* published news of Joseph Priestley's discovery that plants and animals complement each other in maintaining a healthy balance among the various properties of air, and recommended that the city's inhabitants plant trees, shrubs, and grass of whatever kind in order to remove the "nasty vapors" from the air. Other articles told new arrivals in the city how to preserve their health.[65]

The garbage that accumulated in streets and empty lots was both dangerous to health and unsightly. Government agencies constantly sought to clean it up. Thus, in plans for improving the city, property owners were held responsible for keeping "sweepings" cleared from streets facing their property. An instruction from the Commerce College to one of its functionaries shows its attempts to clean up areas under its jurisdiction: "In the stone bazaar and along the galleries that are on the bourse there are often disorderly discarded mats, beams, and planks; there are deposits of sandalwood, wheel rims, girders, and other things which all make for a great disorder, and further carries the danger of fire; so over all this have careful watch, so that as much as possible the sellers of beams, mats, and other Russian wood be diminished, as well as sellers of *kvas* and marketers of various supplies (foodstuffs), and those who are making the mess."[66]

There was no single agency responsible for removing garbage on a regular basis. Surely individual homeowners and government chancelleries alike did not always dispose of garbage, leftover building materials, and accumulated junk in areas under their jurisdiction. A memorandum written in 1793 reveals that the Neva embankment at the Winter Palace was filled with refuse and discarded materials.[67] If this area, supposed to be one of the most beautiful and well tended in the city, was in such a state of neglect, what must the remainder of the city have looked like? An answer was provided by the son of A. T. Bolotov, who commented on St. Petersburg's size in 1762. Petr Andreevich Bolotov first visited the city in 1789. Like almost every other tourist, he lavishly praised the magnificent public buildings. Suddenly he changed his tone, however, by noting with disgust, "Here every day the rainwater and garbage in the streets are great."[68] The central areas of St. Petersburg may have been well conceived and well constructed, and they may have appeared beautiful from a distance, but poor sanitary conditions detracted from the beauty of public buildings and the palaces of the wealthy. In the outer reaches of the city, there was a total lack of cleanliness.

News of the glory of St. Petersburg spread far, however. Contemporary foreign visitors praised its magnificence. The French royal geographer Didier Robert de Vaugndy wrote to St. Petersburg asking for full information about the "monuments with which Catherine decorated the capital, the communications canals which she had dug, the laws which she had established, the edicts, ordinances, and regulations which had emanated from the wisdom of her Imperial Majesty for the prosperity of the State and the good of the people," for the article "Pétersbourg," which he was writing for an encyclopedia.[69] Many historians have likewise praised the reordering of St. Petersburg, the architectural splendors and ensembles that were added to the city during Catherine's reign.[70] This acclaim can suggest misleading conclusions. It is true that some parts of St. Petersburg before 1800 had been made to be quite magnificent. But it has been shown that this was far from universally the case. In many other places the city was unsightly. Whatever the city's size, some areas remained quite rural in appearance, economy, and manner of living. St. Petersburg was by no means fully urban, but it was in the process of developing into a complete city.

9

"Its name . . . not one of ours": The Impact of St. Petersburg

IN LESS THAN A CENTURY AFTER ITS FOUNDING, IN A LOCATION WITH virtually no urban tradition or even dense rural population, St. Petersburg became one of the ten largest cities in Europe. On the entire European continent there were only two cities, Paris and London, larger in 1700 than St. Petersburg would become by 1800. The rapid rate of growth exhibited by the new Russian capital was unparalleled not just in Russian but also in European history. The very concept of the metropolis—the megacity—with the power to bring a huge hinterland under its sway was uncommon in European history until the early modern era. The ancient world had its Rome and the Byzantine Empire its Constantinople, but in their time these two cities were unique centers in the landscape of human settlement, able to compel entire empires to do their will to an extent unmatched elsewhere. Neither city, of course, was built in a day, nor were the cities that succeeded them as the largest in Europe able to acquire influence over their surrounding countrysides overnight. In a European world that remained essentially rural, touched but not dominated by the city, such centers of people and power as London or Paris, Venice or Vienna, Naples or Genoa, developed over a long period of time, waxing and waning cyclically, growing in a series of spurts. Like the ancient capitals before them, they could be seen as aberrations from the normative pattern of human settlement, urban islands in a rural sea where even ten thousand inhabitants made a town large.

But the metropolis, ancient or modern, was able, through the powers vested in it by the concentration of life, wealth, and often political power, to reverse the relationship between town and countryside, assuming the stronger position. The city's growing domination over a hinterland that offered its vitality as food for the city, to be nourished in turn by the city's vigor, was tied in the seventeenth and eighteenth centuries to massive changes in Europe's economy, society, and, in particular, its political order.

Prior to the reign of Peter the Great, Moscow was the only city in Russia that could have had pretensions of sustaining this role. The tsar's creation of St. Petersburg, however, and the subsequent blossoming of the "Window on the West" provided Russia with a second urban giant. Unlike Moscow, London, Paris, Venice, Vienna, or other European cities—Amsterdam alone could boast of a comparable history—St. Petersburg rose to prominence rapidly. The preceding chapters have examined the changes manifested in St. Petersburg's appearance, administration, economy, and population in the reign of Catherine II. Now it is time to view the city's development from a different vantage point, from the perspective of the city's relationship with the empire as a whole.

The principal reasons for St. Petersburg's rapid development were interwoven with economic, social, and political developments affecting all of Russia. Just as rural Russia influenced the evolution of St. Petersburg, so did the city increasingly have its own impact on Russia. That effect is revealed even more clearly if the discussion is extended beyond the eighteenth century to suggest the role of St. Petersburg in casting the mold for nineteenth-century developments.

Reasons for Growth

Peter the Great founded the city on the Neva as a "Window on the West," expecting it to play a critical role in helping pull Russia out of Asia and into Europe by implementing the technological, social, and administrative advancements of western Europe that Peter wanted Russia to emulate. As a potential commercial center, the site of the city was well chosen. An adequate natural harbor already existed; the port remained ice-free longer than other Russian ports with which it competed; and a system of rivers, soon supplemented and improved by canals, provided easy access from the interior. The city offered a natural place to transfer merchandise from one mode of transportation to another, as goods arriving from inland areas by river craft, cart, or sledge were loaded onto seagoing vessels, and imports were carried from ships to warehouses and stores.

In addition to serving as an exchange point for merchants, St. Petersburg offered advantages in manufacturing. Since all exports and imports had to be unloaded and reloaded, it was natural that industries developed to process raw materials from the interior before their exportation overseas. Manufactured or semifinished goods were not as bulky as raw materials and had greater pound-for-pound value. Thus hemp was fashioned into rope, hides and pelts were dressed, timber was split, and flax was woven into cloth.

Catherine the Great certainly seems to have preferred that industrial activity be set up in Russia's villages, where it would not draw people away from agriculture, a condition she saw as "harmful to the state"; she wanted peasants to perform industrial labor in their free time from the fields. This was her conscious policy, but it was often put to the test by the vitality of economic life in St. Petersburg, where the scale of commerce inevitably invited the creation of new industrial enterprises as well. Much of the industrial activity in the city existed without the official blessing of the state, if not in outright violation of its policy.

During the city's first hundred years, commerce developed much faster than industry. Peter I had ordered that all foreign trade pass through St. Petersburg. Although many of his restrictions were lifted later in the century, merchants became aware of St. Petersburg's easy access to western Europe and left other towns for the new capital. In the latter half of the century, far more international business was conducted in St. Petersburg than in any other Russian town.[1]

Military considerations also motivated Peter I to found St. Petersburg. If Russia was to become a commercial power in the Baltic, it had to construct a defensible bastion there to protect the empire's interests. Throughout the eighteenth century, St. Petersburg never lost its distinct military flavor, and still in the 1790s nearly a fifth of the city's population either served in or worked for the army and navy. The fleet commands in Russia's largest naval base and the line units stationed at the primary northwestern army post had the mission of defending Russia against any attacker. Indeed, in 1790 residents of the city were jolted into a new appreciation of this task by the distant rumble of naval artillery audible in St. Petersburg during the battle with Sweden's navy off the coastal town of Kotka.

The city's military function was visible in other ways too. Elite troops, the guards regiments, provided protection for the imperial family and other dignitaries and participated in parades on special occasions. Hundreds of civilians were employed in the large industrial enterprises serving the military: the Admiralty shipyard, gunpowder and ammunition factories, and cannon and gun foundries. The military and naval academies and an extensive military hospital completed the capital's complement of troops. Men in uniform were often accompanied by families and camp followers, further swelling the city's population.

The occasions for commerce, industry, and national defense alone, however, could not have inspired such instantaneous, dramatic expansion as occurred in St. Petersburg. The single most important cause of this impressive growth lay in the decision by Peter I and succeeding rulers to move the residence of the court to St. Petersburg from Moscow. This decision directly affected far more people than just those with official business at court. Other decrees ordered merchants, craftsmen, nobles, and laborers to move to the new capital. Such laws compelled mass migration only during the reign of Peter I, yet new residents continued to be drawn by the court's presence in succeeding years. Builders, laborers, and artisans constructed buildings to house government organs; merchants provided goods for the people of the court; servants and domestics catered to their needs and whims. The embassies and consulates of foreign governments moved to the new capital. A small army of clerks, copyists, secretaries, and other functionaries manned the chancelleries and departments of government.

But St. Petersburg did not wholly supplant Moscow as capital. While the newer city retained its role as the imperial residence after 1733, many governmental offices remained in the older capital. Russia in effect had two capitals, and the imperial court swelled the population of whichever of the two cities the sovereign happened to be in at the time. Catherine much preferred St. Petersburg, whence at least the direction of all foreign policy emanated, but Moscow could be viewed as the seat of the "opposition." As *Residenzstadt*—and by far the grandest example of that genre built in eighteenth-century Europe—St. Petersburg naturally attracted those people who were drawn by visible wealth in the hope of appropriating some of it for themselves.

This fact helps explain St. Petersburg's attractiveness to people from more westerly parts of Europe. In Russia's new capital they could begin a new life; craftsmen and merchants in particular could hope to earn a better living than in their native cities.[2] Contemporaries estimated that foreigners comprised from one-tenth to one-eighth of the city's population. Immigration from western Europe thus contributed greatly to the growth of the city, even though most of those European immigrants did not arrive in the capital with the idea of becoming permanent residents. Foreigners influenced in particular the development of commerce, industry, and science and the arts. The distinctive Western flavor of St. Petersburg among Russian cities evident in architecture simply mirrored a characteristic evident in other spheres of activity as well. This ethnic heterogeneity gave the capital a distinctively more urbanized cast than other Russian towns.

Growth can also be attributed to the state's changing policy regarding towns. Although Peter I had encouraged the development of an urban population, under Anna Ioannovna and Elizabeth the economic activities open to artisans were reduced, the rights and privileges of merchants remained unclear, and industry was, to a great extent, barred from the new capital. Under Catherine II these policies were changed, so that from the 1760s new laws broadened the rights and privileges of both merchants and artisans. Catherine's reforms culminated in the Charter to the Towns, with its comprehensive redefinitions of each urban estate and its rights and duties. Tariffs in 1762 and 1766 tended to encourage international commerce and the establishment of industry in the capital in comparison with those that preceded them. Credit institutions were created or enlarged for the benefit of traders and industrialists, creating further inducement to enter into commerce and production. Legislation enacted during this period, providing for urban self-regulation, remained the basis of town government in St. Petersburg, as well as in all other Russian towns, until 1870.[3]

The fact that St. Petersburg was a new city certainly facilitated rapid growth. Older Russian towns were built as fortresses, around which gathered trading and artisan communities. As urban fortresses declined in military significance, it was difficult for these towns to adapt to new and different functions. The best location for a fortress is not always the ideal site for a town. Furthermore, the old fortress walls themselves and the constricted streets bound by them often impeded expansion. The planners of St. Petersburg did not have to destroy old structures before raising new ones. The street pattern could be laid out in a manner much more conformable to future needs, as straight and broad avenues, without concern for devising the costly and time-consuming projects to align the narrow, winding alleyways of older towns. The very newness of St. Petersburg provided it with an advantage over other Russian towns.

Underlying what has been said about the importance of St. Petersburg in Russia's political life is a deeper significance stemming from a fundamental shift during the eighteenth century in the perception of the nature of the state as an institution. Marc Raeff has elucidated this change in his studies of the development of the notion of *Polizeistaat* and its transplantation from the smaller states of German-speaking Europe to the Russian Empire.[4] The policies embodied in the theories of the well-policed state could be implemented effectively only in a manageable setting: limited geographical extent with a well-developed and reliable transportation network, a population density exceeding certain minimal norms, a sufficiently large cadre of competent officials, and a coherent and rational organizational structure. Indeed, the eventual failure of Russia's rulers to succeed in implementing a well-policed state to the extent that their neighboring German princes did is explained by the absence of or shortcomings in these preconditions.

The well-policed state of the Enlightenment envisioned a society characterized most fully by vigorous town life. The Muscovite model of governmental rule preexisting in Russia was hopelessly inadequate for this new, rationalized conception of the state's role and functions. From the beginning the reforms of Peter I drew on the not yet full-blown theories and applications of the well-regulated state. The most vivid metaphor for Petrine reforms was of course St. Petersburg itself.[5] Without fully understanding so, Peter sensed that since the proper setting for his reforms did not exist, he had to create one. Of those who followed him on the Russian throne, Catherine II alone devoted her attention to the theory of government. She was fully aware of the necessity of town life for the viability of the *Polizeistaat,* devoting several chapters in her *Nakaz,* for example, to the nature of towns and cities, describing in detail the various functions towns performed, and professing that Russia needed towns of all sizes and broad geographical distribution.

The Russian state had no experience in governing large cities, however. Moscow, with all its population, had always been regarded as an overgrown village. No particularly urban functions of administration were developed prior to Peter's reign. Other than collecting taxes, maintaining order, and preserving the security of princely power, Peter I failed to address other problems of administration characteristic of cities. Russia's immediate neighbors, themselves possessing no large cities, provided little help in this regard. In fact, to find any example of a city as large as St. Petersburg was to become under Catherine the Great, Russians had to look as far afield as Amsterdam and Vienna.

Yet St. Petersburg grew, presenting a challenge to the state to find an administrative organization to manage it, and to do so with an apparatus structured primarily to deal with a rural setting and an agricultural society. This notion of the adequacy of a single administrative apparatus was apparently what Catherine had in mind when she attempted to link town government with *guberniia* administration in the provincial reform law of 1775. A similar clarification and expansion of administrative functions in towns was issued in the police statute of 1782, as clear an example of Catherine's use of the principles of the well-policed state as can be seen. Finally, the Charter to the Towns of 1785, an outgrowth of a more specific draft law intended to be applied to St. Petersburg alone, represents the culmination of Catherine's efforts to harness urban vitality to the interests of the state. It was a matter, however, of the state never quite understanding sufficiently the nature of the processes that caused St. Petersburg to become such a large city so quickly, and of its misapprehension that the same administrative structure could be fashioned appropriately for it as for other, more moribund Russian towns.

The Russian Equation

As was suggested above, because Peter the Great did not find St. Petersburg already existing, it was necessary for him to create it. The changes reshaping eighteenth-century Russia necessitated the presence of St. Petersburg or something very nearly resembling it. Better than any other town or city in the Russian Empire, St. Petersburg developed at a place and time that permitted it to profit from those changes. Surely, without the combination of changes taking place in rural Russia, significant growth would have been impossible for St. Petersburg. Without those changes, the capital would have remained simply a residence town.

Studies by B. N. Mironov have shown that a revolution in prices transformed Russian agriculture during the eighteenth century, leading to the production of cash crops for the market, increased concern on the part of landowners to administer their estates more efficiently, and a net drain of population away from towns to the countryside as the economic underpinnings of serfdom were strengthened.[6] As the city of St. Petersburg grew, rural production of foodstuffs more than met the needs of its expanding population, and in fact became a major source of exports for the city's commercial elite.[7] Indeed, international commercial activity consisted significantly of the exchange of grains, flax, hemp, honey, wool, wax, and other agricultural products and derivatives for items of foreign production.

For the capital to grow in population, and especially for it to become a major commercial port, there had to be suitable transportation links with the rest of the empire. The vital link in the water transportation system, the Vyshnii Volochek Canal, had been completed just prior to Catherine's accession to the throne, so that Astrakhan on the Volga near the Caspian Sea, not to speak of towns nearer the heart of Russia, such as Moscow, Novgorod, Kazan', and Iaroslavl', could be reached without portage.[8] A network of primitively surfaced roads supplemented the rivers and canals.

The first large-scale industrial activity in the Russian interior began in the eighteenth century.[9] Large quantities of iron, sailcloth, and silk were exported, primarily to Great Britain. St. Petersburg was the port of departure for most of these industrial products. The water route from the Urals, the center of iron mining, led more simply and directly to the mouth of the Neva than to any other Russian port with access to western Europe. Grain was the sole exported commodity in which Riga and Arkhangel'sk had a competitive advantage.

Not only were agricultural and industrial goods directed to St. Petersburg; so was manpower. Conditions in the countryside were such that large numbers of people were enabled and even encouraged to migrate to the capital. Regulatory measures affecting peasants, both estate serfs and state and crown peasants, permitted movement to the city. Landlords in the former case and village elders, estate stewards, and other government officials in the latter granted passports to serfs and peasants to seek temporary work and take up temporary residency in town, the well-known phenomenon of *otkhodnichestvo.* Many serfs on *obrok* (that is, paying their obligations to landowners in cash or kind or a combination of both) went to nearby towns to earn money, but in the northwest of Russia, that is, in the region around St. Petersburg, where *obrok* was apparently utilized more extensively than *barshchina* (the payment of obligations through labor), serfs took advantage of the opportunity for work in the new capital.[10] Employment in the capital—or sale of produce there—also provided money to pay the soul tax.

Undoubtedly substantial numbers of migrants from the countryside came to St. Petersburg for just these reasons. Their residence did not have to be permanent; indeed, most serfs and state peasants were required to return home periodically for renewal of passports. Local officials in at least one area were beginning to realize the opportunity the capital offered peasants, and urged migration there in order to earn quitrent and tax payments more easily.[11] Furthermore, some provinces suffered from relatively overcrowded conditions in rural areas. This was more true north of Moscow, in the nonblack soil region, than south, toward the relatively unsettled and fertile Ukraine. Insufficiency of land was cited as a major cause of migration to St. Petersburg from Iaroslavl' province, to name at least one place, by a special commission studying peasant movements at the time.[12]

Finally, the subjective elements of curiosity, exaggeration, and the lure of the unknown undoubtedly played a role also. Peasants who had been to St. Petersburg spread tales of its wealth and opportunity. A sojourn there provided respite for those who sought it from the closeness of village life, and back in the village as they related their impressions of the new capital, perhaps they embellished their tales slightly. Listeners, hearing about the marvels of the city, determined that they too one day would visit—or even move to—St. Petersburg. In his study of the town of Bezhetsk, Aleksandr Kamenskii emphasizes that the majority of the local residents who went to St. Petersburg did so for economic reasons rather than in search of adventure, but that at the same time "it is obvious that to remove oneself from the familiar and place oneself in the unknown one had to possess a certain type of character, in particular a readiness to reject the familiar tenor of life."[13]

Relatively few peasants took up permanent residence in the capital the first time they went there. They retained strong ties to their villages; usually passports to leave the estate or village were good only for a season or a year. Landlords feared that too much freedom would encourage serfs to forget entirely to remit their quitrent payment. Likewise, state peasants were kept responsible for rendering their soul taxes by having to return periodically to the village to renew their passports. For these reasons, many peasants became seasonal residents of the city, living there while work was plentiful and wages were at their highest, but returning to the countryside for the remaining months of the year. The most common pattern was to spend the spring and summer months in the city and the winter in the village; a smaller number reversed the paradigm, working all summer on the land and spending the winter employed in the city, usually as cabmen. As these people developed more ties to the city, increasing numbers of them ceased their semiannual trek and became permanent Petersburgers.

Not all peasants attained or held their residency legally. Many simply fled from estates; others, in the capital on passports for a season, a year, or a few years, allowed their passports to lapse and thereafter lived in the city illegally. Apparently a number of people tried to migrate to the city illegally, because laws were repeatedly passed to apprehend such people.[14] The promulgation of similar laws year after year seems to indicate further that the authorities met with little success in their efforts to limit the number of "illegal" residents.

In sum, numerous developments in the economy of the Russian hinterland contributed substantively to St. Petersburg's remarkable expansion: an increased presence of money in the economy, the abolition of internal tolls, a greater dependence on sale of goods than on simple subsistence living, increased industrial activity, an improved transportation network, a surplus of agricultural products, and the existence of a potential labor force. These interrelated shifts in the national economy help to illustrate the close linkage between overall economic and social change and urban growth.

One final explanation of St. Petersburg's growth follows from the interaction of all the above factors. Significant increases in any one sector of the city's population—the armed forces, the civil bureaucracy, peasants seeking a better life, merchants in search of profits, artisans making use of their skills, and so forth—necessitated increases in one or more other sectors. Of course, the population grew unevenly. Yet a certain proportionality had to exist among the various economic services. An increase in the bureaucracy, for example, tended to cause an increase in the number of merchants to supply them with food and clothing, artisans to produce furniture, workers to construct housing, and so on. This snowball effect, impossible to trace in detail, worked itself out not by government fiat but by the laws of supply and demand. Fernand Braudel noted that a city could be "more than the sum of its parts; it acts as an economic multiplier, 'a transformer.'"[15] Writing a century before Catherine's reign, the French thinker Alexandre Le Maître asked in *La Metropolitée* what happens "when the capital city of a State is not only the seat of political power but the center of economic power and of learning? . . . 'If the three parts are brought together in a single body,' the capital will benefit from a positive effect of size which ensures both an extension of its area of influence—'good order, pomp, wealth, trade and glory' will attract foreigners—and a disproportionate growth, the increased and diversified demand causing more artisans to set up there and more capital to be invested."[16]

The Impact on Russia

Whether Peter the Great himself ever used the term, the concept of St. Petersburg as Russia's "Window on the West" soon captured the general imagination. Significantly, the new capital was not seen as a door, permitting free access to an unlimited quantity of outside influences, practices, technologies, ideas, and things, but as a window, more constricted, posing greater difficulty of access, more subject to control, less risky. But a window can transform a room as thoroughly as a door, although differently. St. Petersburg may have been recognized as a window on the West, but it had far greater importance than simply as an agent through which Western ways entered Russia. The city assumed an importance and developed an identity of its own, eventually shaping Russian life in its own fashion. This is most easily seen in the world of politics and administration, in which it is usual to speak of the two centuries following the reign of Peter the Great as the St. Petersburg period in Russian history, the era of the empire. Especially in the nineteenth century, the capital dominated political and administrative life, since all power flowed from the emperor through the many-chambered chanceries and ministries of the capital city into the empire.

But the empire symbolized by St. Petersburg coexisted uneasily with earlier notions of what Russia was and ought still to be, and therefore the city that had usurped the role of Moscow, or at least a portion of that role, was not welcomed by everyone. In some cases opposition to the nature of the tsarist administration or a specific policy was translated into hostility to St. Petersburg, the seat of that administration, as if the place had somehow poisoned the politics. Catherine the Great clearly preferred the new capital to the old, however, seeing in it more that was modern, secular, harmonious, and livable, but for her opponents the new city was to be distrusted, feared, or even anathematized.

Already by the beginning of Catherine's reign, hardly sixty years after the city's founding, the conviction was taking shape among some critics that St. Petersburg was artificial, a monstrous construct of arbitrary power, a gigantic maw consuming whatever it could from the Russian countryside and returning nothing in exchange. It was a gargantuan leech sucking Russia's vitality, and if it gave anything in exchange for what it took, that thing was likely to be poisonous or deformed or otherwise dangerous. This pattern of interpretation began with such contemporaries—and opponents—of Catherine as Prince M. M. Shcherbatov and A. N. Radishchev. It was fueled by the writer A. S. Pushkin, who held an ambivalent attitude toward St. Petersburg. In the famous "Bronze Horseman" poem, Pushkin first sings lyrically of his love for the city as Peter's creation, then has the horseman, symbol of the city, chase a terrified Evgenii through the night streets, as though the city would bring the individual in it only terror and woe. Elsewhere Pushkin popularized the impression that the city's very existence had sacrificed the lives of tens of thousands (if not hundreds of thousands) of peasant workers, on whose very bones the city was constructed. But it was above all the Slavophiles who found no good in Russia's imperial capital.

Slavophiles disparaged Peter the Great for many things, not least of them the founding of St. Petersburg. It became the ultimate symbol of what for them lay outside Russian tradition but had been imposed on Russia. St. Petersburg was the emblem of an entire period in Russian history that should be abandoned and forgotten. Ivan Kireevskii, Ivan Aksakov, and A. S. Khomiakov all expounded upon this view.[17] For Konstantin Aksakov the removal of government to St. Petersburg had created a breach between tsar and people, because the location, the indigenous population, and the name of the new capital were all foreign to Russia and thus false and corruptive.[18] The breach could only be healed by abandoning St. Petersburg. Even more to the point in its wish for St. Petersburg was the poem "Underwater City" by Mikhail Dmitriev. A small boy, taken fishing by an aged companion, hears from the old fisherman the story of a proud city, now submerged, with only a thin spire still breaking through the water's surface to mark the spot. Mesmerized and horrified by the story, the lad asks the name of the drowned city, and hears in reply:

> Its name was—well, not one of ours,
> One I've not recalled for years.
> Its sound was not one we would know,
> And so 'twas lost long, long ago.[19]

These and similar views of St. Petersburg, often expressed, inevitably found their way into popular histories of the city and of Russia.[20]

But these views of the relationship between the city and the country were based less on historical research than on a priori political philosophies or personal predispositions. The myth of St. Petersburg in Russian culture is a subject in itself;[21] to the extent that this myth has portrayed the city as a parasite on Russian life and economy, it should now be reassessed. Several generalizations demonstrating that the capital had a significant positive impact on Russia's further development can be made.

A Catalyst for Change

The relationship between St. Petersburg and the Russian hinterland was symbiotic. Changes in the countryside, as demonstrated earlier, helped make possible the capital's rapid growth. Yet it is also true that the needs of the city helped bring about that very change in the interior. Agriculture was spurred to produce increasing amounts of foodstuffs and other supplies precisely because a growing market for those goods existed in St. Petersburg. Canals were built so that goods could be transported to the capital with greater certainty and less effort and expense. Merchants from the interior increased the turnover of money in the countryside after receiving it as payment for contracted or delivered goods.[22] The capital's labor needs induced considerable migration from the interior. In these ways, the economic activities vital to the city's continued growth contributed also to the development of the entire Russian economy.

Record-keeping in the eighteenth century was too incomplete and inexact to permit us to formulate a precise statistical relationship between the heightening presence of St. Petersburg and the metamorphosis that was slowly beginning to reshape the Russian economy toward the end of the eighteenth century, but there is little doubt that without the stimulation provided by the new capital's economic demands and potentialities those changes would have been less profound. None other than Adam Smith discussed the significance of trade relations between town and countryside, terming it "the great commerce of every civilized society."[23] Smith divided cities into those that had "productive" and those with "unproductive" labor, meaning by the first those that manufactured and by the second those that consumed. These concepts are close to those of "parasitical" and "generative" cities developed later by B. F. Hoselitz and E. A Wrigley.[24] St. Petersburg boasted both features, although it has been argued here that the city contributed far more to Russia than it sapped from it.

The new structure of city administration brought about by the 1785 Charter to the Towns stemmed in part from the central government's recognition that St. Petersburg was inadequately administered under earlier legislation. Rather than prepare a new system of administration for the capital alone, Catherine chose, in typical eighteenth-century manner, to offer a wholesale restructuring of urban government applicable to all Russian towns.[25] Similarly, the commission named by Catherine in 1762 to work on plans for both St. Petersburg and Moscow devoted most of its early work to the former city; but within six years its role was expanded to include all towns in the empire. For many of these towns, the layout of St. Petersburg served as a model, particularly in the arrangement of streets.[26] Attempts to bridle unchecked growth in St. Petersburg contributed substantially to what a Soviet historian has termed the "formative period of the new history of Russian urban construction, when the Russian art of planning was formulated."[27]

Urban planning on a large scale had far greater success in St. Petersburg than in most other Russian towns. The new city was successfully established by imperial fiat and to a great extent planned according to the wishes of a centralized commission. Planners gained the impression that other cities and towns could be laid out the same way, according to the same blueprint. For this reason the St. Petersburg pattern, particularly the concepts of three radial streets extending from the Admiralty and the grid street pattern on Vasil'evskii Island, provided inspiration for the layout of many other Russian towns.[28] But many of these plans were never fully implemented, because the towns for which they were intended simply did not develop. They did fill roles as administrative centers, but hardly proceeded beyond that into commercial relations. If Catherine's fame as a builder of cities could be tied to any one city, it was St. Petersburg, because of her extensive projects to harmonize and beautify the capital.

Catherine and her urban planners never did fully appreciate that St. Petersburg was intrinsically different from other Russian towns. In their thinking and their legislation they operated under the assumption that a city is a city; the structure for administering one can be used for administering all. This belief was only a corollary of the great eighteenth-century thesis that universal laws underlay all forms of societal existence. If this general assumption is true, there is no need to particularize laws for one city. Yet because of its uniqueness in the Russian setting, St. Petersburg was qualitatively different from other towns in Russia. It was far more cosmopolitan than any of them. In sheer size it far outstripped all other Russian cities save Moscow. As William Blackwell has pointed out, its role as capital, with autocrat, court, bureaucracy, and the military in residence, gave it additional political preponderance far out of proportion to the weight of its population alone.[29] For most of the century it was by far the leading port dealing in international trade. It had problems of provisioning, hygiene, and transport that were faced by no other city. Measures designed for the other towns of Russia frequently did not fit St. Petersburg. Conversely, measures developed expressly for St. Petersburg were futilely expected to succeed elsewhere. Much of the planning done by the Commission for the Masonry Construction of St. Petersburg and Moscow that pertained to other Russian towns remained a dead letter simply because it was patterned exactly after the large cities and was of no use in a provincial capital or district town.

More than it could be said of any other Russian municipality, St. Petersburg helped tie the country together. Gilbert Rozman has developed a theory about the nature of development of urban life in premodern societies, finding seven stages of urbanization. According to his reckoning, St. Petersburg was at the most complex and advanced stage. Because this was so, Russia itself was fully prepared for the forces of modernization when they began to make themselves felt.[30] It could be argued with equal conviction that the degree of urbanization that St. Petersburg gave to Russian society did not so much illustrate Russia's readiness to modernize as it imparted that readiness, through the responses aroused in the national economy to the city's needs, appetites, and extensive role in quickening and animating life in Russia.

With no adjacent hinterland to speak of, St. Petersburg turned to the greater part of European Russia to draw its own sustenance and to distribute the fruit of its activities. As handler of half the nation's foreign commerce, locus of its emerging banking and other financial institutions, disseminator of new productive techniques and methods through its academies and societies, innovator in industrial production, St. Petersburg extended an economic influence to the distant reaches of the empire.[31] Furthermore, in the newspaper *Sanktpeterburgskie vedomosti,* published by the St. Petersburg Academy of Sciences, the capital provided an advertisement medium for all Russia. The newspaper's role as facilitator of commercial activity developed almost entirely during Catherine's reign. *Sanktpeterburgskie vedomosti* consisted prior to the 1760s of two major sections, one reproducing news dispatches from various cities throughout Europe, and the other listing commercial opportunities of all sorts. Whereas the former section remained essentially the same length throughout Catherine's reign—four to eight pages—and related more foreign than domestic news, the latter section expanded steadily from four to twenty pages and more.

The content of the second section also changed. At the beginning of Catherine's reign most advertisements were placed by government agencies offering contracts for constructing state buildings, transporting goods, coins, and bullion, and supplying food, firewood, and other necessities to state agencies and institutions. These contracts extended, for the most part, only to St. Petersburg and its immediate environs. But by the late 1770s most advertisements were placed by private individuals seeking to sell goods and sell or rent real estate, by contractors offering their services, and such like. Government agencies rarely made use any longer of the advertisement supplement.[32] Furthermore, many of the goods and services and much of the real estate tendered were located not just in St. Petersburg and its environs but in such distant places as Moscow, the Volga region, and the Urals. By the end of the century, opportunities in industry and commerce throughout Russia were presented to the readers of the capital's newspaper.

The Cultural Impact

One of the consequences of urban development is the accumulation of enough wealth to permit a greater allocation of resources into cultivation of the arts, education, public health, and the sciences.[33] Literary life flourished in the new capital; indeed, the development of a Russian national literature centered in St. Petersburg. Although as yet there was no "St. Petersburg school" of authors, it is significant (and not unexpected) that more noteworthy writers lived in St. Petersburg than in any other town, drawn there by the patronage of the court and a concentration of potential readers; among the authors were Nikolai Ivanovich Novikov (until 1779), Mikhail Dmitrievich Chulkov, Aleksandr Petrovich Sumarokov, Denis Ivanovich Fonvizin, Vasilii Grigor'evich Ruban, Gavriil Romanovich Derzhavin, and Ivan Andreevich Krylov. Aleksandr Nikolaevich Radishchev was head of the St. Petersburg customhouse when he published *A Journey from St. Petersburg to Moscow* in 1790. Satirical journals began to appear in the late 1760s with considerable initial encouragement by Catherine.[34] After 1783, a number of privately owned typographies joined those already operated by government agencies, printing works by Russian authors as well as Russian translations of books popular in western Europe.

If St. Petersburg was only barely beginning to be used as a setting for literary works, it served much more as a subject for artistic creations.[35] The first well-known portrayer of cityscapes from St. Petersburg was

Mikhailo Makhaev, who executed a series of river and street scenes in 1753 in commemoration of the city's first fifty years. In his choice of perspective, composition, and detail, however, he represented the city more as one might wish it to be than as it actually was. His overviews represented one sustained tradition of depicting St. Petersburg in art. Another, more personal, less grandiose, capturing the human dimension, can be seen in the drawings of Giacomo Quarenghi, the architect who came to St. Petersburg from Bergamo in 1779 and soon became Russia's preeminent builder in the classical style.

Increased outlays for welfare and education are mentioned in the second chapter.[36] Yet one segment of that discussion bears repetition in the present context. The 1786 law instituting Russia's first comprehensive public education system, based directly on the Hapsburg adaptation of the Prussian system, followed four years of experimentation with public education in St. Petersburg. Because the system proved workable in the capital, and after an institute ("seminary") for training teachers was set up there, public education was extended to the remainder of the country. In this instance as in others, Catherine used St. Petersburg as a laboratory to test new programs and theories.

In assessing the full impact of St. Petersburg on Russian society, one must also examine its psychological effect, which was great. The intrusion onto the Russian scene of a new and vigorous capital not only set in motion economic changes, but also forced a reorientation of thought and emotion. In the first place, this modern, vibrant, somewhat foreign alternative to Moscow helped set Russians to thinking: What was Russia? Where did Russia really lie? Whence did it derive its "Russianness"? Prince Mikhail Mikhailovich Shcherbatov voiced such questions and rejected the new capital because it was "isolated geographically and spiritually from the nation."[37] Catherine II, among others, indicated her decided preference for the new city, regarding old Moscow as a provincial town inhabited by superstitious people.[38] Denis Fonvizin believed most Russians saw it differently. He posited a state, clearly with Russia in mind, "consisting, one may say, of only two cities, in one of which [St. Petersburg] people live mostly of necessity, and in the other of which [Moscow] they live mostly from inclination."[39] The clash of opinion was even sensed by foreigners; the famous Venetian Giovanni Casanova wrote during his visit to Russia:

> Whoever has not seen Moscow has not seen Russia, and whoever knows Russians only through Petersburg does not know the Russians of real Russia. Here [in Moscow] the inhabitants of the new capital are regarded as foreigners. Mother Moscow will for a long time yet remain the true capital for Russians. If old Muscovites do not proclaim against the new capital

> the sentence of Cato the Elder against Carthage, they at least relate to Petersburg with hostility and aversion. These two cities are not only rivals because of difference in location and purpose, but also for other reasons—reasons religious and political. Moscow stretches back into the misty past; this is a city of legends and reminiscences, the city of tsars, of the species of Asia, with amazement seeing herself in Europe.[40]

The opponents of the new capital can be separated into two large, rather amorphous groups. The first, represented by Prince Shcherbatov, consisted of members of the old nobility from central areas of the country. To them, no other city could replace Moscow. It was the center of everything Russian: traditional capital, seat of Orthodoxy, repository of their values. St. Petersburg on the other hand was singularly un-Russian. Furthermore—and a fact that could not remain unnoticed by those magnates with experience managing households in both capital cities—prices were markedly higher in the new capital than in the old.

The second group made unhappy by St. Petersburg's rise to primacy over Moscow was made up of nonnobles who stood to lose economically from St. Petersburg's growth. Mostly Muscovite merchants and artisans, this group also included individuals from other central Russian towns.

Both groups' rejection of St. Petersburg stemmed in part from aversion to any innovation whatever. They often ignored the benefits and looked with distaste on the ills that they believed St. Petersburg had introduced into Russia: dishonesty and avarice (as exhibited by the merchants in the opera "sanktpeterburgskii gostinyi dvor"), the callousness and inhumanity of the new bureaucracy, and the capital's "urban evils" (as compared with "rural virtues").[41]

The St. Petersburg–Moscow competition for allegiance had overtones even in the eighteenth century of a foreigner-nationalist conflict, a clash that carried over into the nineteenth-century struggle between Slavophiles and Westernizers. The city on the Neva did have a large foreign population, and these non-Russians were integrated into the city to a far greater extent than the foreign community in Moscow had ever been. Not only were many of the new capital's merchants and artisans foreigners, but also many architects, artists, scientists, and even civil servants and military and naval officers.

The Challenge to Tradition

The psychological dimension of St. Petersburg's impact must have been particularly acute for the tens of thousands of ordinary Russians who were affected by the city economically or otherwise. Although Russia remained predominantly rural and economically underdeveloped for decades following Catherine's reign, the city unquestionably began to affect the ways in which Russians who came under its influence viewed themselves and the world around them. For those who came to the city to live, there was at least a partial breakup of traditional familial and associational ties in the village. *Otkhodnichestvo,* the departure from the village for a season to earn money, became a recognizable phenomenon of village life in the eighteenth century and continued to expand throughout the nineteenth.[42] In St. Petersburg the *otkhodnik* found a pattern of life different even from Moscow, not to speak of the smaller industrial and commercial towns. St. Petersburg was far more secular; other than a few churches soon replaced by imperial cathedrals, the center of the city was relatively devoid of Russian Orthodox parish churches. In the heart of town the Catholic, Lutheran, and even Armenian churches of the non-Russian were far more visible. Russian parish churches may have ringed the city's core, but only those ecclesiastical institutions with functions useful for the state—the Synod, the Cathedral of St. Peter and St. Paul containing the sepulchres of deceased emperors and empresses, the church of St. Isaac, where infants of the imperial family were christened, the church of Our Lady of Kazan', rapidly becoming a monument to Russian military prowess—were safely ensconced at the center. Nor did St. Petersburg contain numerous monastic institutions. Far from dominating the middle of town, the few monasteries that did exist there—whether for men or women—were located on the periphery nearest the heart of Russia. Rather than being a city of clerics, St. Petersburg was a monument to the power of the state.

This was not lost on the peasants who came to the new capital. How mighty was this imperial state that could erect one of the great cities of Europe in less than a century, so that it began to resemble Babylon or Paris![43] Peasants living in the vicinity of St. Petersburg are said to have sung a song about this toward the end of the eighteenth century:

> How good is God in Russia!
> On swampy meadows
> Where lay water and ooze,
> Where nor cattle nor people set foot,
> There we sow grain and reap
> And we lay the sheaves in stooks;
> We even sow flax seed.
> O our golden age!
> Our soul aspires after the one
> Who founded Petersburg!

> We ever burn for him,
> We heartily love the time of Peter.
> We love his age sincerely;
> It is worthy of this love.
> Long live his descendants in the flesh,
> Their time will be counted in centuries not years.[44]

Peter and his generation were far more responsible for the transformation of bogs into fields and woods into houses than was God.

But running as a contrapuntal theme to the secular city was the development during Catherine's reign of one of the most radical religious sects in Russia's history, the castration sect, or *skopchestvo,* which consciously chose St. Petersburg as its New Jerusalem, the holy city for its new Children of Israel. For the last two decades of Catherine's reign the acknowledged leader of this least enlightened of sects, Kondratii Selivanov, is reported to have spread his heresy among merchants, craftsmen, and peasants in the capital, having well chosen this city for the access it gave him to people from every part of European Russia.[45]

St. Petersburg also provided refuge for "holy fools," those people who in the medieval Russian tradition had become "fools for the sake of Christ." The best known of the "holy fools" during Catherine's era was Blessed Kseniia, finally made an official saint of the Russian church in 1988. According to the oral tradition she adopted the role of "holy fool" several years before Catherine assumed power and outlived Catherine by several years. She is said to have been quite popular among the common people, the tradesmen, cabbies, shopkeepers, and workmen of St. Petersburg Side where she lived. In the city Catherine praised for its lack of religious fanaticism and its enlightenment, Kseniia, apparently unknown to Catherine, was sought out by people for religious solace in a purely Russian traditional manner.[46]

Selivanov's success at evading the authorities and Kseniia's invisibility to officialdom demonstrate another characteristic of St. Petersburg inimical to traditional village life, the anonymity provided by the city. One could go there to hide. Conversely, the connectional life of the village found no place in the city. Its anonymity can be seen in several ways. The police reported finding numerous bodies on city streets or in waterways that remained unclaimed. With no identification among personal effects and in the absence of friends or relatives to claim bodies, many corpses were delivered to one or another of the various hospitals for anatomical research, or, more rarely, were buried quietly in a potter's field. Certainly many of the foreigners who came to St. Petersburg sought the anonymity of a new start. As a Frenchman wrote circa 1757,

> Upon the arrival of the envoy, the Marquis de l'Hôpital, we were besieged by lots of Frenchmen of every shade, who for the most part, having fallen into altercation with the Paris police, turned up to infect the countries of the north with their presence. We were astonished and distressed to find that fugitives, bankrupts, debauchees, and not a few women of such like, are living in the homes of many eminent persons; to these people, owing to the local partiality towards the French, has been entrusted the upbringing of the children of important people; it is likely that these outcasts of our homeland have settled all the way to China.[47]

Europeans of all sorts discovered Russia through Peter's "Window on the West," which became for them a window on Russia. Catherine may have been aggrieved that numerous foreign visitors, having seen the two capitals, thought they knew Russia, but at least in visiting the two capitals they were marking a growing awareness of Russia in the West, and in most cases St. Petersburg comprised the most favorable part of those impressions. For many young upper-class Englishmen, St. Petersburg became a way station on the Grand Tour, or an integral part of the alternative Northern Tour. Foreign, especially German, members of the St. Petersburg Academy of Sciences set out from St. Petersburg on their expeditions to Tartary and Siberia, and on their return published scholarly studies that added significantly to Europe's knowledge of Russia. Others, like the mathematician Leonhard Euler, the historian Gerhard Friedrich Müller, and the statistician Heinrich Storch, lent their prestige to the academy by their long affiliation with it, and thus contributed to the image of St. Petersburg as one of Europe's coming great cities.

In summary, by the end of Catherine's reign St. Petersburg had reached sufficient proportions to wield considerable power over a large hinterland. It achieved this in part by sheer size, through the concentration of large numbers of people. But its influence was far vaster than its population alone would seem to have warranted. Because of its economic functions—port, manufacturer, banker—it drew goods and services like a magnet from all over Russia. It had the additional advantage of being a seat of ultimate political power, and measures designed to facilitate life in the capital affected a much larger area. This was so because of one characteristic unique to St. Petersburg: the inhospitable northland in the vicinity of the city simply could not support it. Turning this potentially fatal weakness to its singular advantage, the city learned to draw its sustenance from a vast supporting base, and many far-flung parts of the empire, not to speak of Europe generally, thus came into contact with the capital. St. Petersburg by its very existence made its presence felt both near and far.

Conclusion: A Most Intentional City

So prevalent has been autocracy throughout Russian history that virtually every era seems bound inseparably to and guided unalterably by the will of a ruler. The importance of the state, personified by the tsar, is so strong that any other guiding or directing force is seen as exceptional. Ever since the rise of the Muscovite state in the fifteenth century, periods when the tsar and state lost the ability to control events occurred only rarely. Thus the Time of Troubles or the revolutions of 1917 exemplify short, "uncharacteristic" periods in Russia's past, whereas the era of a given ruler, whether Ivan the Terrible or Peter the Great or Stalin, seems to fit more comfortably as a term for dressing Russian historical interpretation. Christianity came to Russia when a prince forcibly baptized his subjects; scholars debate whether serfdom developed organically or, more probably, was imposed by a series of princes; the iconoclast Lev Tolstoi felt compelled to deny at great length the historical importance of the leader in *War and Peace.* The verity of "The Era of ——" is seen even in viceroys, hence the origin of *Bironovshchina, Arakcheevshchina,* and *Ezhovshchina.*

Nowhere is this generalization more apparent than when looking at the history of St. Petersburg. The city's very existence bears witness to the will and design of Peter the Great, and even under the name of Lenin it did not escape the overseeing gaze and haunting memory of the Bronze Horseman, although in fact little remains of the Sankt-Piter-Burkh envisioned and brought to reality by Peter. Still more than to Peter's, the city is linked to the name of Alexander Sergeevich Pushkin. True, he was not a political ruler, but the mythologized memory of his power and influence over Russian cultural life continues to be built with time. A mountain of books and articles has used in some way the words "Pushkin's Petersburg" in their titles. The reign of Pushkin's nemesis Emperor Nicholas I left its mark on the architecture, the personality, and the reputation of the city, with its spacious parade grounds, colonnaded barracks, regimented bureaucracy, and cold officialdom. And in this study, St. Petersburg is addressed as a city developing under the rule of Catherine the Great.

Catherine certainly was an active ruler. Historians have long recognized her concern for Russia's towns, her recognition of the contribution that cities make to the welfare and prosperity of a state and its citizens, and her legislation designed to bring urban life in Russia to a flourishing condition. Living in St. Petersburg much of the time, she could not avoid a certain familiarity with the patterns of its daily and seasonal life, with the impressions it made upon visiting foreigners, with its economic and political significance in Russia. While she refrained from taking on St. Petersburg as a personal project, she clearly attempted to put her stamp on the city in several ways.

But was the hand of the empress the most decisive force in shaping the city during the last third of the eighteenth century? Were the policies and regulations that her appointed officials imposed upon the city's life decisive in shaping the degree and direction of its growth? In short, did St. Petersburg continue to be a "planned city," even to the extent that the term applied to it before Catherine's reign? To what extent were the authorities really in control of the city's life? Or to put the matter differently, to what extent was St. Petersburg what it appeared to be (and what it was widely believed to be), a creation of the state and a reflection of its views of society, economy, and cultural life?

To pursue these questions it is helpful to review Catherine's sense of what cities were supposed to be. Briefly stated, Catherine had a dualistic view of towns. On the one hand, they implied a higher level of culture than the countryside or village. They created wealth through trade and production that contributed to the enhancement of the state. Catherine even defined town residents—genuine city residents—as those people who owned real property in towns and paid taxes; that is, people who contributed to the wealth of the state. On the other hand, Catherine shared with many people of her century an aesthetic aversion to overly large cities, preferring medium-sized towns. The chaos and disorder of unregulated marketplace and clamorous manufactory offended her sense of harmony and symmetry. She especially wanted to limit the number of vagrants in towns, since in her view they were responsible for most of the commotion, confusion, crime, and unsightliness in urban areas. Vagrants included all those who played no useful social or economic role, all those whose place could not be defined in law and whose way of life could not be recognized as contributing to the betterment of society. Catherine's definition of vagrants would thus include mendicant monks, beggars on city streets, prostitutes, and those erstwhile peasants lacking jobs in town and therefore likely to turn to crime there. But those who followed useful occupations were welcomed, and Catherine's legislation attempted to give new status and dignity to merchants and artisans. Catherine recognized that all towns were not the same, that some were basically administrative points, others were centers of industrial activity, while still others concentrated on commerce. But the ideal city assumed all these functions and more.

Among Russian towns, St. Petersburg was undoubtedly Catherine's favorite. She certainly knew it more intimately than she did others. It combined port facilities, administrative offices, commercial markets, industrial enterprises (but not too many), and cultural amenities to make up what she considered to be the complete city. The symmetrical layout of its better districts Catherine frequently recommended as a model for other towns to follow. Its cosmopolitan spirit also appealed to the empress. Next to it, other Russian towns, among which she specifically included Moscow, seemed to her hopelessly provincial and backward. Catherine liked in particular the industriousness of the capital's inhabitants. She was willing to overlook certain urban evils there because St. Petersburg had "disseminated into the Russian Empire more money and industry" during its short existence than had Moscow in five hundred years.[1] Moscow she despised; it lacked all the new capital's virtues. In old Moscow people were superstitious, gossipy, and inclined to disorderliness and riot. Moscow was a place of refuge for her critics; they retired to Moscow, far from the court, to complain and dispute with her.

More laws were issued during Catherine's reign to deal with St. Petersburg than with any other town. Moscow ran it a close second, but when the numerous manifestos combating the plague there in the early 1770s are discounted, the number of laws specifically regarding Moscow is reduced to just over half of those for St. Petersburg.[2] It is difficult to say to what extent these laws reveal the hand of Catherine. Most of them were drawn up by commissions and individual officials directly appointed by her. She at least read and approved the provisions of most of them, because her *byt' po semu* (so be it) frequently appears in her own hand in the margins of copies of the laws preserved in archives. There is justification therefore in saying that the legislation reflected Catherine's will and intent for St. Petersburg, if not for all Russian towns.

This legislation may be considered under four rubrics: administrative reorganization, urban planning, regulation of economic and social activity, and the improvement of the level of culture (*prosveshchenie*) of the citizens. Each category of legislation was suited to a different purpose. The goals of the provincial reform of 1775, Police Statute of 1782, and Municipal Charter of 1785 were to bring greater order to government. If the state were better organized at all levels, it would be more responsive to the sovereign's dictates. The planning commission was created to guide the growth of St. Petersburg and keep it under close control, pliable to the will of the ruler. A well-planned city would yield maximal economic gain, bringing more money into the state treasury. Regulatory measures were introduced to provide each subject with clearly defined status and function in society. If people knew what they were allowed to do and what was expected of them, they could work together in harmony. Finally, the attention to cultural concerns, to the "enlightenment" of subjects, stemmed from the Cameralistic concern for every facet of subjects' lives. It was the duty of the sovereign in a well-run state to provide schools and hospitals, and to care for orphans, widows, and the aged, especially in towns.

Thus Catherine's intent in framing urban legislation went far beyond a desire to have a grand capital. Her greater goal was to subordinate all social and economic activity to state regulation so that it would benefit the state and therefore society. She introduced change not to augment the city's expansion, but to facilitate administration and raise revenue. The concept of urbanization as such did not concern her, yet in the attempt to achieve her ultimate goal, she instituted numerous measures that also encouraged urban growth.

In the most obvious sense, Catherine left her imprint on St. Petersburg by refashioning its physical appearance. As historians have long pointed out, to speak of the existence in our day of a Petrine St. Petersburg is anachronistic, since few buildings constructed in the reign of Peter still stand. From Catherine's reign date close to fifty palaces, state buildings, churches, and other structures. During her reign the canals were integrated into the city's plan and several were spanned by noteworthy bridges. The Neva and the canals were given their granite embankments. The major streets were laid, street lighting and paving were expanded, and a sewage system was introduced. Some monuments associated with subsequent reigns—Kazan'skii, Nikol'skii, and Isakievskii cathedrals, the public library, the bourse, Mikhailovskii Castle, and others—were the fruition of projects inaugurated by Catherine.

These building programs, whether public works projects or palaces for the imperial family and its favorites, provided seasonal employment for tens of thousands of laborers, who in turn had to be housed, fed, and have their other needs met. This swelled population remains almost invisible in the laws defining the city's administration, regulating the pulse of economic life and providing social services, yet it was the vitality exemplified by the coming and going of these construction workers and the people accessory to them that distinguished

St. Petersburg from any other artificially created residence town of the baroque and classical ages.

In making of St. Petersburg a planned city, Catherine dealt in categories of architecture, the patterning of streets and squares, and the legislative regulation of economic and social activities. It was implicitly assumed that governmental fiat could regulate change, rearrange social structures, and shape life in conformity with current enlightened or Cameralist theories. In short, Catherine and her administrators were not all that different from urban planners of any other age. Her program for St. Petersburg, however, was not predicated primarily on what was best for that city's residents, but was subordinated to a more comprehensive view in which St. Petersburg played only a part. Many of Catherine's decisions, because they were taken with other goals in mind, proved to be detrimental to the city's growth. The measures limiting the kinds of economic activities open to peasants and the lower orders of urban residents, the decrees ordering that runaway serfs be apprehended and returned to their estates, the establishment of rigid hierarchies in the corporative rights and obligations of merchants and artisans, the enforced removal of unemployed people from the city—all derive from a vision of society more attuned to a traditional rural order than to maximal urban development. And all tended to retard the natural development of St. Petersburg.

But to attribute to Catherine the ability either to plan and regulate St. Petersburg's growth or to subordinate it to other goals is to credit her with much more power over the city's vitality than she actually had. In the final analysis the city took on a life and will of its own. Neither Catherine nor her planners or administrators seem to have anticipated the tremendous growth in population that took place there during her reign. From time to time she requested information on the number of people in the capital and received figures that even their producers recognized as grossly understated. The attempts to control passage into and out of the city by setting up roadblocks on the major highways and a moat and wall were laughably ineffective. Aware that unchecked growth was influencing price rises on grain and firewood, the government could do little more than create commissions to study the matter.

There seems to have been no awareness whatever that the city's adult population was becoming overwhelmingly male. The concerns of administrative bodies reached down only marginally to the level on which many of these men lived. Their hovels and makeshift quarters appeared overnight near the city's edges without the knowledge, apparently, even of the police. The social organization of workingmen's artels, so simple yet so effective for cutting living costs and dealing with employers, lay outside the view of officialdom.

Repeated attempts to delimit the space where trade could take place proved ineffective. Marketplaces were laid out in each section of the city, but some of them remained devoid of shopkeepers or of customers, while others spilled over into neighboring streets and buildings. The bazaar on Admiralty Side very early outgrew its massive masonry structure, long before it was even finished, so that row upon row of petty merchants' shops offered goods in nearby alleys, many of them fencing stolen goods, even those nabbed right from under the eyes of the empress herself, from the Winter Palace. And the prevalence of smuggling in and around the port was so great that many historians caution against using any of the official statistics for eighteenth-century trade, seeing them as highly unrepresentative of the real exchange of goods, since they include only merchandise on which excise duties were paid.

St. Petersburg bore the imprint of Catherine's rule, but also developed independently of that mold. In that respect, much had changed since the early years of the century. Under Peter I the new capital had depended upon his continued patronage for its existence; he arbitrarily created and sustained it, and had Anna Ioannovna not made it again the capital in the 1730s after a hiatus of several years, it might have remained no more than a sequestered provincial town. But by the last third of the century the city had assumed a vitality, an identity, and a role in Russian life all its own. To be sure, the presence of the court contributed momentum, but St. Petersburg was becoming much more than a baroque *Residenzstadt.* It had achieved recognition as one of the great cities of Europe.

Because St. Petersburg attained this size and significance in less than a century, one might expect to find that there was considerable social flux in the new Russian capital, and indeed there was. But the inferred expectation that this social flux gave rise to riots and massive disorders, especially in view of the high proportion of single males, is unfulfilled. St. Petersburg certainly had its share of crime, but no evidence has been found of large-scale unrest or rebellion. This absence strikes one as unusual in a period when Emelian Pugachev over the course of two years gained massive support in southeastern Russia, and Moscow was wracked by the Plague Riot. Soviet historians placed considerable emphasis on a growing sense of frustration in the "bourgeoisie," leading to their making demands for recognition upon the state, but offered little evidence to support this alleged conflict. Unlike Moscow or, for that matter, cities like Paris and London, St. Petersburg preserved a sense of outward calm. The closest thing to a riot in

St. Petersburg was a work stoppage by four thousand laborers, and that incident seems to have been isolated.

The absence of violent confrontation is explained first by the presence of the court. Simple Russians stood in awe of the sovereign; she was at the same time *matushka* and *Imperatritsa,* little Mother and Her Imperial Majesty, Empress of All the Russias. The magnificent Winter Palace, Tsarskoe Selo's Summer Palace, gilded carriages drawn by six or eight matching horses, and other trappings of royalty further awed urban subjects. So did the large number of imperial guards troops and regular army soldiers stationed in the capital who at regular intervals staged drills and parades for the entertainment of the court and the apprehension of the populace. Additionally, the court sponsored periodic public festivals and entertainments for the common people, gaining their gratitude rather than their envy.

Second, few major famines, pestilences, or periods of political instability struck St. Petersburg during Catherine's reign. In her early years when Vasilii Mirovich tried to liberate the former infant tsar Ivan VI from Shlisselburg Fortress, the matter was dealt with quickly, and no repercussions were felt in the city nearby. Other plots were found out from time to time before they could be hatched and the general population become involved in them. To maintain social stability Catherine ensured that the public granaries were kept full, thereby inhibiting the formation of hunger-driven mobs. The one natural disaster to strike St. Petersburg, the destructive flood of September 1777, was over in a mere eight hours, before fear and want could give rise to violence. Shock and bewilderment did not give way to blame-placing and anger. Russian urban riots traditionally were spawned by these bad economic conditions, not by ideologies. Finally, power struggles over access to the ruler and the exercise of authority, which had often led to riots in western European cities, were next to impossible in a state where virtually all power was in the hands of one person. In Russia, only a pretender to this power could legitimately offer himself to the public as an alternative. Of the numerous pretenders during Catherine's reign, none was able to secure support in St. Petersburg, the city perhaps least susceptible in Russia to the mythmaking of the "lost tsar," because of its western orientation.

Catherine controlled police, guards, and army. Foreigners, who made up a sizable minority of the city and might have instigated trouble because they were used to different forms of urban government, did nothing of the sort. They tolerated Russian conditions because they often held favorable positions (with commensurate salaries) and because most planned a residency of short duration. They recognized that they were strangers or guests in the city. For all these reasons there were no mass outbreaks of violence in St. Petersburg during the last third of the eighteenth century. It was this orderliness that so impressed Catherine.

A broader evaluation of the changes in St. Petersburg during the late eighteenth century takes one far beyond the capacity of the ruler to control and determine those changes. The very process of urbanization extends beyond any government's ability to command.

It is clear that urbanization in St. Petersburg was marked by much more than simple population growth. Urbanization is never characterized by size alone, but by fundamental shifts in the way of life that break the old patterns of the village. It is possible for a population center to be quite large without becoming fully urban, as though it were a macrovillage. Eighteenth-century Moscow frequently was characterized as an overgrown village. As for St. Petersburg, the heterogeneity of its population, the high degree of specialization in its labor force, the increased attention that was paid to education, higher cultural activities, and public welfare, all characterize a high degree of urbanization. It is much more difficult to determine how much the value systems of people living in St. Petersburg changed as a result of their being there. No evidence has been found, for example, of a decline in the importance of religion in their lives or a lessening of familial and village ties. A sense was developing at least among Russian writers that something about living in St. Petersburg was different from life elsewhere in Russia. The city somehow made people different. But the values of the majority of St. Petersburgers probably changed little. Too many legal—not to mention psychological—ties with the village still persisted. If there is no evidence for change, there is equally little to maintain emphatically that an urban mind-set did not develop. On this issue the silence of the sources urges caution in making either case.

Applying the same criteria of urbanization, no other eighteenth-century Russian town, with the possible exception of Moscow, could be called urban. That the capital should have urbanized first, despite its late start, was natural. No other town lay in such close proximity to the central administration, or had its advantages for maritime trade (until the founding of Odessa late in the century). Certainly no other Russian town experienced its rate of growth during this period. Indeed, no other city in Europe could match its transformation. St. Petersburg's growth was made all the more remarkable by the natural barriers that would seem to have impeded expansion: the harsh climate, the absence of a heavily populated countryside nearby from which to draw people, and the vast distances over which the goods to sustain the city's life had to be brought.

Within Russia urbanization had not yet begun in any other center of population except Moscow. That city continued to be termed an overgrown village even into the twentieth century, an appellation wholly unsuitable for St. Petersburg at any time in its existence. Moscow proved unable to keep pace with the new capital. During Catherine's reign St. Petersburg surpassed Moscow in population, economic importance, and cultural awareness. The usurper, less than a century old, was more dynamic and had greater impact on rural Russia than its six-hundred-year-old competitor. Russia received its new ideas, technology, and luxuries through St. Petersburg.

The vigorous and growing economic relationship between St. Petersburg and a large part of rural Russia has been one the themes of this study. The capital could not have survived without deriving sustenance from many parts of the empire, but the Russian interior also grew to be dependent upon St. Petersburg to supplement, if not provide, its livelihood. A study by the Soviet historian L. V. Milov argued that labor obligations (*barshchina*) of peasants were developed as fully as possible in northwestern Russia by the mid-eighteenth century. Profitability from labor was comparatively low in that part of the country because of the poor soil and the short growing season. In order to increase their profits, therefore, landowners had to turn to quitrent (*obrok*).[3] The peasants who were now supposed to pay their rents in cash rather than labor naturally turned to the largest hired labor market in Russia, St. Petersburg, where Catherinian construction projects alone provided cash incomes for tens of thousands of peasant households during the years of her reign. Milov describes a preparedness in the rural economy for movement to a city, a situation that worked to the advantage of a burgeoning St. Petersburg.

Another study, by Gilbert Rozman, speculated that just prior to 1800, Russia was in the last stage of premodern development.[4] Russia was able to modernize fast in the nineteenth century because its level of development was at the highest stage of the premodern before modernization's forces hit it. St. Petersburg best exemplifies Rozman's thesis as related to urbanization. Rozman sees Russia as having been at the highest stage of premodern urbanization in the seven levels he distinguishes. Rather than just illustrating Rozman's thesis, it has been suggested, St. Petersburg was of crucial importance in imparting the readiness of which he speaks, through the market's responses to St. Petersburg's needs and appetites and the city's support for economic activities throughout the country.

The capital city's cultural impact on the countryside was decidedly weaker. A uniquely Russian literature and theater were developing in St. Petersburg, but their effect as a whole was felt only in a later generation. That dimension of the city's effect on Russia awaited a Pushkin. This limitation of St. Petersburg's impact on the Russian countryside does not render any less pertinent, however, one final question: if St. Petersburg was obviously responding to needs in Russian life by its sustained rapid growth during the final third of the eighteenth century, why did urbanization not spread early in the nineteenth century to other Russian towns?

Although St. Petersburg was a major force in transforming Russia in the eighteenth century, it did not sustain this vitality in the nineteenth century. The reason lies partly in what Kingsley Davis and Hilda Golden some years ago termed "over-urbanization."[5] The phenemenon occurs in preindustrial societies that achieve a higher urban population than is to be expected in such societies, where cities otherwise tend to remain small and tied to a local economy. Over-urbanization generally occurs in a single city. The prime example given by Davis and Golden was Cairo, Egypt, in the mid-twentieth century. Over-urbanization is caused not only by an attraction to the city, but also by a push from a depressed rural economy. Although the present study has emphasized the former, it has drawn attention to the latter as a factor in St. Petersburg's expansion.

The inadequacy of the rural economy was due in large part to Russia's social structure. As countless historians have pointed out, the institution of serfdom seriously hindered modernization, and hence prevented extensive urbanization. The new estates and corporations created by Catherine II for townsmen in the 1785 charter did not supersede "rural" estates. Thus a migrant to a city or town might register as a merchant or an artisan, but he remained legally a peasant or serf. This dual role made migration to towns less attractive and more difficult than was the case in western Europe in earlier centuries, where a migrant's former status as peasant lapsed (expressed in the phrase, *Stadtluft macht frei*). Furthermore, urban peasants not registered in an urban estate gained few economic privileges under Catherine's legislation; the right to commerce and industry in towns remained reserved for the "middle class" (*srednii rod liudei, meshchane*): merchants, artisans, and *posad* people. Only with the abolition of serfdom in 1861 and subsequent urban legislation could Russia develop the psychological, social, and political prerequisites for massive urbanization.

Thus the reason for urbanization's failure to continue apace is to be found more in the countryside than in the city itself. The nature of rural society rather than deficiencies in the administrative structure of towns prevented a more vital urban life from developing. Beyond the one city of St. Petersburg, furthermore, the economy lacked the means to transport the necessities of life from countryside to city. The constant attention to the details of supply that we have seen for St. Petersburg demonstrates this point.

In sum, the growth of St. Petersburg, as much as the failure of other towns to develop, may have depended less on administrative measures, imperial edicts, and the will of a monarch than on underlying social and economic realities. On the surface St. Petersburg was a planned city, but the dynamics of its development far exceeded the capacity of planners to plan or the police to control or an empress to foresee.

Notes

Introduction

1. The oft-quoted citation is from the first paragraph of the second chapter of *Notes from the Underground.*

2. S. R. Epstein, ed., *Town and Country in Europe, 1300–1800* (New York: Cambridge University Press, 2001); David Harvey, *The Urban Experience* (Baltimore: Johns Hopkins University Press, 1989); Paul M. Hohenburg and Lynn Hollen Lees, *The Making of Urban Europe* (Cambridge, MA: Harvard University Press, 1985); R. J. Holton, *Cities, Capitalism, and Civilization* (London: Allen and Unwin, 1986); Richard Lawton, ed., *The Rise and Fall of Great Cities: Aspects of Urbanization in the Western World* (New York: Bellhaven Press, 1989); and Bernard Lepetit, *The Preindustrial Urban System: France, 1740–1840,* translated by Godfrey Rogers (New York: Cambridge University Press, 1994), to name but a few.

3. A standard definition of urbanization was formulated by Hope Tisdale Eldridge in 1942. For a discussion of its ramifications, see Jan De Vries, *European Urbanization, 1500–1800* (Cambridge, MA: Harvard University Press, 1984).

4. See E. A. Wrigley, "Brake or Accelerator? Urban Growth and Population Growth Before the Industrial Revolution," in Ad van der Woude, Akira Hayami and Jan de Vries, eds., *Urbanization in History* (New York: Oxford University Press, 1990), pp. 101–12.

5. Theoretical treatment of urbanization and urbanism in historical perspective may be found in Oscar Handlin and John Burchard, eds., *The Historian and the City* (Cambridge: M.I.T. Press, 1967); Gideon Sjoberg, *The Preindustrial City Past and Present* (Glencoe, NY: Free Press, 1960); and Sjoberg, "The Rise and Fall of Cities: A Theoretical Perspective," in Nels Anderson, ed., *Urbanism and Urbanization* (Leiden: E. J. Brill, 1964), 7–20.

6. See Patricia Herlihy, *Odessa: A History, 1794–1914* (Cambridge, MA: Harvard University Press, 1986).

7. On Magnitogorsk, see Stephen Kotkin, *Magnetic Mountain: Stalinism as a Civilization* (Berkeley: University of California Press, 1985).

8. Andrei Petrovich Bogdanov, *Istoricheskoe, geograficheskoe i topograficheskoe opisanie Sanktpeterburga, ot nachala ego, s 1703 po 1751 god, sochinennoe g. Bogdanovym, so mnogimi izobrazheniiami pervykh zdanii, a nyne dopolnennoe i izdannoe, nadvornym sovetnikom, praviashchim dolzhnost' direktora novorossiiskimi uchilishchami, vol'nogo rossiiskogo sobraniia, pri Imperatorskom moskovskom universitete i sanktpeterburgskogo vol'nogo ekonomicheskogo obshchestva chlenom Vasil'em Rubanom* (St. Petersburg, 1779).

9. Vasilii Grigor'evich Ruban, *Dopolnenie k istoricheskomu, geograficheskomu i topograficheskomu opisaniiu Sanktpeterburga, s 1751 po 1762 god, sochinennoe A. Bogdanovym* (St. Petersburg, 1903).

10. Anton Friedrich Büsching, *Neue Beschreibung des russischen Reiches nach allen seinen Staaten und Ländern* (Hamburg, 1763); Johann Gottlieb Georgi, *Opisanie rossiisko-imperatorskogo stolichnogo goroda Sankt-Peterburga i dostopamiatnostei v okrestnostiiakh onogo,* 3 vols. in 1 (St. Petersburg, 1794); Gerhard-Friedrich Müller [Gerard Friderik Miller], *Geograficheskii leksikon rossiiskogo gosudarstva ili slovar', opisaiushchii poazbuchnomu poriadku reki, ozera, moria, gory, kreposti, znatnye monastyri, ostrogi, iasashnye zimoviia, rudnye zavody i prochie dostopamiatnye mesta obshirnoi rossiiskoi imperii s ob"iavleniem i tekh mest, kotorye v prezhniuiu i nyneshniuiu turetskoiu voinu, a nekotorye prezhnogo i ot Persii rossiiskoiu khrabrost'iiu obladaemu byli* (Moscow, 1773); Heinrich von Reimers, *St. Petersburg am Ende seines ersten Jahrhunderts,* 2 vols. (St. Petersburg, 1805); Benedikt Franz Hermann, *Statistische Schilderung von Russland, im Rücksicht auf Bevölkerung, Landesbeschaffenheit, Bergbau, Manufakturen und Handel* (St. Petersburg and Leipzig, 1790); and Heinrich Friedrich von Storch, *Historisch-Statistische Gemälde des russischen Reiches am Ende des XVIII Jahrhunderts: Statistische Übersicht der Statthalterschaften des russischen Reichs nach ihren merkwürdigsten Kulturverhältnissen in Tabellen,* 9 vols. (Riga and Leipzig, 1797–1803).

11. Mikhail Dmitrievich Chulkov, *Istoricheskoe opisanie rossiiskoi kommertsii pri vsekh portakh i granitsakh ot drevnikh vremen do nyne nastoiashchego i vsekh preimushchestvennykh uzakonenii po onoi Gosudaria Petra Velikogo i nyne blagopoluchno tsarstvuiushchei gosudariny Imperatritsy Ekateriny Velikoi,* 7 vols. (St. Petersburg, 1781–86); and Afanasii Shchekatov, *Slovar' geograficheskii rossiiskogo gosudarstva, sochinennyi v nastoiashchego onogo vida,* 7 vols. in 6 (Moscow, 1801–09).

12. Aleksandr Pavlovich Bashutskii, *Panorama Sanktpeterburga,* 2 vols. (St. Petersburg, 1834).

13. Mikhail Ivanovich Pyliaev, *Staryi Peterburg: Rasskazy iz byloi zhizni stolitsy,* 2nd ed. (St. Petersburg, 1885).

14. For example, Vasilii Grigor'evich Avseenko, *200 let Peterburga: Istoricheskii ocherk* (St. Petersburg, 1903); Ivan Nikolaevich Bozherianov, *K dvukhsotletiiu stolitsy: S.-Peterburg v Petrovo vremia, 1703–1903* (St. Petersburg, 1901); also Bozherianov, *"Nevskii Prospekt," Kul'turno-istoricheskii ocherk dvukhvekovoi zhizni S.-Peterburga,* 5 vols. (St. Petersburg, 1902); A. S. Shustov, *Sanktpeterburgskoe kupechestvo i torgovo-promyshlennye predpriiatiia goroda k 200–letnomu iubileiu stolitsy* (St. Petersburg, 1903); and Ivan Petrovich Vysotskii, *S.-Peterburgskaia stolichnaia politsiia i gradonachal'stvo: Kratkii istoricheskii ocherk* (St. Petersburg, 1903).

15. Petr Nikolaevich Stolpianskii, *Zhizn' i byt peterburgskoi fabriki za 210 let ee sushchestvovaniia, 1704–1914 gg.* (Leningrad, 1925).

16. Petr Nikolaevich Petrov, *Istoriia Sanktpeterburga s osnovaniia goroda do vvedeniia v deistvie vybornogo gorodskogo upravleniia po uchrezhdeniiam o guberniiakh, 1703–1782* (St. Petersburg, 1885).

17. Ivan Ivanovich Ditiatin, *Stoletie S.-Peterburgskogo gorodskogo obshchestva. 1785–1885* (St. Petersburg, 1885).

18. Aleksandr Aleksandrovich Kizevetter, *Gorodovoe polozhenie Ekateriny II* (Moscow, 1909); and *Posadskaia obshchina v Rossii XVIII st.* (Rostov-na-Donu, 1904).

19. For example, Iurii Alekseevich Egorov, *The Architectural Planning of St. Petersburg,* trans. Eric Dluhosch (Athens: Ohio University Press, 1969); N. I. Gusev, *Peterburg* (Kiev, 1899); Vladimir Iakovlevich Kurbatov, *Peterburg: Khudozhestvenno-istoricheskii ocherk i obzor khudozhestvennogo bogatstva stolitsy* (St. Petersburg, 1913); Georgii Kreskent'evich Lukomskii, *Sankt-Peterburg: Istoricheskii ocherk arkhitektury i razvitiia goroda* (Munich, 1923); and Pavel Petrovich Svin'in, *Dostopamiatnosti Sanktpeterburga i ego okrestnosti,* 5 vols. in 2 (St. Petersburg, 1816–28).

20. Iurii Robertovich Klokman, *Ocherki sotsial'no-ekonomicheskoi istorii gorodov severo-zapada Rossii v seredine XVIII v.* (Moscow, 1960); and *Sotsial'no-ekonomicheskaia istoriia*

russkogo goroda, vtoraia polovina XVIII veka (Moscow, 1967); Pavel Grigor'evich Ryndziunskii, *Gorodskoe grazhdanstvo doreformennoi Rossii* (Moscow, 1958); and S. P. Luppov, *Istoriia stroitel'stva Peterburga v pervoi chetverti XVIII veka* (Moscow-Leningrad, 1957).

21. To cite only a few examples: Fedor Iakovlevich Polianskii, *Gorodskoe remeslo i manufaktura v Rossii XVIII v.* (Moscow, 1960); Stolpianskii, *Zhizn' i byt peterburgskoi fabriki;* V. K. Iatsunskii, "Rol' Peterburga v promyshlennom razvitii dorevoliutsionnoi Rossii," *Voprosy istorii,* 1954, no. 9: 95–103; Vadim Viacheslavovich Pokshishevskii, "Territorial'noe formirovanie promyshlennogo kompleksa Peterburga XVIII–XIX vv.," *Voprosy geografii* 20 (1950): 122–62.

22. See, for example, the excellent study by Lidiia Nikolaevna Semenova, *Rabochie Peterburga v pervoi polovine XVIII veka* (Leningrad, 1974). Of lesser value is A. V. Safonova, "Polozhenie trudiashchikhsia Peterburga i ikh klassovaia bor'ba v 60–70e gody XVIII veka," *Uchenye zapiski vologodskogo gosudarstvennogo pedagogicheskogo instituta* 14 (1954): 3–46.

23. See, for example, N. B. Golikova, *Ocherki po istorii gorodov Rossii kontsa XVII - nachala XVIII v.* (Moscow, 1982); and B. N. Mironov, *Russkii gorod v 1740–1860e gody: Demograficheskoe, sotsial'noe i ekonomicheskoe razvitie* (Leningrad, 1990). An annual volume of articles on urban history, *Russkii gorod,* began publishing in 1978.

24. M. P. Viatkin et al., eds., *Ocherki istorii Leningrada,* 5 vols. (Moscow-Leningrad, 1955–58); *Istoriia Moskvy,* 5 vols. (1952–55).

25. Solomon Volkov, *St. Petersburg: A Cultural History,* trans. Antonina W. Bouis (Glencoe, NY: Free Press, 1995); Moisei Kagan, *Grad Petrov v istorii russkoi kul'tury* (St. Petersburg, 1996); and G. Z. Kaganov, *Images of Space: St. Petersburg in the Visual and Verbal Arts,* trans. Sidney Monas (Stanford, CA: Stanford University Press, 1997).

26. Reginald E. Zelnik, *Labor and Society in Tsarist Russia: The Factory Workers of St. Petersburg, 1855–1870* (Stanford, CA: Stanford University Press, 1971); Victoria E. Bonnell, *Roots of Rebellion: Workers' Politics and Organizations in St. Petersburg and Moscow, 1900–1914,* (Berkeley: University of California Press, 1983); James H. Bater, *St. Petersburg: Industrialization and Change* (Montreal: McGill-Queens University Press, 1976); Gilbert Rozman, *Urban Networks in Russia, 1750–1800, and Premodern Periodization* (Princeton: Princeton University Press, 1976); Josef W. Konvitz, *Cities and the Sea: Port City Planning in Early Modern Europe* (Baltimore: Johns Hopkins University Press, 1978); J. Michael Hittle, *The Service City: State and Townsmen in Russia, 1600–1800* (Cambridge, MA: Harvard University Press, 1979). Rozman's and Hittle's articles in Michael F. Hamm, ed., *The City in Russian History* (Lexington: University Press of Kentucky, 1976) encapsulate the arguments of their books.

27. Evgenii Viktorovich Anisimov et al., *Sankt-Peterburg: 300 let istorii* (St. Petersburg: Nauka, 2003) and Feliks Moiseevich Lur'e, *Peterburg, 1703–1917: Istoriia i kul'tura v tablitsakh,* 2 vols. (St. Petersburg: "Zolotoi vek"; "Diamant," 2000) are perhaps the most significant of them.

28. Naum Aleksandrovich Sindalovskii, *Istoriia Sankt-Peterburga v predaniiakh i legendakh* (St. Petersburg: "Norint," 1997) and *Legendy i mify Sankt-Peterburga* (St. Petersburg: "Norint," 1997).

Both have also appeared in several other editions in various guises.

29. K. K. Rotikov, *Drugoi Peterburg* (St. Petersburg: Liga Plius, 1998).

30. Emily D. Johnson, *How St. Petersburg Learned to Study Itself: The Russian Idea of Kraevedenie* (University Park: Pennsylvania State University Press, 2006).

31. W. Bruce Lincoln, *Sunlight at Midnight: St. Petersburg and the Rise of Modern Russia* (New York: Basic Books, 2000).

32. Julie A. Buckler, *Mapping St. Petersburg: Imperial Text and Cityshape* (Princeton: Princeton University Press, 2005).

33. J. Thomas Shaw, *The Transliteration of Modern Russian for English-Language Publications* (Madison: University of Wisconsin Press, 1967).

Chapter 1

1. Bolotov was excused from work the next day. Andrei Timofeevich Bolotov, *Zhizn' i prikliucheniia Andreia Bolotova, opisannye samim im dlia svoikh potomkov, 1738–1795,* 4 vols. (St. Petersburg: V. S. Balashev, 1870), 2: 188.

2. Ibid., 2: 187.

3. See Tamara Goryshina, "Bolota 'Severnoi Pal'miry,' " *Neva,* 1997, no. 2: 216–20.

4. Georgi, *Opisanie,* 173.

5. Iu. I. Smirnov, ed., *Sankt-Peterburg: Zanimatel'nye voprosy i otvety* (St. Petersburg, 2000).

6. Shoals at the extreme mouth of the Neva prevented heavily-laden ships from proceeding up the river, however. William Thomson, *Letters from Scandinavia, On the Past and Present State of the Northern Nations of Europe,* 2 vols. (London: For G. G. and J. Robinson, Paternoster Row, 1796), 1: 229.

7. Rossiiskii gosudarstvennyi istoricheskii arkhiv (hereafter RGIA), *fond* 485, *opis'* 2, *dela* 10, 11 ("Petersburg. Graviury Vasil'eva, Ia., s risunka Makhaeva, M. I."). These engravings were published in Galina Nikolaevna Komalova, *Vidy Peterburga i ego okrestnostei serediny XVIII veka: Graviury po risunkam M. Makhaeva* (Leningrad: "Sovetskii khudozhnik," 1968). An interesting commentary on Makhaev's engravings may be found in Grigorii Zosimovich Kaganov, *Images of Space: St. Petersburg in the Visual and Verbal Arts,* translated by Sidney Monas (Stanford, CA: Stanford University Press, 1997), 19–22.

8. The law is cited in RGIA, *fond* 467, *opis'* 4, *delo* 10, *listy* 232–32*ob.*

9. Arkhiv Sankt-Peterburgskogo filiala, institut russkoi istorii, Rossiiskoi akademii nauk (hereafter Arkhiv SPbF IRI RAN; formerly called Arkhiv leningradskogo otdeleniia instituta istorii [LOII]), *fond* 36 (Vorontsovy), *opis'* 1, *delo* 556/429, *listy* 500–507.

10. Mikhail Vasil'evich Danilov, "Zapiski Mikhaila Vasil'evich Danilova, artillerii maiora, napisannye im v 1771 godu (1722–1762)," in Evgenii Viktorovich Anisimov, ed. and intro., *Bezvremen'e i vremenshchiki. Vospominaniia ob "epokhe dvortsovykh perevorotov" (1720-e-1760-e gody)* (Leningrad, 1991), 315, 323–24.

11. Ivan Pushkarev, *Opisanie Sanktpeterburga i uezdnykh gorodov S. Peterburgskoi gubernii* (St. Petersburg: By the author, 1839), 25–26; and Storch, *Picture,* 22.

12. Amsterdam served as a model not only for Petersburg; the plan drawn up by Sir Christopher Wren for the reconstruction of London after the great fire of 1666 showed strong evidence of influence from Amsterdam; canals, despite the topographical difficulties, were an integral part of the plan: Harold Priestley, *London: The Years of Change* (New York: Barnes & Noble, 1966), 200. It is not surprising, then, that the development of St. Petersburg should follow the same pattern, particularly given Peter's admiration of the Dutch.

13. John Perry, *The State of Russia under the Present Czar* (London: Benjamin Tooke, 1716), 40; Afanasii Shchekatov, "Sankt Peterburg," in *Slovar' geograficheskii rossiiskogo gosudarstva,* vol 4, (1807), 678; and Viacheslav Alekseevich Shkvarikov, *Ocherk istorii planirovki i zastroiki russkikh gorodov* (Moscow, 1954), 131ff. "Line" was and is a name peculiar to the island. The streets running north and south are not named, but are numbered beginning from the easternmost of the streets joining the three main east-west avenues. The buildings on one side of the street are on one "line"; on the other

side of the street they are on the next "line." "First Line" is the western side of the street, the eastern side of which was "Cadet Line." The next street is made up of "Second Line" and "Third Line," and so forth. Even-numbered lines are always on the east side of the street, odd numbers on the west side.

14. See the reproduction of his plan in Konvitz, *Cities and the Sea,* 155.

15. *Sloboda* is an untranslatable word that refers to a settlement near or just beyond the edge of a town where people of a single social-legal category lived. They were often under the control and administration of a governmental office, fulfilling their obligations to the state for the most part to that office. One of the best known groups, which had its own *slobody* in many different towns, were the postmen, or *iamshchiki,* responsible for providing and caring for horses and their equipage for official travel by government officials throughout the realm. Rossiiskii gosudarstvennyi arkhiv drevnikh aktov (hereafter RGADA), *fond* 16, *delo* 447, *chast'* 1, *list* 54.

16. For example, Egor Rastorguev, *Progulki po Nevskomu prospektu* (St. Petersburg, 1846); Al'bin M. Konechnyi, ed. and intro, *Progulki po Nevskomu prospektu v pervoi polovine XIX veka* (St. Petersburg: "Giperion," 2002); Georgii Kreskent'evich Lukomskii, *Staryi Peterburg: Progulki po starinnym kvartalam stolitsy,* 2nd ed. (Petrograd, n.d.); Pavel Iakovlevich Kann, *Progulki po Peterburgu* (St. Petersburg: Palitra, 1994); Anatolii Viktorovich Darinskii, *Progulki po staromu Sankt-Peterburgu* (St. Petersburg: Ekam, 1995); Liubov' Konstantinovna Ermolaeva and I. M. Lebedeva, *Progulki po Peterburgu: Progulka vtoraia; Zdes' budet gorod* (St. Petersburg: Khimiia, 1997); Marina Burenina, *Progulki po Nevskomu prospektu* (St. Petersburg: Litera, 2002); Andrei Grechukhin, *Progulki po Petrogradskoi* (St. Petersburg: Severnaia zvezda, 2002); El'vira Rimmer and M. Borodulin, *Progulki po Voskresenskomu prospektu* (Cherepovets: Izdatel'skii dom ID Cherepovets, 2002); Oleg Rostislavovich Khromov, *Progulki po Sankt-Peterburgu: Akvareli, graviury, litografii* (Moscow: Interbuk-biznes, 2002).

17. The word *posad* comes from the word "to plant." The *posad* people were permanently "planted" next to the kremlin, where they were subject to their own form of obligations to the state and, at least from the seventeenth century, their own form of limited self-administration. See Hittle, *The Service City,* chapters 1–2.

18. *Sloboda* residents were originally free from obligations imposed on *posad* people while enjoying the same urban privileges. This situation, not at all to the liking of *posad* residents, ended with the *Ulozhenie* (Code of Laws) of 1649, when *sloboda* residents were put under the same tax and service obligations as *posad* people. Aleksandr Aleksandrovich Kizevetter, "Gorodovoe polozhenie Ekateriny II," in *Tri veka: Rossiia ot smut' do nashego vremeni,* ed. Vladimir Vladimirovich Kallash, vol. 4, *XVIII vek: Vtoraia polovina* (Moscow: Izdanie I. D. Sytin, 1913), 252–53. See also Hittle, *The Service City,* 66–67.

19. Hittle, *The Service City,* 234–36.

20. On this point, see Viacheslav Alekseevich Shkvarikov, *Ocherk istorii planirovki i zastroiki russkikh gorodov* (Moscow, 1954), 62.

21. The differentiation is clearly delineated by T. P. Efimenko, "K istorii gorodskogo zemleustroistva vremen Ekateriny II," *Zhurnal ministerstva narodnogo prosveshcheniia,* 1914, no. 12 (December): 286–87.

22. Andrei Bogdanov and Vasilii Ruban enumerated the bazaars, meat shops, bread stores, hay markets, and places where bricks, clay, and sand were sold for construction, and their location at the beginning of Catherine's reign. Each type of enterprise appeared in each of the four sections comprising the center of the city (except that there was no bazaar in Foundry district). The same cannot be said for the outskirts of the city. Ruban, *Dopolnenie,* 109–11, 119–20, 112–24, and 126–28.

23. See the short historical sketch in Hans Blumenfeld, "Russian City Planning of the Eighteenth and Early Nineteenth Centuries," *Journal of the American Society of Architectural Historians* 4, no. 1 (January 1944): 26.

24. *Plan stolichnogo goroda Sanktpeterburga s izobrazheniem znatneishikh onogo prospektov, izdannyi trudami Imperatorskoi akademii nauk i khudozhestv* (St. Petersburg: Imperatorskaia akademiia nauk, 1753), includes nine maps and several engravings on which this discussion of land use in St. Petersburg is partially dependent; see also Bogdanov, *Opisanie,* 200–201; and Aleksandr Pavlovich Bashutskii, *Panorama Sanktpeterburga,* 2 vols. (St. Petersburg: V tipografii vdovy Pliushara s synom, 1834), 2: 103–04.

25. An attempt to describe the layout of St. Petersburg in 1762 was begun by Petr Nikolaevich Petrov. His work was never completed, but his notes are available in the Russian National Library (Rossiiskaia natsional'naia biblioteka; hereafter cited as RNB), Manuscripts Division, *fond* 575 (Petrov, P. M.), no. 124; see also *Plan stolichnogo goroda;* and RGIA, *fond* 485, *opis'* 2, *delo* 3.

26. Shchekatov, *Slovar',* 1: 53. For a glimpse of how the building of the twelve colleges appeared to contemporaries, see Komalova, *Vidy,* 26. (The original engraving is in RGIA, *fond* 485, *opis'* 2, *delo* 18.)

27. Shchekatov, *Slovar',* 1: 38–49; Elizabeth Craven, *A Journey through the Crimea to Constantinople in a Series of Letters* (London: G. G. J. and J. Robinson, 1789), 125; Jonas Hanway, *An Historical Account of the British Trade over the Caspian Sea: With a Journal of his Travels,* 4 vols. (London: By the author, 1753), 2: 135; and William Richardson, *Anecdotes of the Russian Empire in a Series of Notes* (London: W. Strahan and T. Cadell, 1784), 27n. See also Anthony Cross, *By the Banks of the Neva: Chapters from the Lives and Careers of the British in Eighteenth-Century Russia* (Cambridge: Cambridge University Press, 1997), 11.

28. *Plan stolichnogo goroda;* RNB, Manuscripts Division, *fond* 40, no. 95. See also G. E. Kochin, "Naselenie Peterburga v 60–90kh godakh XVIII v., in *Ocherki istorii Leningrada,* 5 vols. (Leningrad and Moscow, 1955–67), 1: 316 (hereafter *OIL*); and Kurbatov, *Peterburg,* 100–101. The only cemetery in St. Petersburg expressly for foreigners, Smolensk German Cemetery, was located on Vasil'evskii Island.

29. Examples of all three are depicted in Bunin, *Istoriia gradostroitel'nogo iskusstva,* 372.

30. Bolotov, *Zhizn',* 2: 186.

31. RGIA, *fond* 485, *opis'* 2, *delo* 14; Andrei Vladimirovich Bunin, *Istoriia gradostroitel'nogo iskusstva* (Moscow, 1953), 134; and Kurbatov, *Peterburg,* 47.

32. Blumenfeld, "Russian City Planning," *Journal of the American Society of Architectural Historians* 4, 30.

33. RGIA, *fond* 485, *opis'* 2, *delo* 18.

34. It must be noted that although Russian sources without exception refer to the structures as stone houses, they were, with the exception of the limestone or granite foundations, constructed not of stone, but of the much less expensive brick faced with painted plaster. Among the buildings of this type were the Winter Palace and the Admiralty; William Coxe, *Travels into Poland, Russia, Sweden, and Denmark,* 3 vols. (Dublin: S. Price et al., 1784), vol. 2, bk. 4, 465–66.

35. Joseph Marshall, *Travels through Holland, Flanders, Germany, Denmark, Sweden, Lapland, Russia, the Ukraine, and Poland, in the Years 1768, 1769, and 1770,* 4 vols. (London: J. Almon, 1772), 3: 110.

36. Storch, *The Picture of Petersburg: From the German* (London, 1801), 25–27; RGADA, *fond* 294, *opis'* 2, *delo* 530. Only two months before Catherine's accession to the throne, the first steps were made to require all buildings in the center of the city

to be built of masonry. In the aftermath of a disastrous fire, Peter III learned that the fire originated in a wooden building; therefore he decreed that henceforth all buildings constructed in Admiralty Section were to be of stone or brick; Bozherianov, *Nevskii Prospekt,* 1: 174.

37. RNB, Manuscripts Division, *fond* 40, nos. 70, 71, 95.

38. Kochin, "Naselenie Peterburga," *OIL,* 1: 308.

39. RGIA, *fond* 485, *opis'* 2, *dela* 15, 1363, consisting of an engraving and a detailed map of the property. Included in the property was the land now belonging to the park containing the statue of Catherine the Great (1873) designed by Mikhail Mikeshin and executed by Matvei Chizhov and Aleksandr Opekushin, as well as the block occupied by the Russian National Library, formerly the State Public Library.

40. Bunin, *Istoriia gradostroitel'nogo iskusstva,* 107.

41. In 1764 Count Kirilla Grigor'evich Razumovskii had his wooden house redone in masonry. The old house had stood a long time without substantial weathering effects in its exterior. A. A. Vasil'chikov, "Semeistvo Razumovskikh: I grafy Aleksei i Kiril Grigor'evichi," in *Osmnadtsatyi vek: Istoricheskii sbornik,* ed. Petr Bartenev, 4 vols. (Moscow: Tipografiia T. Ris, D. Voeikova, 1868–69), 2: 603. Besides bedrooms, houses of these two types commonly included drawing rooms, receiving rooms, dining rooms, antechambers for the servants of company, workrooms for the masters, dressing rooms for mistresses, nurseries, and rooms for servants. Storage areas included ice cellars, carriage garages, and places for storing fuel, either coal or wood. Often these latter rooms were in outbuildings, not in the main house. Georgi, *Opisanie,* 602–03; Storch, *Picture,* 493–507.

42. Petr Nikolaevich Stolpianskii, *Revoliutsionnyi Peterburg: U kolybeli russkoi svobody* (Petrograd: Izdatel'skoe tovarichestvo "Kolos," 1922), 10–11. Kolomna was a section in the extreme westernmost part of Admiralty Quarter; see Shchekatov, *Slovar',* 5: 628.

43. Storch, *Picture,* 24–25; Luppov, *Istoriia stroitel'stva,* refers to the same phenomenon in an earlier era.

44. Early in the eighteenth century, laborers lived in the center of St. Petersburg. The nobility, living on the banks of the Neva, objected to the settlement of workers so close as an "eyesore." After two ruinous fires in 1736 and 1737 land was taken from the poor and sold to gentry and wealthy merchants or kept by the state; the displaced people were forced away from the center. Bunin, *Istoriia gradostroitel'nogo iskusstva,* 107.

45. See Emrys Jones, *Towns and Cities* (London: Oxford University Press, 1966), on this point. Among twentieth-century cities, Jones specifically mentions the cases of Caracas and Petare, Venezuela, and Rio de Janeiro, Brazil, among others.

46. B. Mansurov, *Okhtenskie admiralteiskie stroeniia* (St. Petersburg, 1855), 7; A. I. Gegello and V. I. Piliavskii, "Arkhitektura Peterburga 60–90kh godov XVIII vv.," *OIL,* 1: 351–52.

47. *Plan stolichnogo goroda,* 7–9, 11–13, 15–16; RNB, Manuscripts Division, *fond* 40, *dela* 73, 81, 82, 85, 95 (maps); RGIA, *fond* 485, *opis'* 2, *delo* 1012.

48. See the section on planning in chapter 4. A discussion of the growth problem as it confronted Russian cities in general is contained in Klokman, *Sotsial'no-ekonomicheskaia istoriia,* 56–59.

49. *Plan stolichnogo goroda,* 96. Most of Vyborg Side was simply devoid of construction. See Kurbatov, *Peterburg,* 102.

50. It is highly probable that most of the planned *slobody* and barracks areas never went beyond the planning stage. Buildings were laid out in an orderly arrangement, but far fewer were erected than were depicted in the plans. RGIA, *fond* 485, *opis'* 2, *dela* 686, 1002, 1013 (maps); and *Plan stolichnogo goroda,* 16.

51. *Plan stolichnogo goroda,* 12–16; and RNB, Manuscripts Division, *fond* 40, *dela* 73, 81, 82, 85, 95 (maps).

52. In Russian, an ordinary convent or monastery was called a *monastyr;* four or five of the greatest and most revered monasteries, in a sense the monastery-laureates, were called instead by the term *lavra.* The Alexander Nevskii received that designation early in the nineteenth century but was still a *monastyr* during Catherine's reign.

53. Sellers placed the frozen carcasses in the snow in poses as lifelike as possible so that they would appeal to buyers. This meat market occupied the same large field year after year. Georgi, *Opisanie,* 126–27.

54. A. L. Shapiro, "'Zapiski o peterburgskoi gubernii' A. N. Radishcheva," *Istoricheskii arkhiv* 5 (1950): 267–68.

55. RGIA, *fond* 485, *opis'* 2, *delo* 783. The same pattern is borne out for the *sloboda* of the Chancellery on Construction in RGIA, *fond* 485, *opis'* 2, *delo* 1002.

56. RGIA, *fond* 1329, *opis'* 2, *delo* 104, no. 38, *listy* 111–14.

57. Bolotov, *Zhizn',* 2: 191–92.

Chapter 2

1. Evgenii Viktorovich Anisimov, *The Reforms of Peter the Great: Progress through Coercion in Russia,* Trans. and intro. John T. Alexander (Armonck, NY: M. E. Sharpe 1993), 184.

2. Vasilii Kirillovich Tradiakovskii, "Pokhvala Izherskoi zemle i tsarstvuiushchemu gradu Sankt-Peterburgu," cited in M. G. Kachurin et al., *Sankt-Peterburg v russkoi literature: Khrestomatiia dlia uchashchikhsia 9–11 klassov, gimnazii, litseev i kolledzhei,* 2 vols. (St. Petersburg: "SVET," 1996), 1: 45.

3. The figures of 120,000 and 220,000, first published in Ministerstvo vnutrennikh del, *Statisticheskie svedeniia o Sanktpeterburge* (St. Petersburg, 1832), 113, were accepted by Pushkarev, *Opisanie,* 41, and Adol'f Grigor'evich Rashin, *Formirovanie rabochego klassa Rossii: Istoriko-ekonomicheskie ocherki,* ed. S. G. Strumilin (Moscow, 1958), 111, among others. A. I. Kopanev, limiting his figures to the Orthodox population, quoted a population for 1801 of 202,038. See his *Naselenie Peterburga v pervoi polovine XIX veka* (Moscow-Leningrad, 1957). These figures are quoted by Arcadius Kahan, *The Plow, the Hammer, and the Knout,* 30. Elsewhere (31) Kahan quotes figures of 211,635 for 1792 and 217,948 for 1789. P. N. Petrov, basing his statistics on parish registers, gave a much lower figure of 60,000 at the beginning of the reign in *Istoriia Sanktpeterburga,* 668. At the other extreme, Bashutskii in *Panorama,* 2: 71, claims that the city held 162,000 in 1765 and 295,000 in 1795. John T. Alexander gives a figure of 150,000 for 1771 in *Bubonic Plague in Early Modern Russia: Public Health and Urban Disaster* (Baltimore: Johns Hopkins University Press, 1980), 245.

4. Population estimates for areas beyond the city limit are difficult to find. Mansurov (*Okhtenskie stroeniia,* 13) says that Okhta had 741 adult males in 1785, with perhaps 2,592 people in all. Galley Haven was estimated to be somewhat larger than Okhta. *Slobody* not included in official reports ranged from the Moscow Postman *sloboda,* with two hundred houses and well over a thousand people, to the Construction Chancellery *sloboda,* with twenty-six houses and fewer than two hundred people. The number of people in all these *slobody* can only be estimated. In addition to them, people attached to the court and members of the science and art academies were not included in police reports. Storch, *Picture,* 85.

5. N. A. Varlamova, in "Ispedoval'nye vedomosti 1737 g. kak istochnik po istorii naseleniia Peterburga," in I. I. Froianov, *Genezis i razvitie feodalizma v Rossii: Problemy*

istorii goroda; Mezhvuzovskii sbornik, Vypusk 2 of the series Problemy otechestvennoi i vseobshchei istorii (Leningrad, 1988), 187–96.

6. Varlamova, "Ispovedal'nye vedomosti," 190. The archival source is RGIA, *fond* 19, *opis'* 2327, *listy* 2–3; *opis'* 112, *delo* 90, *list* 167; and *opis'* 1, *delo* 8986, *listy* 3*ob.*-4.

7. See chapter 9, 264–66.

8. On September 7, 1775, for example, there were 24,193 men from the following regiments: Preobrazhenskii Guards, Semenovskii Guards, Izmailovskii Guards, Horse Guards, naval and galley fleets, artillery engineers, Kazan' cuirassiers, Don Cossacks, Vologda infantry, Kexholm infantry, and garrison battalions. RGADA, *fond* 16, *delo* 500, *list* 28.

9. RGADA, *fond* 16, *delo* 521, *chast'* 1, *listy* 51*ob.*, 82, 90, 106, 110, 166, 176*ob.*, 179*ob.*, 183.

10. Georgi, *Opisanie,* 148–51.

11. "Vedomost' o dvizhenii narodonaseleniia v Sanktpeterburge s 1764 do 1790 god," in Ministerstvo vnutrennikh del, *Tablitsy k statisticheskim svedeniiam o Sanktpeterburge* (St. Petersburg: Izdatel'stvo pri ministerstve vnutrennikh del, 1836), table 27.

12. Table 27, "Vedomost' o dvizhenii narodonaseleniia v Sanktpeterburge s 1764 do 1790 god," in Ministerstvo vnutrennikh del, *Tablitsy k statisticheskim svedeniiam.*

13. Rashin, *Naselenie Rossii, za 100 let, 1811–1913 gg.: Statisticheskie ocherki,* ed. S. G. Strumilin (Moscow: Gosudarstvennoe statisticheskoe izdatel'stvo, 1956), p. 233. From *Statisticheskii sbornik po Petrogradu i Petrogradskoi gubernii* (Petrograd, 1922), 1–2, 12–14. Rashin assumes a population about the same as I in the 1760s but does not agree on the rate of growth. He estimated the population in the 1780s at about 188,000, which was from 40,000 to 50,000 too low. Therefore his birth and death rates per thousand are increasingly high towards the end of the period. The general fact of natural increase in population remains unaffected by his use of figures. For comparison, see the figures cited in Kahan, *The Plow, the Hammer, and the Knout,* 32, table 1.27.

14. For every 1,000 babies less than a year old, 279 in St. Petersburg died. Among foreigners living there the rate was reported as higher, 309 per 1,000. In large cities of western Europe the figure of 370 deaths per 1,000 male babies and 227 for females was cited by Storch, who was a professional statistician. From age 1–15, 215 of 1,000 Russian youths in the capital died; among foreigners there the figure was 346 per 1,000. In Stockholm, by way of comparison, 258 of every 1,000 expired and in London the figure was 435 per 1,000 youngsters dying between the ages of 1 and 15. Storch, *Picture,* 91–93. Herrmann, *Statistische Schilderung,* found that in 1781–1785, of 1,000 male children in St. Petersburg, 756 survived to age 5. For 1791–1796, the figure was 762. This child mortality rate was only half that of Russia as a whole; figures cited in Kahan, *The Plow, the Hammer, and the Knout,* 31.

15. Petrov, *Istoriia Sanktpeterburga,* 607. Only one-sixth of the military personnel were married.

16. Ministerstvo vnutrennikh del, *Statisticheskie svedeniia,* 113. Police Chief Ryleev's figures for 1786 show that the city's population was 64.9 percent male in January, 67.5 percent male in April, and 71.0 percent male by mid-summer. RGADA, *fond* 16, *delo* 521, *chast'* 1, *listy* 51*ob.*, 82, 110. The figures cited by Georgi, *Opisanie,* 148–51 concur.

17. RGADA, *fond* 16, *delo* 478, *list* 50; *fond* 248, *delo* 4078, *listy* 364–69; Ministerstvo vnutrennikh del, *Tablitsy k statisticheskim svedeniiam,* table 27; Storch, *Picture,* 93.

18. Allan Sharlin, "Natural Decrease in Early Modern Cities: A Reconsideration," *Past and Present,* no. 79 (May 1978): 126–38.

19. The figures and explanation are cited in Kahan, *The Plow, the Hammer, and the Knout,* 32–33; see especially tables 1.27 and 1.29.

20. Rashin, *Naselenie Rossii,* 126–27. Not totally reliable, these figures do show proximate relationships between legal categories.

21. Gregory L. Freeze, "The *Soslovie* (Estate) Paradigm and Russian Social History," *American Historical Review* 91, no. 1 (February 1986): 11–36.

22. *Raznochintsy* were defined in 1800 as "Lower court, civil, and retired military servants and the like, who were not enrolled in the merchant trading estate" (*PSZ* 26, no. 19.692: 473), a definition suitable for this context. However, the definition of who was a *raznochinets* varied with time, circumstance, place, and legislative purpose; see Elise Kimerling Wirtschafter, *Structures of Society: Imperial Russia's "People of Various Ranks"* (De Kalb: Northern Illinois University Press, 1994).

23. TsGIA SPb, *fond* 781, *opis'* 2, *delo* 680, *listy* 1–2; Shapiro, "Zapiski," *Istoricheskii arkhiv* 5 (1950): 256–57.

24. The best study in English of this process is Walter McKenzie Pintner and Don Karl Rowney, eds., *Russian Officialdom: the Bureaucratization of Russian Society from the Seventeenth to the Twentieth Century* (Chapel Hill: University of North Carolina Press, 1980), especially chapter 7, by Helju Bennett, and chapter 8, by Pintner.

25. A. A. Vasil'chikov, "Semeistvo Razumovskikh," in Bartenev, ed., *Osmnadtsatyi vek,* 2: 603; and Georgi, *Opisanie,* 608.

26. A detailed accounting of who attended court functions and where Catherine went on social occasions was kept in the *Kamer-fur'erskii tseremonial'nyi, banketnyi i pokhodnyi zhurnal,* published in annual volumes for Catherine's reign by the Ministry of the Imperial Court in the nineteenth century. I am grateful to John T. Alexander for drawing this source to my attention.

27. Roger Parkinson, *The Fox of the North: The Life of Kutuzov, General of War and Peace* (New York: David McKay, 1976), 20.

28. The article is cited in Aleksandr Nikolaevich Afanas'ev, "Cherty russkikh nravov XVIII stoletiia," *Russkii vestnik,* 1857, no. 10 (August): 263–64.

29. For a brief analysis of the role of nobles in this business, see George E. Munro, "The Role of the *Veksel'* in Russian Capital Formation: A Preliminary Inquiry," in R. P. Bartlett, A. P. Cross, and Karen Rasmussen, eds., *Russia and the World of the Eighteenth Century* (Columbus, OH: Slavica, 1988): 551–64.

30. For the etymology of the term *chinovnik,* see Christopher Becker, "*Raznochintsy:* Word and Concept," *American Slavic and East European Review* 18, no. 1 (February 1959): 63–74. Becker's work has been superseded by that of Elise Kimerling Wirtschafter, *Structures of Society* (see note 22 above).

31. For an excellent brief statistical survey of the social composition, qualifications, and career patterns of the St. Petersburg bureaucracy, see Walter M. Pintner, "The Social Characteristics of the Early Nineteenth-Century Russian Bureaucracy," *Slavic Review* 29, no. 3 (September 1970): 429–43.

32. Becker, "Raznochintsy," *American Slavic and East European Review* 18: 66; Petrov, *Istoriia Sanktpeterburga,* 668; Rashin, *Naselenie,* 126–27.

33. Pushkarev, *Opisanie,* 368; RGIA, *fond* 1329, *opis'* 1, *delo* 118, no. 16, *list* 28 contains references to Senate employees who lived in the attic and basement of that building.

34. Pintner, "Social Characteristics," *Slavic Review* 29, no. 3, especially 442–43 and tables 7 and 9.

35. The figure represents an estimate rather than a precise enumeration. A specific number cannot be rendered because of wide variation in eighteenth-century records. Storch in *Picture,* 104, and Karl German in *Statisticheskie issledovaniia otnositel'no rossiiskoi imperii* (St. Petersburg: Akademiia nauk, 1819), 151, agreed that between 1,700 and 1,750 merchants were registered in guilds around the year 1790. By adding

the number of *meshchane* (petty tradesmen) to this figure, one arrives at a total of nearly 6,500 people. But the figures cited in the "General'naia vedomost' po provintsiiam o chisle muzheska polu, dush po nyneshnei tretei revizii," in RNB, Manuscripts Division, *fond* Ermitazhnoe sobranie, no. 244, *list* 7, dated 1782, indicate the presence of 2,156 registered merchants in the city. It is unlikely that the number of merchants declined in a fast growing city. Contemporaries noted, moreover, that all these figures remained significantly lower than the actual number of trading people in the capital. Thus Storch: "by far the greater part of the trading inhabitants live without the pale of these associations, . . ." *Picture,* 104. Furthermore, these figures include only adult males. Including wives and families, the estimate of 17,000 seems feasible. Rashin, cited earlier, gives a figure of 14,300 merchants based on a total population of 202,100. This figure becomes 17,600 by the acceptance of this chapter's assertion that the city's population reached 250,000. This higher figure also accords with statistics cited in German, *Statisticheskie issledovaniia,* 151.

36. RGIA, *fond* 558, *opis'* 2, *delo* 206, *listy* 125–26. Merchants wishing to transfer to the St. Petersburg merchant guilds had to present briefs documented with letters showing that they were in good standing in the old place of residence. RGIA, *fond* 467, *opis'* 4, *delo* 301.

37. Georgi, *Opisanie,* 608–10. According to James Brogden, who visited St. Petersburg in 1787, the English merchants had a "stile of living . . . far superior to the common mode of living in England." James Cracraft, "James Brogden in Russia, 1787–1788," *Slavonic and East European Review* 47, no. 108 (January 1969), 228.

38. One of the purposes of regulatory legislation was to protect merchants from overextending themselves. Nevertheless, notices of bankruptcies and auctions of property appeared often in *Sanktpeterburgskie vedomosti.* See, for example, the issues of September 17, 1764 (no. 75), and February 14, 1772 (no. 13).

39. RGADA, *fond* 16, *delo* 482, *listy* 3–4.

40. Artisan life is discussed in more detail in chapter 7, 217–24.

41. There existed here a great similarity to Berlin, where in the 1740s nearly a quarter of the population was on military duty: Lewis Mumford, *The City in History: Its Origins, Its Transformations, and Its Prospects* (New York: Harcourt, Brace & World, 1961), pp.362–63.

42. Korff suggested that each homeowner pay a proportional share for his district of town, according to the number of people living in the house. From the monies thus collected, barracks would be built or separate flats rented for soldiers: RGADA, *fond* 16, *delo* 473, *listy* 112–17.

43. Numerous examples can be found throughout RGADA, *fond* 16.

44. Elise Kimerling Wirtschafter, *From Serf to Russian Soldier* (Princeton: Princeton University Press, 1990), 35–38.

45. For example, a soldier released from service in May 1764 by a guards regiment was told to find his own means of support. Claiming he had no capital, could hardly walk, and was old and sick, he petitioned for a place in the almshouse at the Church of the Resurrection, which request was granted. RGIA, *fond* 470, *opis'* 6, *delo* 28, *list* 6.

46. Wages averaged around a ruble per week. RGADA, *fond* 16, *delo* 494, *listy* 13–14; *fond* 17, *delo* 78, *list* 15; Storch, *Picture,* 122–23; and Giovanni Giacomo Casanova, "Zapiski venetsiantsa Kazanova o prebyvanii ego v Rossii, 1765–1766," *Russkaia starina* 9 (1874): 539. See also the discussions in Kochin, "Naselenie," *OIL,* 1: 305–06; and H. Rosovsky, "The Serf Enterpreneur in Russia," *Explorations in Enterprise,* ed. Hugh G. J. Aitken (Cambridge, MA: Harvard University Press, 1954), 341–70.

47. For examples, see RGIA, *fond* 467, *opis'* 4, *delo* 76, No. 30, *listy* 144–74 (instructions not to hire such people); *delo* 10, *listy* 67, 101, 236; V. N. Kashin, ed., *Materialy*

po istorii krest'ianskoi promyshlennosti, XVIII i pervoi poloviny XIX v. (vol. 15 of *Trudy istoriko-arkheograficheskogo instituta;* Moscow-Leningrad, 1935), 28–40; and Andrei Grigor'evich Iatsevich, *Krepostnye v Peterburge* (Leningrad: Obshchestvo staryi Peterburg-novyi Leningrad, 1933), 12–13.

48. W. Bruce Lincoln, "The Russian State and its Cities: A Search for Effective Municipal Government, 1786–1842," *Jahrbücher für Geschichte Osteuropas* 17, no. 4 (December 1969): 531–41; and "N. A. Miliutin and the St. Petersburg Municipal Act of 1846: A Study in Reform Under Nicholas I," *Slavic Review* 33, no. 1 (Winter 1974): 55–68.

49. N. I. Pavlenko, "Odvorianivanie russkoi burzhuazii v XVIII v.," *Istoriia SSSR* 6, no. 2 (1961): 71–87 discusses attempts by rich merchants and factory owners to become ennobled. The procedure was long and involved and did not always end successfully. Pavlenko concludes that these people sought ennoblement both for economic (to buy land, to own serfs) and for legal (freedom from corporal punishment, freedom from billeting, freedom from taxes, etc.) reasons. It is noteworthy that ennobled commoners often flaunted their wealth and status before poorer, but more proper, *dvoriane.*

50. Storch, *Picture,* 588–90. On Africans see Allison Blakely, *Russia and the Negro: Blacks in Russian History and Thought* (Washington, DC: Howard University Press, 1986), chapter 2.

51. Examples of people who had changed addresses often may be found in RGADA, *fond* 8, *delo* 128, *listy* 2–3; *delo* 160; RGIA, *fond* 1329, *opis'* 2, *delo* 104, no. 6, *listy* 19–22; *Sanktpeterburgskie vedomosti,* February 14, 1772 (no. 13); February 23, 1784 (no. 16).

52. John Parkinson, *A Tour of Russia, Siberia, and the Crimea, 1792–1794,* ed. and intro. William Collier (London: Frank Cass, 1971), 93. The latter figure is certain to be a glaring overestimation, because it is far out of line with the figures kept by the chaplaincy of the British factory in St. Petersburg. Anthony Cross takes 1,500 to be the "upper limit of the British community in Russia in the last years of Catherine's reign," most but by no means all of whom lived in St. Petersburg. Anthony Cross, *By the Banks of the Neva: Chapters from the Lives and Careers of the British in Eighteenth-Century Russia* (Cambridge: Cambridge University Press, 1997), 16.

53. Examples are drawn from RGADA, *fond* 16, *delo* 473, *list* 59; and *Sanktpeterburgskie vedomosti,* February 23, 1784 (no. 16), 138. Also Cracraft, "Brogden," *Slavonic and East European Review* 47, no. 108 (January 1969): 226–28; and Jean-François Georgel, *Voyage à Pétersbourg,* vol. 6 of *Mémoires,* 6 vols. (Paris, 1818), 178–81, among others.

54. Cross, *By the Banks of the Neva,* 36–39.

55. Cracraft, "Brogden," *Slavonic and East European Review* 47: 232.

56. For more on the English Club see its official history, *Stoletie S.-Peterburgskago angliiskago sobraniia, 1770–1870* (St. Petersburg, 1870); and Cross, *By the Banks of the Neva,* 28–29.

57. See also chapter 7, 218, 223–24.

58. Storch, *Picture,* 476–77.

59. See, for example, Robert Eugene Johnson, *Peasant and Proletarian: the Working Class of Moscow in the Late Nineteenth Century* (New Brunswick: Rutgers University Press, 1979).

60. See note 49, this chapter.

61. Stolpianskii, *Vverkh po Neve ot Sankt-Piter-Burkha do Shliushina: Putevoditel',* 2 vols. (Petrograd, 1922), 1: 7; Storch, *Picture,* 271–73. Storch commented that several Russians had been as successful as Iakovlev, but did not give particulars.

62. RGIA, *fond* 558, *opis'* 2, *delo* 206, *listy* 125–26.

63. Complaints by merchants are contained in articles 26 and 27 of the St. Petersburg instruction to its delegate to the Legislative Commission. *Sbornik Imperatorskago russkago istoricheskago obshchestva,* 148 vols. (St. Petersburg, 1897–1916), 107 (1900): 222–23 (cited hereafter as *Sbornik IRIO);* see also Rosovsky, "Serf Entrepreneur," *Explorations in Enterprise,* 351.

64. RGIA, *fond* 467, *opis'* 4, *delo* 10, *listy* 67, 101; Mikhail Garnovskii, "Zapiski Mikhaila Garnovskago," *Russkaia starina* 15 (1876): 237–38; Aleksandr Vasil'evich Khrapovitskii, *Pamiatnye zapiski A. V. Khrapovitskago, stats-sekretaria imperatritsy Ekateriny vtoroi,* notes by G. I. Gennadi (Moscow, 1862), 35–36, 41; Iatsevich, *Krepostnye v Peterburge,* 19–20. The Soviet historian A. V. Safonova argues that the exploited workers of the capital had to be kept in line forcibly by the police, fought side by side with their peasant brethren against the exploiters, and protected revolutionary peasants sought by police. Her evidence is spotty at best. "Polozhenie trudiashchikhsia," *Uchenye zapiski vologodskogo gosudarstvennogo pedagogicheskogo instituta* 14: 3–46. Vladimir Vasil'evich Mavrodin, *Klassovaia bor'ba i obshchestvenno-politicheskaia mysl' v Rossii v XVIII v. (1725–1773 gg.): Kurs lektsii* (Leningrad, 1964), demonstrates the general lack of any revolt at all in cities, in distinction from the countryside.

65. As nearly as can be determined from inadequate source materials, mortality rates were lower in St. Petersburg than in most western European cities. Two hypotheses might be offered in explanation. First, the climate of St. Petersburg was more rigorous, lessening the incidence of bacterial disease or insect- and rodent-borne germs. Second, although sanitary conditions in Russia's capital fell short of the eighteenth-century ideal, they remained much better than conditions in many other cities, including Paris and London. The fact that Russia's capital was new contributed to its superior position, as did the fact that land was used much less intensively there than elsewhere.

66. Stone (brick) houses averaged just over twenty rooms each; wooden between three and four. An estimate in 1778 indicated that people were crowded seven to a room throughout the city. Ministerstvo vnutrennikh del, *Statisticheskie svedeniia,* 81–82; RNB, Manuscripts Division, *Shifr* Ermitazhnoe sobranie, no. 286.

67. Storch, *Picture,* 477–78.

68. *Sbornik IRIO* 27 (1880): 469. The first eight paragraphs of the city's instruction to its delegate to the 1767 Legislative Commission (there were thirty-five paragraphs in all) had to do with improving sanitary conditions in the city. *Sbornik IRIO* 107 (1900): 213–16.

69. Parkinson, *Tour,* 38–39, 55.

70. Georgel, *Voyage,* 242.

71. Storch, *Historisch-statistische Gemälde,* part 1, 399. On April 26, 1786 Catherine ordered Prince G. A. Potemkin to remove the hospital from its building on Vyborg Side to Strel'na, outside the city, where a masonry palace had been readied for it by I. I. Betskoi. The reasons cited for the move were the inconvenience of the hospital's location upstream from the entire city and its overcrowded accommodations. See Catherine II, "Iz bumag Imperatritsy Ekateriny II khraniashchikhsia v gosudarstvennom arkhive, ministerstva inostrannykh del," *Sbornik IRIO* 27 (1880): 368. Storch's description indicates that the move had not taken place in the early 1790s, nor has it to this very day.

72. Storch, *Historisch-statistische Gemälde,* 400.

73. Georgi, *Opisanie,* 233.

74. Ibid., 423.

75. Guro, "Istoriia Imperatorskikh vospitatel'nykh domov," ed. V. N. Basnin, *Chteniia,* bk. 2 (1860), 97–98; RGIA, *fond* 758 contains the annual journal of the

home. Betskoi's activities in this regard are evaluated in David L. Ransel, "Ivan Betskoi and the Institutionalization of the Enlightenment in Russia," *Canadian-American Slavic Studies* 14, no. 3 (Fall 1980): 327–38. Betskoi's hospital and orphanage were no less successful than the Foundling Hospital in London, where a similar percentage of infants died. M. Dorothy George, *London Life in the Eighteenth Century* (New York: Harper and Row, 1964), 44–45.

76. Storch, *Historisch-statistische Gemälde,* part 1, 390–91, 394.

77. A. Nechaev, *Ocherki po istorii Obukhovskoi bol'nitsy* (Leningrad, 1952), 7–10, 234; Georgi, *Opisanie,* 297–304. By way of comparison, fewer than 10 percent of patients in the London City Hospital died.

78. Storch, *Historisch-statistische Gemälde,* part 1, 392–93.

79. George E. Munro, "The Quest for the Historical Prostitute: Some Barriers to Research in Soviet Archives," *Research in Action* 3, no. 1 (Fall–Winter 1977–8): 10–17.

80. Georgi, *Opisanie,* 297–304.

81. Storch, *Historisch-statistische Gemälde,* part 1, 418.

82. Georgi, *Opisanie,* 230.

83. The St. Petersburg audience from all reports appreciated the theater much more than Muscovites, attesting to the new capital's greater openness to new and "foreign" forms of diversion. For a comparison of theater in the two cities, see Malcolm Burgess, "Russian Public Theater Audiences of the 18th and Early 19th Centuries," *Slavonic and East European Review* 37, no. 88 (December 1958): 160–83.

84. Burgess, "Russian Public Theater Audiences," *Slavonic and East European Review* 37, no. 88: 160.

85. Cracraft, "Brogden," *Slavonic and East European Review* 48: 228–29, especially footnotes 27 and 28 on 229. A list of the productions put on the stage in St. Petersburg during Catherine's reign may be found in Robert Aloys Mooser, *Opéras, intermezzos, ballets, oratorios joués en Russie durant le XVIIIe siècle* (Geneva: R. Kister, 1955).

86. V. A. Bogoliubov, *N. I. Novikov i ego vremia* (Moscow: Izdatel'stvo M. & S. Sabashnikovykh, 1916); W. Gareth Jones, *Nikolay Novikov, Enlightener of Russia* (Cambridge: Cambridge University Press, 1984; Aleksandr Nikolaevich Pypin, *Russkoe masonstvo XVIII i pervaia chetvert' XIX v.,* ed. and notes by G. V. Vernadskii (Petrograd: Izdatel'stvo "Ogni," 1916); and Georgii V. Vernadskii, *Russkoe masonstvo v tsarstvovanie Ekateriny II* (Petrograd: Tipografiia Dela, 1917). Pypin counted as many as thirty-five lodges in St. Petersburg during Catherine's reign and only twenty-four in Moscow.

87. Georgi, *Opisanie,* 422–25, 626–38; *Stoletie S.-Peterburgskago angliiskago sobraniia, 1770–1870* (St. Petersburg: Pechatnia V. I. Golovina, 1870), 1–2; A. V. Predtechenskii, "Obshchestvennaia i politicheskaia zhizn' Peterburga v 60–90kh godov XVIII v.," *OIL,* 1: 396.

88. Keller, Elena Edvinovna, *Prazdnichnaia kul'tura Peterburga: Ocherki istorii* (St. Petersburg: Izdatel'stvo Mikhailova V. A., 2001), 105.

89. Svin'in, *Dostopamiatnosti Sanktpeterburga,* 4: 174.

90. Typical events of this nature are described in RGADA, *fond* 14, *delo* 222; RGIA, *fond* 1329, *opis'* 2, *delo* 54, no. 78, *list* 122; Georgi, *Opisanie,* 650–56; Parkinson, *Tour,* 91–92. Ice hills were as high as thirty-five feet. Parkinson found the descent "frightful." See also Anna Fedorovna Nekrylova, *Russkie narodnye gorodskie prazdniki, uveseleniia i zrelishcha: Konets XVIII–nachalo XX veka* (Leningrad, 1988).

91. On the use of processions for this purpose, see Robert Darnton, "A Bourgeois Puts His World in Order: The City as a Text," in his *The Great Cat Massacre and Other Episodes in French Cultural History* (New York: Basic Books, 1984), 107–43. The same point is made for Russia in Richard S. Wortman, *Scenarios of Power: Myth and Ceremony*

in Russian Monarchy, vol. 1, *From Peter the Great to the Death of Nicholas I* (Princeton: Princeton University Press, 1995).

92. For examples, see Ministerstvo imperatorskogo dvora, *Kamer-fur'erskii tseremonial'nyi zhurnal,* 1763, 131–46, 177–79, 213–14; 1764, 1–2, 6–7, 119–20, 160, 174–81; 1765, 14–15, 123–25; 1766, 86–87, 109–11, 195–96; 1767, 30.

93. Ibid., 1766, 109–11.

94. RGIA, *fond* 470, *opis'* 124/558, *delo* 4.

95. Parkinson, *Tour,* 41.

96. Ibid.

97. Laws governing taverns are recorded in *PSZ* 16, no. 11.713: 115; 23, no. 16.917: 183–88; Bogdanov, *Opisanie,* 150–51; see also Georgi, *Opisanie,* 577–78, 580–81; Storch, *Picture,* 176–81; and Stolpianskii, *Staryi Peterburg: Admiralteiskii ostrov, sad trudiashchikhsia; Istoriko-khudozhestvennyi ocherk* (Moscow: Gosudarstvennoe izdatel'stvo, 1923), 139–40; Georgel, *Voyage,* 178–81.

98. Isabel de Madariaga, "The Foundation of the Russian Educational System by Catherine II," *Slavonic and East European Review* 57, no. 3 (July 1979): 369–95.

99. Georgi, *Opisanie,* 310, 398; A. Voronov, *Istoriko-statisticheskoe obozrenie uchebnykh zavedenii Sanktpeterburgskogo uchebnogo okruga s 1715 po 1828 g. vkliuchitel'no* (St. Petersburg: V tipografii Iakova Treia, 1849), 10–11, 32–33, 77–79; V. N. Bernadskii, I. I. Liubimenko et al., "Kul'turnaia zhizn' Peterburga v 60–90kh godakh XVIII v.," *OIL,* 1: 416–18. For the significance of these schools for the rest of Russia, see chapter 9, 272.

100. Pavel N. Miliukov, *Ocherki po istorii russkoi kul'tury* (Paris: Sovremennye zapiski, 1931), vol. 2, part 2, 758–64. This part of the *Ocherki,* trans. Norman K. Sloan, appears in Marc Raeff, ed., *Catherine the Great: A Profile* (New York: Hill and Wang, 1972), 93–112.

101. *Sochineniia i perevody, k pol'ze i uveseleniiu sluzhashchikhsia,* August 1762, 140–64; September 1762, 251–68; and December 1762, 564–65.

102. Georgi, *Opisanie,* 405–06; RGIA, *fond* 467, *opis'* 4, *delo* 10, *listy* 10–20; Voronov, *Obozrenie,* 6–7; Bernadskii, Liubimenko et al., "Kul'turnaia zhizn'," *OIL,* 1: 415.

103. RGADA, *fond* 14, *delo* 218, *listy* 11–16; *fond* 17, *delo* 78; Georgi, *Opisanie,* 301, 330–32, 404–05. The mining institute is still in operation, the medical school has expanded into a huge complex, and the drama school was the forerunner of the Conservatory and the Mariinskii (before the revolution "Imperial Mariinskii" and during the last decades of Soviet power the "Kirov") Opera and Ballet Company.

104. The Academy's title in full: Russian Imperial Academy for the Furtherance and Preservation of the Russian Language.

105. RGADA, *fond* 17, *delo* 257.

106. Efimenko, "K istorii zemleustroistva," *Zhurnal ministerstva narodnogo prosveshcheniia,* 1914, no. 12 (December): 286–87. See also chapter 8, 8.7–8.9.

Chapter 3

1. David Griffiths and George Munro, trans. and eds., *Catherine the Great's Charters of 1785 to the Nobility and the Towns* (Bakersfield, CA: Charles Schlacks, Jr., 1991), 22.

2. Hittle, *The Service City,* 190–95.

3. A. A. Kizevetter, *Posadskaia obshchina v Rossii XVIII st.* (Moscow, 1903). *Posad* means "settlement" or "suburb," but referred historically to the community (the

meaning of *obshchina*) of tradesmen, craftsmen, merchants, and others not in direct civil or military service who lived next to—but always outside—a kremlin.

4. Kizevetter, *Posadskaia obshchina*, 90–93; Marc Raeff, "The Well-Ordered Police State and the Development of Modernity in Seventeenth- and Eighteenth-Century Europe: An Attempt at a Comparative Approach," *American Historical Review* 80, no. 5 (December 1975): 1234, and the fuller statement in Raeff, *The Well-Ordered Police State: Social and Institutional Change Through Law in the Germanies and Russia, 1600–1800* (New Haven: Yale University Press, 1983); Konvitz, *Cities and the Sea*, 152–56.

5. These reports are preserved in RGADA, *fond* 16.

6. Catherine II, "Iz bumag Imperatritsy Ekateriny II khraniashchikhsia v gosudarstvennom arkhive, ministerstva inostrannykh del," *Sbornik IRIO* 27 (1880): 347–48, 368; and Bashutskii, *Panorama*, 2: 135.

7. RGADA, *fond* 16, *delo* 504, *list* 30.

8. RGADA, *fond* 16, *delo* 529. *list* 1.

9. Ibid., *listy* 2–18. The city plan of 1793 shows the ditch but no mills.

10. Catherine II, letter to N. I. Panin of May 24, 1771, *Sbornik IRIO* 13 (1874): 100.

11. Catherine II, "Sobstvennoruchye pis'ma Imperatritsy Ekateriny k Grafu Ivanu Grigor'evichu Chernyshevu," *Russkii arkhiv*, 1871, no. 9 (September): 1345.

12. To cite one example among many contained in archival sources: in the spring of 1775 the Senate ordered the police to repair and maintain properly the bridges in St. Petersburg, granting 10,000 rubles for this purpose and denying a police request to rebuild Kharlamskii Bridge, at that time a wooden span, in stone. The police failed to follow these instructions, reporting to the Senate the next year that the bridge was too hazardous to use and not worth repairing. This intransigence on the part of the lesser body prompted the Senate's query as to how the bridge could have become so dilapidated if the police were doing their duty. The Senate simultaneously decided to withhold further sums for repairing the bridge; the police would have to find surplus funds in their own budget. RGADA, *fond* 16, *delo* 503, *listy* 1–2. To demonstrate its unwillingness to be subjected to the Senate, the police allowed the bridge to collapse; by 1777 it was totally unusable and a path had to be paved along the canal's bank to the next bridge for people to use. RGADA, *fond* 248, *delo* 5570, *listy* 205–06.

13. For examples of its responsibility in St. Petersburg, see Polianskii, *Gorodskoe remeslo*, 196–98; and V. N. Kashin, ed., *Materialy po istorii krest'ianskoi promyshlennosti*, 17–21; 28–40.

14. RGIA, *fond* 467, *opis'* 4, *delo* 10, *list* 10.

15. Typical of its demands in its relations with the magistracy were the provincial administration's repeated requests for price lists of goods on sale in St. Petersburg contained in Tsentral'nyi gosudarstvennyi istoricheskii arkhiv Sankt-Peterburga (hereafter TsGIA SPb), formerly the Gosudarstvennyi istoricheskii arkhiv leningradskoi oblasti (GIA LO), *fond* 221, *opis'* 2, *delo* 18.

16. RGADA, *fond* 248, *delo* 5693, *listy* 567–68.

17. RGIA, *fond* 796, *opis'* 44, *delo* 13; *PSZ* 16, No. 11.723. In 1762 the commission's name was "Commission for the Arrangement of St. Petersburg and Moscow"; in 1764 the name was changed to "Commission for the Institution of Masonry Construction in St. Petersburg and Moscow." *Sanktpeterburgskie vedomosti*, September 28, 1764, 1. The Commission is dealt with further in chapter 4.

18. For a synopsis, see George E. Munro, "Russia's Non-Russian Capital: Petersburg and the Planning Commission," *Eighteenth-Century Life* 2, no. 3 (March 1976): 49–53.

19. Blumenfeld, "Russian City Planning," *Journal of the American Society of Architectural Historians* 4: 27.

20. *PSZ* 6, no. 3.520 (February 13, 1720); 11, no. 8.734 (May 21, 1743); Ditiatin, *Ustroistvo i upravlenie gorodov Rossii,* 2 vols. (vol. 1, St. Petersburg, 1875; vol. 2, Iaroslavl', 1877), 1: 343; Klokman, *Sotsial'no-ekonomicheskaia istoriia,* 56; Hittle, *The Service City,* 133–34.

21. The provincial reforms of 1775 slightly changed the composition of the magistracy. From then on there were only two burgomasters (*burgomistry*) and four councillors (*ratmany),* instead of four burgomasters and two councillors: *PSZ* 20, no. 14.392 (November 7, 1775): 259; Ditiatin, *Stoletie S.-Peterburgskogo gorodskogo obshchestva, 1785–1885* (St. Petersburg: Tipografiia Shredera, 1885), 24.

22. According to Kizevetter, most important decisions and many trivial ones were made for the magistracies of smaller towns by the Main Magistracy in St. Petersburg. Hittle, *The Service City,* 133. John P. LeDonne, *Ruling Russia: Politics and Administration in the Age of Absolutism, 1762–1796* (Princeton: Princeton University Press, 1984), 51, erroneously places the Main Magistracy in Moscow and a "branch" in St. Petersburg.

23. Hittle, *The Service City,* 208. The magistracy did continue to carry out its administrative and judicial functions within St. Petersburg.

24. The magistracy was not empowered to initiate cases, either civil or criminal, upon its own volition. See *PSZ* 20, no. 14.392, chapter 20, article 283.

25. Instructions in 1777, for example, forbade peasants to trade in the city or within five versts of it. *PSZ* 20, no. 14.595 (March 9, 1777): 506; Nikolai Ivanovich Pavlenko, "O nekotorykh storonakh pervonachal'nogo nakopleniia v Rossii (po materialam XVII–XVIII vv.)," *Istoricheskie zapiski* 54 (1955): 386.

26. *PSZ* 22, no. 15.932 (February 21, 1784): 26–27.

27. RGADA, *fond* 10, *opis'* 3, *delo* 201. TsGIA SPb, *fond* 221, *opis'* 2, *delo* 18, *listy* 1–18.

28. Raeff, "The Well-Ordered Police State," *American Historical Review* 80, no. 5 (December 1975): 1221–43. Much the same point is made in John P. LeDonne, *Ruling Russia,* 115ff.

29. Police duties included the following: (1) to ensure regular building by all the citizenry; (2) to guarantee the protection of riverbanks; (3) to clean streets; (4) to regulate people bringing things to market, tavern owners, and their places of business; (5) to ensure that foodstuffs on sale remained uncontaminated; (6) to prevent fights, arguments, and disturbances; (7) to inspect stoves and chimneys; (8) to watch over property in the city; (9) to be on the lookout for people who acted suspiciously; (10) to check the documents of all arrivals; and (11) to set up local police officials. Bogdanov, *Opisanie,* 478–79; *PSZ* 5, no. 3.203 (May 25, 1718): 569–71.

30. A brief synopsis of the changes in organizational structure is contained in Vysotskii, *S.-Peterburgskaia politsiia.* For the police reforms under Peter III see Marc Raeff, "The Domestic Policies of Peter III and his Overthrow," *American Historical Review* 75, no. 5 (June 1970): 1305–07; and Carol Scott Leonard, "A Study of the Reign of Peter III of Russia," unpublished Ph.D. dissertation, Indiana University, 1976, 172–73.

31. Ditiatin, *Ustroistvo,* 1: 354–70.

32. Vysotskii, *S.-Peterburgskaia politsiia,* 51; RGADA, *fond* 16, *delo* 473.

33. Raeff, "Domestic Policies," *American Historical Review* 75, no. 5: 1305; *PSZ* 16, no. 11.871 (July 4, 1763): 308; Vysotskii, *S.-Peterburgskaia politsiia,* 28. The office (*rozysknaia ekspeditsiia*) existed until 1782, when its functions were handed over to the office of criminal affairs.

34. Korff computed the "fair share" of each householder by surveying lands and measuring buildings, from which the proportionate share of each house was determined. Not so incidentally, the plan provided a convenient way to register all people

living in the city and eliminate those who were unregistered. RGADA, *fond* 16, *delo* 473, *listy* 112–17.

35. A complete list of those who chose to pay additional taxes instead of providing manpower is contained in RGADA, *fond* 16, *delo* 473, *listy* 120–37.

36. Vysotskii, *S.-Peterburgskaia politsiia,* 49–51.

37. RGADA, *fond* 248, *delo* 5570, *list* 450.

38. RGADA, *fond* 248, *delo* 5693, *listy* 141–57 contains the police requests and Senate replies.

39. RGADA, *fond* 16, *delo* 477; and RGIA, *fond* 1329, *opis'* 2, *dela* 52–62, passim.

40. RGADA, *fond* 248, *delo* 5570, *listy* 395–96.

41. *PSZ* 21, no. 15.379 (April 8, 1782): 461–88. The new structure imposed by the reform is synopsized in John P. Le Donne, "The Provincial and Local Police Under Catherine the Great, 1775–1796," *Canadian Slavic Studies* 4, no. 3 (Fall 1970): 513–28, on which portions of the following are dependent. In 1781 a minor reform of the administrative structure of the police did away with the chancellery, the offices of which were subordinated directly to the police chief. He in turn was answerable to the *guberniia* chancellery. RGADA, *fond* 248, *delo* 5693, *listy* 99–99*ob.*

42. The divisions into quarters, or districts, were as follows: (1) First Admiralty, the land between the Neva and the Moika; (2) Second Admiralty, between the Moika and the Ekaterininskii Canal; (3) Third Admiralty, between the Ekaterininskii and the Fontanka; (4) St. Petersburg Side; (5) Vyborg Side; (6) Vasil'evskii Island; (7) Moscow Side; (8) Rozhestvenskaia; (9) Foundry; and (10) Karetnaia. See maps 2 and 3. Note that each district was supposed to contain from 200–700 houses, not households, as LeDonne erroneously ascribed: LeDonne, "Provincial and Local Police," *Canadian Slavic Studies* 4, no. 3 (Fall 1970): 517.

43. S. P. Luppov, "Gorodskoe upravlenie i gorodskoe khoziaistvo Peterburga v 60–90kh godakh XVIII v.," *OIL,* 1: 364; LeDonne, "Provincial and Local Police," *Canadian Slavic Studies* 4, no. 3 (Fall 1970): 517–18.

44. Le Donne, "Provincial and Local Police," *Canadian Slavic Studies* 4, no. 3 (Fall 1970): 519–20.

45. This figure represents about one-fourth of the houses in the city. The remainder either paid the tax in lieu of service or were excused for one reason or another. Less than one-tenth of the buildings were state-owned.

46. The law is contained in RGADA, *fond* 248, *delo* 5693, *listy* 287–90.

47. Vysotskii, *S.-Peterburgskaia politsiia,* 67–68.

48. *PSZ* 20, no. 14.392 (November 7, 1775): art. 38–39; I. E. Andreevskii, "O pervykh shagakh deiatel'nosti S.-Peterburgskogo prikaza obshchestvennogo prizreniia," *Russkaia starina* 63 (1889): 449, 453–55; Aleksandr S. Lappo-Danilevskii, *Ocherk vnutrennei politiki Imperatritsy Ekateriny II* (St. Petersburg, 1898), 14.

49. Originally (until 1785), only homeowners could vote for the mayor. *Sanktpeterburgskie vedomosti,* February 27, 1767, supplement; June 11, 1780, 75; Bozherianov, *Nevskii prospekt,* 2: 218–19.

50. LeDonne, *Ruling Russia,* 157n.

51. Ibid., pp. 152–53.

52. *PSZ* 20, no. 14.392, chapter 26; Indova, *Zakonodatel'stvo,* 316–17; LeDonne, *Ruling Russia,* 161.

53. These fees are referred to indirectly in *PSZ* 20, no. 14.392, chapter 20, articles 286, 289.

54. For example, the merchant and fabricant Sava Iakovlev headed a company for collecting taxes under a contract for 1758–65. Besides himself and his two sons, the

company of Iakovlev included some dozen men, most of them likewise merchants. Petrov, *Istoriia Sanktpeterburga,* 600.

55. References to treasury grants are contained in RGADA, *fond* 16, *delo* 482, *listy* 1–5; *delo* 516, *list* 2; *fond* 248, *delo* 5570, *listy* 86, 403. At times the question of finances seems not to have been important on a construction project. In 1765 the correspondence between the Chancellery on Construction and the Office for erecting stone embankments on the Neva does not include any accounting for the money received or spent on the work. RGIA, fond 467, *opis'* 4, *delo* 10.

56. Boris Borisovich Kafengauz, "Goroda i gorodskaia reforma 1785 g.," in *Period feodalizma: Rossiia vo vtoroi polovine XVIII v.,* vol. 9 of *Ocherki istorii SSSR,* ed. N. M. Druzhinin, A. L. Sidorov, A. M. Pankratova et. al. 9 vols. (Moscow, 1953–58), 157.

57. Obviously large numbers of all three groups were not paying taxes. Among merchants, forty-three wealthy foreigners paid no taxes. Fewer than seven hundred craftsmen paid taxes; more than fifteen hundred were excused. In addition, many nonregistered people did not pay taxes either; more will be said about them in chapter 7. RGIA, *fond* 558, *opis'* 2, *delo* 203, *listy* 2–4.

58. *PSZ* 19, no. 14.056 (October 30, 1773): 851–52.

59. Examples of such financial arrangements can be found in RGADA, *fond* 248, *delo* 5570, *list* 403; and RGIA, *fond* 1329, *opis'* 2, *delo* 62, no. 28, *list* 35.

60. *Sbornik IRIO* 27 (1880): 347–48. Catherine herself initiated this idea, but waited until Potemkin expressed his approval of it before applying the plan. See RNB, Manuscripts Division, *fond* O.IV.82, *listy* 17–19.

61. *PSZ* 22, no. 15.933 (February 21, 1784): 37–38.

62. *PSZ* 22, no. 16.188 (April 21, 1785): 359–84. The Charter and its sources are examined extensively in Kizevetter, *Gorodovoe polozhenie;* Kafengauz, "Gorodskaia reforma," *Period feodalizma,* 151–65, and Hittle, *The Service City,* 216–34. Various drafts of the Charter are among the personal papers of Catherine in RGADA, *fond* 10.

63. George E. Munro, "The Charter to the Towns Reconsidered: The St. Petersburg Connection," *Canadian-American Slavic Studies* 23, no. 1 (Spring 1989): 17–35.

64. Used in this sense, *obshchestvo* is untranslatable, but its essence is best conveyed as "city-at-large" or "city association," referring to a gathering of all those who were considered citizens. A full English translation of the charter is provided in David Griffiths and George Munro, trans. and eds., *Catherine the Great's Charters of 1785 to the Nobility and the Towns,* (Bakersfield, CA: Charles Schlacks, Jr., 1991), 24–59.

65. *PSZ* 22, no. 16.188 (April 21, 1785): 362.

66. Courts of conscience, or equity courts, handled both criminal affairs and civil suits. See chapter 4 and Vasilii Osipovich Kliuchevskii, *Sochineniia,* 8 vols. (Moscow, 1956–59), 5: 118. Oral courts handled misdemeanors. The orphans court looked after the rights and welfare of orphans and widows of petty townsmen (*meshchane*).

67. The six groups, or estates, were: (1) genuine city resident, meaning those who owned real property in the city; (2) those registered in the merchant guilds; (3) workers and artisans registered in craft guilds (*tsekhi);* (4) merchants from other towns and countries; (5) eminent citizens; and (6) *posad* people.

68. Guild members were not necessarily merchants; artisans could register in guilds too, as could anyone wanting to declare his wealth and pay his taxes on that basis (1 percent of declared wealth). All the students of the Charter have assumed that the majority of guildsmen were merchants, and that representatives of the guilds thus reflected a merchant point of view.

69. By statute there were only ten genuine city dwellers, ten *posad* people, three merchants from St. Petersburg, and no more than seven honorable citizens. The re-

maining sixty-odd delegates came from artisans and foreign merchants. The foreign and out-of-town merchants together elected only seven delegates in the 1786 city council elections. Munro, "The Charter to the Towns Reconsidered," *Canadian-American Slavic Studies* 23, no. 1 (Spring 1989): 28.

70. Janet M. Hartley, "The Implementation of the Laws Relating to Local Administration, 1775–1796: With Special Reference to the Guberniia of St. Petersburg," unpublished Ph.D. dissertation, University of London, 1980), 215–17.

71. A copy of one of the earliest registers of real estate is in RNB, Manuscripts Division, O.IV.56.

72. For each person the following information was to be recorded: (1) spouse; (2) number, ages, and sex of children; (3) address of real property in the city and how it had been acquired; (4) whether the person lived within the city limits; (5) occupation; and (6) exact nature of all jobs held, past and present, in or out of St. Petersburg.

73. Kafengauz, "Gorodskaia reforma," in *Period feodalizma,* 157. Ditiatin mistakenly says the register was compiled, if only for the years 1785–88: Ditiatin, *Stoletie,* 199–200.

74. George E. Munro, "Compiling and Maintaining St. Petersburg's 'Book of City Inhabitants': The 'Real' City Inhabitants," in Anthony Cross, ed., *St. Petersburg, 1703–1825* (New York: Palgrave Macmillan, 2003), 83–4, 96–7.

75. TsGIA SPb, *fond* 781, *opis'* 2, *delo* 680, *listy* 1–2.

76. *PSZ* 22, no. 16.188 (April 21, 1785): article 123, with 117 sub-articles, 369–79. The principal source for this section of the Charter was the Swedish statute for Estonia and Finland, issued in 1669. For an article-by-article demonstration of the relationship between the two, see Kizevetter, *Gorodovoe polozhenie,* chapter 5. For an English translation, see the relevant passages in Griffiths and Munro, trans. and eds., *Catherine the Great's Charters,* 39–53.

77. The old *posadskaia obshchina* apparently ceased to function after 1785, although it was never abolished. Yet the terms *posad* and *posadskie liudi* continued to be used. Hittle, *The Service City,* 234–36. The meanings of the terms were by this time undergoing change, however; the connotation of the term *posadskie liudi* was grasped by Georgi, who rendered it in French with the word *menant,* a medieval word meaning boor or villager, or familiarly a yokel or churl. The word was negatively connotative, undoubtedly referring to the recent move to the city of the *posad* people and their continuing rural habits. Georgi, *Opisanie,* 177.

78. The ukase, not included in *PSZ,* was dated October 23, 1790. Lappo-Danilevskii, *Ocherk vnutrennei politiki Ekateriny,* 23.

79. Nor did the Charter mention soldiers and sailors, who comprised approximately one-fifth of city residents throughout the period.

80. *PSZ* 22, no. 16.188 (April 21, 1785): articles 18–21, 23–27, on pp. 360–61.

81. Luppov, "Gorodskoe upravlenie," *OIL,* 1: 367. See also the next chapter, 144.

82. *PSZ* 23, no. 17.043 (May 4, 1792): 330.

83. Instances of police recalcitrance to cooperate are recorded in RGADA, *fond* 248, *delo* 5693, *listy* 567–68; and Ditiatin, *Stoletie,* 77.

84. Hermann, *Statistische Schilderung,* 430; *PSZ* 22, no. 16.457 (November 9, 1786): 708–09. This amount of revenue alone sufficed to meet the council's obligations in these years.

85. Georgi, *Opisanie,* 600–601.

86. *PSZ* 22, no. 16.457 (November 9, 1786): 708–09; 23, no. 16.894 (August 9, 1790): 192–93.

87. This is borne out by the budget for 1803, the first year when the combined figure was kept: income was over a million rubles, expenditure, nearly 800,000 rubles: Ditiatin, *Stoletie,* 194, 200, 205–08; *PSZ* 25, no. 18.664 (September 12, 1798).

88. Kafengauz, "Gorodskaia reforma," in *Period feodalizma,* 156.

89. *PSZ* 22, no. 16.188 (April 21, 1785): 359.

90. Kizevetter's views are summarized in "Gorodovoe polozhenie," *Tri veka,* 1: 250–51, 265–67, and 272–73. For Hartley's position, see her "Town Government in St. Petersburg Guberniya after the Charter to the Towns of 1785," *Slavonic and East European Review* 62, no. 1 (January 1984): 61–84. See also her "Governing the City: St. Petersburg and Catherine II's Reforms," in Anthony Cross, ed., *St. Petersburg, 1703–1825* (New York: Palgrave Macmillan, 2003), 99–118.

91. Ditiatin, *Stoletie,* 82–86. For the ways in which St. Petersburg's city government increased its effectiveness in the first half of the nineteenth century, see W. Bruce Lincoln, "The Russian State and its Cities: A Search for Effective Municipal Government, 1786–1842," *Jahrbücher für Geschichte Osteuropas* 17, no. 4 (December 1969): 531–41.

Chapter 4

1. Hittle, *The Service City,* 5–11.

2. Vysotskii, *S.-Peterburgskaia politsiia,* 49–51; *PSZ* 16, no. 11.991 (December 15, 1763): 468; 44, part 2: 65–66.

3. I. N. Artamonova, "Chicherin, Nikolai Ivanovich," in *Russkii biograficheskii slovar',* 25 vols. (Moscow-St. Petersburg, 1896–1918) (hereafter *RBS*), 22: 430; M. Popov, "Lopukhin, Petr Vasil'evich," *RBS,* 11: 686–87; P. Maikov and B. M-i, "Ryleev, Nikita Ivanovich," *RBS,* 17: 697–701. Khrapovitskii's full assessment of the capital's police chiefs: "If regimental officers have little intellect, then from practice they are made suitable for being senior chiefs of police—but the one here is a very fool, *celui ne profitera pas.*" Cited in P. Maikov and B. M-i, "Ryleev," *RBS,* 17: 700.

4. In the wake of her coup she issued an *ukaz* establishing sentinels in the streets at regular intervals for the "prevention of drunkenness, arguments and brawls": *PSZ* 16, no. 11.585 (June 30, 1762): 4. The draft of the law is in RGIA, *fond* 1329, *opis'* 2, *delo* 52, *list* 21.

5. Police reports from the time are contained in RGADA, *fond* 16, *delo* 477.

6. In one such episode, a group of carousers attacked and beat to death a watchman who had challenged them: RGADA, *fond* 16, *delo* 477, *list* 56.

7. These figures, extrapolated from archival evidence, appear in an unpublished paper delivered by the author at the American Historical Association in 1978, "Crime in the City, or Urban Crime? The Case of St. Petersburg."

8. "Pis'ma Imperatritsy Ekateriny IIi k I. F. Glebovu," *Russkii arkhiv,* 1867, no. 5 (May): 342–43.

9. RGIA, *fond* 467, *opis'* 4, *delo* 76, no. 30, *listy* 144–74. Embarrassed officials strengthened laws dealing with theft from royal sources.

10. See, for example, *Sanktpeterburgskie vedomosti,* December 31, 1764, no. 105.

11. See the story about a Russian courier robbed in Westphalia run side by side with a report of the European reaction to an attack on a French diplomat outside St. Petersburg. *Sanktpeterburgskie vedomosti,* March 2, 1764, no. 18.

12. Bozherianov, *Nevskii prospekt,* 2: 201–02. Panin in particular was familiar with Scandinavian cities, having spent much of his life in Copenhagen and Stockholm.

13. One night in 1787 during *maslianitsa* (Shrovetide), 160 people were picked up lying drunk on city streets. RGADA, *fond* 16, *delo* 533, *chast'* 1, *listy* 25*ob*.-26. In November 1778, following a three-day holiday, 370 people who had apparently died from overdrinking were found in the city's streets. Letter of Catherine II to police chief D. V. Volkov, November 27, 1778, in *Russkaia starina* 18 (1877): 744.

14. *PSZ* 16, no. 11.949 (October 15, 1763): 397.

15. *PSZ* 16, no. 12.218 (July 30, 1764): 856; 17, no. 14.938 (November 2, 1779): 877; 18, no. 12.957 (August 11, 1767): 183–88; Vysotskii, *S.-Peterburgskaia politsiia*, 70.

16. RGIA, *fond* 467, *god* 1765, *opis'* 4, *delo* 10, *listy* 236–36*ob.*

17. RGADA, *fond* 16, *delo* 521, *chast'* 1, *listy* 198–98*ob.*; *delo* 535, *list* 18.

18. For references to public disorders, see Bozherianov, *Nevskii prospekt*, 2: 279–80; Khrapovitskii, *Pamiatnye zapiski*, 11; and Safonova, "Polozhenie trudiashchikhsia," *Uchenye zapiski vologodskogo gosudarstvennogo pedagogicheskogo instituta* 14 (1954): 3–46, although she gives no concrete examples.

19. Shchekatov, *Slovar'*, 1: 43, 45–46; Georgi, *Opisanie*, 325–26. Derek Lionel Howard, *John Howard: Prison Reformer* (London: Christopher Johnson, 1958), 91–94.

20. Mikhail Garnovskii, "Zapiski," *Russkaia starina* 15 (1876): 703–04.

21. Georgi, *Opisanie*, 325–26.

22. Ibid., 322–25.

23. RGADA, *fond* 16, *delo* 521, *chast'* 1, *listy* 198–98*ob.*; *delo* 535, *list* 18.

24. *PSZ* 21, no. 15.379 (April 8, 1782): 468 (article 72).

25. For example, see the figures cited for St. Petersburg region in 1786 in Hartley, "The Implementation of the Laws," 148.

26. RGADA, *fond* 16, *delo* 499, *list* 7.

27. This and the following are drawn from the Instruction for St. Petersburg's oral courts, RGADA, *fond* 16, *delo* 504, *chast'* 1, *listy* 194–98.

28. RGADA, *fond* 16, *delo* 528, *listy* 6–7*ob.*

29. Bogoslovskii, *Tri veka*, 242–43; Storch, *Picture*, 129–32.

30. RGADA, *fond* 16, *delo* 528, *listy* 6–7*ob.*

31. Thereafter the task fell to the *guberniia* magistracy. RGADA, *fond* 16, *delo* 504, *chast'* 1, *list* 194*ob.*

32. RGADA, *fond* 16, *delo* 499, *listy* 4–9*ob.*

33. For example, a year and a half after the *ukaz* of March 17, 1775, permitting peasants to register as merchants, the magistracy did not know how to go about registering them and had to turn to the Senate for instructions. RGADA, *fond* 248, *delo* 3797, *listy* 191–96. In 1782 the elders of the merchant guilds refused to provide information about prices requested by the magistracy for the guberniia board, and the magistracy did nothing to punish their insolence. TsGIA SPb, *fond* 221, *opis'* 2, *delo* 18, *listy* 14–18.

34. RGADA, *fond* 16, *delo* 504, *chast'* 1, *list* 194*ob.*

35. Hartley, "The Implementation of the Laws," 261, 335.

36. The records of many such cases are housed in RGADA, *fond* 248, *delo* 5693. See especially the rulings in favor of a third-guild merchant and against the Admiralty (*listy* 200–202); for the policy of the city police and against the widow of a general (*listy* 613–35); and for a merchant and against the poet and eminent personage Gavriil Derzhavin (*listy* 461–97). John LeDonne states that the Second Department of the Senate handled transferred and appellate cases, but in a footnote raises the question whether this was so; see his *Ruling Russia*, 146–47.

37. Regulations over commerce and industry are treated in more detail in chapters 6 and 7. Building regulations fall into the section on city planning below in this chapter.

38. An example of such notification can be found in *Sanktpeterburgskie vedomosti,* February 7, 1763, 4. See also John Williams, *The Rise, Progress, and Present State of the Northern Governments: viz, The United Provinces, Denmark, Sweden, Russia and Poland,* 2 vols. (London, 1777), 2: 326.

39. There were even gates at all entrances to the city, where officers checked the documents of all entering and exiting people before allowing them to proceed. See Georgi, *Opisanie,* 578–79; Stolpianskii, *Vverkh po Neve,* 1: 29. Also Georgel, *Voyage,* 177.

40. Georgel, *Voyage,* 332.

41. Typical examples of documents of this type can be found in RGIA, *fond* 467, *opis'* 4, *delo* 10; and *fond* 1329, *opis'* 2, *delo* 54.

42. The ukase is in RGIA, *fond* 467, *opis'* 4, *delo* 10, *list* 236. In 1790 large numbers of such people were mobilized to defend the city from possible attack from the Swedes: Garnovskii, "Zapiski," *Russkaia starina* 16 (1876): 431.

43. Bertram Wolfe once made the curious statement that during this period people fled from cities rather than flocked to them. See his "Backwardness and Industrialization in Russian History and Thought," *Slavic Review* 26, no. 2 (June 1967): 177–203. Nothing in my research bears out his contention. For another view emphasizing the constraints upon townsmen so that "in Russia town air did not make men free," see Samuel H. Baron, "The Town in Feudal Russia," *Slavic Review* 28, no. 1 (March 1969): 116–22. His point has some validity, but demonstrably there was in St. Petersburg wholesale violation of the law which, for the most part, escaped unnoticed and unpunished, thereby rendering the law of no effect. See, for example, the police report, RGADA, *fond* 16, *delo* 473, *list* 116, article 11.

44. *Sbornik IRIO* 107 (1900): 213.

45. Bashutskii, *Panorama,* 2: 135–37; Pushkarev, *Opisanie,* 84–85; Luppov, "Gorodskoe upravlenie," *OIL,* 1: 370–71.

46. RGADA, *fond* 16, *delo* 504, *chast'* 1, *listy* 62–63*ob.* The state had to buy the wagons to be used for this purpose because no contractors could be found who would supply their own wagons.

47. RGADA, *fond* 16, *delo* 481, *chast'* 3, *listy* 34–35*ob.;* Shustov, *Sanktpeterburgskoe kupechestvo,* 52.

48. RGADA, *fond* 16, *delo* 521, *chast'* 1, *list* 39.

49. Gospodin Shreter, "O moshchenii ulits v gorodakh," *Trudy vol'nogo ekonomicheskogo obshchestva,* Part 51 (1796): 177–95.

50. RGADA, *fond* 16, *delo* 504, *chast'* 1, *listy* 66–67.

51. Gospodin Shreter, "O moshchenii ulits v gorodakh," *Trudy vol'nogo ekonomicheskogo obshchestva,* Part 51 (1796): 177–212.

52. Georgel, *Voyage,* 254.

53. For a cross-sectional drawing of the disposition of the embankment made by B. F. Rastrelli showing the embankment along the frontage of the Winter Palace, see B. B. Piotrovskii, gen. ed., *Ermitazh: Istoriia stroitel'stva i arkhitektura zdanii* (Leningrad, 1991), 70.

54. RGIA, *fond* 470, *opis'* 6, *delo* 28, *list* 6.

55. For the law setting up the poorhouses, see *PSZ* 17, no. 12.334 (February 24, 1765): 61–63. See also Georgi, *Opisanie,* 142–43, 313–15; and Bozherianov, *Nevskii prospekt,* 2: 207–08.

56. Andreevskii, "O pervykh shagakh," *Russkaia starina* 63 (1889): 449–55; RGADA, *fond* 16, *delo* 533, *list* 18; Lappo-Danilevskii, *Ocherk vnutrennei politiki Ekateriny,* 14; Georgi, *Opisanie,* 305–07; and Janet M. Hartley, "Philanthropy in the Reign of Catherine the Great: Aims and Realities," in Roger Bartlett and Janet M. Hartley, eds., *Rus-*

sia in the Age of Enlightenment. Essays for Isabel de Madariaga (New York: St. Martin's Press, 1990), especially 180–82, 186–87.

57. See A. P. Piatkovskii, "S.-Peterburgskii vospitatel'nyi dom pod upravleniem I. I. Betskogo," *Russkaia starina* 12 (1875): 146–59, 359–80; 13 (1875): 177–99, 532–53. Also Georgi, *Opisanie,* 308–10; and V. N. Basnin, ed., "Istoriia Imperatorskikh vospitatel'nykh domov," *Chteniia v Imperatorskom obshchestve istorii i drevnostei rossiiskikh pri moskovskom universitete* 2, (1860): 93–98.

58. *PSZ* 16, no. 11.901 (August 19, 1763): 337–38. The new provisions shared many common points with those of other large European cities, as for example London after the great fire of 1666. See Harold Priestley, *London.*

59. Catherine II, letter to N. I. Panin, May 24, 1771, *Sbornik IRIO* 12 (1874): 99. She expressed it slightly differently the same day in a hand-written note to Ivan Chernyshev, "Yesterday I resembled Job: tiding after tiding came to me, each worse than the preceding one, and from our windows three or four parts of the capital could be seen aflame." *Russkii arkhiv,* 1871, no. 9 (September): 1345.

60. Catherine II, letter to Voltaire, May 25, 1771, *Sbornik IRIO* 13 (1874): 134–35.

61. The measures are recorded in RGADA, *fond* 16, *delo* 479, *listy* 229–30.

62. I. Mordvinov, ed., "Peterburgskoe navodnenie Ekaterininskago vremeni v opisanii ochevidtsa," *Russkii arkhiv,* 1916, nos. 1–3 (January–March): 209–10.

63. Petr Petrovich Karatygin, *Letopis' peterburgskikh navodnenii 1730–1879 gg. P. P. Karatygina* (St. Petersburg, 1889), 17–32; Pyliaev, *Staryi Peterburg,* 114–18. This was the third worst flood in the city's history after those of 1824 and 1924: *Atlas leningradskoi oblasti* (Moscow, 1967), 26. Although officially only a handful of people died, Catherine soon relieved police chief Chicherin of his duties, blaming him for the state of unpreparedness that cost the lives of thousands.

64. *PSZ* 20, no. 14.653 (September 21, 1777): 554–55; RNB, Manuscripts Division, *fond* 40, contains the maps.

65. See chapter 5, 165–68; also George E. Munro, "Feeding the Multitudes: Grain Supply to St. Petersburg in the Era of Catherine the Great," *Jahrbücher für Geschichte Osteuropas* 35, no. 4 (1987): 481–508.

66. *PSZ* 17, no. 12.790 (November 27, 1766): 1065. The law was widened later to provide for peasants to buy grain under terms of repayment in kind with interest. The grain warehouses were to act as "banks" in this exchange: *PSZ* 18, no. 13.238 (January 21, 1769): 808–10.

67. The story of this epidemic, in the context of eighteenth-century medicine, is well told in John T. Alexander, *Bubonic Plague.*

68. *PSZ* 19, no. 13.663 (September 30, 1771): 316–18; no. 13.674 (October 10, 1771): 327–29); Alexander, *Bubonic Plague,* 245–47.

69. *PSZ* 19, no. 13.679 (October 14, 1771): 334–40; no. 13.686 (October 22, 1771): 350–56); no. 13.706 (November 25, 1771): 383; no. 13.745 (January 19, 1772): 437–29; *Sanktpeterburgskie vedomosti,* November 11, 1771 (no. 90), supplement; January 10, 1772 (no. 3), supplement. Also Alexander, *Bubonic Plague,* 247–48.

70. Alexander, *Bubonic Plague,* 249.

71. These figures and the following paragraphs draw from Philip H. Clendenning, "Dr. Thomas Dimsdale and Smallpox Inoculation in Russia," *Journal of the History of Medicine and Allied Sciences* 28 (April 1973): 109–25. See also Cross, *By the Banks of the Neva,* 137–40.

72. Clendenning, "Dimsdale," 124.

73. A gardener apprentice's son died from smallpox and his master tried to bury the boy's body secretly. The only official reaction to the event was an order to the in-

spector of gardeners to reprimand the master craftsman and mete out "proper punishment" to the father. RGIA, *fond* 467, *opis'* 4, *delo* 10, *list* 57.

74. RNB, Manuscripts Division, Arkhiv I. V. Pomialovskogo, no. 23, *list* 230; Georgi, *Opisanie,* 731; Luppov, "Gorodskoe upravlenie," *OIL,* 1: 377.

75. See the account of the journey kept by his wife, Baroness Elizabeth Dimsdale, *An English Lady at the Court of Catherine the Great: The Journal of Baroness Elizabeth Dimsdale, 1781,* ed., intro., and notes A. G. Cross (Cambridge: Crest Publications, 1989).

76. Catherine was not the first ruler of Russia to express concern about St. Petersburg's appearance. Some orderly construction dated from an earlier commission established in 1736 by Anna Ioannovna. Hers was an important and farsighted move, but by the 1760s the commission had long since ceased to function. Bunin, *Istoriia gradostroitel'nogo iskusstva,* 120; Pushkarev, *Opisanie,* 11.

77. The commission was also known as the Commission on the Building of St. Petersburg and Moscow. See Robert E. Jones, "Urban Planning and the Development of Provincial Towns in Russia, 1762–1796," in John G. Garrard, ed., *The Eighteenth Century in Russia* (Oxford: Clarendon Press, 1973), 332ff.

78. It is unclear whether this final provision was carried out; it may have been, for Catherine indicated that it had been done previously. In neither case do records survive.

79. In 1764 when Dashkov suddenly died, two new members were added, Nikolai Erofeevich Murav'ev and Nikolai Ivanovich Chicherin. RGIA, *fond* 1329, *opis'* 2, *delo* 104, no. 4, *list* 1; *Sanktpeterburgskie vedomosti,* September 28, 1764 (no. 78): 1.

80. *PSZ* 16, no. 11.723 (December 11, 1762): 127–28; Bozherianov, *Nevskii prospekt,* 1: 186; Egorov, *Architectural Planning,* 42–43; Pushkarev, *Opisanie,* 13–14; Shkvarikov, *Ocherk istorii planirovki,* 84.

81. Shkvarikov, *Ocherk istorii planirovki,* 87–88.

82. Kvasov died in 1772 and was replaced as chief architect by Ivan Egorovich Starov. Kvasov designed no buildings of note. Starov was the architect for the Holy Trinity Cathedral in the Aleksandronevskii Monastery and the Tavricheskii Palace: L. S. Shaumian, ed., *Leningrad: Entsiklopedicheskii spravochnik* (Moscow-Leningrad, 1957), 177, 178, 542, 731.

83. Munro, "Russia's Non-Russian Capital," *Eighteenth Century Life* 2, no. 3 (March 1976): 49–53.

84. RGIA, *fond* 1329, *opis'* 2, *delo* 104, no. 3, *listy* 3–4. The task of making maps was still in progress in 1772, at which time the draftsmen estimated that it would take another year. It was originally supposed to be completed by 1768.

85. Blumenfeld, "Russian City Planning," *Journal of the American Society of Architectural Historians* 4, no. 1: 27. The materials of the commission are housed in RGADA, *fond* 1310.

86. RGADA, *fond* 16, *delo* 475, *listy* 1–4.

87. *PSZ* 17, no. 12.324 (February 8, 1765): 21–22. The same report in a fuller version is in RGIA, *fond* 1329, *opis'* 2, *delo* 104, no. 4, *listy* 5–10.

88. For a long time unable to agree whether squares should be built by the government or by private individuals, the members approved the latter course, also presenting a minority report for all government construction.

89. *PSZ* 17, no. 12.546 (January 19, 1766): 531–34.

90. *PSZ* 17, no. 12.645 (May 13, 1766): 692–94.

91. *PSZ* 18, no. 12.883 (April 26, 1767): 115–17.

92. *PSZ* 17, no. 12.659 (May 25, 1766): 716–94; Efimenko, "K istorii zemleustroistva," *Zhurnal Ministerstva narodnogo prosveshcheniia* 12: 291.

93. *PSZ* 18, no. 13.080 (March 24, 1768): 485–86; the proposal is also found, in slightly different form, in RGIA, *fond* 1329, *opis'* 2, *delo* 104, no. 18, *listy* 48–49.

94. *PSZ* 18, no. 13.125 (May 27, 1768): 679, contains the core of the revised plan. More comprehensive copies are in RGIA, *fond* 1329, *opis'* 2, *delo* 104, nos. 20 and 25, *listy* 54, 74–82. The proposal also advocated moving the glass factory, a request for which had been made in the St. Petersburg instruction to delegate A. G. Orlov in the Legislative Commission. The detailed plan was completed almost a year after Catherine's rejection of the first one.

95. *PSZ* 18, no. 13.323 (July 17, 1769): 924; RGADA, *fond* 248, *delo* 5570, *list* 1. Obvodnyi and Ligovo canals were the principal ones dug for this purpose. Nine years later construction began on the earthen wall alongside the canals. That project, never completed as proposed, is a story in itself: its plans called for a large mound with footpaths on top and some dozen mills operated by water and wind power along its southern extremity. See RGADA, *fond* 16, *delo* 504, *chast'* 1, *listy* 29–58*ob.*

96. The edict recognized that many inhabitants were not wealthy by permitting small masonry houses without majestic adornment. No house could be less than forty-two feet in height, however, with eaves at least twenty feet above the ground. When built on line, houses were required to have firewalls between them. At the end of the century the French churchman Georgel noted that poorer people continued to roof their houses with wooden planks, but that they painted them to look like sheet iron. Georgel, *Voyage,* 253.

97. *PSZ* 19, no. 13.631 (July 26, 1771): 292; RGIA, *fond* 1329, *opis'* 2, *delo* 104, no. 33, *list* 101.

98. RGIA, *fond* 1329, *opis'* 2, *delo* 104, no. 38, *listy* 111–14; RGADA, *fond* 16, *delo* 516, *list* 2.

99. *PSZ* 19, no. 13.982 (May 15, 1773): 762–63. RNB, Division of Prints and Engravings, "Vue de la place et du grand théatre de l'opéra a St. Pétersbourg," by Courvoisier and Dubois.

100. Soviet scholars ordinarily conclude that the instructions represented merchant interests. It is curious to note therefore that to ensure merchant representation at all, so dominated was the electorate by nonmerchants, two merchants were selected before the general election, in which the remaining three committee members were chosen. Unanimously selected outright were merchants Grigorii Nikonov and Semen Galaktionov. Chosen in the general election were A. V. Olsuf'ev, D. A. Merlin, and a third merchant, Ivan Shchukin. Thus it turned out that a majority of members were merchants, but only because the mayor was concerned that at least two merchants be chosen to ensure merchant cooperation with the commission: Vasilii Nikolaevich Latkin, *Zakonodatel'nye kommissii Rossii XVIII stoletiia: Istoriko-iuridicheskoe issledovanie* (St. Petersburg, 1887), 199.

101. The first twelve articles asked for such things as greater cleanliness in the city, more pastureland, masonry houses, bread in time of famine, an increase in the number of doctors, midwives, and apothecaries, and precautions against fire. Of the remainder, some fourteen applied to merchants, six to craftsmen, and two to the aristocracy. The instructions are reproduced in full in *Sbornik IRIO* 107 (1900): 213–26.

102. Kizevetter, *Gorodovoe polozhenie,* 153–54.

103. The instructions to this effect are housed in RGADA, *fond* 248, *delo* 5693, *list* 105.

104. N. D—v, "Proshloe Peterburga," *Zhurnal Ministerstva narodnogo prosveshcheniia* 240 (July 1885): 152.

105. RGADA, *fond* 16, *delo* 530, *list* 19.

106. In fact, the register was not completed for several years. The list of property owners, for example, proved to be extremely difficult to compile. See Munro, "Compiling and Maintaining St. Petersburg's 'Book of City Inhabitants'," in A. G. Cross, ed., *St. Petersburg, 1703–1825,* 82–84.

107. Besides the sixty-one *tsekhi,* another twelve trades had an insufficient number of practitioners in the capital (fewer than five) to form a *tsekh.* RGADA, *fond* 16, *delo* 530, *listy* 14–16*ob.;* TsGIA SPb, *fond* 221, *opis'* 1, *delo* 115, *listy* 1–4.

108. TsGIA SPb, *fond* 788, *opis'* 1, *delo* 2, *listy* 4–5.

109. RGADA, *fond* 16, *delo* 535, *list* 3.

110. Hartley, "The Implementation of the Laws," 215–19.

111. Ibid., 261.

112. Khrapovitskii, *Zapiski,* 35.

113. Hartley, "The Implementation of the Laws," 244.

114. *PSZ* 22, no. 16.188 (April 21, 1785): 383, article 167. The English translation is taken from Griffiths and Munro, trans. and eds., *Catherine the Great's Charters,* 58.

115. *PSZ* 23, no. 16.917 (May 20, 1790): 164–68. In order to ensure that decency and good order were maintained in taverns, Catherine shortly put their operation back under the authority of the police: *PSZ* 23, no. 16.957 (November 9, 1790): 183–88; Vysotskii, *S.-Peterburgskaia politsiia,* 70.

116. *PSZ* 22, no. 16.457 (November 9, 1786): 708–09.

117. RGADA, *fond* 16, *delo* 533, *chast'* 2, *listy* 17–18*ob.*

118. According to tables compiled by Arcadius Kahan, St. Petersburg's share of revenues collected at that port from exports alone averaged slightly over 80,000 rubles per year in the period 1786–90. See his *The Plow, the Hammer, and the Knout,* table 4.90, 244.

119. D——v, "Proshloe Peterburga," *Zhurnal Ministerstva narodnogo prosveshcheniia* 240 (July 1885): 157. Money for snow removal from First Admiralty in 1786, a total of 4230 rubles, and cleaning streets in summer (3045 rubles) came directly from the Cabinet. RGADA, *fond* 16, *delo* 533, *chast'* 1, *list* 84.

120. RGADA, *fond* 16, *delo* 536, *list* 16.

121. RGADA, *fond* 16, *delo* 536, *listy* 1, 3, 5, 8, 9, 13, 20, 27.

122. This criticism of much of the historiography of Russian towns is presented more fully in Hittle, *The Service City,* 5–7.

123. Cited in E. Kurganova and N. Okhotina, eds., *Russkii literaturnyi anekdot kontsa XVIII-nachala XIX veka,* intro. E. Kurganova (Moscow: "Khudozhestvennaia literatura," 1990), 61–62. Originally published in S. P. Zhikharev, *Zapiski sovremmenika,* ed. B. M. Eikhonbaum (Moscow, 1955), 149–51.

Chapter 5

1. This issue is treated thoroughly in Robert E. Jones, "Getting the Goods to St. Petersburg: Water Transport from the Interior 1703–1811," *Slavic Review* 43, no. 3 (Fall 1984): 413–33.

2. Klokman, *Ocherki,* 105–06.

3. Stolpianskii, *Vverkh po Neve,* 47.

4. Georgi, *Opisanie,* 588–93.

5. Hanway, *Historical Account,* 2: 139.

6. These products were all imported in noticeable quantities: Georgi, *Opisanie,* 588–93. Also RGIA, *fond* 602, *opis'* 1, *delo* 196.

7. *Sanktpeterburgskie vedomosti,* February 6, 1764 (no. 11). Later the same year a foreign merchant offered exotic cheeses and other goods. *Sanktpeterburgskie vedomosti,* December 28, 1764 (no. 104).

8. Thomas Dimsdale was told while dining with Catherine at the Winter Palace that the cantaloupes on the table were among those supplied in great number from Astrakhan, and that the apples and pears came from the Ukraine. Fresh grapes also came from Astrakhan. "Zapiska Barona Dimsdelia," *Sbornik IRIO* 2 (1868): 302.

9. Arkhiv SPbF IRI RAN, *fond* 36, *opis'* 1, *delo* 547, *list* 42. The information is from 1778.

10. Georgi, *Opisanie,* 672; Pushkarev, *Opisanie,* 49–77; Kopanev, *Naselenie Peterburga,* 29; A. L. Shapiro, "Zapiski," *Istoricheskii arkhiv* 5: 258.

11. For a brief survey of eighteenth-century legislation on this matter prior to Catherine's reign, see Hittle, *The Service City,* 170–71.

12. Kizevetter, *Gorodovoe polozhenie,* 176–77.

13. *PSZ* 20, no. 14.476: 392. Presumably peasants could sell only what they could carry on their person, a restriction that would in itself limit their share of urban commerce to a trifling amount.

14. Georgi, *Opisanie,* 212.

15. RGADA, *fond* 16, *delo* 511, *list* 6. The process is described more fully in Jones, "Getting the Goods to St. Petersburg," 420–24, and Munro, "Feeding the Multitudes: Grain Supply to St. Petersburg in the Era of Catherine the Great," *Jahrbücher für Geschichte Osteuropas* 35, no. 4 (1987): 486–89.

16. Munro, "Feeding the Multitudes," 488.

17. *Sanktpeterburgskie vedomosti,* July 9, 1764 (no. 55). *Kharchevye* were in many ways predecessors of Soviet-era *stolovye* or today's basement cafés; cheaply run establishments serving poorer sorts of food, the connotation of their meaning can be freely translated into "chophouse," or "eatery."

18. The basis for this information is TsGIA SPb, *fond* 781, *opis'* 2, *delo* 680, *listy* 9–39. See also the discussion in George E. Munro, "Food in Catherinian St. Petersburg," in Musya Glants and Joyce Toomre, eds., *Food in Russian History and Culture* (Bloomington: Indiana University Press, 1997), especially 41–44.

19. Georgi, *Opisanie,* 172–77; Kochin, "Naselenie Peterburga," *OIL,* 1: 305.

20. Kochin, "Naselenie Peterburga," *OIL,* 1: 310.

21. Bashutskii, *Panorama,* 2: 112–13.

22. The same point is discussed further in chapter 9, 263–65.

23. Examples of people appearing at the state orphanage offering their services are contained in RGIA, *fond* 758, *opis'* 1, *delo* 1, *list* 5.

24. The examples cited are contained consecutively in RGADA, *fond* 248, *delo* 3610, *list* 61; RGIA, *fond* 758, *opis'* 1, *delo* 1, *list* 15; and *Sanktpeterburgskie vedomosti,* February 8, 1793 (no. 11), 231.

25. Aleksandr Nikolaevich Afanas'ev, "Cherty russkikh nravov XVIII stoletiia," *Russkii vestnik,* 1857, no. 11 (September): 264.

26. As cited in ibid., 253–54.

27. As cited in ibid., 258–59. The Frenchman and German appear in a similar vein in another conversation analyzed in Walter J. Gleason, *Moral Idealists, Bureaucracy, and Catherine the Great* (New Brunswick: Rutgers University Press, 1981), 178.

28. Georgi, *Opisanie,* 140. RGADA, *fond* 16, *delo* 482, *listy* 3–4.

29. John Cook, *Voyages and Travels through the Russian Empire,* 1: 61–62.

30. Shops in the new masonry building were leased for five rubles per year; a merchant could hold his shop as long as he paid rent on it: Bogdanov, *Opisanie,* 113–17; *PSZ* 18, no. 13.149: 701–04.

31. Arkhiv SPbF IRI RAN, *fond* 36, *opis'* 1, *delo* 550, *listy* 143–57.
32. Ibid., *delo* 556, *list* 299.
33. Shchekatov, *Slovar',* 1: 51–53.
34. Arkhiv SPbF IRI RAN, *fond* 36, *opis'* 1, *delo* 556, *list* 298*ob.*
35. RGADA, *fond* 16, *delo* 504, *chast'* I, *listy* 79ff.
36. *PSZ* 21, no. 15.451: 616; Vysotskii, *S.-Peterburgskaia politsiia,* 66–67.
37. *PSZ* 21, no. 15.576: 737–41.
38. Georgi, *Opisanie,* 109.
39. Ibid, 126–27.
40. Bogdanov, *Opisanie,* 126–28; 134–35.
41. See Petrov, *Istoriia Sanktpeterburga,* 730.
42. *PSZ* 21, no. 15.451: 616.
43. The section that follows is based on George E. Munro, "Compiling and Maintaining St. Petersburg's 'Book of City Inhabitants': The 'Real' City Inhabitants," in Anthony Cross, ed., *St. Petersburg, 1703–1825* (New York: Palgrave Macmillan, 2003), 80–98.
44. Michelle Lamarche Marrese, *A Woman's Kingdom: Noblewomen and the Control of Property in Russia, 1700–1861* (Ithaca, NY: Cornell University Press, 2002).
45. Kochin, "Naselenie Peterburga," *OIL,* 1: 305.
46. Georgi, *Opisanie,* 581–82; *PSZ* 16, No. 11.949: 397. An ukase from the Senate in 1783 accused "people of various ranks" of renting cabs in order to race, encouraging the drivers to go so fast "that from fast driving many are dying," and beating those drivers who refused to race: see P. N. Menshikov, "Neostorozhnaia ezda v starinu, 1683–1800 gg.," *Russkaia starina* 18 (1877): 742–43.
47. Police Chief Chicherin asked in 1766 to raise the licensing fee to four rubles; he sought to force cabmen to use fewer horses and to drive out from their number local peasants who, after their agricultural duties for the year were over, came to the city in the winter to work as cab drivers. Georgi, *Opisanie,* 581–82; RGADA, *fond* 16, *delo* 487, *listy* 3–4.
48. Pushkarev, *Opisanie,* 104–05.
49. RGADA, *fond* 16, *delo* 511, *list* 3.
50. Munro, "Feeding the Multitudes," 488–89.
51. The shortage of the 1766 harvest was the subject of an article by "Gospodin Oleshov" in part 5, no. 3, of *Trudy Imperatorskago vol'nago ekonomicheskago obshchestva* ("O neurozhae rzhi, osoblivo 1766 god"). RGIA, *fond* 91, *opis'* 1, *delo* 273, no. 1, *list* 11; and RGIA, *fond* 466, *opis'* l, *delo* 105, no. 39, *list* 58.
52. Catherine II, "Pis'ma k I. F. Glebovu," *Russkii arkhiv,* 1867, no 5 (May): 347–50.
53. RNB, Manuscripts Division, Ermitazhnoe sobranie, no. 332.
54. Gosudarstvennyi arkhiv iaroslavskoi oblasti, *fond* 55, *opis'* 1, *delo* 81, *listy* 27–27 *ob.* The units of measure used here have the following equivalents. A *chervert'* (quarter) was a unit of measure equal to approximately eight bushels. A *kul'* was a bag usually weighing between 300 and 325 pounds. A *pud* was a unit of weight, approximately 36.11 pounds, and a *funt* was a Russian pound, equal to about nine-tenths of a pound avoirdupois.
55. In fact, Russia was experiencing a shortfall in grain harvests that lasted for several years. Harvests began to return to normal only at the end of the decade.
56. Munro, "Feeding the Multitudes," 505.
57. RGIA, *fond* 467, *opis'* 4, *delo* 10 *list* 147.
58. Georgi, *Opisanie,* 592–93. Nearly one-fourth of all alcoholic beverages sold in Russia were provided to St. Petersburg. Petrov, *Istoriia Sanktpeterburga,* 730.
59. TsGIA SPb, *fond* 781, *delo* 934, *sviaz'ka* 204 (1790).

60. The use of anthracite and bituminous coal was virtually unknown. Even manufactories and smithies using fire extensively in the manufacturing process burned wood. There was some attempt to introduce charcoal, as is evidenced by an article on the subject in the *Trudy Imperatorskogo vol'nogo ekonomicheskogo obshchestva* (I. G. Leman, "Kak luchshim sposobom zhech' iz drov ugol'e," part 4, 1766: 1–29). But the use of charcoal was not extensive.

61. Hittle, *The Service City,* 169. The law also applied to Moscow, and may have been intended as well to reduce the threat of social unrest from too large concentrations of workers; this is argued in John T. Alexander, "Catherine II, Bubonic Plague, and the Problem of Industry in Moscow," *American Historical Review* 79, no. 3 (June 1974): 637–71.

62. Georgi, *Opisanie,* 320–21; Shchekatov, *Slovar',* 1: 46.

63. RGADA, *fond* 16, *delo* 517, *listy* 3–16.

64. In the last year of her reign, Catherine put the warehouse under the supervision of the vice-governor because of complaints about the continued rising cost of wood.

65. RGADA, *fond* 16, *delo* 477, *listy* 33, 96; Bozherianov, *Nevskii Prospekt,* 2: 203–25.

66. RNB, Manuscripts Division, *fond* Shtelin, Iakov Iakovlevich, no. 28.

67. RGIA, *fond* 1329, *opis'* 2, *delo* 52, *list* 27*ob.* Complete listings of prices in 1763 and 1764 are found in RGADA, *fond* 16, *delo* 477, *listy* 29ff.

68. Storch, *Picture,* 189. Storch seems to be referring to a black market, in which proprietors demanded higher prices than the law allowed for goods in particular demand.

69. TsGIA SPb, *fond* 1731, *opis'* 1, *delo* 16, *listy* 20–23. A "head" of sugar was a sugar loaf, a conically-shaped piece of hard, refined sugar.

70. TsGIA SPb, *fond* 221, *opis'* 2, *delo* 19, *listy* 78–83.

Chapter 6

1. For a discussion of this "prehistory" of St. Petersburg, see Saulo Kepsu, *Pietari ennen Pietaria: Nevansuun vaiheita ennen Pietarin kaupungin perustamista* (Helsinki, 1995).

2. Slightly over 40 percent of urban dwellers registered as *posad* people (prior to the establishment of merchant guilds) made their living from commerce. Only 2 percent participated in international trade. Nearly 2 percent of Russia's towns had no merchants (*torguiushchie*) in them at all. Included in the *posad* population were all residents of *posady* except gentry, ecclesiastics, peasants, and civil servants. Besides merchants, those registered included craftsmen and artisans (15 percent) and unemployed (*zhivushchie v prazdnosti*) (42 percent). These figures are cited in Kashin, ed., *Materialy,* 248–49.

3. Subsistence urbanization, like subsistence agriculture, "connotes a level of living . . . on which [the inhabitants] can barely exist and . . . no surplus [is] exported, sold, or otherwise disposed of . . . to improve the standard of living." Gerald Breese, *Urbanization in Newly Developing Countries* (Englewood Cliffs, NJ: Prentice-Hall, 1966), 5.

4. The largest merchant ships put in at Kronshtadt, fourteen miles west of the city, and sent their wares to market in galleys, which were in extensive use nowhere else in Europe at that time; they were indispensable in St. Petersburg, where they offered the primary means of water transport of goods within the city and were used in the gulf, rivers, and canals alike.

5. This picture of activity is drawn from a mid-century engraving of the docks in RGIA, *fond* 485, *opis'* 2, *delo* 19.

6. Arkhiv SPbF IRI RAN, *fond* 36, *opis'* 1, *delo* 547, *list* 42.

7. Ibid., *fond* 36, *opis'* 1, *delo* 556, *listy* 482–86.

8. They often escaped the notice of contemporary observers because of their dispersion throughout the city. But their importance in the city's economic life is clearly demonstrated by the number of advertisements they placed in *Sanktpeterburgskie vedomosti* and the frequency with which their names appear in registers of real estate.

9. For example, see *Sanktpeterburgskie vedomosti* January 10, 1763, 1.

10. David L. Ransel, "An Eighteenth-Century Russian Merchant Family in Prosperity and Decline," in Jane Burbank and David L. Ransel, eds., *Imperial Russia: New Histories for the Empire* (Bloomington: Indiana University Press, 1998), 256–80.

11. Georgi, *Opisanie,* 206; Storch, *Picture,* 269; Büsching, *Neue Beschreibung,* 633–34; and Shchekatov, *Slovar',* 5: 675.

12. RGADA, *fond* 16, *delo* 497, *listy* 12–225.

13. The workings of *veksel'* law are set forth in Philipp Heinrich Dilthey, *Nachal'nye osnovaniia veksel'nogo prava, a osoblivo rossiiskogo, kupno i shvedskogo, s pribavleniem raznykh rossiiskikh ukazov i s dvumia dissertatsiiami, k onomu prinadlezhashchimi, dlia upotrebleniia v Moskovskom iuridicheskom fakul'tete po udobneishemu sposobu raspolozhennye,* 3rd ed. (Moscow, 1781).

14. Thomson, *Letters,* 287; Parkinson, *A Tour of Russia,* 48–49. Yet one Englishman noted that the "citizens and merchants are not at all intelligent in trade and commerce, nor would they be able to carry on the foreign commerce of their country without the assistance of strangers. . . ." Williams, *Northern Governments,* 3: 307. In the fall of 1762 sworn brackers were instituted in the city to note the exact terms of commercial agreements in sales and deliveries. This apparently was intended more to protect illiterate provincial merchants against unscrupulous foreigners than it was to defend merchants in the capital against those from the interior. The notes written by brackers had full legal power in disputes: Petrov, *Istoriia Sanktpeterburga,* 658.

15. John Richard, *A Tour from London to Petersburgh, and from Thence to Moscow* (Dublin, 1781), 36; Büsching, *Beschreibung,* 633.

16. Storch, *Picture.* 270; Shchekatov, *Slovar',* 5: 675.

17. Further description of these river rafts may be found in George E. Munro, "Feeding the Multitudes," *Jahrbücher für Geschichte Osteuropas* 35, no. 4 (1987): 487; and Robert E. Jones, "Getting the Goods to St. Petersburg," *Slavic Review* 43, no. 3 (Fall 1984): 416.

18. Storch, *Picture,* 265.

19. RGADA, *fond* 16, *delo* 511, *list* 1.

20. RGADA, *fond* 16, *delo* 479, *listy* 36–38.

21. Georgi, *Opisanie,* 140–41.

22. Winter effectively closed down most large-scale commercial activity. Rivers and the gulf remained frozen from November to April. The only way to convey goods was by sledge. Transportation of wares to the interior continued, utilizing frozen rivers and overland routes. Each year three to five merchant ships were forced to winter in St. Petersburg, not having left soon enough to escape the ice.

23. Georgi, *Opisanie,* 140; *Chteniia,* 1880 (part 4), 60. The diplomatic crisis had to do with Catherine's attempting to set up a league of armed neutrality to counterpoise British highhandedness on the seas. See Isabel de Madariaga, *Britain, Russia, and the Armed Neutrality of 1780: Sir James Harris's Mission to St. Petersburg during the American Revolution,* foreword by Samuel Flagg Bemis (New Haven: Yale University Press, 1962).

24. Figures are for 1781, 1794, and 1795. Arkhiv SPbF IRI RAN, *fond* 36, *opis'* 1, *delo* 565, *listy* 6 *ob*.-7, 43, 64. In 1792 and 1793 from the start of the navigational year through July 1 the figures were 40.4 percent and 58.3 percent carrying only ballast, respectively. See *list* 24. In general the Baltic trade was characterized by more freight exiting than entering. Declarations by skippers entering and exiting the Sound in 1795 reveal that 19.3 percent of ships headed for Copenhagen but only 6.2 percent of those exiting the Sound from Copenhagen were laden solely in ballast. Comparative figures for Rostock were 16.7 percent and 6.2 percent, for Lubeck 19.6 percent and 4.8 percent, for Swedish ports 24.6 percent and 3.0 percent, for Prussian ports 68.3 percent and 1.3 percent, for Danzig (Gdansk) 76.5 percent and 0 percent, for Kurland 47.5 percent and 0 percent, and for Russian ports 70.6 percent arriving in ballast but only .5 percent departing that way. See *listy* 70–73.

25. The charges for off-loading were set at half an efimok (62.5 kopecks) per last. Arkhiv SPbF IRI RAN, *fond* 36, *opis'* 1, *delo* 556, *listy* 74–80.

26. The real ruble value of imports and exports through St. Petersburg in selected years (in thousands of rubles) is as follows:

year	export	import	year	export	import
1764	5,585	5,460	1782	11,467	12,204
1768	6,630	6,328	1783*	10,099	11,485
1775	8,300	6,893	1784	12,942	12,172
1776	n.a.	5,257	1785	13,498	10,063
1777	12,960	8,640	1786	13,360	11,776
1779	n.a.	8,857	1787	16,087	15,565
1780	10,941	8,656	1788	n.a.	15,474
1781	12,204	9,582	1789	18,720	15,371

*The figure for 1783 given here differs slightly from that provided by A. R. Vorontsov in note 27.

Sources include Georgi, *Opisanie,* 149; Hermann, *Statistische Schilderung,* 429; Joshua Jepson Oddy, *European Commerce, Shewing New and Secure Channels of Trade With the Continent of Europe; Detailing the Produce, Manufactures and Commerce, of Russia, Prussia, Sweden, Denmark, and Germany.* 2 vols. (Philadelphia, 1807), 2: 128; and Makarov, "Ekonomicheskaia zhizn'," *OIL,* 1: 288.

27. Report to Catherine II by Alexander Vorontsov on behalf of the Commerce Commission, April 8, 1784: Arkhiv SPbF IRI RAN, *fond* 36, *opis'* 1, *delo* 637, *list* 271.

28. Ibid., *list* 277.

29. Oddy, *European Commerce,* 1: 203; Makarov, "Ekonomicheskaia zhizn'," *OIL,* 1: 289.

30. Oddy, *European Commerce,* 1: 115; Richard, *Tour,* 8–9; Hanway, *Historical Account,* 2: 167–68; and *Observations on the Present State of Denmark, Russia and Switzerland, in a Series of Letters* (London, 1784), 146–47.

31. Arkhiv SPbF IRI RAN, *fond* 36, *opis'* 1, *delo* 556, *listy* 467–77. The size of a last varies according to the product measured, but it is generally about two tons. The ships carried 100–150 tons each.

32. Storch, *Picture,* 255–56. In 1769 a list of Russian merchants engaged in international commerce made for the Commerce Commission included only eight men. Nikolai Leonidovich Rubinshtein, "Vneshniaia torgovlia Rossii i russkoe kupechestvo vo vtoroi polovine XVIII v.," *Istoricheskie zapiski* 54 (1955): 354.

33. Peter Henry Bruce, *Memoirs of Peter Henry Bruce, Esq., A Military Officer, In the Services of Prussia, Russia, and Great Britain, Containing an Account of His Travels in Germany, Russia, Tartary, Turkey, and the West Indies, etc.* (London, 1782), 387.

34. Arkhiv SPbF IRI RAN, *fond* 36, *opis'* 1, *delo* 556, *list* 21.

35. N. L. Rubinshtein was the first to make this point. The traditional interpretation holds that foreigners, particularly Englishmen, dominated the trade scene. True, in the 1770s only 40 percent of the total value of imports was registered in the names of Russian merchants. The figure rose to 70 percent by the 1790s, however. Exports, also controlled by foreigners in the 1770s (Russians declared only 10 to 15 percent of export value during that decade), were still in foreign hands by the 1790s, the Russian share having increased to 40 percent. Because the value of exports during the total period exceeded that of imports fully by one-half, it is clear that foreign merchants maintained their overall position of superiority, yet it is equally clear that Russian merchants cut deeply into foreign domination. Foreign-controlled commerce increased in absolute value, but declined in its proportionate share of overseas commerce. Rubinshtein, "Vneshniaia torgovlia," *Istoricheskie zapiski* 54: 348–49. Georgi (published in 1793) lists the following number of exporters: hemp and linen—16 Russians and 14 foreigners; oil and tallow—5 Russians and 3 foreigners; herring—4 Russians and 3 foreigners; tobacco—1 Russian and 2 foreigners; Russia leather—5 Russians and 3 foreigners; horsehair and silk—2 Russians and 1 foreigner; rabbit skins—1 Russian and 2 foreigners. Georgi's evidence supports Rubinshtein's conclusion: Georgi, *Opisanie,* 151.

36. Iosif Mikhailovich Kulisher, *Istoriia russkoi torgovli do deviatnadtsatogo veka vkliuchitel'no* (Petrograd, 1923), 189.

37. See the discussion in Herbert Kaplan, *Russian Overseas Commerce with Great Britain during the Reign of Catherine II* (Philadelphia: American Philosophical Society, 1995), chapter 10. In 1789 the State Council during the war with Sweden toughened the requirements for merchantmen flying the Russian flag because of reports of ships otherwise registered as Russian sailing to Swedish ports under the flags of their skippers' real nationalities. Arkhiv SPbF IRI RAN, *fond* 36, *opis'* 1, *delo* 406, *listy* 156–57.

38. Arkhiv SPbF IRI RAN, *fond* 36, *opis'* 2, *delo* 9, *listy* 51–56.

39. Shapiro, "Zapiski," *Istoricheskii arkhiv* 5 (1950): 256–57.

40. TsGIA SPb, *fond* 781, *opis'* 2, *delo* 680, *listy* 1–2.

41. Although statistics are incomplete, a number of sources suggest this conclusion, among them: RNB, Manuscripts Division, *fond* O.IV.56; RGADA, *fond* 16, *delo* 473; *fond* 294, *opis'* 2, *delo* 79, listy 5–25; and RGIA, *fond* 558, *opis'* 2, *delo* 206, *listy* 125–26, 162.

42. RGADA, *fond* 16, *delo* 479, *listy* 36–38.

43. Ibid., *listy* 31–35.

44. Ibid., *list* 3.

45. Georgi, *Opisanie,* 156; Storch, *Picture,* 271–73. Grigorii Stepanovich Vinskii claimed that merchants charged as high as ten percent per month interest; see his *Moe vremia: Zapiski G. S. Vinskogo,* ed. and intro. P. E. Shchegoleva (St. Petersburg, 1914.), 34.

46. The background of the law is contained in RGIA, *fond* 467, *opis'* 4, *delo* 76, no. 30, *listy* 144–74.

47. Robert Aloys Mooser, *Opéras, intermezzos, ballets, cantates, oratorios joués en Russie durant le XVIIIe siècle* (Geneva: R. Kister, 1955), 75, 124–25. The title of the revival was, "As You Live, So Shall You Be Judged" [*Kak pozhivesh', tak i proslivesh'*].

48. Mikhail Matinskii, *Opera komicheskaia: S.-Peterburgskii gostinyi dvor,* 2nd ed. (Odessa, 1890), 87–89.

49. Storch, *Picture,* 271–73; Pyliaev, *Staryi Peterburg,* 334–35; Petrov, *Istoriia Sanktpeterburga,* 598; Klokman, *Ocherki,* 142–44; Rubinshtein, "Vneshniaia torgovlia," *Istoricheskie zapiski* 54, 351; and RNB, Manuscripts Division, *fond* O.IV.56.

50. TsGIA SPb, *fond* 781, *opis'* 2, *delo* 1014, *list* 1.

51. Bruce, *Memoirs,* 382.

52. Of the 267 British mercantile firms operating in Russia in the course of the eighteenth century, A. V. Demkin identifies ninety-one of them specifically as doing business in St. Petersburg in Catherine's reign. Andrei Vladimirovich Demkin, *Britanskoe kupechestvo v Rossii XVIII veka* (Moscow: Rossiiskaia akademiia nauk, Institut rossiiskoi istorii, 1998).

53. Arkhiv SPbF IRI RAN, *fond* 36, *opis'* 1, *delo* 556, *listy* 394–99*ob.*; 402–08*ob.*

54. Storch, *Picture,* 268–69.

55. Commercial activity by tutors, governesses, and other foreign servants was prohibited in 1756. Petrov, *Istoriia Sanktpeterburga,* 570. *Koshelek,* a satirical journal, created a fictional Frenchman who, though nearly illiterate, posed as a teacher while building up a lucrative business in smuggled goods. The satire undoubtedly resulted from actual cases of that type. Afanas'ev, "Cherty," *Russkii vestnik,* 1857, no. 11 (September): 258–59.

56. *Sanktpeterburgskie vedomosti,* June 21, 1764 (no. 62), supplement.

57. *PSZ* 18, no. 13.219 (December 29, 1768): 787.

58. *PSZ* 22, no. 16.407 (June 28, 1786): 616.

59. Bashutskii, *Panorama,* 2: 159–60.

60. Storch, *Picture,* 226.

61. The laws are contained in *PSZ* 19, no. 13.575: 233–34; and 20, no. 14.481, 395–97.

62. For an introduction to this problem, see Arcadius Kahan, "The Costs of 'Westernization' in Russia: The Gentry and the Economy in the Eighteenth Century," *Slavic Review* 25, no. 1 (March 1966): 40–66.

63. A. Semenov, *Izuchenie istoricheskikh svedenii o rossiiskoi vneshnei torgovle i promyshlennosti s poloviny XVII-go stoletiia po 1858 god* (St. Petersburg, 1859), 38–39; *PSZ* 17, no. 12.735: 951; and RGIA, *fond* 467, *opis'* 4, *delo* 10, *list* 53.

64. Issued September 10, 1789.

65. SPbF IRI RAN Arkhiv, *fond* 36, *opis'* 1, *delo* 556, *listy* 114–15. Two other petitions may be found on *listy* 330–31 and 336–37.

66. Munro, "Feeding the Multitudes," *Jahrbücher für Geschichte Osteuropas* 35 (1987): 500, 502.

67. The ban lasted only for a few days, until Catherine was assured that supply was adequate: *PSZ* 23, no. 17.378 (September 5, 1795): 761.

68. RGADA, *fond* 16, *delo* 479, *listy* 196a, 205–07, 216–32*ob.*

69. *PSZ* 22, no. 16.237 (August 5, 1785): 436–37, is an example of such a law.

70. Bruce, *Memoirs,* 386–87; Büsching, *Beschreibung,* 627–28; Storch, *Picture,* 260–62; Richardson, *Anecdotes,* 261–62; Richard, *Tour,* 24–26; Oddy, *European Commerce,* 1: 43, Marshall, *Travels,* 3: 113; Hermann, *Statistische Schilderung,* 428; Kulisher, *Istoriia russkoi torgovli,* 217–18.

71. Georgi, *Opisanie,* 213–14; Williams, *Northern Governments,* 324–25.

72. Georgi, *Opisanie,* 213–14; Storch, *Picture,* 185–87.

73. Storch, *Picture,* 277–78. Storch's reference to a developed luxury goods industry indicates the extent of industrial response to the tendency toward conspicuous consumption during Catherine's reign. The argument developed here is also based on Bruce, *Memoirs,* 386–87; and Damaze de Raymond, *Tableau historique, géographique, militaire et morale de l'empire de Russie* (Paris, 1812), 413–16.

74. RGADA, *fond* 10, *opis'* 3, *delo* 202.
75. Bruce, *Memoirs,* 383.
76. RGIA, *fond* 758, *opis'* 1, *delo* 3, *list* 16. Interest rates, although agreed upon in advance, were not recorded in the journal.
77. Examples are found in RGIA, *fond* 467, *opis'* 4, *delo* 10, *listy* 160–61; and Vinskii, *Moe vremia,* 31–34.
78. RGADA, *fond* 16, *delo* 482, *listy* 1–5.
79. The third explanation, that a disgruntled worker angry with his merchant employer had set the fire, was no more complimentary to the merchants. RGADA, *fond* 16, *delo* 479, *list* 196a.
80. Aleksandr Nikolaevich Radishchev, *Puteshestvie iz Peterburga v Moskvu* (Moscow-Leningrad, 1961), 40–42.
81. The Amsterdam merchant-banking firm of Hope & Company regularly maintained accounts for several Russian merchants in St. Petersburg, discounting their bills, providing them with shipping insurance, selling shipments on consignment, and carrying out other mercantile services. See my unpublished paper, "Buy Now, Pay Later: Financing Russia's Baltic Trade," delivered at the American Association for the Advancement of Slavic Studies annual meeting in Honolulu, Hawaii, November 18, 1988.
82. Kulisher, *Istoriia russkoi torgovli,* 188.

Chapter 7

1. Mikhail Ivanovich Tugan-Baranovskii devoted only the first seventy-five pages of *Russkaia fabrika v proshlom i nastoiashchem* (Moscow: Moskovskii rabochii, 1922) to the eighteenth century. The more recent two-volume *Istoriia rabochikh Leningrada, 1703–1965,* ed. S. N. Valk, et al. (Leningrad, 1972) gives a similar amount of space to the period. Likewise, Stolpianskii, *210 let,* concentrated far more heavily on the nineteenth century than the eighteenth. A notable exception to this generalization is Makarov, "Ekonomicheskaia zhizn'," *OIL,* 1: 251–93.
2. Kizevetter, *Posadskaia obshchina,* 243, thought that there was little industrial activity at all. Rural manufactories owned by the gentry replaced small merchant manufactories. Ryndziunskii argues that there was industry in the capital city. See his *Gorodskoe grazhdanstvo,* 34. Pokshishevskii agrees, and offers the further qualification that these concerns were small and often short-lived, operated by individual craftsmen. The few large factories were state-owned. "Territorial'noe formirovanie," *Voprosy geografii,* Sbornik 20 (1950): 136. Evgenii Viktorovich Tarle argued that manufacturing was at least as advanced in Russia as in France; see "Byla li ekaterininskaia Rossiia ekonomicheski otstaloiu stranoiu?" in his *Zapad i Rossiia: Stat'i i dokumenty iz istorii XVIII–XX vv.* (Petrograd, 1918), 122–49. In addition there is a long-standing debate among Soviet historians over whether such industrial production as existed was basically capitalist or feudal in its organization; see the comments by A. G. Man'kov in N. F. Nosov et al., eds., *Remeslo i manufaktura v Rossii, Finliandii, Pribaltike* (Leningrad, 1975), 147; and the introduction to Gerasim Sergeevich Isaev, *Rol' tekstil'noi promyshlennosti v genezise i razvitii kapitalizma v Rossii, 1760–1860* (Leningrad, 1970), 9–24. The debate among Soviet historians is summarized by David M. Griffiths in his introduction to Hugh D. Hudson, Jr., *The Rise of the Demidov Family and the Russian Iron Industry in the Eighteenth Century* (Newtonville, MA: Oriental Research Partners, 1986), 1–26.

3. Variant definitions can be found in M. D. Chulkov, *Istoricheskoe opisanie rossiiskoi kommertsii,* 5: 10–11; Kashin, *Materialy po istorii krest'ianskoi promyshlennosti,* 247; and Fedor Sukin, vice-president of the Manufactures College during part of Catherine's reign, quoted in Polianskii, *Gorodskoe remeslo,* 159.

4. RNB, Manuscripts Department, *fond* F.II.146, *list* 339*ob.*

5. Quoted in Polianskii, *Gorodskoe remeslo,* 159.

6. For example, in 1774 five hatmakers brought a petition to the Manufactures College alleging that thirteen manufacturers of hats had not registered with the College and therefore were escaping taxation. They also, of course, fail to appear on lists of hat factory owners compiled by the College the year before. Dmitrii Baburin, *Ocherki po istorii Manufaktur-kollegii* (Moscow, 1939), 149–50. The absence of comprehensive data has forced historians to limit the scope of their studies. Thus N. N. Dmitriev, *Pervye russkie sitsenabivnye manufaktury XVIII veka* (Moscow-Leningrad, 1935), examines in detail a minute topic for which materials do exist. Similar works include G. S. Isaev, *Rol' tekstil'noi promyshlennosti* and Elena Ivanovna Zaozerskaia, *Rabochaia sila i klassovaia bor'ba na tekstil'nykh manufakturakh v 20–60 gg. XVIII veka* (Moscow, 1960). More generalized works are based on representative information, not complete data. Such studies include Polianskii, *Gorodskoe remeslo;* Stolpianskii, *210 let;* and L. N. Semenova, *Rabochie Peterburga v pervoi polovine XVIII veka.*

7. The work of the Manufactures College is examined in Baburin, *Ocherki.*

8. For 1775, E. I. Indova, "O rossiiskikh manufakturakh vtoroi poloviny XVIII v.," in A. L. Narochnitskii et al., eds., *Istoricheskaia geografiia Rossii XII-nachala XX v. Sbornik statei k 70–letiiu L. G. Beskrovnogo* (Moscow, 1975), 326–45, a list of factories under the Manufactures College in 1775; for 1779, RGADA, *fond* 294, *opis'* 2, *delo* 79, *listy* 5*ob.*-25.

9. Separate factories turned out artillery, ships and boats, gunpowder and ammunition, rope and cable, firearms, and sail and canvas. Georgi, *Opisanie,* 157–59; Klokman, *Sotsial'no-ekonomicheskaia istoriia,* 248–49; Makarov, "Ekonomicheskaia zhizn'," *OIL,* 1: 262, 264–75.

10. Shchekatov, *Slovar',* 5: 683–84; and RGADA, *fond* 19, *delo* 403, *list* 1.

11. Pokshishevskii, "Territorial'noe formirovanie," *Voprosy geografii,* sbornik 20, 139; Georgi, *Opisanie,* 100–101, 159–61; and Makarov, "Ekonomicheskaia zhizn'," *OIL,* 1: 262, 264–75.

12. Such enterprises were established long before this period even in St. Petersburg; elsewhere in Russia they existed long before the time of Peter I.

13. Georgi, *Opisanie,* 159–62; Chulkov, *Istoricheskoe opisanie rossiiskoi kommertsii,* 6, part 3, 663–97; RGADA, *fond* 294, *opis'* 2, *delo* 79, *listy* 5–25; *delo* 71, *listy* 1–17.

14. Georgi, *Opisanie,* 158–62; RGADA, *fond* 294, *opis'* 2, *delo* 79, *listy* 5–25.

15. Altogether more than fifteen million bricks were baked annually in St. Petersburg kilns. Klokman, *Sotsial'no-ekonomicheskaia istoriia,* 248–49; Stolpianskii, *210 let,* 15–17.

16. *PSZ* 22, no. 15.932 (February 21, 1784): 26–37; Mansurov, *Okhtenskie stroeniia,* 49–50. Georgi records (*Opisanie,* 114) that the shipyard was state-subsidized, undoubtedly to ensure economic viability.

17. One such shipyard is documented in David M. Griffiths, "American Commercial Diplomacy in Russia, 1780–1783," *William and Mary Quarterly,* 3rd series, 27, no. 3 (July 1970): 387. Very likely there were others, small ones, records of which have not survived.

18. This particular factory had great significance for industrial development in St. Petersburg, serving as prototype for the establishment of the machine-building industry there. V. K. Iatsunskii, "Rol' Peterburga," *Voprosy istorii,* 1954, no. 9 (September): 99–100.

19. Pokshishevskii, "Territorial'noe formirovanie, *Voprosy geografii,* sbornik 20, 139.

20. Petr Mikhailovich Maikov, *Ivan Ivanovich Betskoi: Opyt' ego biografii* (St. Petersburg, 1904), 95–96; RGIA, *fond* 467, *opis'* 4, *delo* 48, no. 29, *listy* 206–07; and Makarov, "Ekonomicheskaia zhizn'," *OIL,* 1: 260. At least one factory owner argued that his factory was not polluting the Neva, but he was forced to relocate along with the others. RGADA, *fond* 294, *opis'* 2, *delo* 164.

21. Stolpianskii, *210 let,* 62–63. Catherine II reconfirmed Elizabeth's prohibition in an edict of November 23, 1762, but lack of enforcement continued. See the discussion in Polianskii, *Gorodskoe remeslo,* 196–98. In 1767 the instruction to the city's delegate to the Legislative Commission asked him to secure the removal of the glass factory, still located in the heart of the city at that time. *Sbornik IRIO* 107 (1900): 215.

22. The state-owned rope factory was moved by the Admiralty to Kronshtadt in 1786 because part of its building was needed for a new grain warehouse. Other parts of the building were razed and replaced by housing. RGADA, *fond* 16, *delo* 502, *list* 33.

23. TsGIA SPb, *fond* 781, opis' 2, *delo* 550.

24. Sources for the preceding discussion include: RGADA, *fond* 19, *delo* 403; *fond* 294, *opis'* 2, *delo* 16, *listy* 1–19; *delo* 49, *listy* 5–101, 162–73, 179, 213, 263, 308, 367, 405, 448, 493, 536; *delo* 71, *listy* 1–17: *delo* 79, *listy* 5–25; RGIA, *fond* 467, *opis'* 4, *delo* 48, no. 29, *listy* 206–07; K. K. Zlobin, ed., "Vedomost' sostoiashchim v S.-Peterburge fabrikam, manufakturam i zavodam 1794 goda sentiabria dnia, *Sbornik IRIO* 1 (1867): 352–61; Indova, "O rossiiskikh manufakturakh," 326–45; Bogdanov, *Opisanie.* 126–27, 129–33; Chulkov, *Opisanie kommertsii,* 6, part 3, 663–97: Georgi, *Opisanie,* 105, 159–62, 669–70; Klokman, *Ocherki,* 143: Kurbatov, *Peterburg,* 552; Makarov, "Ekonomicheskaia zhizn'," *OIL,* 1: 259–63, 272–73; Kashin, *Materialy,* 617–21; *PSZ* 16, no. 12.013 (January 13, 1764): 494–95; Shchekatov, *Slovar',* 1: 1225–26; 5: 683–89; Stolpianskii, *210 let,* 17–24, 29–30, 31, 34, 36; Stolpianskii, "Iz istorii proizvodstv v S. Peterburge za XVIII vek i pervuiu chetvert' XIX veka," *Arkhiv istorii truda v Rossii,* bk. 2 (1921): 89.

25. Indova, "O rossiiskikh manufakturakh," 326–45; Zlobin, "Vedomost'," *Sbornik IRIO* 1 (1867): 352–61; and RGADA, *fond* 294, *opis'* 2, *delo* 79, *listy* 5*ob.*-25.

26. *Sbornik IRIO* 107 (1900): 222–23.

27. Westhof, Meux, and Stephens are all identified in Anthony Cross, *By the Banks of the Neva,* 67, 69.

28. A. V. Safonova, "Polozhenie trudiashchikhsia," *Uchenye zapiski vologodskogo gosudarstvennogo pedagogicheskogo instituta* 14 (1954): 7.

29. Ibid.

30. In all locations the Admiralty had as many as 10,000 workers at a time. A. A. Preobrazhenskii, "Razvitie manufaktury v Rossii (konets XVII - pervaia polovina XVIII vv.)," in N. E. Nosov et al., eds., *Remeslo i manufaktura v Rossii, Finliandii, Pribaltike* (Leningrad, 1975), 53.

31. V. M. Paneiakh, "Masterovye i rabotnye liudi vo vtoroi polovine XVIII veka," in S. N. Valk et al., eds., *Istoriia rabochikh Leningrada, 1703–1965,* 2 vols. (Leningrad, 1972); vol. 1, *1703–fevral' 1917,* 47–48.

32. Indova, "O rossiiskikh manufakturakh," 326–45.

33. The lowest ratio existed in Count Sergei Pavlovich Iaguzhinskii's silk stocking factory, where the capital was reported at 10,325 rubles, or 95.60 rubles for each of the workers. Next lowest were the waxed paper and wallpaper factories of Ivan Chirkin, with a capital of 10,000 rubles and nine workers, or 111.11 rubles per worker. All the other factories known to have employed serfs had a ratio of more than 200 rubles per worker, often substantially higher. Indova, "O rossiiskikh manufakturakh," 326–45.

34. TsGIA SPb, *fond* 781, *opis'* 2, *delo* 550.

35. The government was also interested in keeping brick prices high enough that the state-run kilns could compete. RGADA, *fond* 16, *delo* 484, *list* 2; RGIA, *fond* 467, *opis'* 4, *delo* 76, no. 45, *listy* 208–09.

36. A. Prussak, "Petrovskaia instrumental'naia izba v Peterburge," *Sovetskaia meditsina* 6 (1948): 38. When Russian goods did exhibit high quality, the fact was specially noted. Thus Georgi (*Opisanie,* 114) spoke highly of tapestries turned out in the state-owned factory.

37. In the glass factory owned by Prince Potemkin, manager Garnovskii reported that the German workers were better than any Russians. He wanted them to train Russian blowers. Mikhail Garnovskii, "Zapiski," *Russkaia starina* 16 (1876): 434–35.

38. Paneiakh, "Masterovye i rabotnye liudi," 47.

39. RGADA, *fond* 19, *delo* 403.

40. These reports are housed in RGIA, *fond* 1329, *dela* 58189, 58190, 58195, 58196, 58197, 58201, 58206, 58213, and 58214.

41. Petr Stepanovich Kolotov, *Deianiia Ekateriny II, Imperatritsy i samoderzhitsy vserossiiskoi,* 6 vols. (St. Petersburg, 1811).

42. Ibid., 6: 217.

43. To clock makers Sando (Sandome?) and Basselier and to the manufacturer of clothing accessories Jean-Pierre Ador. Indova, "O rossiiskikh manufakturakh," 342–43. Roger Bartlett has discovered numerous cases of foreigners coming to St. Petersburg who requested financial aid and loans from the state to help them set up factories or workshops, most of which were denied. Roger P. Bartlett, *Human Capital: The Settlement of Foreigners in Russia, 1762–1804* (Cambridge, 1979), 158ff.

44. In one open-and-shut case, Christian Lehman tried to have the cotton-spinning factories of Brauer and Miller expelled from the city, without success. RNB, Manuscripts Department, Arkhiv G. R. Derzhavina, vol. 38, *listy* 224–25.

45. An excellent example is K. A. Petroev's attempt to obtain a shop for selling his leather goods. RGADA, *fond* 248, *delo* 5570, *list* 243.

46. Hittle, *The Service City,* 127.

47. Polianskii, *Gorodskoe remeslo,* 134–35.

48. Ibid., 142–43.

49. Pokshishevskii, "Territorial'noe formirovanie," 136; Polianskii, *Gorodskoe remeslo,* 134–36; Makarov, "Ekonomicheskaia zhizn'," *OIL,* 1: 280–81; TsGIA SPb, *fond* 221, *opis'* 1, *delo* 115, *listy* 1–4; RGADA, *fond* 291, *delo* 12005.

50. See Bartlett, *Human Capital.*

51. This practice is illustrated in RGADA, *fond* 248, *delo* 3380, *listy* 1–23, 42.

52. *PSZ* 19, no. 13.421 (March 7, 1770): 18–19. The original is in RGIA, *fond* 1329, *opis'* 2, *delo* 62, no. 7, *list* 9.

53. Polianskii, *Gorodskoe remeslo,* 142–43.

54. RGADA, *fond* 19, *delo* 40, *listy* 84–86.

55. RGIA, *fond* 1329, *opis'* 2, *delo* 62, no. 7, *list* 9 contains the order.

56. Catherine's interest in creating a stronger urban artisan estate and various projects to do so are discussed in David M. Griffiths, "Eighteenth-Century Perceptions of Backwardness: Projects for the Creation of a Third Estate in Catherinian Russia," *Canadian-American Slavic Studies* 13 (1979): 452–72.

57. Georgi, *Opisanie,* 168.

58. *Sbornik IRIO* 107 (1900): 216–17. This request was technically granted with the issuance of a regulation for artisans as a section of the Charter to the Towns. The concern over quality appeared in a second article of the *nakaz* also, in the request that all rebuilt houses be inspected to ensure that the work met certain standards.

59. See, for example, RGIA, *fond* 470, *delo* 34.

60. Edict of April 17, 1767, cited in V. A. Kondrat'eva and V. I. Nevzorov, eds., *Iz istorii fabrik i zavodov Moskvy i moskovskoi gubernii (konets XVIII-nachalo XX v.): Obzor dokumentov* (Moscow, 1968), 7.

61. Polianskii, *Gorodskoe remeslo,* 145–46.

62. The Artisan Regulation made up Article 123 (with 117 subarticles) of the Charter to the Towns. *PSZ* 22, no. 16.188 (April 21, 1785): 369–79. The regulation guaranteed the work of registered craftsmen, but was unable to control the work of unregistered artisans, *posad* people and peasants living in the city temporarily. These part-time artisans undoubtedly created many of the problems in behavior and quality of work.

63. An English translation of the Artisan Regulation is available in Griffiths and Munro, trans. and eds., *Catherine the Great's Charters of 1785,* 39–53.

64. RNB, Manuscripts Department, *fond* F.II.146, *listy* 325–90.

65. I could only decipher the signatures of nine of the men, of whom I could identify only two: Ivan Dolgoi (or Dolgov), who served on the St. Petersburg *guberniia* magistracy from 1780–83 and owned a glass factory; and Petr Rogovikov (d. 1797), son of the famous merchant Semen Rogovikov and owner during this period of a passementerie factory in Foundry district. The others were Dmitrii Nikonov, Semen Klevtsov, Martyn Eizerman, Stepan Elizarev, Grigorii Iakimovich Demidov, Andrei Salinkov, and Il'ia Ivanovich Aleksiev(?).

66. The complete list: bookbinders, coopers, lacquerers, copper-beaters, copper-pot makers, smithies, makers of rough cast-iron pots and dishes, weavers, spinners, thread makers, tobacconers, carriage makers, joiners, ceramicists, glass and brick makers, saddlers, printers, chandlers, fensterers, simple potters, bast-shoemakers, cobblers, tailors, furriers, other cloth makers, bone-smiths, metalworkers who simply beat their products to shape them (without using heat), glovers, barbers, metal stampers, cooks, sailors, fruit and vegetable gardeners, brewers, bakers, bartenders, and dyers.

67. RNB, Manuscripts Department, *fond* F.II.146, *listy* 335–90.

68. Chulkov, *Istoricheskoe opisanie rossiiskoi kommertsii,* vol. 6, part 3, 699–701. See also Storch, *Picture,* 277–88.

69. Safonova, "Polozhenie trudiashchikhsia," *Uchenye zapiski vologodskogo gosudarstvennogo pedagogicheskogo instituta* 14: 16.

70. Pokshishevskii, "Territorial'noe formirovanie," *Voprosy geografii,* sbornik 20, 126, 128; and S. I. Kolotilova, "Sotsial'nyi sostav rabotnikov chastnovladel'cheskoi promyshlennosti Peterburga i Peterburgskoi gubernii v 1750–1770–kh godakh," *Uchenye zapiski Pskovskogo gosudarstvennogo pedagogicheskogo instituta, Kafedra istorii,* vypusk 23 (1964), 43–54.

71. Paneiakh, "Masterovye i rabotnye liudi," *Istoriia rabochikh Leningrada,* 1: 54–55; Kolotilova, "Sotsial'nyi sostav," 46–48.

72. Paneiakh, "Masterovye i rabotnye liudi," *Istoriia rabochikh Leningrada,* 1: 54–55.

73. Ibid., 48–50.

74. Makarov, "Ekonomicheskaia zhizn'," *OIL,* 1: 258–73.

75. The complexities of the interlocking "capitalist" and "feudal" modes of labor organization are raised by L. N. Semenova and A. G. Man'kov, among others, in the symposium of Finnish and Soviet historians held in Leningrad in 1972. See the discussion in N. E. Nosov et al., eds., *Remeslo i manufaktura,* 142–43, 147–49.

76. Paneiakh, "Masterovye i rabotnye liudi," *Istoriia rabochikh Leningrada,* 1: 66.

77. Ibid., 57–59; Kolotilova, "Sotsial'nyi sostav," 46–48.

78. Dmitriev, *Sitsenabivnye manufaktury,* 135.

79. Paneiakh, "Masterovye i rabotnye liudi," *Istoriia rabochikh Leningrada,* 1: 56.

80. Kolotilova, "Sotsial'nyi sostav," 49.

81. Paneiakh, "Masterovye i rabotnye liudi," *Istoriia rabochikh Leningrada,* 1: 56.

82. Safonova, "Polozhenie trudiashchikhsia," *Uchenye zapiski vologodskogo gosudarstvennogo pedagogicheskogo instituta* 14: 16.

83. Georgi, *Opisanie,* 312; Stolpianskii, *210 let,* 66; Kochin, "Naselenie," *OIL,* 1: 300. All these aspects of apprenticeship had of course been practiced in western Europe for years.

84. RNB, Manuscripts Department, *fond* NSRK 1947.207 F. Poorly paid workers did often receive housing at the factory as additional compensation. See Stolpianskii, *210 let,* 34; and Kochin, "Naselenie," *OIL,* 1: 301, 303–04.

85. Those advertising their abilities in *Sanktpeterburgskie vedomosti* rarely had to place advertisements more than once. On the other hand, those offering to sell unskilled serfs were forced to run the same announcement over and over again; see, for example, the issues of *Sanktpeterburgskie vedomosti* for early 1793, beginning with January 7.

86. RGADA, *fond* 248, *delo* 3380, *listy* 27a–31.

87. Kopanev, *Naselenie Peterburga,* 80.

88. Bashutskii, *Panorama,* 2: 112–13; Pavel Grigor'evich Liubomirov, *Ocherki po istorii russkoi promyshlennosti: XVII, XVIII i nachalo XIX veka,* ed. S. G. Strumilin (Moscow, 1947), 101.

89. Safonova, "Polozhenie trudiashchikhsia," *Uchenye zapiski vologodskogo gosudarstvennogo pedagogicheskogo instituta* 14: 16.

90. Paneiakh, "Masterovye i rabotnye liudi," *Istoriia rabochikh Leningrada,* 1: 67–68.

91. Safonova, "Polozhenie trudiashchikhsia," *Uchenye zapiski vologodskogo gosudarstvennogo pedagogicheskogo instituta* 14: 24–28. Runaways often turned to crime if honest labor could not be found: specific instances are cited in *Materialy,* 28–40.

92. See, for example, RGIA, *fond* 467, *opis'* 4, *delo* 10, *listy* 67, 101; *fond* 1329, *opis'* 2, *delo* 54, no. 77, *list* 121.

93. Paneiakh, "Masterovye i rabotnye liudi," *Istoriia rabochikh Leningrada,* 1: 70.

94. Hartley, "The Implementation of the Laws," 171, 180–81.

95. Khrapovitskii, *Pamiatnye zapiski,* 35–36, 41; Garnovskii, "Zapiski," *Russkaia starina* 15 (1876): 237–38; Bozherianov, *Nevskii prospekt,* 2: 279–80.

96. Examples are found in RGIA, *fond* 467, *opis'* 4, *delo* 48, *listy* 30–31; and *Materialy,* 28–40.

97. Storch, *Picture,* 190–91; Shchekatov, *Slovar',* 5: 654–55, 674.

98. Storch, *Picture,* 190–91; RGADA, *fond* 248, *delo* 5570, *list* 480; RGIA, *fond* 467, *delo* 664, *listy* 28, 29, 32; *fond* 758, *opis'* 1, *delo* 1, *listy* 12, 14, 15, 16, 19, 22, contain contracts of this nature.

99. RGADA, *fond* 16, *delo* 494.

100. N. A. Rozhkov, *Gorod i derevnia v russkoi istorii (kratkii ocherk ekonomicheskoi istorii Rossii),* 7th ed. (Petrograd, 1923), 97.

Chapter 8

1. Catherine II to Frau Bielcke, July 13, 1770, in *Sbornik IRIO* 13 (1874): 23.

2. General sources for the discussion in this chapter include RNB, Manuscripts Department, *fond* 40, nos. 74–75, 78, 80, 82–83, 107, 111, and 437–39, which consist of maps dating from 1777 and 1796; RGIA, *fond* 1293, *opis'* 167, *delo* 5; and Shchekatov, *Slovar',* 5: 55–57.

3. Shchekatov, *Slovar'*, 5: 630.

4. Even in the relatively undeveloped areas inside the city ditch, one could find buildings irregularly and at intervals, despite the absence of regular construction. Storch, *Picture*, 13–14.

5. Georgel, *Voyage*, 177.

6. Mikhail Ivanovich Pyliaev, *Zabytoe proshloe okrestnostei Peterburga* (St. Petersburg, 1889), 117. See also Eric Amburger, *Ingermanland: Eine junge Provinz Russlands im Wirkungsbereich der Reszidenz und Weltstadt St. Petersburg-Leningrad*, 2 vols. (Köln, 1980), 2: 924–26.

7. RGIA, *fond* 1399, *opis'* 1, *delo* 160, *list* 6.

8. Ibid.; Amburger, *Ingermanland*, 2: 927.

9. Storch, *Picture*, 53–54, says that the island offered at once "forest and morass, village and hamlet, town and residence." See map 3 at front of book.

10. The order is found in RGIA, *fond* 467, *opis'* 3/5, *delo* 2, *list* 1. Construction did not actually begin until 1764.

11. Each section took about two years to complete. Actual costs are difficult to determine, but it would seem that about one hundred rubles were expended for each linear foot of embankment. The project was extremely expensive, but it must be remembered that no additional work was needed to shore up banks for many years. Money for the task came from the state treasury. Details are available in RGADA, *fond* 16, *delo* 485a.

12. RGADA, *fond* 248, *delo* 5693, *listy* 200–202; Pushkarev, *Opisanie*, 93–94. The burst of energy in 1780 that supplied the impetus to complete the Catherine Canal project was applied to the Fontanka too. Construction of its banks in granite began the same year and was completed by 1789.

13. Bunin, *Istoriia gradostroitel'nogo iskusstva*, 137–38; Pushkarev, *Opisanie*, 93–94; and Shkvarikov, *Ocherk istorii planirovki*, 134, all claim the Moika was quayed with granite. Storch asserts that in the 1790s there were still wooden pilings along it and it was choked with mud. Storch, *Picture*, 20–22. See also "Moika," in Shaumian, ed., *Leningrad: Entsiklopedicheskii spravochnik*, 611.

14. Shkvarikov, *Ocherk istorii planirovki*, 132ff., discusses this point lucidly.

15. A plan for the construction of several such canals is in RGADA, *fond* 248, *delo* 5570, *list* 1.

16. Pushkarev, *Opisanie*, 96, 99, 100. The two still standing are Kalinkin and Obukhov (now Lomonosov) bridges.

17. Instead of repairing the bridge, a small sum of money was provided in 1777 to pave the bank of the canal as far as the next bridge so that people could at least go around without becoming mired in mud: RGADA, *fond* 248, *delo* 5570, *list* 205*ob*.

18. Georgii Kniazev, "Dom akademikov," *Belye nochi: Ocherki, zarisovki, dokumenty, vospominaniia*, no. 2 (1972): 82–83.

19. Luppov, "Gorodskoe upravlenie," *OIL*, 1: 362; *PSZ* 16, no. 12.038: 530–31; J. Cooke, engraver, "Plan of the City of St. Petersburg, the Imperial Residence" (London, 1801).

20. Andrei Timofeevich Bolotov, *Pamiatnik pretekshikh vremen, ili kratkie istoricheskie zapiski o byvshikh proizshestviiakh i o nosivshikhsia v narode slukhakh* (Moscow, 1875), 39.

21. Bashutskii, *Panorama*, 2: 102; B. Vasil'ev, "K istorii planirovki Peterburga vo vtoroi polovine XVIII veka," *Arkhitekturnoe nasledstvo*, no. 4 (1953): 24.

22. Kurganov's own house on Sixteenth Line burned, taking with it all his wealth and labors accumulated over thirty years. Iurii Stennik, "Entsiklopediia vsiakoi mudrosti," *Belye nochi*, no. 4 (1975): 363. This fire was also described in *Sanktpeter-*

burgskie vedomosti, May 27, 1771, 1; other major conflagrations are enumerated in Bashutskii, *Panorama,* 3: 184–90, and Pyliaev, *Staryi Peterburg,* 92.

23. Efimenko, "K istorii zemleustroistva," *Zhurnal ministerstva narodnogo prosveshcheniia,* no. 12 (1914): 286–87; Luppov, "Gorodskoe upravlenie," *OIL,* 1: 379; Shkvarikov, *Ocherk istorii planirovki,* 82–83.

24. RNB, Manuscripts Department, OLDP.0.XXXVI ("Plan S. Peterburga"), lists all canals, rivers, streets, bridges, churches, administrative districts, and important state buildings in the city in the years 1762, 1777, and 1796.

25. In the first half of Catherine's reign, for example, Moscow Side more than tripled in size; its new districts were Moscow, Narva, and Karetnaia: Gegello and Piliavskii, "Arkhitektura," *OIL,* 1: 349.

26. See Cooke, "Plan of St. Petersburg;" Georgi, *Opisanie,* 123–24; Pushkarev, *Opisanie,* 77, 93; Storch, *Picture,* 57.

27. RGIA, *fond* 466, *opis'* 1, *delo* 113, no. 39; and Vasil'ev, "K istorii planirovki," *Arkhitekturnoe nasledstvo,* no. 4, 24. Government efforts to reduce the size of large estates in the city are discussed in chapter 3.

28. The lack of such legislation had not prevented merchants from circumventing the law in earlier years; this pressure to make *de jure* conform to *de facto* was another factor behind the enactment of the edict. According to the law, merchants were still not to keep the lands expressly for themselves, but "for the general use of the city." *PSZ* 21, no. 15.848. Merchants could follow the letter of the law, of course, and at the same time utilize the land more specifically for their own purposes. See Klokman, *Sotsial'no-ekonomicheskaia istoriia,* 61.

29. Ministerstvo vnutrennikh del, *Statisticheskie svedeniia,* xxxviii–xxxix.

30. Storch, *Picture,* 53–54; Thomson, *Letters,* 229.

31. Storch, *Picture,* 29, 44, 45.

32. Ibid., 44.

33. Shchekatov, *Slovar',* 1: 51–53.

34. Storch, *Picture,* 47.

35. The wharf at Smolnyi is depicted in a watercolor painting by F. K. Neelov, done in 1803, entitled, "Vid tavricheskogo dvortsa so storony Nevy" [View of the Tauride Palace from the Neva] hanging in the State Hermitage in St. Petersburg.

36. *PSZ* 21, no. 15.451 (June 28, 1782): 616.

37. RGIA, *fond* 1293, *opis'* 167, *delo* 5; Shchekatov, *Slovar',* 1: 38.

38. *PSZ* 18, no. 12.883 (April 26, 1767): 117; Georgi, *Opisanie,* 100–101; Makarov, "Ekonomicheskaia zhizn'," *OIL,* 1: 272–73.

39. RGIA, *fond* 467, *opis'* 4, *delo* 48, no. 29, *listy* 206–07; RGADA, *fond* 16, *delo* 493.

40. I. F. Rybakov, "Nekotorye voprosy genezisa kapitalisticheskogo goroda v Rossii," *Voprosy genezisa kapitalizma v Rossii,* ed. Vladimir Vasil'evich Mavrodin (Leningrad, 1960), 230. Although describing outlying areas in "the majority of towns at the end of the eighteenth century," Rybakov's comments apply to sections of St. Petersburg with accuracy. Sections of Vyborg Side fitted best into this description. See also Storch, *Picture,* 57.

41. Efimenko, "K istorii zemleustroistva," *Zhurnal ministerstva narodnogo prosveshcheniia,* 12: 304–06.

42. Mansurov, *Okhtenskie stroeniia,* 10.

43. RGADA, *fond* 16, *delo* 504, *chast'* 1, *list* 55.

44. RGADA, *fond* 16, *delo* 529, *list* 18.

45. For a particularly interesting argument that Russia's wooden towns were significantly less "urban" than Western Europe's masonry cities, see Otto Brunner, *Neue*

Wege der Verfassungs- und Sozialgeschichte, 2nd enlarged ed. (Göttingen: Vandenhoeck & Ruprecht, 1968), chapter 12, "Europäisches und russisches Bürgertum."

46. RNB, Manuscripts Department, *fond* 40, no. 83, *list* 2.

47. RGADA, *fond* 16, *delo* 516; RGIA, *fond* 1329, *opis'* 2, *delo* 104, no. 38.

48. Georgi, *Opisanie,* 173; Shchekatov, *Slovar',* 5: 630; Bashutskii, *Panorama,* 2: 103–04; and Bozherianov, *Nevskii prospekt,* 2: 228.

49. RNB, Prints/Engravings Department, "Panoramic View of St. Petersburg, Dedicated by Permission to His Imperial Majesty Alexander 1st, by His Much Obliged Humble Servant, J. A. Atkinson," 1801, plate 3.

50. Pushkarev, *Opisanie,* 93.

51. A *sazhen'* was equal to seven feet, so a square *sazhen'* was forty-nine square feet.

52. Unfortunately the sources do not reveal the disposition of the suit: RGADA, *fond* 248, *delo* 5693, *listy* 49–95.

53. Pushkarev, *Opisanie,* 93; RGIA, *fond* 1329, *opis'* 2, *delo* 104, no. 25. In 1793, a resident of Seventh Line on Vasil'evskii Island offered for sale a cow with calf, maintained at that address. *Sanktpeterburgskie vedomosti,* February 8, 1793, 225.

54. The original owner had five years after the enactment of the law (1766) to erect buildings. RGADA, *fond* 248, *delo* 5693; *PSZ* 17, no. 12.497: 364–65.

55. RGADA, *fond* 248, *delo* 5693, *listy* 461–97.

56. The story of the planning and construction of the monument is told in Alexander M. Schenker, *The Bronze Horseman: Falconet's Monument to Peter the Great* (New Haven: Yale University Press, 2003).

57. Stolpianskii, "Bibliografiia 'Sankt-Piter-Burkha'," manuscript, library of the State Museum of the History of the City of St. Petersburg. Stolpianskii argues specifically against speaking about "Petrine style" or the "Petersburg of Peter"; his comments also pertain to Catherinian St. Petersburg.

58. RNB, Manuscripts Department, OLDP.0.XXXVI; Bunin, *Istoriia gradostroitel'nogo iskusstva,* 108.

59. *PSZ* 17, no. 12.324 (February 24, 1765): 21–22; no. 12.546 (January 19, 1766): 531–34; 18, no. 12.883 (April 26, 1767): 115–18. On St. Petersburg Side wooden structures were permitted in the region of the Petropavlovsk Fortress. All the provisions were again stated for reconstruction of Vasil'evskii Island after the great fire there in 1771: *PSZ* 19, no. 13.631 (July 26, 1771): 292.

60. *PSZ* 17, no. 12.324 (February 24, 1765): 21–22; no. 12.546 (January 19, 1766): 531–34; no. 12.629 (April 27, 1766): 668–69. Vasil'ev, "K istorii planirovki," *Arkhitekturnoe nasledstvo,* no. 4, 24. Only the plan for First Admiralty detailed the mechanism to guarantee enforcement of the building code. Architects were to work with the people living in the area; together they were to draw up plans street by street to determine the external facade. Only the chief of police could grant revisions of accepted blueprints. The internal construction of houses was left up to owners, as well as minor external adornments.

61. RNB, Manuscripts Department, Ermitazhnoe sobranie, no. 286; Vasil'ev, "K istorii," *Arkhitekturnoe nasledstvo,* no. 4, 24.

62. Lukomskii, *Staryi Peterburg: Progulki po starinnym kvartalam,* 2nd ed. (Petrograd, n.d.), 37.

63. RGIA, *fond* 466, *opis'* 1, *delo* 184, *list* 37; *fond* 1329, *opis'* 2, *delo* 62, nos. 27, 28; Shchekatov, *Slovar',* 5: 654.

64. It was the weather that wrought such havoc with pavement. First cobblestones were tried, but the next spring or autumn rains loosened them up. Stone squares were tried next, with a foundation and cement to ensure durability. They too were unsuccessful. Other attempts involved wheel tracks of granite, wide slabs of stone,

and wooden planks. Each was short-lived. Not until the nineteenth century was a relatively permanent form of pavement found in the macadam surface. Pushkarev, *Opisanie,* 83–84; Shchekatov, *Slovar',* 5: 655.

65. *Sanktpeterburgskii vestnik,* February 1778, "O ochishchenii vozdukha v gorodakh i domakh," 116–19. An example of the second type of article was a short note by a man named Peken appearing in *Trudy Imperatorskogo vol'nogo ekonomicheskogo obshchestva* 1 (1765): part 4.

66. RGADA, *fond* 16, *delo* 479, *listy* 201–201*ob.*

67. RGIA, *fond* 470, *opis'* 124/558, *delo* 4, *list* 15.

68. Bolotov, *Zhizn',* 4: 651.

69. RGADA, *fond* 17, *delo* 108. The letter was signed simply, "Robert."

70. Lukomskii, *Progulki,* 18, 29; Ditiatin, "Russkii doreformennyi gorod," *Russkaia mysl',* 5 (1884), no. 5: 17; Vissarion Grigor'evich Belinskii, "Peterburg i Moskva," *Fiziologiia Peterburga, sostavlennaia iz trudov russkikh literatorov,* ed. Nikolai Alekseevich Nekrasov (St. Petersburg, 1845), 22–99; Egorov, *Architectural Planning;* and W. Bruce Lincoln, *Sunlight at Midnight: St. Petersburg and the Rise of Modern Russia* (New York: Basic Books, 2000).

Chapter 9

1. Contemporaries familiar with port cities elsewhere commented on the volume of trade in St. Petersburg. Büsching, *Neue Beschreibung des russischen Reiches,* 636; Coxe, *Travels,* 37; de Raymond, *Tableau,* 425–26; and Georgi, *Opisanie,* 140.

2. In fact, some craftsmen ended up casting themselves on the mercy of the state for income; see the brief discussion of German artisans in St. Petersburg in Bartlett, *Human Capital,* 158ff.

3. The next major reform (discounting the brief rule of Paul I), in 1846, retained Catherine's basic organizational structure. Lincoln, "The Russian State and its Cities," *Jahrbücher für Geschichte Osteuropas,* band 17, no. 4: 531–41; Manfred Hildermeier, *Bürgertum und Stadt in Russland, 1760–1870: Rechtliche Lage und soziale Struktur* (Köln-Vienna: Böhlau Verlag, 1986).

4. Marc Raeff, "The Well-Ordered Police State and the Development of Modernity in Seventeenth- and Eighteenth-Century Europe: An Attempt at a Comparative Approach," *American Historical Review* 80, no. 5 (December 1975): 1221–43; and *The Well Ordered Police State: Social and Institutional Change Through Law in the Germanies and Russia, 1600–1800* (New Haven: Yale University Press, 1983).

5. James Cracraft deals with this matter at length in chapter 6, "St. Petersburg," of his *The Revolution of Peter the Great* (Cambridge, MA: Harvard University Press, 2003).

6. Boris Nikolaevich Mironov, *Vnutrennii rynok Rossii vo vtoroi polovine XVIII-pervoi polovine XIX v.* (Leningrad: Nauka, 1981; "Sotsial'naia struktura gorodskogo naseleniia Rossii vo vtoroi polovine XVIII-pervoi polovine XIX v.," in I. Ia. Froianov, ed., *Genezis i razvitie feodalizma v Rossii: Problemy istorii goroda,* Problems of National and General History, no. 11 (Leningrad, 1988), 197–224; "Revoliutsiia tsen v Rossii XVIII v. i ee ekonomicheskie, sotsial'nye i politicheskie posledstviia," unpublished paper delivered at the IV International Conference of the Study Group on Eighteenth-Century Russia, Hoddesdon, England, July 1989; and *Russkii gorod v 1740–1860e gody: Demograficheskoe, sotsial'noe i ekonomicheskoe razvitie* (Leningrad: Nauka, 1990).

7. See Berngard Borisovich Kafengauz, "Nekotorye voprosy genezisa kapitalizma v Rossii," in Mavrodin, ed., *Voprosy genezisa,* 9. Some of the food consumed in the

capital came from the so-called agrarian towns, towns that specialized in vegetable gardening. See L. V. Milov, "O tak nazyvaemykh agrarnykh gorodakh Rossii XVIII veka," *Voprosy istorii,* 1968, no. 6 (June): 56–64.

8. E. G. Istomina, "Vyshnevolotskii vodnyi put' vo vtoroi polovine XVIII-nachale XIX v.," in A. L. Narochnitskii et al., eds., *Istoricheskaia geografiia XII-nachalo XX v.: Sbornik statei k 70–letiiu Professora Liubomira Grigor'evicha Beskrovnogo* (Moscow, 1975), 204–06. See also Robert E. Jones, "Getting the Goods to St. Petersburg," *Slavic Review* 43, no. 3 (Fall 1984): 413–33.

9. For example, Russia's Ural mines were the greatest extractors of iron ore in the world at the time, before the introduction of coke smelting. Alexander Baykov, "The Economic Development of Russia," in *Russian Economic Development from Peter the Great to Stalin,* ed. and intro. William L. Blackwell (New York, 1974), 11.

10. There was an upsurge in *obrok* usage in the first half of Catherine's reign, followed by an increase in *barshchina* near the end of the century. For an explanation of these changes see Michael Confino, *Domaines et seigneurs en Russie vers la fin du XVIIe siècle: Etude de structures agraires et de mentalités économiques* (Paris, 1963), as well as his *Systémes agraires et progrès agricole: L'assolement triennal en Russie aux XVIIIe–XIXe siècles: Etude d'économie et de sociologie rurales* (Paris, 1969). Also Marc Raeff, "Pugachev's Rebellion," in *Preconditions of Revolution in Early Modern Europe,* ed. Robert Forster and Jack P. Greene (Baltimore: Johns Hopkins University Press, 1970), 161–202.

11. RGADA, *fond* 259, *delo* 3676, *listy* 913*ob.*-14; cited in Makarov, "Economicheskaia zhizn'," *OIL,* 1: 252. For the various ways that peasants legally obtained passports to live in towns see Klokman, "Gorod v zakonodatelst've russkogo absoliutizma vo vtoroi polovine XVII–XVIII vv.," in *Absoliutizm v Rossii (XVII–XVIII vv.): Sbornik statei k semidesiatiletiiu so dnia rozhdeniia i sorokopiatiletiiu nauchnoi i pedagogicheskoi deiatel'nosti B. B. Kafengauza,* ed. N. M. Druzhinin (Moscow, 1964), 337.

12. RGIA, *fond* 1258, *opis'* 1, *delo* 112, *kniga* 2, *list* 43*ob.*: cited in Makarov, "Ekonomicheskaia zhizn'," *OIL,* 1: 252.

13. A. B. Kamenskii, *Povsednevnost' russkoi gorodskikh obyvatelei. Istoricheskie anekdoty iz provintsial'noi zhizni XVIII veka* (Moscow: Rossiiskii gosudarstvennyi gumanitarnyi universitet, 2006), 322.

14. RGIA, *fond* 467, *opis'* 4, *delo* 10, *listy* 67, 101, 236, and passim.

15. Cited in Bernard Lepetit, *The Pre-Industrial Urban System: France, 1740–1840,* trans. Godfrey Rogers (New York: Cambridge University Press, 1994), 81.

16. Ibid., 82.

17. Nicholas V. Riasanovsky, *Russia and the West in the Teaching of the Slavophiles: A Study of Romantic Ideology* (Cambridge, MA: Harvard University Press, 1952), especially 78–82.

18. Konstantin Sergeevich Aksakov, "On the Internal State of Russia," trans. Valentine Snow, in *Russian Intellectual History: An Anthology,* ed. Marc Raeff (New York: Harcourt, Brace & World, 1966), 243.

19. N. A. Engel'gardt, "Dvukhsotletie S.-Peterburga," *Istoricheskii vestnik* 112 (June 1903): 925.

20. For example, see Angelo S. Rappoport, *The Curse of the Romanovs* (London, 1907), 12; Ian Grey, *Catherine the Great: Autocrat and Empress of All Russia* (Philadelphia, 1962), especially chapters 13 and 15; and Joseph Wechsberg, *In Leningrad* (Garden City, NJ: Doubleday, 1977), chapter 1.

21. This theme can be found, for example, in Nikolai Alekseevich Nekrasov, *Fiziologiia Peterburga, sostavlennaia iz trudov russkikh literatorov* (St. Petersburg, 1845); Mikhail Ivanovich Pyliaev, *Staryi Peterburg: Rasskazy iz byloi zhizni stolitsy,* 3rd ed. (St. Petersburg: Izdanie A. S. Suvorina, 1887); Nikolai Pavlovich Antsiferov, *Byl i mif Peterburga* (Petrograd: Brikgauz-Efron, 1924); and Hans Rogger, *National Consciousness in*

Eighteenth Century Russia (Cambridge, MA: Harvard University Press, 1960). *Belye nochi: Ocherki, zarisovki, dokumenty, vospominaniia,* an annual serial begun by I. I. Slobozhan in 1973 (Leningrad: Lenizdat), continued to build upon this tradition. More recently Naum Aleksandrovich Sindalovskii has popularized it in such works as *Istoriia Sankt-Peterburga v predaniiakh i legendakh* (St. Petersburg: "Norint," 1997) and *Legendy i mify Sankt-Peterburga* (St. Petersburg: "Norint," 1997). Several essays in the volume edited by Iu. N. Bespiatykh, *Fenomen Peterburga* (St. Petersburg: Russko-Baltiiskii informatsionnyi tsentr BLITs, 2000), the proceedings of an international conference held at the Pushkin Museumm in November 1999, also address the theme, as does Dmitrii Leonidovich Spivak, *Severnaia stolitsa: Metafizika Peterburga* (St. Petersburg: "TEMA," 1998).

22. The role of the capital's commerce in creating a money economy in Russia is stressed by A. L. Shapiro, "O roli Peterburga v razvitii vserossiiskogo rynka v XVIII i pervoi polovine XIX vv.," in *Goroda feodal'noi Rossii: Sbornik statei pamiati N. V. Ustiugova,* ed. V. I. Shunkov (Moscow, 1966), 386–96. See also Georgi, *Opisanie,* 586–87.

23. Adam Smith, *An Inquiry into the Nature and Causes of the Wealth of Nations,* 2 vols. (London: W. Strahan and T. Cadell, 1776), 1: 401.

24. See E. A. Wrigley, "Brake or Accelerator? Urban Growth and Population Growth before the Industrial Revolution," in Ad van der Woude, Akira Hayami, and Jan de Vrees, eds., *Urbanization in History: A Process of Dynamic Interactions* (New York: Oxford University Press, 1990), 101–12.

25. Munro, "The Charter to the Towns Reconsidered," *Canadian-American Slavic Studies* 23, no. 1 (Spring 1984): 17–34.

26. More than three hundred towns received a total of 416 plans, many of them with ray streets like St. Petersburg's.

27. Shkvarikov, *Ocherki istorii planirovki,* 77.

28. This idea is developed by E. A. Gutkind, *Urban Development in Eastern Europe, Bulgaria, Romania, and the U.S.S.R.,* vol. 8 of the *International History of City Development* (New York, 1972), 300ff.

29. William L. Blackwell, "Modernization and Urbanization in Russia: A Comparative View," the conclusion of Hamm, ed., in *The City in Russian History,* 302–03.

30. Rozman, *Urban Networks,* 18.

31. It is noteworthy that Russia's first economically useful railroad began in St. Petersburg, extending from there to Moscow, and later to other areas. Blackwell, *The Beginnings of Russian Industrialization, 1800–1860* (Princeton: Princeton University Press, 1968), 116.

32. Perhaps government contracts were made known by other means, or it may be that governmental agencies had begun to supply their needs with their own people. Either explanation remains conjectural until more is known about the personnel policies of governmental agencies.

33. Kingsley Davis and Hilda H. Golden, "Urbanization and the Development of Preindustrial Areas," *Economic Development and Cultural Change* 3 (October 1954): 23–24.

34. A detailed analysis of the role of satirical journals in Russia's literary development may be found in Aleksandr Nikolaevich Afanas'ev, *Russkie satiricheskie zhurnaly 1769–1774 godov: epizod iz istorii russkoi literatury XVIII veka,* 2nd ed. (Kazan', 1921).

35. For insightful commentary on both see Kaganov, *Images of Space,* 19–38.

36. Chapter 2, 73–77, 81–84.

37. Mikhail Mikhailovich Shcherbatov, *On the Corruption of Morals in Russia,* trans. and ed. A. Lentin (London: Cambridge University Press, 1969), 79.

38. For a summary of Catherine's views comparing the two cities see Rogger, *National Consciousness,* 18. Reasons for Catherine's preferences are elucidated in John

T. Alexander, "Petersburg and Moscow in Early Urban Policy," *Journal of Urban History* 8, no. 2 (February 1982): 145–69.

39. Denis Ivanovich Fonvizin, "A Discourse on Permanent Laws of State," trans. Ronald Hingley, in Marc Raeff, ed., *Russian Intellectual History: An Anthology,* intro. Isaiah Berlin (New York: Harcourt, Brace & World, 1966), 103.

40. G. G. Casanova, "Zapiski Kazanova," *Russkaia starina* 9 (1874): 548. Casanova's comments were unusually perceptive.

41. Radishchev pointed to such evils in his *Journey from St. Petersburg to Moscow.* His indictment was much less severe than the later diatribe against St. Petersburg by Ivan Petrovich Kornilov, a high official in the Ministry of Public Education in the late nineteenth century: "Petrovgrad [*sic*], heretically speaking Piterburkh: that is an abominably obscene receptacle of an insidious spectacle, of tremulous singing which is harmful to the soul, and of all sorts of sinful lechery and gluttony. Blow and spit!" "Blow and spit" are ritual actions taken three times against the devil and the evils of the world in the ceremony of baptism into the Russian Orthodox Church. Kornilov considered St. Petersburg part of the realm of the devil to be rejected by all Orthodox Russians. RGIA, *fond* 970, *delo* 294, *list* 2.

42. See, for example, the discussion in Daniel Morrison, "'Trading Peasants' and Urbanization in Eighteenth-Century Russia: The Central Industrial Region," unpublished Ph.D. dissertation, Columbia University, 1981, especially chapter 6; for the later time period, see Robert Eugene Johnson, *Peasant and Proletarian: The Working Class of Moscow in the Late Nineteenth Century* (New Brunswick: Rutgers University Press, 1979).

43. V. Sreznevskii, ed., "Prazdnovanie stoletiia Peterburga," *Russkaia starina* 114 (1903): 369.

44. Szreznevskii, "Prazdnovanie," 368.

45. For more on the Skoptsy see Laura Engelstein, *Castration and the Heavenly Kingdom: A Russian Folktale* (Ithaca: Cornell University Press, 1999).

46. George E. Munro, "The Petersburg of Catherine II: Official Enlightenment versus Popular Cults," in Ian Lilly, ed., *Moscow and Petersburg: The City in Russian Culture* (Nottingham, England: Astra Press, 2002), 49–64.

47. D. F. Kobeko, "Frantsuzskaia koloniia v Peterburge," *Russkii arkhiv,* 1874, no. 1 (January): 952–55, quoting from La Messelière's *Voyage a Pétersbourg* (Paris, 1803), 124–245.

Conclusion

1. Aleksandr Nikolaevich Pypin, ed., *Sochineniia imperatritsy Ekateriny II,* 12 vols. (St. Petersburg, 1901–1907), 12: 643. See also the evaluation of this document in John T. Alexander, "Petersburg and Moscow in Early Urban Policy," *Journal of Urban History* 8, no. 2 (February 1982): 145–69.

2. Based on the index of the first series of *PSZ* (vol. 42), eighty-eight laws dealt specifically with St. Petersburg during Catherine's reign; there are eighty-seven for Moscow, but forty of those were issued in 1770–1771 to combat the plague there. Only seven of St. Petersburg's laws dealt with that crisis.

3. L. V. Milov, *Issledovaniia ob "ekonomicheskikh primechaniiakh" k general'nomu mezhevaniiu (K istorii russkogo krest'ianstva i sel'skogo khoziaistva vtoroi poloviny XVIII v.)* (Moscow, 1965), 270–71.

4. Rozman, *Urban Networks,* chapter 1.

5. Davis and Golden, "Urbanization," in *Economic Development and Cultural Change,* 3:6–26.

Bibliography

FOUR BRIEF EXPLANATORY REMARKS ARE IN ORDER. FIRST, RUSSIAN archives underwent changes in name after the collapse of the Soviet Union. They are cited by their current names, with their former (Soviet) names in brackets. Second, archival sources are indicated only by the broadest category of fund (*fond*) number, together with a brief summary of the kinds of materials used from each *fond*. The more precise citations may be found in the chapter notes, where the index number (*opis'*) and file number (*delo*) are also given. Third, for published sources, the name of the publisher is given only for Western publishers for the past century. Otherwise the publisher's name has been omitted in order to save space. Finally, where an article appears within a larger edited work, volume and article are cited separately.

PRIMARY WORKS

Unpublished

ST. PETERSBURG [LENINGRAD]

Arkhiv Sankt-peterburgskogo filiala instituta russkoi istorii rossiiskoi akademii nauk (cited as Arkhiv SPbF IRI RAN).
Fond 36 (The Vorontsovs).
Tsentral'nyi gosudarstvennyi istoricheskii arkhiv Sanktpeterburga [formerly Gosudarstvennyi istoricheskii arkhiv leningradskoi oblasti, or GIA LO] (cited as TsGIA SPb).
Fond 221 (Materials of the St. Petersburg merchant board).
Fond 781 (Materials of the St. Petersburg city *duma*).
Fond 788 (Materials of the St. Petersburg city magistracy).
Fond 1731.
Rossiiskaia natsional'naia biblioteka [formerly the Gosudarstvennaia ordena Trudovogo Krasnogo znameni Publichnaia biblioteka imeni M. E. Saltykova-Shchedrina] (cited as RNB).
Department of Prints
"Panoramic View of St. Petersburg Dedicated by Permission of His Imperial Majesty Alexander lst by his Much Obliged Servant J. A. Atkinson."

"Vue de la place et du grand théatre de l'Opéra à St. Pétersbourg." Drawn by Courvoisier. Printed by Dubois.
Manuscripts Department
Fond 40 (Maps, charts, and plans of St. Petersburg in various years).
Fond 575 (Papers of Petr Nikolaevich Petrov).
Fond Ermitazhnoe sobranie (Population lists).
Fond F.II.146 (Papers of the St. Petersburg city *duma*).
Fond NsRK 1947.207 F (Papers pertaining to the history of the St. Petersburg tapestry factory).
Fond 0.IV.56 (Real estate list for St. Petersburg).
Fond Sobranie OLDP.0 (Explanations of various maps of St. Petersburg).
Fond 1966.62 (Plans for St. Petersburg at various times).
Fond Arkhiv G. R. Derzhavina (Papers of G. R. Derzhavin).
Fond Shtelin, Iakov Iakovlevich (Prices in St. Petersburg).
Fond Arkhiv Petra Nikolaevicha Stolpianskogo (Bibliography of works about St. Petersburg).
Rossiiskii gosudarstvennyi istoricheskii arkhiv [formerly Tsentral'nyi gosudarstvennyi istoricheskii arkhiv] (cited as RGIA).
Fond 91 (Minutes of meetings of the Free Economic Society).
Fond 466 (Imperial edicts).
Fond 467 (Documents of the Chancellery on Construction).
Fond 470 (Documents of the court administrative office).
Fond 485 (Maps, charts, and plans of St. Petersburg).
Fond 488 (Documents of the Sofiia city council).
Fond 571 (Tax registers).
Fond 588 (Materials concerning the registration by peasants as merchants and artisans).
Fond 758 (Records of the public orphanage).
Fond 970 (Papers of Ivan Petrovich Kornilov).
Fond 1281 (Information concerning public education in St. Petersburg).
Fond 1293 (Maps and plans of St. Petersburg).
Fond 1329 (Laws and drafts of laws).
Fond 1350 (Economic information on St. Petersburg city and district).
Fond 1399 (Maps and plans of St. Petersburg).

Moscow

Rossiiskii gosudarstvennyi arkhiv drevnikh aktov [Rossiiskii gosudarstvennyi arkhiv drevnikh aktov] (cited as RGADA).
Fond 8 (Kalinkin House and matters concerning crimes against morality).
Fond 10 (The cabinet of Catherine II and its continuation).
Fond 14 (Affairs at court).
Fond 16 (Reports from commissions, police, and others about construction, births and deaths, crime, welfare, etc., made to the Senate).
Fond 17 (Developments in science, literature, and the arts).
Fond 19 (Financial reports of industrial concerns).
Fond 248 (Affairs brought before the chancellery of the Senate).
Fond 277 (Journals of the Senate).
Fond 291 (Magistracy reports).

Fond 294 (Manufactures College information concerning developments in industry).
Fond 1329 (Information about state-owned factories).

Iaroslavl'

Gosudarstvennyi arkhiv iaroslavskoi oblasti.
Fond 55 (Magistracy reports).

Published

Akademiia nauk. *Plan stolichnogo goroda Sanktpeterburga s izobrazheniem znatneishikh onogo prospektov, izdannyi trudami Imperatorskoi akademii nauk i khudozhestv.* St. Petersburg, 1753.

Atkinson, John Augustus, and James Walker. *A Picturesque Representation of the Manners, Customs and Amusements of the Russians.* 3 vols. London, 1803–4.

Barsukov, Aleksandr Platonovich, ed. *Pis'ma brat'ev Orlovykh k grafu Petru Aleksandrovichu Rumiantsevu (1764–1788).* St. Petersburg, 1897.

Beliavskii, Mikhail Timofeevich, ed. *Dvorianskaia imperiia XVIII veka (osnovnye zakonodatel'nye akty): Sbornik dokumentov.* Moscow, 1960.

Bogdanov, Andrei Petrovich. *Istoricheskoe, geograficheskoe i topograficheskoe opisanie Sanktpeterburga, ot nachala zavedeniia ego, c 1703 po 1751 god, sochinennoe g. Bogdanovym, so mnogimi izobrazheniiami pervykh zdanii, a nyne dopolnennoe i izdannoe, nadvornym sovetnikom, praviashchim dolzhnost' direktora novorossiiskimi uchilishchami, vol'nogo rossiiskogo sobraniia, pri Imperatorskom moskovskom universitete i sanktpeterburgskogo vol'nogo ekonomicheskogo obshchestva chlenom Vasil'em Rubanom.* St. Petersburg, 1779.

Bolotov, Andrei Timofeevich. *Pamiatnik pretekshikh vremen, ili kratkie istoricheskie zapiski o byvshikh proizshestviiakh i o nosivshikhsia slukhakh.* Moscow, 1875.

———. *Zhizn' i prikliucheniia Andreia Bolotova, opisannye samim im dlia svoikh potomkov, 1738–1795.* 4 vols. St. Petersburg, 1870.

Bruce, Peter Henry. *Memoirs of Peter Henry Bruce, Esq. a Military Officer, in the Services of Prussia, Russia, and Great Britain, containing an Account of his Travels in Germany, Russia, Tartary, Turkey, and the West Indies, etc.* London, 1782.

Büsching, Anton Friedrich. *Neue Beschreibung des russischen Reiches nach allen seinen Staaten und Ländern.* Hamburg, 1763.

Carr, John. *A Northern Summer: or Travels round the Baltic, through Denmark, Sweden, Russia, Prussia, and Part of Germany, in the Year 1804.* Philadelphia, 1805.

Casanova, Giovanni Giacomo [Kazanova, G. G]. "Zapiski venetsiantsa Kazanova: Prebyvanie ego v Rossii, 1765–1766 gg.," *Russkaia starina* 9 (1874): 532–61.

[Catherine II]. "Iz bumag Imperatritsy Ekateriny II khraniashchikhsia v gosudarstvennom arkhive, ministerstva inostrannykh del." *Sbornik Imperatorskogo russkogo istoricheskogo obshchestva* 13 (1874) and 27 (1880).

———. "Pis'ma Ekateriny II k senatoru Dmitriiu Vasil'evichu Volkovu, 1771–1779." Compiled by S. A. Rudakov. *Russkaia starina* 18 (1877): 372, 576, 744.

———. "Pis'ma Imperatritsy Ekateriny II-i k I. F. Glebovu," *Russkii arkhiv,* 1867, no. 5 (May): 342–64.

———. "Sobstvennoruchnye pis'ma Imperatritsy Ekateriny k Grafu Ivanu Grigor'evichu Chernyshevu," *Russkii arkhiv,* 1871, no. 9 (September): 1313–48.

Chantreau, Pierre Nicholas. *Philosophical, Political and Literary Travels in Russia, during the Years 1788–1789.* London, 1794.

Chulkov, Mikhail Dmitrievich. *Istoricheskoe opisanie rossiiskoi kommertsii pri vsekh portakh i granitsakh ot drevnikh vremen do nyne nastoiashchego i vsekh preimushchestvennykh uzakonenii po onoi Gosudaria Petra Velikogo i nyne blagopoluchno tsarstvuiushchei gosudariny Imperatritsy Ekateriny Velikoi.* 7 vols. St. Petersburg, 1781–86.

Cook, John. *Voyages and Travels through the Russian Empire, Tartary, and Part of the Kingdom of Persia.* 2 vols. Edinburgh, 1770.

Coxe, William. *Travels into Poland, Russia, Sweden and Denmark.* 3 vols. Dublin, 1784.

Craven, Elizabeth. *A Journey through the Crimea to Constantinople in a Series of Letters.* London, 1789.

Danilov, Mikhail Vasil'evich. "Zapiski Mikhaila Vasil'evicha Danilova, artillerii maiora, napisannye im v 1771 godu (1722–1762)." In *Bezvremen'e i vremenshchiki: Vospominaniia ob "epokhe dvortsovykh perevorotov" (1720–e-1760–e gody),* edited and introduction by Evgenii Viktorovich Anisimov. Leningrad, 1991.

Dashkova, Ekaterina Romanovna. *Memoirs of the Princess Daschkaw. Lady of Honor to Catherine II, Empress of All the Russias: Comprising Letters of the Empress and Other Correspondence.* Translated and edited by Mrs. W. Bradford. 2 vols. London, 1840.

Derzhavin, Gavriil Romanovich. *Zapiski Gavriila Romanovicha Derzhavin, 1743–1812.* Moscow, 1860.

Dilthey [Dil'tei], Philipp Heinrich. *Nachal'nye osnovaniia veksel'nogo prava, a osoblivo rossiiskogo, kupno i shvedskogo, s pribavlenîem raznykh rossiiskikh ukazov i s dvumia dissertatsiiami, k onomu prinadlezhashchimi, dlia upotrebleniia v Moskovskom iuridicheskom fakul'tete po udobneishemu sposobu raspolozhennye.* 3rd ed. Moscow, 1781.

Dimsdale, Elizabeth. *An English Lady at the Court of Catherine the Great: the Journal of Baroness Elizabeth Dimsdale, 1781.* Edited, introduction, and notes by A. G. Cross. Cambridge: Crest Publications, 1989).

Dimsdale, Thomas. "Zapiska Barona Dimsdelia," *Sbornik Imperatorskogo russkogo istoricheskogo obshchestva,* 2: 302.

Fonvizin, Denis Ivanovich. "A Discourse on Permanent Laws of State" [Rassuzhdenie o nepremennykh gosudarstvennykh zakonakh]. Translated by Ronald Hingley. In *Russian Intellectual History, an Anthology,* edited by Marc Raeff, 96–105. Introduction by Isaiah Berlin. New York: Harcourt, Brace & World, 1966.

Fries, Jakob. *Eine Reise durch Sibirien im achtzehnten Jahrhundert.* Munich, 1955.

Garnovskii, Mikhail. "Zapiski Mikhaila Garnovskogo," *Russkaia starina* 15(1876): 9–38, 237–65, 471–99, 687–720; 16 (1876): 1–32, 207–38, 399–440.

Georgel, Jean-François. *Mémoires.* Vol 6, *Voyage à Pétersbourg.* Paris, 1818.

Georgi, Johann Gottlieb. *Opisanie rossiisko-imperatorskogo stolichnogo goroda Sankt-Peterburga i dostopamiatnostei v okrestnostiakh onogo.* 3 vols. in 1. St. Petersburg, 1794.

———. *Opisanie vsekh obitaiushchikh v Rossiiskom gosudarstve narodov, ikh zhiteiskikh obriadov, obyknovenii, odezhd, zhilishch, uprazhnenii zabav, veroispovedanii. i drugikh dostopamiatnostei. Tvorenie, za neskol'ko let pered sim na nemetskom iazyke, v perevode na rossiiskii iazyk ves'ma vo mnogom ispr. i v nov' sochinennoe.* St. Petersburg, 1799.

Gmelin, Samuil Georg. *Puteshestvie po Rossii dlia issledovaniia 3kh tsarstvovanii estestva.* 3 vols. St. Petersburg, 1777–84.

Gosudarstvennyi sovet. *Arkhiv gosudarstvennogo soveta.* 5 vols. in 16. St. Petersburg, 1869–1904.

Grekov, Boris Dmitrievich, ed. *Materialy po istorii volnenii na krepostnykh manufakturakh v XVIII v.* Moscow-Leningrad, 1937.

Gribovskii, Adrian Moiseevich. "Vospominaniia i dnevniki Adriana Moiseevicha Gribovskogo," *Russkii arkhiv,* 1899, no. 1, (January): 1–166.

Griffiths, David, and George Munro, trans. and eds. *Catherine the Great's Charters of 1785 to the Nobility and the Towns*. Bakersfield, CA: Charles Schlacks, Jr., 1991.

Hanway, Jonas. *An Historical Account of the British Trade over the Caspian Sea, with a Journal of his Travels*. 4 vols. London, 1753.

Harris, James. *Diaries and Correspondence of James Harris*. London, 1845.

Hermann, Benedikt Franz. *Statistische Schilderung von Russland, im Rücksicht auf Bevölkerung, Landesbeschaffenheit, Bergbau, Manufakturen und Handel*. St. Petersburg and Leipzig, 1790.

Imperatorskaia akademiia nauk. *Plan stolichnogo goroda Sanktpeterburga s izobrazheniem znatneishikh onogo prospektov, izdannyi trudami Imperatorskoi akademii nauk i khudozhestv*. St. Petersburg, 1753.

Imperatorskaia kantseliariia. *Polnoe sobranie zakonov rossiiskoi imperii s 1649 goda*. First series: 1649–1825. 46 vols. in 48, plus 3 appendices. St. Petersburg, 1830–35 (cited as *PSZ*).

Indova, E. I., ed. *Zakonodatel'stvo perioda rastsveta absoliutizma*. Vol. 5 of *Rossiiskoe zakonodatel'stvo X-XX vekov*, general editor I. Chistiakov. 9 vols. Moscow, 1984–.

Kashin, V. N., ed. *Materialy po istorii krest'ianskoi promyshlennosti, XVIII i pervoi poloviny XIX v*. Vol. 15 of *Trudy istoriko-arkheograficheskogo instituta*. Moscow-Leningrad, 1935.

Khrapovitskii, Aleksandr Vasil'evich. *Pamiatnye zapiski A. V. Khrapovitskogo, stats-sekretaria imperatritsy Ekateriny vtoroi*. Notes by G. I. Gennadi. Moscow, 1862.

Klushin, Aleksandr. "Smes'," *Sanktpeterburgskii merkurii* 1, no. 1 (January 1793): 85–91.

Kolotov, Petr Stepanovich. *Deianiia Ekateriny II, Imperatritsy i samoderzhitsy vserossiiskoi*, 6 vols. St. Petersburg, 1811.

Kraf[f]t, L. Iu. [Wolfgang Ludwig]. "Opyt o tablitsakh brakov i rozhdenii g. Peterburga za 1764–1785 gg.," *Sobranie sochinenii, vybrannykh iz mesiatseslov na raznye gody* 2 (1787), 368–404.

La Messelière, de, Count. *Voyage à Pétersbourg ou nouveaux mémoires sur la Russie*. Paris, 1803.

Le Maître, Alexandre. *La Metropolitée*. Amsterdam, 1682.

Leman, I. G. "Kak luchshim sposobom zhech' iz drov ugol'e," *Trudy Imperatorskogo vol'nogo ekonomicheskogo obshchestva*. Part 4 (1766): 1–29.

Manstein, Christof Hermann von. *Memoirs of Russia, Historical, Political, and Military, from the Year MDCCXXVII to MDCCXLIV*. London, 1770.

Marshall, Joseph. *Travels through Holland, Flanders, Germany, Denmark, Sweden, Lapland, Russia, the Ukraine, and Poland, in the Years 1768, 1769, and 1770*. 4 vols. London, 1772.

Matinskii, Mikhail. *Opera komicheskaia: S.-Peterburgskii gostinyi dvor*. 2nd. ed. Odessa, 1890.

Miller, Gerard Friderik [Müller, Gerhard-Friedrich]. *Geograficheskii leksikon rossiiskogo gosudarstva ili slovar', opisaiushchii poazbuchnomu poriadku reki, ozera, moria, gory, kreposti, znatnye monastyri, ostrogi, iasashnye zimoviia, rudnye zavody i prochie dostopamiatnye mesta obshirnoi rossiiskoi imperii s ob"iavleniem i tekh mest, kotorye v prezhniuiu i nyneshniuiu turetskuiu voinu, a nekotorye prezhnogo i ot Persii rossiiskoiu khrabrost'iiu obladaemu byli*. Moscow, 1773.

Ministerstvo imperatorskago dvora. *Kamer-fur'erskii tseremonial'nyi zhurnal*. Annual vols. for 1762–96. St. Petersburg, 1853–96.

Ministerstvo vnutrennikh del. *Statisticheskie svedeniia o Sanktpeterburge*. St. Petersburg, 1836.

———. *Tablitsy k statisticheskim svedeniiam o Sanktpeterburge*. St. Petersburg, 1836.

Narodnyi Peterburg kontsa XVIII i nachala XIX-go vekov v izobrazheniiakh zhivopistsev i graverov. Moscow, n.d.

Observations on the Present State of Denmark, Russia, and Switzerland. in a Series of Letters. London, 1784.

Oleshov, [Gospodin] Aleksei. "O neurozhae rzhi, osoblivo 1766 god," *Trudy Imperatorskogo vol'nogo ekonomicheskogo obshchestva.* Part 5 (1766): 33–47.

Pallas, Peter Simon. *Reise durch verschiedene Provinzen des russischen Reiches.* St. Petersburg, 1771.

Parkinson, John. *A Tour of Russia, Siberia, and the Crimea, 1792–1794.* Edited and introduction by William Collier. London: Frank Cass, 1971.

Perry, John. *The State of Russia under the Present Czar.* London, 1715.

Poroshin, Semen Andreevich. *Semena Poroshina zapiski, sluzhashchiia k istorii ego imperatorskogo vysochestva blagovernogo gosudaria tsesarevicha i velikogo kniazia Pavla Petrovicha naslednika prestolu rossiiskogo.* St. Petersburg, 1844.

Pypin, Aleksandr Nikolaevich, ed. *Sochineniia imperatritsy Ekateriny II.* 12 vols. St. Petersburg, 1901–07.

Radishchev, Aleksandr Nikolaevich. *Puteshestvie iz Peterburga v Moskvu.* Moscow-Leningrad, 1961.

Reimers, Heinrich von. *St. Petersburg am Ende seines ersten Jahrhunderts mit Rückblicken auf Entstehung und Wachsthum dieser Residenz unter den verschiedenen Regierungen während dieses Zeitraums.* 2 vols. St. Petersburg, 1805.

Richard, John. *A Tour from London to Petersburgh, and from Thence to Moscow.* Dublin, 1781.

Richardson, William. *Anecdotes of the Russian Empire in a Series of Notes.* London, 1784.

Ruban, Vasilii Grigor'evich. *Dopolnenie k istoricheskomu, geograficheskomu i topograficheskomu opisaniiu Sanktpeterburga, c 1751 po 1762 god, sochinennoe A. Bogdanovym.* St. Petersburg, 1903.

Sanktpeterburgisches Journal (1777–82).

Sanktpeterburgskaia adresnaia kniga na 1809 god. Edited by Heinrich von Reimers. St. Petersburg, 1809.

Sanktpeterburgskie vedomosti (1762–96).

S.-Peterburgskii merkurii, ezhemesiatsnoe izdanie (1793).

Sanktpeterburgskii vestnik (1778–80).

Sanktpeterburgskoe ezhenedel'noe sochinenie, kasaiushcheesia do razmnozheniia domostroitel'stva i rasprostraneniia obshchepoleznykh znanii (St. Petersburg, 1778).

Sbornik Imperatorskogo russkogo istoricheskogo obshchestva (1867–1916). Cited as *Sbornik IRIO.*

Schwan, Christian Friedrich. *Anecdotes russes, ou lettres d'un officier allemand a un gentilhomme livonien, écrites de Pétersbourg en 1762; tems du regne et du détronement de Pierre III.* Berlin and Dresden, 1765.

Shchekatov, Afanasii. *Slovar' geograficheskii rossiiskogo gosudarstva, sochinennyi v nastoiashchego onogo vida.* Title varies. 7 vols. in 6. Moscow, 1801–9.

Shcherbatov, Mikhail Mikhailovich. *On the Corruption of Morals in Russia.* Translated and edited by A. Lentin. London: Cambridge University Press, 1969.

———. "Proshenie Moskvy o zabvenii ee." *Chteniia moskovskogo obshchestva istorii i drevnostei rossiiskikh* 1 (1860): 49–52.

Shmelev, G. N., ed. *Akty tsarstvovaniia Ekateriny II: Uchrezhdeniia dlia upravleniia gubernii i zhalovannye gramoty dvorianstvu i gorodam.* Moscow, 1907.

Shreter, Gospodin. "O moshchenii ulits v gorodakh," *Trudy Imperatorskogo vol'nogo ekonomicheskogo obshchestva.* Part 51 (1796): 177–212.

Smith, Adam. *An Inquiry into the Nature and Causes of the Wealth of Nations.* 2 vols. London: W. Strahan and T. Cadell, 1776.

Sochineniia i perevody, k pol'ze i uveseleniiu sluzhashchikhsia (St. Petersburg, 1762).

Storch, Heinrich Friedrich von. *Historisch-statistische Gemälde des russischen Reiches am Ende des XVIII Jahrhunderts: Statistische Übersicht der Statthalterschaften des russischen Reichs nach ihren merkwürdigsten Kulturverhältnissen in Tabellen.* 9 vols. Riga and Leipzig, 1797–1803.

———. *The Picture of Petersburg.* London, 1801.

Swinton, Andrew. *Travels into Norway, Denmark, and Russia in the Years 1788, 1789, 1790, and 1791.* London, 1792.

Thomson, William. *Letters from Scandinavia, on the Past and Present State of the Northern Nations of Europe.* 2 vols. London, 1796.

Tolchenov, Ivan Alekseevich. *Zhurnal ili zapiska zhizhni i prikliuchenii Ivana Alekseevicha Tolchenova.* Introduction by N. I. Pavlenko; commentary by V. Kh. Bodisko. Moscow, 1974.

Trudy Imperatorskogo vol'nogo ekonomicheskogo obshchestva (1765–96).

Vigor, (Mrs.) William (née Rondeau). *Letters from a Lady Who Resided some Years in Russia, to her Friend in England, with some Historical Notes.* London, 1775.

Vinskii, Grigorii Stepanovich. *Moe vremia: Zapiski G. S. Vinskogo.* Edited and introduction by P. E. Shchegoleva. St. Petersburg, 1914.

Williams, John. *The Rise, Progress, and Present State of the Northern Governments: viz, the United Provinces, Denmark, Sweden, Russia, and Poland.* 2 vols. London, 1777.

Wraxhall, Nathaniel. *Tour through the Northern Parts of Europe, particularly Copenhagen, Stockholm and Petersburg (1774).* Vol. 17 of *Mavor's Voyages,* 1774.

Zhikharev, Stepan Petrovich. *Zapiski sovremmenika.* Edited by B. M. Eikhonbaum. Moscow, 1955.

Zlobin, K. K., ed. "Vedomost' sostoiashchim v S.-Peterburge fabrikam, manufakturam i zavodam 1794 goda sentiabria dnia," *Sbornik Imperatorskogo russkogo istoricheskogo obshchestva* 1: 352–61.

Secondary Works

Afanas'ev, Aleksandr Nikolaevich. "Cherty russkikh nravov XVIII stoletiia." *Russkii vestnik,* 1857, no. 10 (August): 623–44; no. 11 (September): 248–82.

———. *Russkie satiricheskie zhurnaly 1769–1774 godov: Epizod iz istorii russkoi literatury XVIII veka.* 2nd ed. Kazan', 1921.

Aksakov, Konstantin Sergeevich. "On the Internal State of Russia." Translated by Valentine Snow. In *Russian Intellectual History: an Anthology,* edited by Marc Raeff, 230–51. New York: Harcourt, Brace & World, 1966.

Alexander, John T. *Bubonic Plague in Early Modern Russia: Public Health and Urban Disaster.* Baltimore: Johns Hopkins University Press, 1980.

———. "Catherine II, Bubonic Plague, and the Problem of Industry in Moscow." *American Historical Review,* 79, no. 3 (June 1974): 637–71.

———. *Catherine the Great: Life and Legend.* New York: Oxford University Press, 1989.

———. "Petersburg and Moscow in Early Urban Policy." *Journal of Urban History,* 9, no. 2 (February 1982): 145–69.

Al'perovich, Moisei Samuilovich. *Fransisko de Miranda v Rossii.* Moscow: "Nauka," 1986.

Alston, Patrick L. *Education and the State in Tsarist Russia.* Stanford, CA: Stanford University Press, 1969.

Amburger, Erik. *Ingermanland: Eine junge Provinz Russlands im Wirkungsbereich der Residenz und Weltstadt St. Petersburg-Leningrad.* 2 vols. Köln-Wien: Böhlau Verlag, 1980.

Anderson, Nels, ed. *Urbanism and Urbanization.* International Studies in Sociology and Social Anthropology. Vol. 2. Leiden: E. J. Brill, 1964.

Andreevskii, I. E. "O pervykh shagakh deiatel'nosti S.-Peterburgskogo prikaza obshchestvennogo prizreniia." *Russkaia starina* 63 (1889): 447–56.

Anisimov, Evgenii Viktorovich, ed. and intro. *Bezvremen'e i vremenshchiki: Vospominaniia ob "epokhe dvortsovykh perevorotov" (1720–e-1760–e gody).* Leningrad, 1991.

———. *The Reforms of Peter the Great: Progress through Coercion in Russia.* Translation and introduction by John T. Alexander. Armonk, NY: M. E. Sharpe, 1993.

Antsiferov, Nikolai Petrovich. *Dusha Peterburga.* Petrograd, 1922.

———. *Byl i mif Peterburga.* Petrograd, 1924.

Arkin, D. E. "Perspektivnyi plan Peterburga 1764–1773 gg. (Plan Sent-Ilera-Gorikhvostova-Sokolova)." *Arkhitekturnoe nasledstvo,* 7 (1950): 1–39.

———. "Zamechatel'nyi dokument russkogo gradostroitel'stva XVIII veka." *Sovetskii arkhitekt,* no. 6 (1955): 99–110.

Artamonov, Mikhail Illarionovich. *Russkaia kul'tura XVIII veka.* Moscow, 1955.

Artamonova, I. N. "Chicherin, Nikolai Ivanovich." *Russkii biograficheskii slovar',* 22: 430.

Atlas leningradskoi oblasti. Moscow: Glavnoe upravlenie geodezii i kartografii pri Sovete Ministrov SSSR, 1967.

Avseenko, Vasilii Grigor'evich. *200 let Peterburga: Istoricheskii ocherk.* St. Petersburg, 1903.

Baburin, Dmitrii. *Ocherki po istorii manufaktur-kollegii.* Moscow, 1939.

Baron, Samuel H. "The Town in Feudal Russia." *Slavic Review,* 28, no. 1 (March 1969): 116–22.

———. "The Weber Thesis and the Failure of Capitalist Development in 'Early Modern' Russia." *Jahrbücher für Geschichte Osteuropas,* 18, no. 3 (September 1970): 322–36.

Barrow, John, ed. *Some Account of the Public Life, and a Selection from the Unpublished Writings of the Earl of MacCartney.* 2 vols. London, 1807.

Bartenev, Petr Ivanovich, ed. *Osmnadtsatyi vek: Istoricheskii sbornik.* 4 vols. Moscow, 1868–69.

Bartlett, Roger P. *Human Capital: The Settlement of Foreigners in Russia, 1762–1804.* Cambridge: Cambridge University Press, 1979.

———, and Janet M. Hartley, eds. *Russia in the Age of Enlightenment: Essays for Isabel de Madariaga.* New York: St. Martin's Press, 1990.

Bashutskii, Aleksandr Pavlovich. *Panorama Sanktpeterburga.* 2 vols. St. Petersburg, 1834.

———. *Sobranie devianosta vos'mi gravirovannykh na stali vidov dlia Panoramy Sanktpeterburga.* St. Petersburg, 1834.

Basnin, V. N., ed. "Istoriia Imperatorskikh vospitatel'nykh domov." *Chteniia v Imperatorskom obshchestve istorii i drevnostei rossiiskikh pri moskovskom universitete,* 2 (1860): 93–98.

Bater, James H. *St. Petersburg: Industrialization and Change.* Montreal: McGill-Queens University Press, 1976.

Baykov, Alexander. "The Economic Development of Russia." In *Russian Economic Development from Peter the Great to Stalin,* edited and introduced by William L. Blackwell. New York, 1974.

Becker, Christopher. "Raznochintsy: Word and Concept." *American Slavic and East European Review,* 18, no. 1 (February 1959): 63–74.

Beliavskii, Mikhail Timofeevich. *Krest'ianskii vopros v Rossii nakanune vosstaniia E. I. Pugacheva.* Moscow, 1965.

Belinskii, Vissarion Grigor'evich. "Peterburg i Moskva." In *Fiziologiia Peterburga,* edited by Aleksei Nikolaevich Nekrasov (n. d.), pp. 29–99.

Berkov, Pavel Naumovich. *Istoriia russkoi zhurnalistiki XVIII veka.* Moscow-Leningrad, 1952.

Bernadskii, V. N., I. I. Liubimenko et al. "Kul'turnaia zhizn' Peterburga v 60-90kh godakh XVIII v." In *Ocherki istorii Leningrada,* edited by M. P. Viatkin et al., 1: 410–46.

Beskrovnyi, L. G., E. I. Zaozerskaia, and A. A. Preobrazhenskii, eds. *K voprosu o pervonachal'nom nakoplenii v Rossii (XVII–XVIII vv.): Sbornik statei.* Moscow, 1958.

Bespiatykh, Iurii Nikolaevich, ed. *Fenomen Peterburga.* St. Petersburg: Russko-Baltiiskii informatsionnyi tsentr BLITs, 2000.

Bil'basov, Vasilii Alekseevich. *Istoriia Ekateriny vtoroi.* Vols. 1 and 12. Berlin, 1890–96.

Blackwell, William L. *The Beginnings of Russian Industrialization, 1800–1860.* Princeton: Princeton University Press, 1968.

———. "Modernization and Urbanization in Russia: A Comparative View." In *The City in Russian History,* edited by Michael F. Hamm. Lexington, KY: University Press of Kentucky, 1976.

———, ed. and intro. *Russian Economic Development from Peter the Great to Stalin.* New York: New Viewpoints, 1974.

Blakely, Allison. *Russia and the Negro: Blacks in Russian History and Thought.* Washington, DC: Howard University Press, 1986.

Blumenfeld, Hans. "Russian City Planning of the Eighteenth and Early Nineteenth Centuries." *Journal of the American Society of Architectural Historians,* 4, no. 1 (January 1944): 22–33.

Bobovich, I. M. "Iz istorii promyshlennosti i rabochego klassa Peterburga pervoi poloviny XIX veka." *Nauchnye zapiski leningradskoi finansovo ekonomicheskogo instituta,* 11 (1956): 218–37.

Bogoliubov, V. N. *N. I. Novikov i ego vremia.* Moscow, 1916.

Bogoslovskii, Mikhail Mikhailovich. *Istoriia Rossii XVIII veka (1725 g.-1796 g.).* Moscow, 1915.

Bonnell, Victoria E. *Roots of Rebellion: Workers' Politics and Organizations in St. Petersburg and Moscow, 1900–1914.* Berkeley: University of California Press, 1983.

Borovoi, Saul Iakovlevich. "Voprosy kreditovaniia torgovli i promyshlennosti v ekonomicheskoi politike Rossii XVIII veka." *Istoricheskie zapiski,* 33 (1950): 92–93.

Bozherianov, Ivan Nikolaevich. *K dvukhsotletiiu stolitsy: S.-Peterburg v Petrovo vremia, 1703–1903.* St. Petersburg, 1901.

———. *"Nevskii prospekt," Kul'turno-istoricheskii ocherk dvukhvekovoi zhizni S.-Peterburga.* 5 vols. St. Petersburg, 1902.

Breese, Gerald. *Urbanization in Newly Developing Countries.* Englewood Cliffs, NJ: Prentice-Hall, 1966.

Brunner, Otto. *Neue Wege der Verfassungs- und Sozialgeschichte.* 2nd, enlarged ed. Göttingen: Vandenhoeck & Ruprecht, 1968.

Buckler, Julie. *Mapping St. Petersburg: Imperial Text and Cityshape.* Princeton: Princeton University Press, 2005.

Bulygin, Il'ia Andreevich et al. "Nachal'nyi etap genezisa kapitalizma v Rossii." *Voprosy istorii,* 1966, no. 10: 65–90.

Bunin, Andrei Vladimirovich. *Istoriia gradostroitel'nogo iskusstva.* Moscow, 1953.

Burbank, Jane, and David L. Ransel. *Imperial Russia: New Histories for the Empire.* Bloomington: Indiana University Press, 1998.

Burenina, Marina. *Progulki po Nevskomu prospektu.* St. Petersburg: Litera, 2002.

Burgess, Malcolm. "Russian Public Theater Audiences of the 18th and Early 19th Centuries." *Slavonic and East European Review,* 37, no. 88 (December 1958): 160–83.

Catteau-Colleville, Jean Pierre Guillaume. *Tableau de la mer baltique.* Paris, 1812.

Chechulin, Nikolai Dmitrievich. *Ocherki po istorii russkikh finansov v tsarstvovanie Ekateriny II*. St. Petersburg, 1906.

———. *Vneshniaia politika Rossii v nachale tsarstvovaniia Ekateriny II, 1762–1774*. St. Petersburg, 1896.

Clendenning, Philip H. "Dr. Thomas Dimsdale and Smallpox Inoculation in Russia." *Journal of the History of Medicine and Allied Sciences*, 28 (April 1973): 109–25.

Confino, Michael. *Domaines et seigneurs en Russie vers la fin du xviii-e siècle: Étude de structures agraires et de mentalités économiques*. Preface by Roger Portal. Paris, 1963.

———. *Systèmes agraires et progrès agricole: L'assolement triennal en Russie aux xviii-ee-xix-e siècles: Étude d'économie et de sociologie rurales*. Paris, 1969.

Cracraft, James. "James Brogden in Russia, 1787–1788." *Slavonic and East European Review*, 67, no. 108 (January 1969): 219–44.

———. *The Revolution of Peter the Great*. Cambridge, MA: Harvard University Press, 2003.

Cross, Anthony G. "The British in Catherine's Russia: A Preliminary Survey." In *The Eighteenth Century in Russia*, edited by J. G. Garrard, 233–63. Oxford: Clarendon Press, 1973.

———. *By the Banks of the Neva: Chapters from the Lives and Careers of the British in Eighteenth-Century Russia*. Cambridge: Cambridge University Press, 1997.

———, ed. *St. Petersburg, 1703–1825*. New York: Palgrave Macmillan, 2003.

Damaze de Raymond. *Tableau historique, géographique, militaire et moral de l'empire de Russie*. 2 vols. Paris, 1812.

Darinskii, Anatolii Viktorovich. *Progulki po staromu Sankt-Peterburgu*. St. Petersburg: Ekam, 1995.

Darnton, Robert. *The Great Cat Massacre and Other Episodes in French Cultural History*. New York: Basic Books, 1984.

Davis, Kingsley, and Hilda H. Golden. "Urbanization and the Development of Preindustrial Areas." *Economic Development and Cultural Change*, 3 (October 1954): 6–26.

D——v, N. "Proshloe Peterburga." *Zhurnal ministerstva narodnogo prosveshcheniia*, 240 (July 1885): 145–61.

De Ligne [De Lin'i], N. N., ed. *Staryi Peterburg (1703–1953): Iubileinyi sbornik vospominanii*. Book 1. Paris, 1953.

Demkin, Andrei Vladimirovich. *Britanskoe kupechestvo v Rossii XVIII veka*. Moscow: Rossiiskaia akademiia nauk, Institut rossiiskoi istorii, 1998.

De Vries, Jan. *European Urbanization, 1500–1800*. Cambridge, MA: Harvard University Press, 1984.

Ditiatin, Ivan Ivanovich. *Russkii doreformennyi gorod*. Vols. 5 and 6 of *Russkaia mysl'*. 1884.

———. *Stoletie S.-Peterburgskogo gorodskogo obshchestva, 1781–1885*. St. Petersburg, 1885.

———. *Ustroistvo i upravlenie gorodov Rossii*. 2 vols. St. Petersburg, 1875 (vol. 1); Iaroslavl', 1877 (vol. 2).

Dmitriev, N. N. *Pervye russkie sitsenabivnye manufaktury XVIII veka*. Moscow-Leningrad, 1935.

Donnert, Erich. *Russia in the Age of Enlightenment*. Translated from the German by Alison and Alistair Wightman. Leipzig: Edition Leipzig, 1986.

Druzhinin, Nikolai Mikhailovich, ed. *Absoliutizm v Rossii (XVII-XVIII vv.): Sbornik statei k semidesiatiletiiu so dnia rozhdeniia i sorokapiatiletiiu nauchnoi i pedagogicheskoi deiatelnosti B. B. Kafengauza*. Moscow, 1964.

——— et al., eds. *Period feodalizma: Rossiia vo vtoroi polovine XVIII v*. Vol. 9 of *Ocherki istorii SSSR*. Moscow, 1958.

Efimenko, T. P. "K istorii gorodskogo zemleustroistva vremen Ekateriny II." *Zhurnal ministerstva narodnogo prosveshcheniia*, 1914, no. 12: 280–315.
Egorov, Iurii Alekseevich. *The Architectural Planning of St. Petersburg*. Translated by Eric Dluhosch. Athens: Ohio University Press, 1969.
Ekimov, A. A. "Iz istorii razvitiia krupnoi mashinnoi industrii v Peterburge v doreformennyi period (1800–1860 gg.)." *Vestnik leningradskogo gosudarstvennogo universiteta*, 1954, no. 3: 79–95.
Engel'gardt, N. A. "Dvukhsotletie S.-Peterburga." *Istoricheskii vestnik*, 92 (June 1903): 901–46.
Engelstein, Laura. *Castration and the Heavenly Kingdom: A Russian Folktale*. Ithaca: Cornell University Press, 1999.
Engman, Maks [Max]. *Finliandtsy v Peterburge*. Translated from Swedish by A. I. Ropasov. St. Petersburg: "Evropeiskii dom," 2005.
Epstein, S. R., ed. *Town and Country in Europe, 1300–1800*. New York: Cambridge University Press, 2001.
Ermolaeva, Liubov' Konstantinovna, and I. M. Lebedeva. *Progulki po Peterburgu: Progulka vtoraia: zdes' budet gorod*. St. Petersburg: Khimiia, 1997.
Fava, Sylvia Fleis, ed. *Urbanism in World Perspective: A Reader*. New York: Thomas Y. Crowell, 1968.
Florovskii, Antonii Vasil'evich. *Iz istorii ekaterininskoi zakonodatel'noi kommissii, 1767 g.: Vopros o krepostnom prave*. Odessa, 1910.
Fokin, Nikolai Nikolaevich. "O pamiatnykh mestakh pushkinskogo Peterburga." In *Pushkin i ego vremia: Sbornik statei*. Edited by M. M. Kalaushin, 1: 541–52. Leningrad, 1962.
Fox, Frank. "French-Russian Commercial Relations in the Eighteenth Century and the French-Russian Commercial Treaty of 1787." Unpublished PhD dissertation, University of Delaware, 1966.
Freeze, Gregory L. "The *Soslovie* (Estate) Paradigm and Russian Social History." *American Historical Review*, 91, no. 1 (February 1986): 11–36.
Friebe, W. Chr. *Über Russlands Handel, landwirtschaftliche Kultur, Industrie und Produkte*. St. Petersburg, 1797.
Garrard, John G., ed. *The Eighteenth Century in Russia*. Oxford: Clarendon Press, 1973.
Gegello, A. I., and V. I. Piliavskii. "Arkhitektura Peterburga 60–90kh godov XVIII v." In *Ocherki istorii Leningrada*, edited by M. P. Viatkin et al., 1: 320–59.
George, M. Dorothy. *London Life in the Eighteenth Century*. New York: Harper & Row, 1964.
German [Herrman], Karl. *Statisticheskie issledovaniia otnositel'no rossiiskoi imperii*. St. Petersburg, 1819.
Gernet, Mikhail Nikolaevich. *Istoriia tsarskoi tiurmy*. 2nd ed. 5 vols. Moscow, 1951.
Gerschenkron, Alexander. "Problems and Patterns of Russian Economic Development." In *The Transformation of Russian Society*, edited by Cyril E. Black. Cambridge, MA: Harvard University Press, 1960.
Gleason, Walter J. *Moral Idealists, Bureaucracy, and Catherine the Great*. New Brunswick: Rutgers University Press, 1981.
Golikova, N. B. *Ocherki po istorii gorodov Rossii kontsa XVII-nachala XVIII v.* Moscow, 1982.
Gooch, George Peabody. *Catherine the Great and Other Studies*. Hamden, CT: Archon Books, 1966.
Gordin, A. M. *Krylov v Peterburge*. Leningrad, 1969.
Goryshina, Tamara. "Bolota 'Severnoi Pal'miry.'" *Neva*, 1997, no. 2: 216–20.
Grabar', Igor' Emmanuilovich. *O russkoi arkhitekture*. Moscow, 1969.

Grach, Aleksandr Danilovich. *Arkheologicheskie raskopki v Leningrade: K kharakteristike kul'tury i byta naseleniia Peterburga XVIII v.* Moscow-Leningrad, 1957.

Grechaniuk, Nikolai Mokeevich, et al. *Baltiiskii flot: Istoricheskie ocherki.* Moscow, 1960.

Grechukhin, Andrei. *Progulki po Petrogradskoi.* St. Petersburg: Severnaia zvezda, 2002.

Grey, Ian. *Catherine the Great: Autocrat and Empress of All Russia.* London: Hodder and Stoughton, 1961.

Griffiths, David Mark. "American Commercial Diplomacy in Russia, 1780–1783." *William and Mary Quarterly,* 3rd series, 27, no. 3 (July 1970): 379–410.

———. "Eighteenth-Century Perceptions of Backwardness: Projects for the Creation of a Third Estate in Catherinian Russia." *Canadian-American Slavic Studies,* 13, no. 4 (Winter 1979): 452–72.

Guro. "Istoriia imperatorskikh vospitatel'nykh domov." Edited by V.N. Basnin. *Chteniia v Imperatorskom obshchestve istorii i drevnostei rossisskikh pri moskovskom universitete,* 2 (1860): 93–117.

Gusev, N. I. *Peterburg.* Kiev, 1899.

Gutkind, E. A., ed. *Urban Development in Eastern Europe, Bulgaria, Romania, and the U.S.S.R.*. Vol. 8 of the *International History of City Development.* New York: Free Press, 1972.

Hamm, Michael F., ed. *The City in Russian History.* Lexington: University Press of Kentucky, 1976.

Handlin, Oscar, and John Burchard, eds. *The Historian and the City.* Cambridge: M.I.T. Press, 1967.

Hans, Nicholas. *The History of Russian Educational Policy (1701–1917).* New York: Russell and Russell, 1964.

Hartley, Janet M. "Governing the City: St. Petersburg and Catherine II's Reforms." In *St. Petersburg, 1703–1825,* edited by Anthony Cross, 99–118. New York: Palgrave Macmillan, 2003.

———. "The Implementation of the Laws Relating to Local Administration, 1775–1796, with Special Reference to the Guberniia of St. Petersburg." Unpublished PhD dissertation, University of London, 1980.

———. "Philanthropy in the Reign of Catherine the Great: Aims and Realities." In *Russia in the Age of Enlightenment. Essays for Isabel de Madariaga,* edited by Roger Bartlett and Janet M. Hartley, 167–202. New York: St. Martin's Press, 1990.

———. "Town Government in St. Petersburg Guberniya after the Charter to the Towns of 1785." *Slavonic and East European Review,* 62, no. 1 (January 1984): 61–84.

Harvey, David. *The Urban Experience.* Baltimore: Johns Hopkins University Press, 1989.

Hassell, James. "The Planning of St. Petersburg." *Historian: A Journal of History,* 36, no. 2 (February 1974): 248–63.

Herlihy, Patricia. *Odessa: A History, 1794–1914.* Cambridge, MA: Harvard University Press, 1986.

Hildermeier, Manfred. *Bürgertum und Stadt in Russland 1760–1870: Rechtliche Lage und soziale Struktur.* Köln and Vienna: Böhlau Verlag, 1986.

Hittle, J. Michael. *The Service City: State and Townsmen in Russia, 1600–1800.* Cambridge, MA: Harvard University Press, 1979.

Hohenburg, Paul M., and Lynn Hollen Lees. *The Making of Urban Europe.* Cambridge, MA: Harvard University Press, 1985.

Holton, R. J. *Cities, Capitalism, and Civilization.* London: Allen and Unwin, 1986.

Howard, Derek Lionel. *John Howard: Prison Reformer.* London: Christopher Johnson, 1958.

Hudson, Hugh D., Jr. *The Rise of the Demidov Family and the Russian Iron Industry in the Eighteenth Century.* Newtonville, MA: Oriental Research Partners, 1986.

Iakovtsevskii, Vasilii Nikolaevich. *Kupecheskii kapital v feodal'no-krepostnicheskoi Rossii.* Moscow, 1953.

Iatsevich, Andrei Grigor'evich. *Krepostnye v Peterburge.* Leningrad, 1933.

Iatsunskii, V. K. "Rol' Peterburga v promyshlennom razvitii dorevoliutsionnoi Rossii." *Voprosy istorii,* 1954, no. 9: 95–103.

Il'in-Zhenevskii, Aleksandr Fedorovich. "Kogda i kak nachal svoe sushchestvovanie Putilovskii zavod." *Krasnaia letopis',* 1930, no. 3: 194–222; no. 4: 153–95; no. 5: 149–77.

Indova, Ekaterina Iosifovna. "O rossiiskikh manufakturakh vtoroi poloviny XVIII v." In *Istoricheskaia geografiia Rossii XII-nachalo XX v. Sbornik statei k 70–letiiu Professora Liubomira Grigor'evicha Beskrovnogo,* edited by A. L. Narochnitskii et al., 248–345. Moscow, 1975.

Isaev, Gerasim Sergeevich. *Rol' tekstil'noi promyshlennosti v genezise i razvitii kapitalizma v Rossii, 1760–1860.* Leningrad, 1970.

Istomina, E. G. "Vyshnevolotskii vodnyi put' vo vtoroi polovine XVIII-nachale XIX v." In *Istoricheskaia geografiia Rossii XII - nachalo XX v. Sbornik statei k 70–letiiu Professora Liubomira Grigor'evicha Beskrovnogo,* edited by A. L. Narochnitskii et al., 193–206. Moscow, 1975.

Istoricheskaia panorama Sanktpeterburga i ego okrestnostei. Part 1. Moscow, 1911.

Istoriia Moskvy. 5 vols. Moscow, 1952–55.

Johnson, Emily D. *How St. Petersburg Learned to Study Itself: The Russian Idea of Kraevedenie.* University Park: Pennsylvania State University Press, 2006.

Johnson, Robert Eugene. *Peasant and Proletarian: The Working Class of Moscow in the Late Nineteenth Century.* New Brunswick: Rutgers University Press, 1979.

Jones, Emrys. *Towns and Cities.* London: Oxford University Press, 1966.

Jones, Robert E. "Getting the Goods to St. Petersburg: Water Transport from the Interior 1703–1811." *Slavic Review,* 43, no. 3 (Fall 1984): 413–33.

———. *Provincial Development in Russia: Catherine II and Jakob Sievers.* New Brunswick: Rutgers University Press, 1984.

———. "Urban Planning and the Development of Provincial Towns in Russia, 1762–1796." In *The Eighteenth Century in Russia,* edited by John G. Garrard. Oxford: Clarendon Press, 1973.

Jones, W. Gareth. *Nikolay Novikov, Enlightener of Russia.* Cambridge: Cambridge University Press, 1984.

Kabuzan, Vladimir Maksimovich. *Narodonaselenie Rossii v XVIII i pervoi polovine XIX v. (Po materialam revizii).* Moscow, 1963.

Kafengauz, Berngard (Boris) Borisovich. "Goroda i gorodskaia reforma 1785 g." In *Istoriia SSSR. Period feodalizma: Rossiia vo vtoroi polovine XVIII v.,* edited by N. M. Druzhinin et al., 151–65. Moscow, 1958.

———. "Nekotorye voprosy genezisa kapitalizma v Rossii." In *Voprosy genezisa kapitalizma v Rossii,* edited by V. V. Mavrodin. Leningrad, 1960.

———. *Ocherki vnutrennego rynka pervoi poloviny XVIII veka.* Moscow, 1958.

Kagan, Moisei. *Grad Petrov v istorii russkoi kul'tury.* St. Petersburg: AO "Slaviia," 1996.

Kaganov, Grigorii Zosimovich. *Images of Space: St. Petersburg in the Visual and Verbal Arts.* Translated by Sidney Monas. Stanford, CA: Stanford University Press, 1997.

Kahan, Arcadius. "Continuity in Economic Activity and Policy During the Post-Petrine Period in Russia." *Journal of Economic History,* 25, no. 1 (March 1965): 61–85.

———. "The Costs of 'Westernization' in Russia: The Gentry and the Economy in the Eighteenth Century." *Slavic Review,* 25, no. 1 (March 1966): 40–66.

———. "Entrepreneurship in the Early Development of Iron Manufacture in Russia." *Economic Development and Cultural Change.* 10, no. 4 (July 1962): 59–77.

———. *The Plow, the Hammer, and the Knout: An Economic History of Eighteenth-Century Russia.* Editorial assistance by Richard Hellie. Chicago: University of Chicago Press, 1985.

Kallash, Vladimir Vladimirovich, ed. *Tri veka: Rossiia ot smut' do nashego vremeni.* 4 vols. Moscow, 1913. Vol. 4, *XVIII vek: Vtoraia polovina.*

Kamenskii, Aleksandr Borisovich. *Povsednevnost' russkoi gorodskikh obyvatelei: Istoricheskie anekdoty iz provintsial'noi zhizni XVIII veka.* Moscow: Russian State Humanities University, 2006.

Kaplan, Herbert. *Russian Overseas Commerce with Great Britain during the Reign of Catherine II.* Philadelphia: American Philosophical Society, 1995.

Kann, Pavel Iakovlevich. *Progulki po Peterburgu.* St. Petersburg: Palitra, 1994.

Karatygin, Petr Petrovich. *Letopis' peterburgskikh navodnenii 1730–1879 gg., P. P. Karatygina.* St. Petersburg, 1889.

Kashpirev, V. *Pamiatniki novoi russkoi istorii: Sbornik istoricheskikh statei i materialov.* 2 vols. St. Petersburg, 1871–72.

Keller, Elena Edvinovna. *Prazdnichnaia kul'tura Peterburga: Ocherki istorii.* St. Petersburg: Izdatel'stvo Mikhailova V. A., 2001.

Kepsu, Saulo. *Pietari ennen Pietaria: Nevansuun vaiheita ennen Pietarin kaupungin perustamista.* Helsinki: Suomalaisen Kirjallisuuden Seura, 1995.

Khromov, Oleg Rostislavovich. *Progulki po Sankt-Peterburgu: Akvareli, graviury, litografii.* Moscow: Interbuk-biznes, 2002.

Kizevetter, Aleksandr Aleksandrovich. "Gorodovoe polozhenie Ekateriny II." In *Tri veka: Rossiia ot smut' do nashego vremeni,* edited by Vladimir Vladimirovich Kallash. 4 vols. Moscow, 1913.

———. *Gorodovoe polozhenie Ekateriny II.* Moscow, 1909.

———. *Istoricheskie ocherki.* Moscow, 1912.

———. *Mestnoe samoupravlenie v Rossii. IX-XIX st.: Istoricheskii ocherk.* 2nd ed. Petrograd, 1917.

———. *Posadskaia obshchina v Rossii XVIII st.* Moscow, 1903.

———. *Russkoe obshchestvo v vosemnadtsatom stoletii.* Rostov-na-Donu, 1904.

Kliuchevskii, Vasilii Osipovich. *Sochineniia.* 8 vols. Moscow, 1956–59.

Klochkov, Mikhail Vasil'evich. *Naselenie Rossii pri Petre velikom po perepisiam togo vremeni.* Vol. 1, *Perepisi dvorov i naseleniia (1678–1721).* St. Petersburg, 1911.

Klokman, Iurii Robertovich. "Gorod v zakonodatel'stve russkogo absoliutizma vo vtoroi polovine XVII–XVIII vv." In *Absoliutizm v Rossii (XVII–XVIII vv.): Sbornik statei k semidesiatiletiiu so dnia rozhdeniia i sorokopiatiletiiu nauchnoi i pedagogicheskoi deiatel'nosti B. B. Kafengauza,* edited by N. M. Druzhinin, 320–54. Moscow, 1964.

———. *Ocherki sotsial'no-ekonomicheskoi istorii gorodov severo-zapada Rossii v seredine XVIII v.* Moscow, 1960.

———. *Sotsial'no-ekonomicheskaia istoriia russkogo goroda: Vtoraia polovina XVIII veka.* Moscow, 1967.

Kniazev, Georgii. "Dom akademikov." *Belye nochi: Ocherki, zarisovki, dokumenty, vospominaniia,* 2 (1972): 79–92.

Kniaz'kov, Sergei Aleksandrovich. *S.-Peterburg i s.-peterburgskoe obshchestvo pri Petre velikom.* St. Petersburg, 1914.

Kobeko, D. F. "Frantsuzskaia koloniia v Peterburge." *Russkii arkhiv,* 1874, no. 1: 952–55.

Kochan, Miriam. *Life in Russia under Catherine the Great.* New York: G. P. Putnam's Sons, 1969.

Kochin, G. E. "Naselenie Peterburga v 60–90kh godakh XVIII v." In *Ocherki istorii Leningrada,* edited by M. P. Viatkin et al., 1: 294–319.

Kolotilova, S. I. "Sotsial'nyi sostav rabotnikov chastnovladel'cheskoi promyshlennosti Peterburga i peterburgskoi gubernii v 1750–1770-kh godakh." *Uchenye zapiski Pskovskogo gosudarstvennogo pedagogicheskogo instituta: Kafedra istorii,* 1963, no. 23: 43–54.

Komalova, Galina Nikolaevna. *Vidy Peterburga i ego okrestnostei serediny XVIII veka: Graviury po risunkam M. Makhaeva.* Leningrad, 1968.

Kondrat'eva, V. A., and V. I. Nevzorov, eds. *Iz istorii fabrik i zavodov Moskvy i moskovskoi gubernii (konets XVIII-nachalo XX v.): Obzor dokumentov.* Moscow, 1968.

Konechnyi, Al'bin M., ed. and intro. *Progulki po Nevskomu prospektu v pervoi polovine XIX veka.* St. Petersburg: "Giperion," 2002.

Konvitz, Josef W. *Cities and the Sea: Port City Planning in Early Modern Europe.* Baltimore: Johns Hopkins University Press, 1978.

Kopanev, A. I. *Naselenie Peterburga v pervoi polovine XIX veka.* Moscow-Leningrad, 1957.

Korf[f] Sergei Aleksandrovich. *Dvorianstvo i ego soslovnoe upravlenie za stoletie, 1762–1855 gg.* St. Petersburg, 1906.

Kotkin, Stephen. *Magnetic Mountain: Stalinism as a Civilization.* Berkeley: University of California Press, 1995.

Koval'chenko, I. D., and L. V. Milov. "Ob intensivnosti obrochnoi ekspluatatsii krest'ian tsentral'noi Rossii v kontse XVIII-pervoi polovine XIX v." *Istoriia SSSR* 11, no. 4 (1966): 55–80.

Kulisher, Iosif Mikhailovich. *Istoriia russkoi torgovli do deviatnadtsatogo veka vkliuchitel'no.* Petrograd, 1923.

Kurbatov, Vladimir Iakovlevich. *Peterburg: Khudozhestvenno-istoricheskii ocherk i obzor khudozhestvennogo bogatstva stolitsy.* St. Petersburg, 1913.

Kurganova, E. and N. Okhotina, eds., *Russkii literaturnyi anekdot kontsa XVIII—nachala XIX veka.* Introduction by E. Kurganova. Moscow, 1990.

Lappo-Danilevskii, Aleksandr S. *Ocherk vnutrennei politiki imperatritsy Ekateriny II.* St. Petersburg, 1898.

Laran, Michel. "La première génération de l'intelligentsia roturière en Russie." *Revue d'histoire moderne et contemporaine,* 13, no. 2 (April-June 1966): 137–56.

Latkin, Vasilii Nikolaevich. *Uchebnik istorii russkogo prava: Period imperii (XVIII i XIX st.).* St. Petersburg, 1899.

———. *Zakonodatel'nye kommissii Rossii XVIII stoletiia: Istoriko-iuridicheskoe izsledovanie.* St. Petersburg, 1887.

Lawton, Richard, ed. *The Rise and Fall of Great Cities: Aspects of Urbanization in the Western World.* New York: Bellhaven Press, 1989.

LeDonne, John P. "The Provincial and Local Police Under Catherine the Great, 1775–1796." *Canadian Slavic Studies,* 4, no. 3 (Fall 1970): 513–28.

———. *Ruling Russia: Politics and Administration in the Age of Absolutism, 1762–1796.* Princeton: Princeton University Press, 1984.

Leningrad: Arkhitekturno-planirovannyi obzor razvitiia goroda. Leningrad, 1943.

Leningradskii ordena Lenina gosudarstvennyi universitet im. A. A. Zhdanova. Geografo-ekonomicheskii nauchno-issledovatel'skii institut. *Peterburg-Leningrad: Istoriko-geograficheskii atlas, chast' pervaia.* Leningrad, 1957.

Leonard, Carol Scott. "A Study of the Reign of Peter III of Russia." Upublished PhD dissertation. Indiana University, 1976.

———. *Reform and Regicide: The Reign of Peter III of Russia.* Bloomington: Indiana University Press, 1993.

Lepetit, Bernard. *The Preindustrial Urban System: France, 1740–1840.* Translated by Godfrey Rogers. New York: Cambridge University Press, 1994.

Letiche, John M., ed. *A History of Russian Economic Thought: Ninth Through Eighteenth Centuries.* Translated by Basil Dmytryshyn and Richard A. Pierce. Berkeley: University of California Press, 1964.

Levin, A. "Chuma." *Entsiklopedicheskii slovar',* 39, 647–48.

Liashchenko, Petr Ivanovich. *Istoriia narodnogo khoziaistva SSSR.* Vol. 1, *Dokapitalisticheskie formatsii.* 4th ed. Moscow, 1956.

Lincoln, W. Bruce. "N. A. Miliutin and the St. Petersburg Municipal Act of 1846: A Study in Reform under Nicholas I." *Slavic Review,* 33, no. 1 (Winter 1974): 55–68.

———. "The Russian State and its Cities: A Search for Effective Municipal Government, 1786–1842." *Jahrbücher für Geschichte Osteuropas,* 17, no. 4 (December 1969): 531–41.

———. *Sunlight at Midnight: St. Petersburg and the Rise of Modern Russia.* New York: Basic Books, 2000.

Liubomirov, Pavel Grigor'evich. *Ocherki po istorii russkoi promyshlennosti: XVII, XVIII, i nachalo XIX veka.* Edited by S. G. Strumilin. Moscow, 1947.

———. "Rol' kazennogo dvorianskogo i kupecheskogo kapitala v stroitel'stve krupnoi promyshlennosti Rossii v XVII–VIII vekakh." *Istoricheskie zapiski,* 16 (1945): 65–69.

Lukomskii, Georgii Kreskent'evich. *Sankt-Peterburg: Istoricheskii ocherk arkhitektury i razvitiia goroda.* Munich, 1923.

———. *Staryi Peterburg: Progulki po starinnym kvartalam.* 2nd ed. Petrograd, n.d.

Luppov, S. P. "Gorodskoe upravlenie i gorodskoe khoziaistvo Peterburga v 60–90kh godakh XVIII v." In *Ocherki istorii Leningrada,* edited by M. P. Viatkin et al., I: 360–79.

———. *Istoriia stroitel'stva Peterburga v pervoi chetverti XVIII veka.* Moscow-Leningrad, 1957.

Lystsov, Vikentii Pavlovich. *M. V. Lomonosov v sotsial'no-ekonomicheskom razvitii Rossii.* Voronezh, 1969.

Madariaga, Isabel de. *Britain, Russia, and the Armed Neutrality of 1780: Sir James Harris's Mission to St. Petersburg during the American Revolution.* Foreword by Samuel Flagg Bemis. New Haven: Yale University Press, 1962.

———. *Catherine the Great: A Short History.* New Haven: Yale University Press, 1990.

———. "The Foundation of the Russian Educational System by Catherine II." *Slavonic and East European Review,* 57, no. 3 (July 1979): 369–95.

———. *Russia in the Age of Catherine the Great.* New Haven: Yale University Press, 1981.

Maikov, Petr Mikhailovich. *Ivan Ivanovich Betskoi: Opyt ego biografii.* St. Petersburg, 1904.

Maikov, P. and B. M-i. "Ryleev, Nikita Ivanovich." *Russkii biograficheskii slovar',* 17: 697–701.

Makarov, V. I. "Ekonomicheskaia zhizn' Peterburga 60–90kh godov XVIII v." In *Ocherki istorii Leningrada,* edited by M. P. Viatkin et al., 1: 251–93.

Mansurov, B. *Okhtenskie admiralteiskie stroeniia.* St. Petersburg, 1855.

Marrese, Michelle Lamarche. *A Woman's Kingdom: Noblewomen and the Control of Property in Russia, 1700–1861.* Ithaca: Cornell University Press, 2002.

Marsden, Christopher. *Palmyra of the North: The First Days of St. Petersburg.* London: Faber & Faber, 1942.

Mavrodin, Vladimir Vasil'evich. *Klassovaia bor'ba i obshchestvenno-politicheskaia mysl' v Rossii v XVIII v. (1725–1773 gg.): Kurs lektsii.* Leningrad, 1964.

———, ed. *Voprosy genezisa kapitalizma v Rossii: Sbornik statei.* Leningrad, 1960.

Mel'gunov, P. E., K. V. Sivkov, and N. P. Sidorov, eds. *Russkii byt po vospominaniiam ovremennikov: XVIII vek.* Vol. 2, *Vremia Ekateriny II.* 2nd ed. Moscow, 1922.

Menshikov, P. N. "Neostorozhnaia ezda v starinu, 1683–1800 gg." *Russkaia starina* 18 (1877): 740–44.

Milov, L. V. *Issledovanie ob "ekonomicheskikh primechaniiakh" k general'nomu mezhevaniiu (K istorii russkogo krest'ianstva i sel'skogo khoziaistva vtoroi poloviny XVIII v.).* Moscow, 1965.
Milov, L. V. "O tak nazyvaemykh agrarnykh gorodakh Rossii XVIII veka." *Voprosy istorii,* 1968, no. 6: 54–64.
Miliukov, Pavel N. *Ocherki po istorii russkoi kul'tury.* 3 vols. Paris, 1931.
Mironov, Boris Nikolaevich. *Russkii gorod v 1740–1860e gody: Demograficheskoe, sotsial'noe i ekonomicheskoe razvitie.* Leningrad, 1990.
———. "Sotsial'naia mobil'nost' rossiiskogo kupechestva v XVIII - nachale XIX veka (opyt izucheniia). In *Problemy istoricheskoi demografii SSSR: Sbornik statei,* edited by R. N. Pullat, 207–17. Tallinn, 1977.
———. "Sotsial'naia struktura gorodskogo naseleniia Rossii vo vtoroi polovine XVIII-pervoi polovine XIX v." In *Genezis i razvitie feodalizma v Rossii: Problemy istorii goroda,* edited by I. Ia. Froianov, 197–224. Leningrad, 1988.
———. *Vnutrennii rynok Rossii vo vtoroi polovine XVIII-pervoi polovine XIX v.* Leningrad, 1981.
Mooser, Robert Aloys. *Opéras, intermezzos, ballets, cantates, oratorios joués en Russie durant le xviii-e siècle.* Geneva: R. Kister, 1955.
Mordvinov, I., ed. "Peterburgskoe navodnenie Ekaterininskogo vremeni v opisanii ochevidtsa" *Russkii arkhiv,* 1916, nos. 1–3: 209–10.
Morrison, Daniel. "'Trading Peasants' and Urbanization in Eighteenth-Century Russia: The Central Industrial Region." Unpublished PhD dissertation, Columbia University, 1981.
Mumford, Lewis. *The City in History: Its Origins, its Transformations, and its Prospects.* New York: Harcourt, Brace & World, Inc., 1961.
Munro, George E. "The Charter to the Towns Reconsidered: The St. Petersburg Connection." *Canadian-American Slavic Studies,* 23, no. 1 (Spring 1989): 17–34.
———. "Compiling and Maintaining St. Petersburg's 'Book of City Inhabitants': The 'Real' City Inhabitants." In *St. Petersburg, 1703–1825,* edited by Anthony Cross, 80–98. New York: Palgrave Macmillan, 2003.
———. "Feeding the Multitudes: Grain Supply to St. Petersburg in the Era of Catherine the Great." *Jahrbücher für Geschichte Osteuropas,* 35, no. 4 (1987): 481–508.
———. "Food in Catherinian St. Petersburg." In *Food in Russian History and Culture,* edited by Musya Glants and Joyce Toomre, 31–48. Bloomington: Indiana University Press, 1997.
———. "The Petersburg of Catherine II: Official Enlightenment versus Popular Cults." In *Moscow and Petersburg: The City in Russian Culture,* edited by Ian Lilly, 49–64. Nottingham, England: Astra Press, 2002.
———. "The Quest for the Historical Prostitute: Some Barriers to Research in Soviet Archives." *Research in Action,* 3, no. 1 (Fall-Winter 1977–78): 10–17.
———. "The Role of the *Veksel'* in Russian Capital Formation: A Preliminary Inquiry." In *Russia and the World of the Eighteenth Century,* edited by R. P. Bartlett, A. P. Cross, and Karen Rasmussen, 551–64. Columbus, OH: Slavica, 1988.
———. "Russia's Non-Russian Capital: Petersburg and the Planning Commission." *Eighteenth Century Life,* 2, no. 3 (March 1976): 49–53.
Nechaev, A. *Ocherki po istorii obukhovskoi bol'nitsy.* Leningrad, 1952.
Nechaev, Vladimir Nikolaevich. *Kak buntovali "fabrichniki" v seredine XVIII veka.* Moscow, 1932.
Nekrasov, Nikolai Alekseevich, ed. *Fiziologiia Peterburga, sostavlennaia iz trudov russkikh literatorov.* St. Petersburg, 1845.
Nekrylova, Anna Fedorovna. *Russkie narodnye gorodskie prazdniki, uveseleniia i zrelishcha: Konets XVIII–nachalo XX veka.* Leningrad, 1988.

Neustroev, Aleksandr Nikolaevich. *Pervyi russkii meditsinskii zhurnal "Sanktpeterburgskie vrachebnye vedomosti" 1793 (1792)-1794 gg.* St. Petersburg, 1874.

Nosov, N. E. et al., eds. *Remeslo i manufaktura v Rossii, Finliandii, Pribaltike.* Leningrad, 1975.

Oddy, Joshua Jepson. *European Commerce, Shewing New and Secure Channels of Trade with the Continent of Europe: Detailing the Produce, Manufactures, and Commerce, of Russia, Prussia, Sweden, Denmark and Germany.* 2 vols. Philadelphia, 1807.

Ozhegov, Sergei Sergeevich. *Tipovoe i povtornoe stroitel'stvo v Rossii v XVIII-XIX vekakh.* Moscow, 1987.

Paneiakh, V. M. "Masterovye i rabotnye liudi vo vtoroi polovine XVIII veka." Chapter 2 of *Istoriia rabochikh Leningrada, 1703–1965,* edited by S. N. Valk et al., 1: 46–71. 2 vols. Vol. 1, *1703 -fevral' 1917.* Leningrad, 1972.

Pankratova, Anna Mikhailovna. *Formirovanie proletariata v Rossii (XVII–XVIII vv.).* Moscow, 1963.

Pantenius, Heinrich, and Grosberg, Oskar. *Deutsches Leben im alten St. Petersburg: Ein Buch der Erinnerung.* Riga, 1930.

Parkinson, Roger. *The Fox of the North: The Life of Kutuzov, General of War and Peace.* New York: David McKay, 1976.

Pavlenko, Nikolai Ivanovich. *Istoriia metallurgii v Rossii XVIII veka: Zavody i zavodovladel'tsy.* Moscow, 1962.

———. "O nekotorykh storonakh pervonachal'nogo nakopleniia v Rossii (po materialam XVII–XVIII vv.)." *Istoricheskie zapiski,* 54 (1955): 382–419.

———. "Odvorianivanie russkoi burzhuazii v XVIII v." *Istoriia SSSR* 6, no. 2 (1961): 71–87.

Pazhitnov, Konstantin Alekseevich. *Ocherki istorii tekstil'noi promyshlennosti dorevoliutsionnoi Rossii: Sherstianaia promyshlennost'.* Moscow, 1955.

———. *Problema remeslennykh tsekhov v zakonodatel'stve russkogo absoliutizma.* Moscow, 1952.

Peterburg i ego zhizn'. St. Petersburg, 1914.

Petrov, A. "Palaty Kikina (neissledovannoe zdanie nachala XVIII veka)." *Arkhitekturnoe nasledstvo,* 4 (1953): 139–47.

Petrov, A. N., ed. *Pamiatniki arkhitektury Leningrada.* Leningrad, 1958.

Petrov, Petr Nikolaevich. *Istoriia Sanktpeterburga s osnovaniia goroda do vvedeniia v deistvie vybornogo gorodskogo upravleniia po uchrezhdeniiam o guberniiakh: 1703–1782.* St. Petersburg, 1885.

Piatkovskii, A. P. "S.-Peterburgskii vospitatel'nyi dom pod upravleniem I. I. Betskogo." *Russkaia Starina* 12 (1875): 146–59, 359–80, 665–80; 13 (1875): 177–99, 532–53.

Piliavskii, V. I. *Arkhitektura Leningrada.* Leningrad, 1953.

Pintner, Walter M. "The Social Characteristics of the Early Nineteenth-Century Russian Bureaucracy." *Slavic Review,* 29, no. 3 (September 1970): 429–43.

———, and Don Karl Rowney, eds. *Russian Officialdom: The Bureaucratization of Russian Society from the Seventeenth to the Twentieth Century.* Chapel Hill: University of North Carolina Press, 1980.

Piotrovskii, Boris Borisovich, gen. ed. *Ermitazh: Istoriia stroitel'stva i arkhitektura zdanii.* Leningrad, 1991.

Ploshinskii, Liudvig Osipovich. *Gorodskoe ili srednee sostoianie russkogo naroda, v ego istoricheskom razvitii ot nachala Rusi do noveishikh vremen.* St. Petersburg, 1852.

Pokshishevskii, Vadim Viacheslavovich. "Territoria'lnoe formirovanie promyshlennogo kompleksa Peterburga v XVIII–XIX vv." *Voprosy geografii,* Sbornik 20 (1950): 122–62.

Polianskii, Fedor Iakovlevich. *Gorodskoe remeslo i manufaktura v Rossii XVIII v.* Moscow, 1960.

Polianskii, Fedor Iakovlevich. "Pokupka krepostnykh manufakturistami v Rossii XVIII veka." *Uchenye zapiski moskovskogo gosudarstvennogo universiteta,* Vypusk 179 (1956): 3–27.

Popov, M. "Lopukhin, Petr Vasil'evich." *Russkii biograficheskii slovar',* 11: 686–87.

Predtechenskii, A. V. "Obshchestvennaia i politicheskaia zhizn' Peterburga v 60–90kh godov XVIII v." In *Ocherki istorii Leningrada,* edited by M. P. Viatkin et al., 1: 380–409.

———. *Peterburg petrovskogo vremeni: Ocherki.* Leningrad, 1948.

Preobrazhenskii, A. A. "Razvitie manufaktury v Rossii (konets XVII-pervaia polovina XVIII vv.)." In *Remeslo i manufaktura v Rossii, Finliandii, Pribaltike,* edited by N. E. Nosov et al., 48–60. Leningrad, 1975.

Priestley, Harold. *London: The Years of Change.* New York: Barnes & Noble, 1966.

Prussak, Anna Vladimirovna. "Petrovskaia instrumental'naia izba v Peterburge." *Sovetskaia meditsina,* no. 6 (1948): 37–40.

Pushkarev, Ivan Il'ich. *Opisanie Sanktpeterburga i uezdnykh gorodov S.-Peterburgskoi gubernii.* St. Petersburg, 1839.

Pyliaev, Mikhail Ivanovich. *Staryi Peterburg: Rasskazy iz byloi zhizni stolitsy.* 2nd ed. St. Petersburg, 1889.

———. *Zabytoe proshloe okrestnostei Peterburga.* St. Petersburg, 1889.

Pypin, Aleksandr Nikolaevich. *Istoriia russkoi literatury.* 4 vols. St. Petersburg, 1898–99.

———. *Russkoe masonstvo XVIII i pervaia chetvert' XIX v.* Petrograd, 1916.

Raeff, Marc, ed. *Catherine the Great: A Profile.* New York: Hill and Wang, 1972.

———. "The Domestic Policies of Peter III and His Overthrow." *American Historical Review,* 75, no. 5 (June 1970): 1289–1310.

———. *Origins of the Russian Intelligentsia: The Eighteenth-Century Nobility.* New York: Harcourt, Brace, & World, 1966.

———. "Pugachev's Rebellion." In *Preconditions of Revolution in Early Modern Europe,* edited by Robert Forster and Jack P. Greene, 161–202. Baltimore: Johns Hopkins University Press, 1970.

———. "The Well-Ordered Police State and the Development of Modernity in Seventeenth- and Eighteenth-Century Europe: An Attempt at a Comparative Approach." *American Historical Review,* 80, no. 5 (December 1975): 1221–43.

———. *The Well-Ordered Police State: Social and Institutional Change Through Law in the Germanies and Russia, 1600–1800.* New Haven: Yale University Press, 1983.

Ransel, David L. "An Eighteenth-Century Russian Merchant Family in Prosperity and Decline." In *Imperial Russia: New Histories for the Empire,* edited by Jane Burbank and David L. Ransel, 256–80. Bloomington: Indiana University Press, 1998.

———. "Ivan Betskoi and the Institutionalization of the Enlightenment in Russia." *Canadian-American Slavic Studies,* 14, no. 3 (Fall 1980): 327–38.

———. *Mothers of Misery: Child Abandonment in Russia.* Princeton: Princeton University Press, 1988.

———. *The Politics of Catherinian Russia: The Panin Party.* New Haven: Yale University Press, 1975.

Rappoport, Angelo S. *The Curse of the Romanovs.* London, 1907.

Rashin, Adol'f Grigor'evich. *Formirovanie rabochego klassa Rossii: Istoriko-ekonomicheskie ocherki.* Edited by S. G. Strumilin. Moscow, 1958.

———. *Naselenie Rossii za 100 let. 1811–1913 gg.: Statisticheskie ocherki.* Edited by S. G. Strumilin. Moscow, 1956.

Rastorguev, Egor. *Progulki po Nevskomu prospektu.* St. Petersburg, 1846.

Reading, Douglas K. *The Anglo-Russian Commercial Treaty of 1734.* New Haven: Yale University Press, 1938.

Reddaway, William Fiddian. “MacCartney in Russia, 1765–1767.” *Cambridge Historical Journal,* 3 (1931): 846–63.

Riasanovsky, Nicholas V. *Russia and the West in the Teaching of the Slavophiles: A Study of Romantic Ideology.* Cambridge, MA: Harvard University Press, 1952.

Rice, Tamara Talbot. “Eighteenth-Century St. Petersburg.” In *Cities of Destiny,* edited by Arnold Toynbee, 242–57. New York: McGraw-Hill, 1967.

Richardson, A. E. “Classic Architecture in Russia.” *Architectural Review,* 38 (1915): 87–99 and plates; 39 (1916): 19–24, 50–55, 95–103 and plates.

Rimmer, El’vira, and M. Borodulin. *Progulki po Voskresenskomu prospektu.* Cherepovets: Izdatel’skii dom ID Cherepovets, 2002.

Rodjestvensky, Sergey, and Anna Ivanovna Lubimenko. “Contributions à l’histoire des relations commerciales franco-russes au XVIII siècle.” *Revue d’histoire économique et sociale,* 17 (1929): 362–402.

Rogger, Hans. *National Consciousness in Eighteenth Century Russia.* Cambridge, MA: Harvard University Press, 1960.

Ronimois, H. E. *Russia’s Foreign Trade and the Baltic Sea.* London, 1946.

Rosovsky, Henry. “The Serf Entrepreneur in Russia.” In *Explorations in Enterprise,* edited by Hugh G. J. Aitken, 341–70. Cambridge, MA: Harvard University Press, 1954.

Rozhkov, Nikolai Aleksandrovich. *Gorod i derevnia v russkoi istorii (Kratkii ocherk ekonomicheskoi istorii Rossii).* 7th ed. Petrograd, 1923.

Rozman, Gilbert. *Urban Networks in Russia, 1750–1800, and Premodern Periodization.* Princeton: Princeton University Press, 1976.

Rubinshtein, Nikolai Leonidovich. “Topograficheskie opisaniia namestnichestv i gubernii XVIII v. pamiatniki geograficheskogo i ekonomicheskogo izucheniia Rossii.” *Voprosy geografii,* 31 (1953): 56–78.

———. “Vneshniaia torgovlia Rossii i russkoe kupechestvo vo vtoroi polovine XVIII v.” *Istoricheskie zapiski,* 54 (1955): 343–64.

Russkii biograficheskii slovar’. 25 vols. St. Petersburg/Petrograd, 1896–1918.

Rybakov, I. F. “Nekotorye voprosy genezisa kapitalisticheskogo goroda v Rossii.” In *Voprosy genezisa kapitalizma v Rossii,* edited by V. V. Mavrodin. Leningrad, 1960.

Ryndziunskii, Pavel Grigor’evich. *Gorodskoe grazhdanstvo doreformennoi Rossii.* Moscow, 1958.

———. “Gorodskoe naselenie.” In *Ocherki ekonomicheskoi istorii Rossii pervoi poloviny XIX veka,* edited by M. K. Rozhkova. Moscow, 1959.

Safonova, A. V. “Polozhenie trudiashchikhsia Peterburga i ikh klassovaia bor’ba v 60–70e gody XVIII Veka.” *Uchenye zapiski vologodskogo gosudarstvennogo pedagogicheskogo instituta,* 14 (1954): 3–46.

Saitov, Vladimir Ivanovich. *Peterburgskii nekropol’: Spravochnyi istoricheskii ukazatel’ lits, rodivshikhsia v XVII i XVIII stoletiiakh, po nadgrobnym nadpisiam Aleksandronevskoi lavry i uprazdnennykh peterburgskikh kladbishch.* Moscow, 1883.

Salias de Turnemir, Evgenii Andreevich. *Peterburgskoe deistvo: Istoricheskii roman, 1762 g.* 3 vols. St. Petersburg, 1884.

Sanktpeterburg: Issledovanie po istorii, topografii, i statistike stolitsy. 3 vols. St. Petersburg, 1870.

S.-Peterburg: Istoriko-statisticheskii ocherk s planami i ukazateliami. St. Petersburg, 1909.

S.-Peterburgskoe angliiskoe sobranie. *Stoletie S.-Peterburgskogo angliiskogo sobraniia, 1770–1870.* St. Petersburg, 1870.

———. *Uchrezhdenie S.-peterburgskogo angliiskogo sobraniia, osnovannogo 1 marta 1770 g. (peresmotreno v 1853 godu).* St. Petersburg, 1878.

Schenker, Alexander M. *The Bronze Horseman: Falconet's Monument to Peter the Great.* New Haven: Yale University Press, 2003.

Scherer, Johann Benedikt. *Geschichte und gegenwärtiger Zustand des russischen Handels.* Leipzig, 1789.

Semenov, A. *Izuchenie istoricheskikh svedenii o rossiiskoi vneshnei torgovle i promyshlennosti s poloviny XVII-go stoletiia po 1858 god.* 3 vols. St. Petersburg, 1859.

Semenova, Lidiia Nikolaevna. "Pravitel'stvo i rabochii liud Peterburga v pervoi polovine XVIII veka." In *Vnutrenniaia politika tsarizma,* edited by N. E. Nosov, 127–67. Leningrad, 1967.

———. *Rabochie Peterburga v pervoi polovine XVIII veka.* Leningrad, 1974.

Semevskii, Vasilii Ivanovich. *Krest'iane v tsarstvovanie imperatritsy Ekateriny II.* St. Petersburg, 1888.

Serman, Il'ia Zakharovich. "Russian National Consciousness and its Development in the Eighteenth Century." In *Russia in the Age of the Enlightenment: Essays for Isabel de Madariaga,* edited by Roger Bartlett and Janet Hartley, 40–56. New York: St. Martin's Press, 1990.

Shapiro, A. L. "O roli Peterburga v razvitii vserossiiskogo rynka v XVIII i pervoi polovine XIX vv." In *Goroda feodal'noi Rossii: Sbornik statei pamiati N. V. Ustiugova,* edited by V. I. Shunkov. Moscow, 1966.

———. "'Zapiski o peterburgskoi gubernii' A. N. Radishcheva." *Istoricheskii arkhiv,* 5 (1950): 190–287.

Sharlin, Allan. "Natural Decrease in Early Modern Cities: A Reconsideration." *Past and Present,* no. 79 (May 1978): 126–38.

Shaumian, L. S., ed. *Leningrad: Entsiklopedicheskii spravochnik.* Moscow-Leningrad, 1957.

Shaw, J. Thomas. *The Transliteration of Modern Russian for English-Language Publications.* Madison: University of Wisconsin Press, 1967.

Shkvarikov, Viacheslav Alekseevich. *Ocherk istorii planirovki i zastroiki russkikh gorodov.* Moscow, 1954.

———. *Planirovka gorodov Rossii XVIII i nachala XIX veka.* Moscow, 1939.

Shunkov, V. I., ed. *Goroda feodal'noi Rossii: Sbornik statei pamiati N. V. Ustiugova.* Moscow, 1966.

———, ed. *Perekhod ot feodalizma k kapitalizmu v Rossii: Materialy vsesoiuznoi diskussii.* Moscow, 1969.

Shustov, A. S. *Sanktpeterburgskoe kupechestvo i torgovo-promyshlennye predpriiatiia goroda k 200–letnomu iubileiu stolitsy: Illiustrirovannyi al'manakh.* St. Petersburg, 1903.

Sindalovskii, Naum Aleksandrovich. *Istoriia Sankt-Peterburga v predaniiakh i legendakh.* St. Petersburg: "Norint," 1997.

———. *Legendy i mify Sankt-Peterburga.* St. Petersburg: "Norint," 1997.

Sjoberg, Gideon. *The Preindustrial City Past and Present.* Glencoe, NY: Free Press, 1960.

———. "The Rise and Fall of Cities: A Theoretical Perspective." In *Urbanism and Urbanization,* edited by Nels Anderson, 7–20. International Studies in Sociology and Social Anthropology. Leiden: E. J. Brill, 1964, 7–20.

Smirnov, Iu. I., ed. *Sankt-Peterburg: Zanimatel'nye voprosy i otvety.* St. Petersburg, 2000.

Sokolovskii, Aleksandr Kazimirovich. *Staryi Peterburg na knizhnykh znakakh.* Leningrad, 1925.

Sokolovskii, Ivan Vladimirovich. "K voprosu o sostoianii promyshlennosti v Rossii v kontse XVII i pervoi polovine XVIII stoletiia." *Uchenye zapiski kazan'skogo universiteta,* 3 (1890): 1–58.

Spivak, Dmitrii Leonidovich. *Severnaia stolitsa: metafizika Peterburga.* St. Petersburg, "TEMA," 1998.

Sreznevskii, V., ed. "Prazdnovanie stoletiia Peterburga." *Russkaia starina* 114 (1903): 363–78.

Statisticheskii sbornik po Petrogradu i petrogradskoi gubernii. Petrograd, 1922.

Stennik, Iurii. "Entsiklopediia vsiakoi mudrosti." *Belye nochi,* 4 (1975): 335–65.

Steveni, William Barnes. *Petrograd Past and Present.* Philadelphia, 1916.

Stolpianskii, Petr Nikolaevich. "Bibliografiia 'Sankt-Piter-Burkha.'" Unpublished manuscript in the library of the State Museum of the History of the City of St. Petersburg.

———. "Iz istorii proizvodstv v S.-Peterburge za XVIII vek i pervuiu chetvert' XIX veka." *Arkhiv istorii truda v Rossii,* book 2 (1921): 86–105.

———. *Petergofskaia pershpektiva: Istoricheskii ocherk.* St. Petersburg, 1923.

———. *Revoliutsionnyi Peterburg: U kolybeli russkoi svobody.* Petrograd, 1922.

———. *Staryi Peterburg: Admiralteiskii ostrov, Sad trudiashchikhsia: Istoriko-khudozhestvennyi ocherk.* Moscow, 1923.

———. *Staryi Peterburg: Torgovlia khudozhestvennymi proizvedeniiami v XVIII veke.* St. Petersburg, 1913.

———. *Vverkh po Neve ot Sankt-Piter-Burkha do Shliushina: Putevoditel'.* 2 vols. Petrograd, 1922.

———. *Zhizn' i byt peterburgskoi fabriki za 210 let ee sushchestvovaniia. 1704–1914 gg.* Leningrad, 1925.

Sukhodrev, Vsevolod Mikhailovich. *Peterburg i ego dostoprimechatel'nosti: Istoricheskoe proshloe i nastoiashchee Peterburga.* St. Petersburg, 1901.

Svin'in, Pavel Petrovich. *Dostopamiatnosti Sanktpeterburga i ego okrestnostei.* 5 vols. in 2. St. Petersburg, 1816–28.

Tarle, Evgenii Viktorovich. "Byla li ekaterininskaia Rossiia ekonomicheski otstaloiu stranoiu?" In *Zapad i Rossiia,* edited by Evgenii Viktorovich Tarle, 122–49. Petrograd, 1918.

———. *Zapad i Rossiia: Stat'i i dokumenty iz istorii XVIII-XX vv.* Petrograd, 1918.

Tikhmenev, Petr Aleksandrovich. *Istoricheskoe obozrenie obrazovaniia rossiisko-amerikanskoi kompanii i deistvii ee do nastoiashchego vremeni.* 2 vols. St. Petersburg, 1861–63.

Tikhomirov, Mikhail Nikolaevich. *The Towns of Ancient Rus'.* Translated by Y. Sdobnikov. Moscow, 1959.

Tisdale, Hope. "The Process of Urbanization." *Social Forces,* 20, no. 3 (March 1942): 311–16.

Tolstoi, Dmitrii Aleksandrovich. *Akademicheskaia gimnaziia v XVIII stoletii, po rukopisnym dokumentam arkhiva akademii nauk.* St. Petersburg, 1885.

Tompkins, Stuart Ramsey. *The Russian Mind: From Peter the Great Through the Enlightenment.* Norman: University of Oklahoma Press, 1953.

Tooke, William. *View of the Russian Empire During the Reign of Catherine the Second.* 3 vols. London, 1800.

Troitskii, S. M. *Finansovaia politika russkogo absoliutizma v XVIII veke.* Moscow, 1966.

———. *Russkii absoliutizm i dvorianstvo v XVIII v. Formirovanie biurokratii.* Moscow, 1974.

Tseitlin, M. A. "Kazennye (imperatorskie) stekliannye i zerkal'nye zavody v S.-Peterburge." *Sbornik nauchnykh trudov leningradskogo finansovo-ekonomicheskogo instituta.* Vypusk 5 (1948): 145–77.

Tugan-Baranovskii, Mikhail Ivanovich. *Russkaia fabrika v proshlom i nastoiashchem.* Moscow, 1922.

Turgenev, Aleksandr Ivanovich, ed. *La cour de la Russie, il y a cent ans 1724–1783: Extraits des dépêches des ambassadeurs anglais et français.* 3rd ed. Leipzig, 1860.

Tsylov, Nikolai Ivanovich. *Plany S.-Peterburga v 1700, 1705, 1725, 1738, 1756, 1777, 1799, 1840 i 1849 godakh, s prilozheniem planov 13 chastei stolitsy 1853 goda.* St. Petersburg, 1853.

Valk, S. N. et al., eds. *Istoriia rabochikh Leningrada, 1703–1965.* 2 vols. Leningrad, 1972.
van der Woude, Ad, Akira Hayami, and Jan de Vrees, eds., *Urbanization in History: A Process of Dynamic Interactions.* New York: Oxford University Press, 1990.
Van Woensel, Pieter. *État présent de la Russie.* St. Petersburg-Leipzig, 1783.
Varlamova, N. A. "Ispovedal'nye vedomosti kak istochnik po istorii naseleniia Peterburga." In *Genezis i razvitie feodalizma v Rossii: Problemy istorii goroda,* edited by I. Ia. Froianov, 187–96. Leningrad, 1988.
Vasil'chikov, A. A. "Semeistvo Razumovskikh: I Grafy Aleksei i Kiril Grigor'evichi." In *Osmnadtsatyi vek: Istoricheskii sbornik,* Edited by Petr Bartenev, 2: 377–630. 4 vols. Moscow: Tipografiia T. Risa, 1868–99.
Vasil'ev, Boris Dmitrievich. "K istorii planirovki Peterburga vo vtoroi polovine XVIII veka." *Arkhitekturnoe nasledstvo,* 4 (1953): 14–29.
Verblovskii, G. "Slovesnye sudy." *Entsiklopedicheskii slovar',* 30: 403–4.
Vernadskii, Georgii V. *Russkoe masonstvo v tsarstvovanie Ekateriny II.* Petrograd, 1917.
Viatkin, M. P. et al., eds. *Ocherki istorii Leningrada.* Vol. 1, *Period feodalizma: 1703–1861 gg.* Moscow-Leningrad, 1955.
Volkov, Solomon. *St. Petersburg: A Cultural History.* Translated by by Antonina W. Bouis. New York: Free Press, 1995.
Volodarskaia, C. G. "Perekhod k vol'nonaemnomu trudu na pervoi russkoi bumagopriadil'ne." *Voprosy istorii,* 1955, no. 11: 76–82.
Von Mohrenschildt, Dmitry S. *Russia in the Intellectual Life of Eighteenth-Century France.* New York: Octagon Books, 1972.
Voronov, A. *Istoriko-statisticheskoe obozrenie uchebnykh zavedenii sanktpeterburgskogo uchebnogo okruga s 1715 po 1828 g. vkliuchitel'no.* St. Petersburg, 1849.
Vysotskii, Ivan Petrovich. *S.-Peterburgskaia stolichnaia politsiia i gradonachal'stvo: Kratkii istoricheskii ocherk.* St. Petersburg, 1903.
Wechsberg, Joseph. *In Leningrad.* Garden City, NY: Doubleday, 1977.
Williams, John. *The Rise, Progress, and Present State of the Northern Governments; viz. The United Provinces, Denmark, Sweden, Russia, and Poland.* 2 vols. London, 1777.
Wirtschafter, Elise Kimerling. *From Serf to Russian Soldier.* Princeton: Princeton University Press, 1990.
———. *Structures of Society: Imperial Russia's "People of Various Ranks."* De Kalb: Northern Illinois University Press, 1994.
Wolfe, Bertram D. "Backwardness and Industrialization in Russian History and Thought." *Slavic Review,* 26, no. 2 (June 1967): 177–203.
Wortman, Richard S. *Scenarios of Power: Myth and Ceremony in Russian Monarchy.* Vol. 1, *From Peter the Great to the Death of Nicholas I.* Princeton: Princeton University Press, 1995.
Wrigley, E. A. "Brake or Accelerator? Urban Growth and Population Growth before the Industrial Revolution." In *Urbanization in History,* edited by Ad van der Woude, Akira Hayami and Jan de Vries, 101–12. New York: Oxford University Press, 1990.
Zaozerskaia, Elena Ivanovna. *Rabochaia sila i klassovaia bor'ba na tekstil'nykh manufakturakh v 20–60 gg. XVIII veka.* Moscow, 1960.
Zelnik, Reginald E. *Labor and Society in Tsarist Russia: The Factory Workers of St. Petersburg, 1855–1870.* Stanford, CA: Stanford University Press, 1971.
Ziablovskii, Evdokim Filippovich. *Statisticheskoe opisanie rossiiskoi imperii.* 2nd ed. St. Petersburg, 1815.
———. *Zemleopisanie rossiiskoi imperii dlia vsekh sostoianii.* 6 parts. St. Petersburg, 1810.
Zlotnikov, M. "Ot manufaktury k fabrike." *Voprosy istorii,* 1946, nos. 11–12: 31–48.
Zolotninskaia, R. L. "Iz rukopisnykh planov Peterburga XVIII veka." *Izvestiia vsesoiuznogo geograficheskogo obshchestva,* 89, Vypusk 3 (May-June 1957): 77–84.

Index